Cotton

Today's world textile and garment trade is valued at a staggering 425 billion dollars. We are told that under the pressure of increasing globalisation, it is India and China that are the new world-manufacturing powerhouses. However, this is not a new phenomenon: until the industrial revolution, Asia manufactured great quantities of colourful printed cottons that were sold to places as far afield as Japan, West Africa and Europe. *Cotton* explores this earlier globalised economy and its transformation after 1750 as cotton led the way in the industrialisation of Europe. By the early nineteenth century, India, China and the Ottoman Empire switched from world producers to buyers of European cotton textiles, a position that they retained for over two hundred years. This is a fascinating and insightful story which ranges from Asian and European technologies and African slavery to cotton plantations in the Americas and consumer desires across the globe.

GIORGIO RIELLO is Professor of Global History at the University of Warwick and a member of Warwick's Global History and Culture Centre. He is the author of *A Foot in the Past* (2006) and has co-edited several books, including *The Spinning World* (2009), *How India Clothed the World* (2009) and *Global Design History* (2011). In 2010 he was awarded the Philip Leverhulme Prize.

COTTON

The Fabric that Made the Modern World

GIORGIO RIELLO

CAMBRIDGE
UNIVERSITY PRESS

CAMBRIDGE
UNIVERSITY PRESS

Shaftesbury Road, Cambridge CB2 8EA, United Kingdom

One Liberty Plaza, 20th Floor, New York, NY 10006, USA

477 Williamstown Road, Port Melbourne, VIC 3207, Australia

314–321, 3rd Floor, Plot 3, Splendor Forum, Jasola District Centre, New Delhi – 110025, India

103 Penang Road, #05–06/07, Visioncrest Commercial, Singapore 238467

Cambridge University Press is part of Cambridge University Press & Assessment, a department of the University of Cambridge.

We share the University's mission to contribute to society through the pursuit of education, learning and research at the highest international levels of excellence.

www.cambridge.org
Information on this title: www.cambridge.org/9780521166706

First published 2013
Paperback edition first published 2015
3rd printing 2018

A catalogue record for this publication is available from the British Library

Library of Congress Cataloging-in-Publication data
Riello, Giorgio.
Cotton : the fabric that made the modern world / Giorgio Riello.
   pages   cm
Includes bibliographical references and index.
ISBN 978-1-107-00022-3 (hardback)
1. Cotton textile industry – History.   2. Cotton trade – History.
3. Cotton – History.   I. Title.
HD9870.5.R54   2013
338.4´767721 – dc23   2012034005

ISBN   978-1-107-00022-3   Hardback
ISBN   978-0-521-16670-6   Paperback

CONTENTS

Part III The second cotton revolution: a centripetal system, *circa* 1750–2000

FIGURES AND COLOUR PLATES

The following list of figures also indicates those illustrations that are reproduced in colour. Colour plates are located between pages 228 and 229.

MAPS

TABLES

PREFACE

Today the world textile and garment trade amounts to a staggering 425 billion US dollars in value. We are told that under the pressure of increasing globalisation, it is Asia – India and China in particular – that is the new world-manufacturing powerhouse. However the recent growth of Asia into the world's leading textile manufacturer is not a new phenomenon. Until the industrial revolution at the end of the eighteenth century, both India and China were leading economic areas and their skills in cotton textile manufacturing were superior to those of Europe. Asia manufactured great quantities of colourful printed and painted cottons that were sold across the Indian Ocean and reached faraway places such as Japan and Europe where they were craved as exotic fashionable goods.

Historians have argued that this ensured for Asia – and in particular India – widespread prosperity, as well as high rates of economic growth and technological development, but that sometime after 1750 Europe experienced a sudden and radical economic transformation: the continent industrialised. Mechanisation was first experienced in the textile sector. The spinning machine allowed one late eighteenth-century European woman to produce as much yarn as three hundred women in India. By the early decades of the nineteenth century, India, China and the Ottoman Empire switched from being world producers to being buyers of European cotton textiles, a position that they retained for the following two centuries.

This book is the first global analysis of cotton textiles. It argues that Europe's engagement with cotton textiles changed the shape of the world we still live in. It brings together the history of European industrialisation and the global significance of cotton textiles. Key to this book is the explanation of when, how and why Europe replaced Asia as the main area of production and trade of cotton textiles and the profound effects that this generated. Cotton was central to the creation of a 'new global system' increasingly presided over by Europe, not Asia. But technological development was just one among the many factors explaining this transition. The importance of raw materials, markets for products and consumers' preferences, and the increasing power of European nations over vast areas of the globe are in this book seen as critical in explaining the divergent paths of Europe and Asia.

This book was researched and written over a period of several years. Its original idea and formulation emerged from the activities of the Leverhulme-funded Global Economic History Network (GEHN) based at the London School of Economics and coordinated by Patrick O'Brien between 2003 and 2007. The network constituted the first truly collaborative platform for research and discussion in the field of global economic history. Over the years, I learned a great deal about global history and about the challenges posed by this relatively new field of historical enquiry. I also learned from Patrick what historians should aim for, a lesson that is more important than any other. Several members of GEHN provided much needed support. I would like to thank in particular Kent Deng, Kenneth Pomeranz, Om Prakash, Kaoru Sugihara and Peer Vries. I have also a considerable debt to the late Larry Epstein.

My move to the University of Warwick in 2007 and the foundation of the Global History and Culture Centre was a second and no less important stage in the shaping of this book. It allowed me to engage with a new agenda in cultural and social history that has greatly enriched my analysis. I also found the best colleagues that one can hope for, in particular Maxine Berg, Anne Gerritsen and Luca Molà. The four of us developed courses and organised sometimes logistically complicated events and trips that entailed cooking dyes in a famous London museum, broken arms, and getting lost in Beijing. The Warwick Global History and Culture Centre has provided the perfect setting for completing the research included in this book.

Adventure and friendship mix together. Beverly Lemire, Peter McNeil and John Styles were great companions in several trips to archives, museums and artisans' workshops in Europe, North America and Asia. We risked our lives on at least a couple of motorways and got lost in dodgy neighbourhoods, all in the name of research. Tirthankar Roy and Prasannan Parthasarathi rescued me from the maze of editing books. My collaboration with both of them has been essential for the writing of this book as has been the intellectual input of over thirty contributors to these edited projects. I would like to thank in particular Prasannan for checking on me every week during the writing of this book, making sure that it was completed.

Maxine Berg, Pat Hudson, Beverly Lemire, Patrick O'Brien, Prasannan Parthasarathi and John Styles read closely the entire manuscript, comment-ing, questioning and correcting it. Needless to say that any remaining errors are entirely their fault! Shengfang Chou, Amy Evans and Sara van Dijk provided much needed research and practical assistance. Glenn Adamson, Alain and Michèle Bresson, Barbara Canepa, Giovanni Luigi Fontana, Kayoko Fujita, Sakis Gekas, Regina Grafe, Hannah Greig, Philippe Minard, Maria Giuseppina Muzzarelli, Liliane Pérez, Jeannie Siegman and the late Tony Siegman, Claudia Stein, Sarah Teasley, Elisa Tosi Brandi and Amanda Vickery have been great friends and have supported this project in different and extraordinary ways. Richard Butler read every single word with enormous patience and care. Finally, my mother, brother, sister-in-law and nieces Eleonora and Anastasia hope that the book will be soon translated into Italian so that they can find out what it is about.

Any heartless economic historian like me should point out that love and friendship do not pay bills. The research and writing of this book has been possible thanks to the financial support and hospitality of the following instutions: Australian National University, Canberra; British Academy; Ecole des Hautes Etudes in Sciences Sociales, Paris; European University Institute; Leverhulme-funded Global Economic History Network, LSE; Fondation Les Treilles, France; Leverhulme Trust; Stanford Humanities Center, Stanford University; University of Technology Sydney; and Warwick Global History and Culture Centre.

Several libraries, archives and museums allowed me to use their collections. I would like to thank in particular: Archives Nationales de France, Paris; Ashmolean Museum, Oxford; Bibliothèque Nationale de France, Paris; Boston Museum of Fine Arts; British Library, London; British Museum, London; European University Institute Library, Florence; Institute of Historical Research, London; London School of Economics Library; Musée de l'Impression sur Etoffes, Mulhouse; National Archives, Kew; National Art Library at the Victoria and Albert Museum, London; The New York Historical Society; The Philadelphia Museum of Art; Royal Ontario Museum, Toronto; School of Oriental and African Studies Library, London; Stanford University Library; University of London Library; Victoria and Albert Museum, London; Warburg Institute Library, London; University of Warwick Library.

Several institutions kindly invited me to present my research. The list over the years has become so long that I will mention only the cities where my research brought me: Aix-en-Provence, Beijing, Bilbao, Binghamton, Boston, Cambridge, Catania, Coventry, Dublin, Edinburgh, Exeter, Florence, Konstanz, Helsinki, Istanbul, Leicester, London, Madrid, Melbourne, Norwich, Osaka, Padua, Paris, Pune, Reading, Santa Cruz, Stanford, Stockholm, Sydney, Uppsala, Utrecht, Wilmington – Delaware, York and Wolverhampton.

I am particularly grateful to the Leverhulme Trust for the Leverhulme Research Fellowship (RF/3/RFG/2010/0089) and the Stanford Humanities Center for the External Fellowship (2010–11) that enabled me to complete this book. This publication has been made possible by a grant from the Scouloudi Foundation in association with the Institute of Historical Research and the financial assistance of the Humanities Research Fund at the University of Warwick.

The majority of this book was written in Palo Alto while a fellow at the Stanford Humanities Center. I was surrounded by a group of absorbing scholars who made me often forget the throbbing toothache that accompanied the slow writing of this work.

To Anastasia and Eleonora
Christmas 2012

ABBREVIATIONS

AHR	*American Historical Review*
ANF	Archives Nationales de France, Paris
BNF	Bibliothèque Nationale de France, Paris
BPP	British Parliamentary Papers
EEIC	English East India Company
EHR	*Economic History Review*
FEIC	French East India Company
IESHR	*Indian Economic and Social History Review*
JAS	*Journal of Asian Studies*
JEEH	*Journal of European Economic History*
JEH	*Journal of Economic History*
JESHO	*Journal of the Economic and Social History of the Orient*
JGH	*Journal of Global History*
JWH	*Journal of World History*
NA	National Archives, Kew, London
P&P	*Past & Present*
TH	*Textile History*
VOC	Dutch East India Company

1 INTRODUCTION: GLOBAL COTTON AND GLOBAL HISTORY

This book is a history of cotton textiles, but also a story narrated through cotton textiles. It is a story of how the world we live in has changed over the last thousand years. Cotton today is a very large industry, the most common material for our clothing and furnishings, a widely traded commodity, as well as the source of the means of living for millions of cultivators, workers and large and small traders. Cotton has also a cultural value: cotton textiles are consumed across the entire world and the cotton fibre has acquired specific social and cultural meanings. We think of it as a fabric softer and more casual than wool or silk, and more 'organic' than synthetics; we like our blue jeans, our T-shirts and cotton underwear.

One strand of this book is a narrative of how cotton came to be such a ubiquitous commodity, material and product. A thousand years ago the presence of cotton was limited. Raw cotton was cultivated and manufactured only in specific parts of the world. Slowly it entered into the consuming habits of millions of people, especially in the Indian subcontinent.[1] This book narrates the success of cotton in becoming global. But what does 'global' mean? Cotton came to be part of the production, exchange and consumption of many societies around the world. By 1300 India had developed a sophisticated series of regional industries specialised in the production of different types of cotton textiles that were traded across the Indian Ocean.[2] Cotton textile production was a flourishing industry also in China and had made inroads into Southeast Asia and in parts of Africa. Cotton and cotton textiles became 'global' not just by virtue of being contemporaneously present in different places, but also by their capacity to connect different corners of the world. Cotton textiles were probably the most traded commodity in the medieval and early modern world. However the 'globalisation' that cotton brought about was a tenuous linking of different places across Asia, some parts of Africa and Europe, rather than a thick web of connections.[3]

A world that produces and exchanges more over time is a world that becomes richer: people are busy at the loom or at cultivating raw cotton; others might buy cloth, allowing them to specialise in producing other commodities; traders earn from exchange; states impose taxes and duties. And this leads us to the second aspect of a story of cotton, one that is not about cotton itself but is narrated *through* cotton. Cotton was over a millennium one of the most important industries in the world. This is not an uncontentious claim, but the geographical extension and later history of industrialisation of cotton textiles makes it an acceptable generalisation. Hence cotton can be used as a lens through which to read other global phenomena that cotton came to exemplify and possibly explain. In this sense, a book on global cotton is also an example of how global economic history can be written.

The wealth that cotton brought about was not equally distributed. We live in a world with profound differences between industrialised, developing, and what used to be called third world countries. As the world 'progressed', some places became richer than others. The western world (Europe, North America and some outposts in East Asia, namely Japan and Australasia) is several times richer than many countries in Africa or Asia. Although more or less everyone has become richer over time, inequality has increased. Right now people living in the western world are approximately fifteen times richer than their ancestors three centuries ago. At the same time, however, there are parts of the world where famine is still a common occurrence and in which vast parts of the population live with less than 2 dollars a day.[4]

What has all of this to do with cotton? This material, commodity and industrial product contributed significantly to the phenomenal economic growth of the world in the last thousand years, but it is also partly to blame for the intensification of inequality. This book tells a story that has a happy ending, but basically for its leading economic character, namely the western world.

Argument

Cotton's primary position in the histories of economic development is hardly news. It has become a truism that cotton was the fuel of the industrial revolution. The story goes that cotton came to be the first mechanised sector of an island economy in the northwestern part of Europe called England. There and for the first time humanity used efficient machines to produce large quantities of textiles that were cheap. Large-scale factories emerged employing (and exploiting) millions of workers. Here was the beginning of what we call a modern industrial society.

I am purposely using the language of primary school texts, as this is the notion in the minds of millions of people. None of the facts are wrong, but the story might not be as transparent as we would like to imagine. It suggests a narrative of how one part of the world – mainly on the basis of its own initiative – became rich. It does not say much, however, about why other parts of the world did not do the same. This book tells a different story, of how cotton changed the way in which economies around the world worked. Europe, by using new technologies and imported raw materials from other continents, and by selling finished products to the entire world, became rich. The balance of economic development tipped away from Asia, especially from India, where cotton had been a very large industry. This marks the beginning not just of modern industrialisation but also of a 'divergence' between different parts of the world: the rich and the poor.

My explanation will be complicated, geographically dislocated and, in an attempt to avoid familiar tropes (modernity; mechanisation, etc.), difficult to simplify. It will not claim any special virtue for Europe (or England); rather, it will attempt to explain what happened in one location by linking it to what happened elsewhere in the world. Global history exposes how events located in a precise space and time (the industrial revolution – England – c. 1780) are in reality the fruit of complex interactions between different parts of the world (for instance between factories in England and artisans in India; between cotton plantations in the Americas and consumers in Africa). A global approach attempts to be *systemic*, that is to say, to consider possible explanations not just by looking inside but also outside the 'black box'. Let me give you an example: in 1931 two fine scholars, Alfred P. Wadsworth and Julia de Lacy Mann, published what is still a highly cited book.[5] Their narrative of the rise of the cotton industry in England came to influence generations of historians and informed the general public. Their way of framing the problem was basically regional. It was about the rise of a region of England, not even England as a whole. Theirs is a story told by a narrating voice standing in Lancashire. This book has a different agenda. While Wadsworth and Mann studied Lancashire in the belief that they could understand how this region changed the world, my book looks at the world with the anticipation that it can explain what happened in Lancashire.

So far I have given particular importance to the role of cotton and cotton textiles in revolutionising the world at a specific time, namely the end of the eighteenth century. I have taken a well-established story – that of industrialisation – and claimed that I wish to explain it in a more global way. Would it not be easier to consider a short span of time, perhaps a couple of centuries, as Wadsworth and Mann did? As my explanation aims to be global, it also needs to go back in time and see the evolution of an industry, a material and a product. The risk taken in concentrating on a specific period is that of producing a truncated and partial account that misses many of the 'backward linkages' to a past that, although not destiny, created a path for future change and development. Plainly said, this book shows how cotton textiles, in the period before the seventeenth century, came to shape a world of exchange, economic welfare and socio-cultural relations that was very different from the one shaped by cotton from the eighteenth century onwards.

The book starts by considering the role of cotton as an industry and commodity to be found in different areas of the world, and especially in India. During the period between 1000 and 1500 CE, the subcontinent came to be regarded as the most efficient manufacturer of cotton textiles in Eurasia, and its products were sought after from the Mediterranean to Japan. Fast-forward in time to the nineteenth century, and the world that cotton helped to form is very different. By the early decades of the nineteenth century Europe had become the main location of production of cotton textiles in the world; cotton textiles were produced through a new system of manufacturing, and were sold by European traders across the entire world. One of the main aims of this book is to understand how and why that happened. The reply depends as much on understanding the end point in England, as understanding the point of departure in India.

There is a second reason why I consider such an enormous swathe of time. Change can either be sudden and quick or protracted and slow. The traditional story of the industrial revolution (and the very term betrays it) is more on the 'sudden and quick' side of the spectrum, though there is an entire body of literature discussing how quick and sudden a revolution must be to qualify as 'revolutionary'. The shift to a more global perspective has not changed this perspective, and Kenneth Pomeranz – to whom we owe the popularisation of the idea of Divergence – thinks that Europe escaped a common path of slow economic growth suddenly at the end of the eighteenth century.[6] This book instead tells a story of change that is rather slow. Factories might have materialised in England suddenly, but they are epiphenomena, the symptoms of something else. Economic historians accord too much importance to measurable outcomes. I am more interested in the process that brought us from a world in which India dominated the production and trade of cottons to a world in which Europe emerged as an industrial powerhouse. Processes take time, and this book argues that the transition built up over several centuries.[7]

The second part of the book shows how the relocation of cotton manufacturing, the changing modalities of production, and the relationships of power that it supported were part of a complex process formed from many different variables, not all of which led to the unidirectional shift of production to Europe. It was a process that was at times quite random, that had no *deus ex machina* type of rationale that gave it purposefulness and direction. In this sense, the story that

I tell in this book is quite different to a more deterministic story still found in many economic histories.

It would be incorrect to say that historians are not interested in processes of change, or that I am the first to care about them. Economic historians are as much interested in measuring outcomes (levels of production) as they are in explaining them. But by and large they tend to explain 'it all' parsimoniously. They attribute all the merit (or blame) to one or a limited range of variables. Both the industrial revolution and divergence have been in turn explained by: culture, technology, resources, consumption, wages, institutions, and so on. The list could continue, but these variables seem to be nearly always exclusive. To see one or a small set of factors as the explananda of everything makes for a memorable narrative and a good argument with rivals who support other variables. Yet, when we are considering complex social, economic and cultural phenomena over the best part of several centuries, it appears to be a rather narrow way of accruing alternative explanations.

This book tells a story of change that is not just about long processes; it sees change itself as the product of a variety of interconnected variables; it deals with consumption, trade, culture, technology, and so on, and argues that it was their interactions that produced momentous change. This way of conceptualising change has the weakness of appearing timid, resistant to admitting its 'real' causes and indifferent at shouldering other explanations. History is not about historians being right or wrong, but about trying to create a convincing explanation of a dynamic past.

Content

The three parts of this book each consider the interrelationship between resources (especially raw cotton), exchange (trade and consumption) and production (technologies, organisations, and the role of institutions and human agency).

Part one entitled 'The First Cotton Revolution: a Centrifugal System', considers the long period from *circa* 1000 to the sixteenth century. During this period cotton textiles were already a global industry and South Asia dominated their production and trade. I call this global system *centrifugal*, as it was based on processes of diffusion of resources, technologies, knowledge and the sharing of profits. India was the core of a global system that was only loosely coordinated by that subcontinent. Whilst enjoying the competitive advantage provided by the high quality of local production, most of the areas with which India interacted engaged in their own right in the cultivation of raw cotton, its processing and manufacturing into cloth. They together formed a system marked by competition and symbiosis. Trade was structured through a network of Asian intermediaries and consumers were keen to integrate local with exotic commodities, and the latter were customised to suit the taste and local meaning attributed to cloth. Cotton textiles were central to the articulation of a global system structuring itself mostly through 'nodes' of trade. India indeed emerged as a core area, but over time its position was weakened by processes of osmosis dominated by a centrifugal logic.

The second part of this book, entitled 'Learning and Connecting: Making Cottons Global', asks what was the contribution of Europeans operating outside the continent's borders to the subsequent rise of Europe as a new global core for cotton textile production. Historians have accorded particular significance to the coming of European traders (Portuguese, and later Dutch, English, French and other state-sponsored trading companies) to the Indian Ocean after 1500.[8] The importation of Indian cottons into Europe was clearly important, but it was not the only contribution deriving from the intensification of world trade. The European chartered companies provided the knowledge necessary to engage with a complex variety of fabrics. Consumers in Europe had to learn how to integrate cotton textiles into their dress and furnishings. European merchants also transformed cotton textiles into an Atlantic commodity for both American and African consumers. And finally Europe acquired techniques of printing and dyeing from Asia that came to transform the aesthetic vocabulary of textile production and consumption.

No one can deny the unprecedented (revolutionary) development of cotton manufacturing in Europe at the end of the eighteenth century. Yet, I argue in the second part of this book that this was the end result of a process that took at least two centuries and in which Europe relied heavily on knowledge, ideas, expertise, materials and commodities from the rest of the world. I call this a process of 'learning' by Europe, in engaging with cotton textiles in terms of production, consumption, trade and in understanding the potential of an 'Asian' fibre. What Europe learned by looking and venturing outside its own borders was of fundamental importance for the subsequent shift (from India to Europe) and reconfiguration (from artisanal to industrial) of a world-important industry such as the cotton textile. Europeans exploited the openness of the Indian Ocean system, as 'late participants' to a continuing centrifugal process, to draw together a series of factors, conditions and structures necessary to make cotton textiles a new and integral part of European manufacturing, trade and consumption. But the continent also relied on endogenous factors such a strong human capital, a specific state-led social and economic structure, and long-standing expertise in the manipulation of other fibres.

Europe could have matured into another area among the many in which cotton spinning and weaving were carried out along proto-industrial lines. This was not to be. The final part of this book, entitled 'The Second Cotton Revolution: a Centripetal System', explains how cotton was central to the story of 'why Europe grew rich', as Parthasarathi puts it.[9] 'Learning' evolved into the structuring of a new system in which Europe became not just the global centre for production and trade in cotton textiles, but also embraced a new system of manufacturing. In the 'second cotton revolution', manufacturing was as central as trade had previously been in the Asian 'first cotton revolution'.

Historians have argued for the centrality of manufacturing, but their explanations have closely focused on the role of technological innovation in spinning and weaving that characterised Europe alone.[10] My book restores an emphasis to the importance of finishing and raw materials and argues that manufacturing positioned itself within the structure of a new global system that differed from its Asian forerunner in several respects. This was a centripetal system, one based on the capacity of the centre to 'exploit' resources and profits towards its productive and commercial core, rather than a centrifugal system based on the diffusion of resources, technologies, knowledge and the sharing of profits. The new system was one of competition and exclusiveness rather than cooperation and symbiosis; it was based on direct connections – often coordinated by the rising European financial centres – rather than on loose areas connected by nodes of exchange. But most of all, it was a system the prosperity of which was based on forms of intensive global exploitation of natural resources and markets.

Europeans learned to exploit raw cotton coming from other parts of the world (mostly the Americas) and the ecological advantages that this generated. Moving to a more comparative methodology, I show how, unlike other world areas of cotton textile production, in Europe the link between trade and manufacturing was consolidated, creating unique conditions for the restructuring of production to cater for global markets. What came to be broken was instead the link between manufacturing and the agrarian economy of Europe. I reflect specifically on the role of raw cotton and how and why within the new system Europe did not cultivate its own raw materials but created a fragmented productive process based on the intercontinental trade of raw materials. Slowly, but surely, a 'western system' centred on Europe and the Atlantic organised and determined by European producers and traders came into existence. The book concludes with a final chapter describing the articulation of this new centripetal system in terms of domination of world markets, leading to an eventual demise of cotton textile production in many areas of the globe.

Debates

Today's world economy – an economy that restructured itself in the early nineteenth century – is very different from the world that preceded it. A key difference is the relative economic and social development of different areas of the globe and their changing relationships. This is in no way a new issue: the emergence of the West (and Europe in particular) to the front stage of world power and wealth has engaged historians in recent decades.[11] Triumphalist narratives of the 'rise of the West' and the relative backwardness of 'the Rest' have in recent times been revised presumably to accommodate the unstoppable development of China and India, back – one might say – to positions of wealth from which they had been dethroned more than two centuries ago. Recent scholarship has had to deal also with the parallel (and far too often separate) issue of the connectivity of the world that we live in. We might called it *globalisation*, a process of intensification of commercial, economic, social and cultural connections between different areas of the world. The trajectory of one world area is often linked to what happens elsewhere. It turns out that historically a world that has become more connected has also become more unequal.[12]

These two issues – divergence and globalisation – have in recent decades been at the centre of intense discussion. Two of the scholars who have most contributed to each of these concepts are Immanuel Wallerstein, with his multi-volume work on world systems published between 1974 and 2011, and Kenneth Pomeranz, with his book *The Great Divergence* published in 2000.[13] I cite only these two authors because it would be unduly tedious to venture into the historiography of globalisation and divergence. I must state outright that my overall argument is not always in line with either Wallerstein's or Pomeranz's ideas, though their preoccupations, methodologies and findings have been fundamental for the research and writing of this book.

Let me start with divergence. Simply put, divergence is the differential between the GDP per capita of Western Europe and that of China, as in Figure 1.1, although the graph for India and other parts of the world would be similar. The graph can be divided into three periods: the widening of difference (divergence; up to the 1820s); a central period in which such difference was maintained (roughly the period from 1825 and 1975); and a final moment of shrinking difference ('convergence'; from 1975 and into the future). For the moment I am concerned with the period of divergence. There is disagreement over the chronology and intensity of such a process, in particular whether Europe was already developing faster than China or India in the sixteenth and seventeenth centuries. Unlike the graph proposed by Angus Maddison, Pomeranz's divergence is located in the late eighteenth century and was 'great' because it was intense over

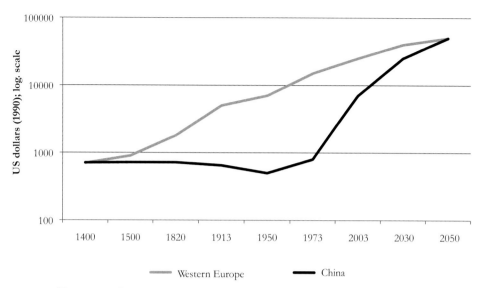

Figure 1.1 Comparative GDP per capita in China and Western Europe, 1400–2050.

a short period of time (a century at best) that coincided with the industrialisation of the British Isles and Europe. This book sees instead a divergence lasting several centuries, a long process that eventually allowed Europe to reap the benefits.

The reason why I am suggesting that divergence was a long process is linked to a second, and perhaps more important debate: what are the reasons for diverging economic results at a global level? I simplify again by saying that over the last century explanations moved between two poles; from the idea of the 'exceptionalism of the West' to the idea that it all happened because of 'contingencies' (Figure 1.2). There is a gradient of 'agency' in the process of divergence on the part of the West. Exceptionalism tends to emphasise that Europe had something special that no one else had (a special culture or religion – Weber and later Landes; a special political ability to conquer – Jones; etc.). Contingencies are lucky coincidences such as the fact that Europe had good and cheap reserves of coal and access to land ('ghost acreages') and markets in the Americas. This is the interpretation of Pomeranz, much loved as it sidelines cultural traits in favour of

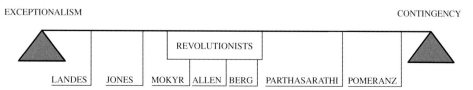

Figure 1.2 Explaining divergence: between 'exceptionalism' and 'contingency'.

hard differences and complies with our ecological awareness. In between exceptionalism and contingency, there is a range of scholars interested specifically in explaining the industrial transition of Europe (I call them 'industrialists' and I underline that they are not a homogenous category). Let me also say that this list is far from complete.

The story told through cotton in this book does not fall in the 'contingency camp': I try to explain how improbable, and in many ways unthinkable, it was for a continent like Europe, with little knowledge of cultivation, processing and consumption of cotton, to specialise in this product. Yet this does not make Europe exceptional: cotton was taken up elsewhere in the world, though it did not become the key sector and product for enormous economic and social transformation. Europe, in many ways, was more *extreme* than *exceptional* on a world scale. I argue in this book that such extreme outcomes were not the result of one specific factor that gave Europe a comparative advantage over other areas of the world (be it religion, culture, force, machines, coal of colonies, just to cite a few). The path that Europe undertook was the result of a 'layering' of different factors and circumstances, some of which were peculiar to the continent, some of which she borrowed from elsewhere, and others of which were quite absent altogether. These factors and circumstances produced synergies and catalysed change. The result was an economic transition that was momentous, but that should not be interpreted as the best possible outcome: the European 'transition' on which global divergence so much depended was also the result of failed attempts and partial successes. I argue, especially in the second part of this book, that many of these opportunities presented themselves from the interaction of Europe with other continents after 1500: the learning of technologies, of products and of raw materials, and the cultural and social changes at home that allowed for products, technologies and resources to be integrated into the socio-economic system of the West.

This leads me to 'globalisation', or better to say the relationship between different areas of the world. The subject matter of this book cannot either support or disprove the coming into place of a 'world economy', as suggested by Wallerstein. The world of cotton was not geographically homogenous. Before the eighteenth century, India had dominated production and trade in the Indian Ocean; after that date northwestern Europe dominated on a truly world scale. These two worlds were very different in their working, size and outcomes. For sure, the development of the European cotton industry looks like a leading sector for the Wallersteinian world-system, though my understanding of it includes not just power and money but also products, fashion and technologies, and Europe's capacity to profit from the physical disintegration of traditional chains of production with its industrial activities connected to raw materials, skills and final markets that were local and regional.

Methodology

Global history is not a history of everything. It is not a summary of history or a history of histories. One might easily repeat the truism that global history considers issues that are of a supranational and even supra-international nature: intercontinental trade, the movement of people worldwide, as well as cultural and social exchange and contact are all topics to be found within the rubric of global history. Perhaps, the global is best defined as a lens through which problems – present and past – are analysed. It is a way to observe and consider phenomena and to pose questions. The method used by global history addresses also a major problem, that of the overabundance of content. Method guides historians on 'what to leave out', a skill that William McNeill sees as central to the production of historical scholarship of a global type.[14] The choice on what to include (and what to exclude) has been motivated by the main argument of the book. Concentrating on India, I have sidelined important textile industries located in the Chinese and Ottoman empires. By integrating the raw materials together with the processes of transformation and the final products, I have given little space to labour. I have also preferred to temper economic sources with cultural and artefactual evidence, and will leave debates unresolved rather than force them to premature conclusions.

My choices assume that there is no uncontaminated bird's eye view of the world. All global histories must have a perspective or point of view. My main issue has been to explain a transition and I have focused mostly on two actors: South Asia and Western Europe. China, Southeast Asia, Africa and the Americas are included and in some cases are analysed in detail, but only in the context of an argument that wishes to reply to specified questions. The identification of a problem, however global it might be, implies the hierarchical pigconholing of places, data and evidence. The space allocated to Europe is something that I have done purposefully and not in a bout of unconscious Eurocentrism. Another book might have considered instead the issue of why Turkey did not start an industrial revolution. That would have been an equally important topic for a global narrative.

A second choice has been not to enter into the nitty-gritty of the complex story of cotton and cotton textiles in the nineteenth and, to a lesser extent, twentieth century. The focus of this book is the European early modern period, *circa* 1500–1800. The enormous increase in the size of cotton cultivation and manufacturing in the nineteenth century and the rise of the US and later Japan to the fore of global production are topics that are only briefly touched upon and hence not considered in great detail. This has been partly done in the interest of brevity and because there is a vast and up-do-date literature on these topics.[15] My main aim is to explain a transition of one of the world's largest industries from Asia to Europe, and I consider this divergence concluded by the early decades of the nineteenth century. I have also consciously sidelined the story of Indian decline, again briefly summarised but not looked at in any detail.[16]

The final issue with global history is about practice. How is research to be done when the remit is so vast? Whilst potentially drawing on large quantities of information, interpretations and historiographies, global history suffers by being often biased. European (western language) scholarship and archival resources are at the core of the problem. This book's reliance on English (and to a certain extent on a handful of other European languages) should be made clear from the outset. I might excuse myself by pointing out the difficulty of surveying historiographies in different languages when the material is so abundant, but I will simply say that lack of linguistic skills and easy access to familiar sources has produced a result that is biased from the start.

I have argued that global history is not about 'doing it all', and I add that it is not about 'doing it all *on your own*'. From the very beginning the research model adopted for this book has been collaborative. I might not be able to read Mandarin, but I know colleagues who can. The engagement with primary sources and secondary literature in different languages has been done by drawing on the expertise of those who can access them. The publication of this book was preceded by two large edited volumes presenting new findings and interpretations from a variety of scholars who have been involved in the LSE Global Economic History Network.[17] What they provided was not just in-depth knowledge of the literature and archival sources connected to their area and/or topic; they also actively participated in a dialogue that has allowed for confrontations and collaborations across geographies and the evaluation of different theoretical models.

Although this book adopts the language of the economy, it also integrates the economic value of cotton within a larger palette, something that I hope approximates a (real) world in which the economic, the cultural, the social are never separated or mutually exclusive. From a methodological point of view, it wishes to be a contribution to the understanding of economic transformation within a matrix that is social and cultural. Many of the recent global histories interested in explaining economic change have positioned themselves well within the domain of economic history. Some of them make use of mathematical and economic modelling that most historians have little familiarity with. My aim has been instead to understand a major episode of economic history within a wider framework. It can only be, of course, a partial and incomplete attempt, but it is visible in at least two ways. Firstly, my research integrates consumption into global (economic) history. The story that I am trying to narrate cannot be explained simply through production and trade, as many global histories of divergence and globalisation are.[18] Secondly, I have made use of artefacts and the methodologies of material culture. This explains the somewhat extravagant number of illustrations in the book. Material culture – as a methodological approach and as a series of sources – is integral to my argument about the importance of taste, the relevance of finishing processes and the significance of linking individual, localised events to wider long-term shifts, modifications and reconfigurations.

I want to conclude with an afterthought on what this book is not about. These days, a global perspective is hardly sufficient to make a case for proposing anything new. The shelves of any bookshop provide eclectic selections of global books. A sub-category of these seems to be dedicated to commodities: from chocolate to salt, from cod to sugar, just to cite a few.[19] Although commodities are a great way to tell a global story, my book is not a history of a commodity called *cotton*. This book does not follow a single commodity, as in many ways there is no commodity called *cotton*. The story gets even more complicated when we consider simultaneously the raw material (always referred to in this book as *cotton*, *cotton fibres* or *raw cotton*), yarn and the finished cloth (referred to as *cotton textiles* or *cottons*) and when we talk about both growing, production and consumption all at once. The literary form of the history of commodities, though appealing and often commercially successful, is unsuitable for the story that I wish to narrate. Yet there is a concession to a genre or mode of narrating 'the global' that is quite different from economic history concerns, as it attempts to understand how specific goods changed the way in which people lived, their tastes, their desires and physical conditions.

PART I

THE FIRST COTTON REVOLUTION: A CENTRIFUGAL SYSTEM, *CIRCA* 1000–1500

From the beginning of the second millennium and over the following six centuries, the cultivation of cotton fibres, the production of cotton textiles and their trade developed across Eurasia. During these centuries, South Asia emerged as the key producer of cotton textiles. Although several other areas came to produce, trade and consume cotton textiles on a large scale, India was the core of a 'global system' that was only loosely coordinated by the subcontinent. Whilst India enjoyed competitive advantages provided by high-quality production, most of the areas with which India interacted engaged in their own right in the cultivation of raw cotton, its processing and manufacture into cloth. Together they formed a system of competition as well as symbiosis. By 'system' I mean the logic that connects different areas through products, technologies and economic relationships. The world's first cotton revolution was 'centrifugal', a difficult word indicating it was based on diffusion. Chapter 1 considers the wide reach of Indian cottons and their ability to complement as well as to compete with similar local products and substitutes. Chapter 2 considers the diffusion of cotton cultivation across Asia to form several poles of production and trade with which India interacted. Finally, Chapter 3 elaborates upon the spread of technologies across most of Asia, Africa and Europe.

Trade and exchange were at the heart of this system and explain why cotton became a key commodity and productive activity across Eurasia in this period. The system did not rest on an international division of labour in which different regions of the world are locked into their respective roles. In this period there was no hierarchical relationship of cores and peripheries and their connections remained rather fluid. India was not the undisputed head or coordinator of the system: its products enjoyed wide appeal and spurred attempts at imitation. South Asia did not triumph over other concentrations of production and the 'open' and participatory nature of the system implies that the hegemony of India was progressively weakened.

2 SELLING TO THE WORLD: INDIA AND THE OLD COTTON SYSTEM

Material culture seems to be a useful concept to investigate the nature of trade and consumption for periods and areas of the world for which we have little documentary or statistical evidence. The object overleaf (Figure 2.1) is not a beautiful palampore or one of the high-quality Indian textiles that illustrate books or adorn major museums and collections. It is a fragment of cloth dating from the fourteenth century. It is rare but not unique: there are at least another 1,225 similar fragments in the storage space at the Ashmolean Museum in Oxford, and more are to be found in other museums around the world.[1] They were acquired in the early twentieth century by P. E. Newberry, the first professor of Egyptology at the University of Liverpool, who donated them to the Ashmolean Museum in 1946. They include printed cottons excavated in Old Fustat, near Cairo, in Egypt. They survive in relatively good condition because of the dry Saharan climate. For decades they remained uncatalogued and unseen. It was only in the 1980s that curator Ruth Barnes went back to them. By then their importance no longer lay within the field of Egyptian medieval archaeology. What is fascinating about these textiles found in Egypt is that their printed designs, use of mordants and colour scheme leave no doubt that they came from several thousand miles away, from Gujarat in northwestern India, and were probably traded all the way to Egypt via the western Indian Ocean and the Red Sea.[2]

The number and variety of their designs suggest that by the fourteenth century cotton textiles produced in India were regularly traded to North Africa. Again this is unremarkable. There are numerous archaeological and literary sources showing that Indian cottons were already exported to the ports of the Red Sea and to Egypt in the first century AD.[3] The trade connecting North Africa and the western coast of India was booming by the eleventh and twelfth centuries, and Indian cotton textiles were traded commodities purchased by ordinary consumers in coastal Asia and in Africa.[4] What is however remarkable about these fragments is that in some cases they are similar to textiles found at the other side of

Figure 2.1 Cotton textile fragment excavated in Old Fustat, fourteenth century. (See also colour plate.)

the Indian Ocean, in the Sulawesi Islands, in Southeast Asia (Figure 2.1 and Figure 2.2). Ruth Barnes, who was trained as an anthropologist of Southeast Asia, connected the artefacts that belong to different collections. Design similarity might be misleading, but in this case carbon dating and scientific analysis have confirmed that several of the Sulawesi fragments are indeed contemporaneous to those found in Old Fustat. In at least a couple of cases, their similarity is such that one might think they may have come from the same hand or printing block. This is the case of the now famous 'goose' (*hamsa*) pattern textiles considered by Ruth Barnes, John Guy and Beverly Lemire, among many others.[5] This is not an isolated episode: the fragment of textile we started with (Figure 2.1) has striking similarities with an artefact in storage at the Victoria and Albert Museum, although this second textile was found in Toraja in central Sulawesi (Figure 2.2).[6] Both textiles are from the first half of the fourteenth century and were produced in Gujarat. What is even more remarkable is that after the publication of these textiles in the book *Woven Cargoes* by John Guy, some of the textile printers in Gujarat have copied the design, literally 'reappropriating'

Figure 2.2 Cotton cloth produced in Gujarat and traded to the Sulawesi islands, *c.* 1340. (See also colour plate.)

their past via museum scholarship, and they now produce wonderful tablecloths in this precise pattern.

These textiles provide yet another reminder that globalisation was medieval. More importantly, the Ashmolean and V&A artefacts are useful material evidence showing the extent to which during a period spanning from at least the twelfth to the seventeenth centuries large quantities of Indian textiles were sold regularly across the Indian Ocean. These were not luxuries but were used as everyday attire and as decorative items by consumers of all social levels and economic standing. This chapter reflects on what sort of economic and material geographies – but also geographies of meaning – were formed through the exchange of cloth produced mostly in India and traded across the vast space of the Indian Ocean and beyond – to continental Asia, Africa and to Europe. It asks in particular why Indian cottons were sought after by consumers across half of the world, how consumers used them and the meanings that they attributed to such commodities. The chapter concludes by reflecting on the world of trade and consumption that Indian cottons created and attempts to understand how such commodities interacted with local products and stimulated (or encroached upon) the economic and commercial development of different parts of Afro-Eurasia.

Producing for the world

The regions of Gujarat in western India, Punjab and Pradesh in the north, Coromandel in its southern parts and from the seventeenth century Bengal in present-day eastern India and Bangladesh were thriving centres of textile manufacturing within a well-articulated system of exchange (Map 2.1).[7]

Some of these areas had produced for international markets since ancient times. The *Periplus Maris Erythraei*, a handbook for Greek-speaking merchants trading in the first and second century CE, cites the fact that 'much cheap cotton goods, all kinds of linen [and] finer cottons' were produced in Tagara (Ter) in India and sold through the port of Baryjaza, later better known as Broach in Gujarat, to the Red Sea.[8] By the Middle Ages the ports of Broach and the nearby Cambay were key nodes of trade both to the western and the eastern parts of the Indian Ocean. From these ports varieties of cotton textiles such as *baftas* produced in the region, and in particular in the city of Ahmedabad in Gujarat, were sold to the Maldives, Mozambique, Abyssinia and southern Arabia.[9] In the seventeenth century Cambay traded cheap printed and white cotton cloth to Arabia, Persia, Melaka, Sumatra and in particular Zanzibar. Better versions were traded to the Philippines, Borneo, Java and Sumatra.[10] Dutch traders were impressed by the variety and profusion of cloths that they could buy in Ahmedabad in the 1620s, which included 'red and black *chelas*, black and white *berams*, black *kannekins*, *baftas* of 28 yards length, black and white *chelas* and *dhoti dholka*, both coarse and fine as well as broad and narrow'.[11]

Western India specialised in low-price varieties, while Malabar, the Coromandel coast and Bengal dedicated themselves to higher-quality products.[12] The ports and manufacturing areas of the Coromandel coast were as well stocked as Gujarat. The European traveller John Huyghen van Linschoten noted in his *Voyage to the East Indies* (1598) a 'great traffique [from the Coromandel coast] into Bengala, Pegu, Sian, and Malacca', adding that 'there is excellent faire linnen of Cotton made in Negapatan, Saint Thomas, and Masulepatan, of all colours, and woven with divers sorts of loome workes and figures, verie fine and cunningly wrought, which is much worne in India, and better esteemed then silke'.[13] The area was well connected both internationally and with other parts of the subcontinent, with a port like Pulicat in Tamil Nadu trading cottons to be sold in Melaka, Sumatra, Pegu, as well as Gujarat and the Malabar coast.[14] Bengal was also an important area for the production and trade of cotton textiles. Although this area entered the international network of exchange later than other regions of the subcontinent, the local availability of high-quality cotton and a well-developed merchant community made it possible to trade about twenty varieties of cotton cloth that ranged from the lower types to the expensive and fine muslins

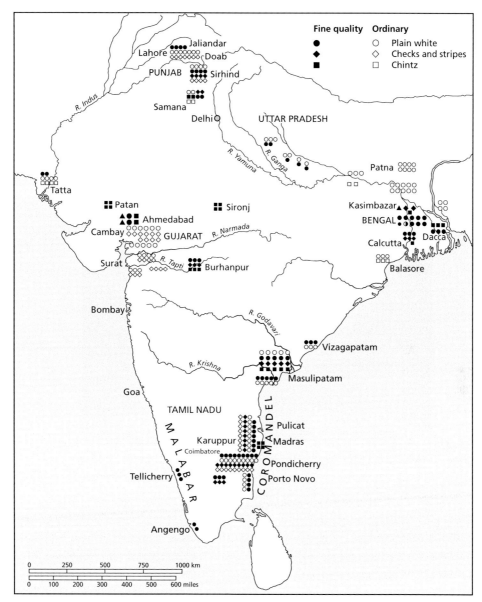

Map 2.1 Key areas of cotton textile production and trade in late seventeenth- and eighteenth-century India.

used for turbans. These were traded to the Malabar and to Southeast Asia by a variety of merchants that included Arabs, Parsees, Turks and Abyssinians.[15]

The main areas of production were not necessarily located on the coasts. The interior town of Sironj and Burhanpur in Madhya Pradesh were major centres

Figure 2.3 Cotton sash produced in Burhanpur, eighteenth century.

of cotton textile production for Indian Ocean markets. Burhanpur specialised in the manufacturing of textiles with small designs, popular as waist sashes, in particular in the seventeenth century, and in brightly coloured chintzes that were sold across Asia as neck or headscarves (Figure 2.3).[16] In the city of Sironj, according to Tavernier, 'the workers print their calicoes according to the design given by the foreign merchants', indicating a high level of connectedness to international markets.[17] The city's production included bed covers, tablecloths, pillowcases, pocket handkerchiefs, and men's and women's waistcoats that were traded to Persia and Anatolia.[18] Other cities both in South and North India specialised in specific markets: Coimbatore in Tamil Nadu produced printed cottons for Java already by the fifteenth century, while Karuppur, also in Tamil Nadu, specialised in the niche production of high-quality turban cloths, saris and dhotis.[19]

The trading world of Indian cottons

The fabrics produced in Gujarat, the Malabar coast, the Coromandel coast, Bengal and other areas of India were traded via land and sea to places as far away as Indonesia and Japan in the east and Saudi Arabia, Ethiopia, Egypt and West Africa to the west (Map 2.2).[20] When Europeans entered the Indian Ocean by circumnavigating the Cape of Good Hope at the end of the fifteenth century, they marvelled at the scale, sophistication and articulation of a trade that was not just geographically more widespread than the trade of woollens in Europe, but that comprised a range of mercantile communities. These included large diasporic communities of Jewish and Armenian merchants, who traded Indian textiles in exchange for a variety of commodities that included spices, foodstuffs, specie and luxuries.

The trade of textiles to the western part of the Indian Ocean, the Middle East, the Red Sea and North Africa was carried out both by land and sea. Cottons from the western coast of India were traded to Persia. In the mid seventeenth century, 25–30,000 camel-loads of cottons coming from India reached Persia every year. Cotton textiles changed hands several times and reached central Asia, China and eastern Europe. They were also traded to Basra and Baghdad and from there via land to as far away as Constantinople via Aleppo.[21] Trade to the Gulf and to the Red Sea via Aden carried textiles to the Horn of Africa. From there, Indian textiles, especially cheap striped cloth, reached Ethiopia along with silver and gold and embroidered luxury cloths used as regal gifts.[22] As early as the fourteenth century, East Africa exchanged primary products for Asian-manufactured goods, cottons, other fine textiles, beads, copperware, Islamic earthenware, glass and Chinese porcelain.[23] Considerable quantities of Asian textiles also arrived in Congo as luxury cloths designed in rich and colourful ways.[24]

Two characteristics distinguish this trade. Firstly, it was based both on land and sea routes. Land and sea were not exclusive ways of trading cottons and other commodities but were complementary to each other, with commodities being unloaded from ships and loaded on camels and vice versa. Secondly, this was a trade based on several intermediaries. Only rarely would a single merchant carry his commodities from the point of origin all the way to the final consumer. There might have been several changes of hands. From Gujarat, for instance, it took an entire season to reach Melaka, and because of the monsoon, merchants had to wait until the following March to go back. It was therefore difficult and financially risky to venture into the Chinese sea, as it would have required a journey and investment of over three years.[25] Trade relied instead on a series of mercantile intermediaries. This created a web of commercial relations across

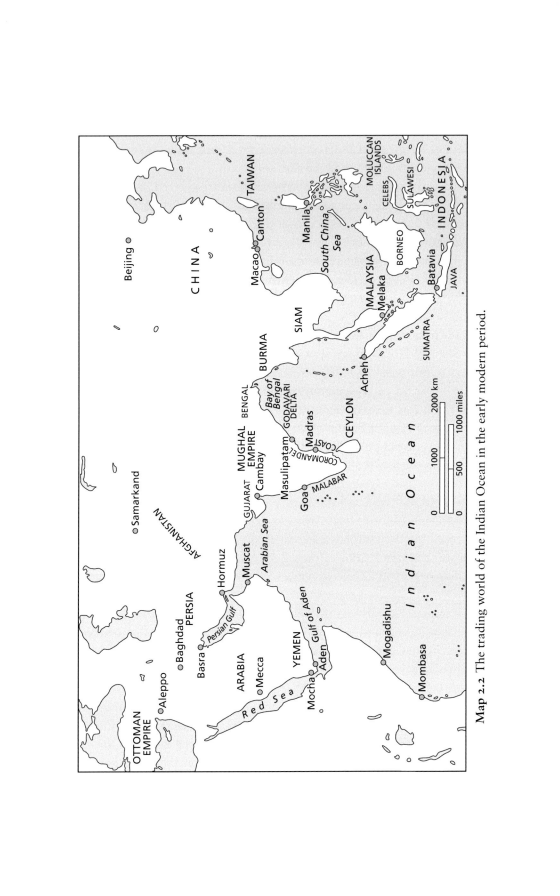

Map 2.2 The trading world of the Indian Ocean in the early modern period.

a vast continental and maritime space, connecting different ports, manufacturing locales and areas of consumption, which acted as 'nodes' in a network of exchange. This was the case for Southeast Asia, which, although geographically situated several thousands of miles away from India, was closely connected to the main economic areas of the subcontinent. The Portuguese Tomé Pires did not fail to notice how the port of Melaka, a hundred miles north of today's Singapore, could not 'live without Cambay, nor Cambay without Malacca'.[26] Cambay was the main port of Gujarat, and Gujarati merchants dominated the rich textile trade with Southeast Asia.[27] Melaka imported rice, sugar and fish as well as cotton textiles in exchange for pepper, camphor, spices, sandalwood, Chinese porcelain, silk and metals; this place also acting as an important connecting point between the Chinese sea and the Indian Ocean.[28]

Through textiles, the Indian Ocean was quintessentially a *space of flux* – a space of commercial exchange but also a space structured by the movement of people and socio-cultural communication. Cotton textiles were central to the dynamics of interaction created within the space of the Indian Ocean. Global historians have seen this space as the cradle of a phase of proto-globalisation. A series of popular as well as academic books underline the global centrality of Asia, and in particular the Indian Ocean, in the period before the eighteenth century.[29] This was a global system in which cotton cloth was the key commodity traded and India was its manufacturing core. But what type of system was it? This was of course a 'global system' that was not global at all, in the sense that it did not extend beyond the landmass of Afro-Eurasia and did not affect the Atlantic or the Americas. But it was also a loosely connected system structured through a series of intermediaries and sub-areas, as suggested by Janet Abu-Lughod (Map 2.3).[30]

Abu-Lughod graphically represents this India-centred system as composed of subsystems and punctuated by a series of cities – what she calls an 'archipelago of towns' – trading ports such as Melaka, Aceh, Canton, Aden, Mocha or Masqat, and land nodes such as Baghdad, Aleppo and Samarkand.[31] Each of these cities received not just diasporic trading communities (merchants from Gujarat, Bengal and Golconda, and Hindu and Muslim merchants from the Coromandel and Malabar coasts), but also what we might call 'diasporic commodities'.[32] The 'scattering' of goods went hand in hand with the movement of people. In a world in which shipping and nautical technologies were still inadequate, it should not surprise us that international and intercontinental trade was structured in flexible ways in which the interaction among the different parts of the system was a more salient feature than the privileged position enjoyed by its manufacturing core. India might have provided large quantities of the textiles, but its manufacturers and merchants were not the undisputed rulers and coordinators of the system.

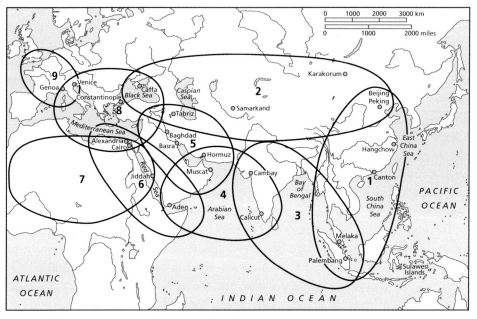

Map 2.3 Systems of exchange in thirteenth-century Eurasia.

It is important to underline that the *space of flux* created by the trade of Indian cottons was not limited to the Indian Ocean, as much of the literature often implies.[33] Abu-Lughod's map allows us to follow Indian cloth as it moved outside the geographical remit of the Indian Ocean and formed a new and extended geography of interaction. Stephen Dale suggests that Southeast Asian imitations of Indian cotton textiles were sold to China early in the Common Era, and that such a trade remained buoyant even after China developed its own cotton industry. The famous silk roads that carried silks from China to central Asia and from there towards the Middle East and Europe (no. 2 in Map 2.3) were, according to Dale, a 'cotton road' when seen in the opposite direction, with cotton textiles reaching present-day Xinjiang, the utmost western province of China in the later Han period (first and second century CE).[34] From India also came high-quality muslins (*po-tieh*) that are frequently mentioned in Tang (618–907 CE) sources. By the European Middle Ages, it was not uncommon for central Asian consumers to use turbans, napkins, handkerchiefs and other textiles such as chintzes, calicoes and muslins produced in India.[35] The trade of Indian cotton cloth via Cambodia and Java was also buoyant in southern China as early as the eleventh and twelfth centuries CE.[36] These were high-quality products manufactured in Bengal, as seen in the case of fine muslin cloth referred to as 'cloth as fine as starched paper' in early Ming sources.[37]

Africa was also heavily connected to the world of cotton exchange. As early as the fourteenth century, ivory, gold and slaves from Africa were exchanged for cloth – both cottons and silks – that was used for apparel and decoration.[38] These textiles were traded to the Red Sea and found their way to sub-Saharan Africa, to the kingdoms of the Yoruba and the Hausa, and to Senegambia via trans-Saharan caravans leaving the entrepôt of Cairo and possibly the towns and cities of Nubia and Abyssinia.

Creating products

The simple understanding of the geographies of exchange of cotton textiles and their importance in structuring a global system of trade are insufficient for appreciating the complex and subtle ways in which people, things and meanings interacted. We know that Indian merchants often produced for specific markets, customising production to suit local preferences.[39] This was done because consumers across Asia and Africa expressed different tastes or assigned different meanings to textiles. The Basra market, for instance, was well known for its liking of deep-blue shades, something that Gujarati merchants were able to provide thanks to the abundant supplies of indigo in their region.[40] Specific areas of India became specialised in production for particular markets. Patola was a type of cloth produced mostly in Patan and Ahmedabad, and traded by Gujarati merchants to Southeast Asia. Patolas were created through an elaborate process of double ikat, a procedure that Indian weavers learned by borrowing the technique from Southeast Asia itself. Yet, customisation could go a step further, as Indian producers also sold block-printed patola imitations to Indonesian markets in order to cater to less affluent consumers (Figure 2.4).[41]

It would therefore be incorrect to see the logic of this system of exchange as simply allocative, that is to say geared towards satisfying local needs. Interaction itself created new designs, new practices and new meanings for cloth.[42] The example of patolas shows how several Indian motifs were integrated into Southeast Asian ikat production.[43] Customisation served to sell more, but the results were sometimes unexpected. The so-called Baju jacket in Figure 2.5 is a good example of material hybridity, but also hybridism of meaning. The cloth of which it is made was produced on the Coromandel coast and traded to Sumatra, where it was tailored into a jacket. Yet, this is not in any sense a Southeast Asian artefact because the design reveals a strong European influence, suggesting that the cloth might have been produced for the European and not the Southeast Asian market. It is difficult to say what consumers in Sumatra might have made of it when the cloth was eventually tailored into a garment. This was not part of

Figure 2.4 Ceremonial hanging with a hunting scene, late seventeenth/ eighteenth century. (See also colour plate.)

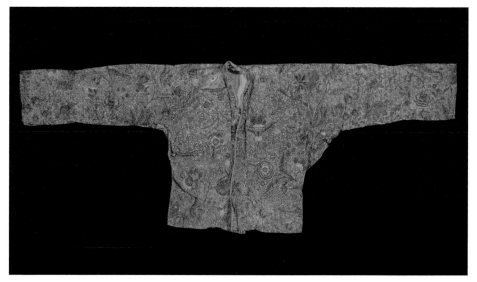

Figure 2.5 Jacket produced on the Coromandel coast, late eighteenth century, and tailored into a jacket in Sumatra. (See also colour plate.)

the Sumatran sartorial repertoire, as sewn garments became available only with the spread of Arabic and Indian types of dress.[44]

For us, textiles have quintessentially a consumer value. However, anthropological studies have revealed that, in most Asian cultures, textiles were not important simply for what economists would call 'use-value', that is to say their ability to fulfil a functional need. They were often seen as powerful objects conveying personal and collective meaning. According to Lotika Varadarajan, cottons were exchanged 'within a cultural matrix in which the semiotics of the object traded provided it with a value which could not at all times be expressed in terms of the price paid'.[45] What she means is that consumption was not so much an act of individual satisfaction or fashionable behaviour; rather, the use of a piece of cloth could be symbolic of wider social principles linking the individual to community, state and religion. This was particularly the case for imported cloth that acted as a sign of 'distinction', not for the individual using it but in the social or ritual practice in which the cloth was used.

Many of the textiles imported to Southeast Asia, one of the areas that has been better studied, were used for a variety of purposes, which included curing diseases, death and other religious rights, the sanctification of icons, ceremonial and diplomatic exchange, as well as the payment of services and taxes and the decoration of royal compounds.[46] These practices suggest that the use of Indian cloth was not simply practical (covering one's body) or decorative (as fashionable apparel). Cloth served to connect people across space and time. In Jambi, in Southeast Asia, a cotton cloth called *Biru*, imported from India, played a key role in the relationship between the king and his subjects. In the Indonesian islands, cotton textiles were sometimes considered precious heirlooms with magical properties that connected multiple generations and acted as ways to represent past events and people.[47] Their value derived from local religions and folk beliefs that shaped the purchase of cloth not just in Southeast Asia but also in other areas of Afro-Eurasia.

By adopting anthropological and material culture methodologies, however, it is sometimes easy to forget that the textiles that today we see in museums are not entirely representative of the large quantities of goods traded in the Indian Ocean. It would be misleading to think that all textiles traded to Southeast Asia or elsewhere entered 'circuits of deep meaning'. The majority of textiles sold across the Indian Ocean were relatively cheap. We have seen the articulation of the trade, though it is more difficult to say how large this was in terms of quantities. The VOC (the Dutch East India Company – Vereenigde Oost-Indische Compagnie) in the 1620s estimated the trade from Masulipatam to Burma on the part of Asian merchants to be worth from £80,000 to £120,000, the majority of which was cloth.[48] Textiles had a real economic function beyond profit for the traders themselves. Similarly to silver, they were indispensable commodities for any merchant who wanted to do business around the Indian Ocean. Javanese and Malays, for instance, would not accept any other product apart from textiles in exchange for foodstuffs and spices. Textiles were therefore a means to an end as well as a commodity to enjoy. In Thailand, imported sarasa cloth from Gujarat supplemented local consumption but was also re-exported to China, the Philippines and Japan.[49] Imported textiles were therefore key to further successful trade and they allowed even remote parts of Asia to find trading partners. This was the case for the indigenous people of Formosa (Taiwan), who would happily barter their deerskins for Guinea cloth and *cangans*. The accumulation, sometimes of hundreds, of cangans and Chinese piece-goods was part of a strategy of display of wealth and social status within local communities.[50]

Cotton textile consumption in India

One of the competitive advantages of Indian cotton textiles was their sheer variety, diversity and assortments and the specialised finishing skills involved in their production.[51] Different areas of the subcontinent specialised in niche products ranging from the fine muslin of Bengal down to the cheap striped Guinea cloth produced in western India. The range of products was made available to consumers in India and elsewhere thanks to a capillary system of distribution based on thousands of merchants who had a clear sense of markets and who acted as merchandising agents.

The many Mughal miniatures and colonial prints in today's museums and private collections show the wide range of textiles used in India in the early modern period. Together with literary evidence, they indicate that consumers had access to a range of cotton textiles. Exchange was not just strong at an international level but connected the different parts of India, which often complemented each other in terms of product specialisation. It is difficult to generalise on the levels of consumption and on the varieties of textiles used in each region. What is certain is that demand was not static, but that consumers expressed personal and regional preferences that changed over time.[52] Cottons were used for interior decoration as well as for clothing. Europeans were quick to notice how textiles structured spaces: buildings in India were not as enclosed as in Europe, and masonry was integrated with textiles in the form of canopies, curtains, floor spreads, tents and other household decorations.[53] The effect that we see in miniatures is dazzling, with a profusion of textile patterns and colours. The highest-quality textiles (both cottons and silks) were used in large quantities by

Figure 2.6 Rai Surjan Hada, the ruler of Ranthambhor, in northwest India, submitting to the Mughal emperor Akbar (r. 1556–1605) in 1569. This scene from the *Akbarnama* (*Book of Akbar*) was designed by the Mughal court artist Mukund and painted by Shankar. It shows the profusion of textiles used by the court. (See also colour plate.)

the Mughal court, which, because of its peripatetic nature, needed a constant supply of soft furnishings and tents (Figure 2.6).[54]

Cottons were similarly used for clothing, integrating different textiles of diverse texture and colours. The Englishman Nicholas Downton reported in the diary of his travels to India in 1610–13 that the clothing worn by the Indians 'is white, light, and thinne, fit for the countryess heate', adding that in winter they wore heavier and more colourful clothing made of 'pintadoes, silke stuffes,

Figure 2.7 Page from an album of sketches of costumes of south India, *c.* 1842. (See also colour plate.)

satins, and damasks, dyed into all sorts of lively and good colers, cloth of gold, silver, and tissue of their own, whereof they have plenty'.[55] The most expensive and most appreciated of the cotton textiles was muslin, though it came in a wide range of qualities and prices, with the finer ones being several times more expensive than cheaper types.

Calico was instead the favourite choice of mid-range consumers, as seen in Figure 2.7. This is a so-called Company School work and therefore should be suitably assessed as a British representation of life in South India in the early nineteenth century. Yet it is a useful depiction of everyday attire. It is part of a collection of twenty-four similar watercolours on a range of castes and tribes living in Malabar, Cochin and Travancore, which include Konkanis, Nazarenes (Syrian Christians), Jonagans, and Chettis. The couple here represented belongs to the Chettis (traders), an occupational term employed as a caste name that included weavers, oil pressers and other artisans. The man wears a dhoti, an angavastram draped on chest and shoulders, earrings and a turban made of printed cloth. His wife wears a sari and carries with her a basket with cotton, perhaps suggesting that the husband is a weaver. The dress is simple but the presence of a turban, the wearing of cloth with a red border (perhaps printed or embroidered in silk) and the use of jewellery distinguish this couple both from consumers of lower rank, represented as wearing coarser varieties of cotton cloth such as *pat*, and from their wealthier counterparts wearing instead embroidered and highly decorated cottons and silks.[56]

Local and imported products

Elsewhere in Asia imported Indian textiles did not replace the local production of cotton cloth carried out by households or small productive centres. The logic of trade and exchange was *complementary* and *supplementary* rather than *competitive* with local manufacturing. This might appear an abstract principle, but we find it repeated not just in the different regions of India but also when we consider the relationship between cotton textile trade and production in other parts of Afro-Eurasia. How is it possible that Indian textiles did not kill off the local – often domestic – industries of the regions they were targeted at? A response to this question can be found by considering two distinct issues: firstly, the competitiveness of Indian production; and secondly, the logic that underpinned the 'old cotton system'.

India's competitiveness in cotton textile manufacturing might appear 'natural' because the cultivation of cotton developed in the subcontinent earlier than in the rest of Asia. However, the local availability of raw cotton cannot be taken as sufficient to explain the success of India in this sector for several centuries. It was also thought that Indian textiles 'clothed the world' because they were cheap: the low cost of labour assured competitiveness. This axiom too has been questioned. Indian wages could be relatively high in Asian terms. Moreover, it was mostly the more expensive varieties of Indian cottons that were traded. Indian cottons were ahead of competitors in terms of the variety on offer and the skills that characterised the artisan production of the subcontinent. It was the quality of the product, the result of local specialisation, and the skilful use of mordants and dyes that made Indian textiles both attractive and striking.[57]

Why import Indian cottons instead of trying to manufacture them at home? We have seen earlier the appeal of the design, the high level of customisation and the 'exotic' nature of such textiles, which could be matched only with difficulty. However, in several places the reason for importing Indian cottons could be simpler. In the Malay peninsula, the dry season was not long enough to grow cotton, which made these areas reliant upon imported cotton textiles. The same could be said of Europe, where the lack of raw cotton presented an opportunity for the trade in cotton cloth to flourish. Perhaps more puzzling is that many areas that imported cloth from India were manufacturers in their own right. The Philippines, for instance, produced raw cotton and manufactured a number of cotton cloths (*lampotes*, *talingas* and *mantles of Ilocos*), but also imported cottons from India.[58] Several areas of Asia produced their own cotton cloth in large quantities, but local production was probably not sufficient to satisfy demand. Similarly, in Persia, the local production of chintzes, *qalamkār* (Indiennes), *qadak* (a narrow calico cloth) and *karbās* (a coarse white calico) were supplemented by imports of Indian cottons.[59]

Local production should not be seen as an alternative to import. In seventeenth-century Samarqand, Indian merchants brought with them Indian master weavers, who were encouraged to settle locally and produce for them.[60] For Southeast Asia, Kenneth Hall has suggested that it was imported textiles that sparked local textile manufacturers to imitate Indian goods.[61] There is little statistical evidence to measure the size of Southeast Asian markets for Indian textiles compared to the domestic market. It is probable – and surviving artefacts confirm this – that Indian imports catered to the high- and medium-quality market, while local production provided for the majority of the medium and lower products.[62] However, we should not oppose imported versus domestic products, as a considerable share of Southeast Asian textiles were also exported to markets in East Java, Bali, Sumbawa, Buton, South Sulawesi and parts of Cambodia as well as South China.[63]

West Africa imported Indian cottons but manufactured also its own distinctive products, such as the locally woven cotton strips used as currency in Kanem in the fourteenth century. Imported Indian cottons were not the only textiles that were traded. West African cloth circulated widely in regional markets that were characterised by distinctive preferences: striped cloths were particularly in demand on the Gold Coast, where they were exchanged for precious metal; indigo-blue cloths were sold mostly in Gabon and Angola in exchange for ivory and slaves.[64] Indian cottons came, therefore, to supplement an already articulated supply of locally woven cloths.[65] It was also a fluid commercial relationship in no way as fixed as modern trading systems. Changes in local production, alliances between tribes, and specific economic conditions could swing the balance between imported and local textiles. This is an argument that in different versions has been proposed both by Joseph Inikori for West Africa and Anthony

Reid for Southeast Asia. In the case of Africa, Inikori supports the idea that the slave trade, while pushing imported textiles, subtracted precious human capital from the local textile industry.[66] Reid instead has emphasised that the integration of specific locales or areas within a wider economic system of exchange was not necessarily permanent.[67] In the case of Southeast Asia, he has argued that in the second half of the seventeenth century several urban centres withdrew local and long-distance trade in what Kenneth Hall calls a 'loss of the indigenous role in international trade'.[68]

A further argument for both the success of Indian cottons and the expansion of local manufacturing across Eurasia is that of complementarity with other available textiles and the flexible use to which cottons were put. Cotton found different uses in different parts of the world. In China, for instance, they were appreciated for their supple texture, which was softer than ramie, and they were widely used for their capacity to insulate against warmth and humidity. Cotton was used in China not only as cloth but also for padding. Raw cotton, once ginned and bowed, was stuffed into mattresses and quilts and even into garments.[69] Cotton was warmer than ramie and was thus suitable for the dress of the common people, especially in the cold northern provinces of China.[70] Woven cotton textiles complemented and competed against silks.[71] Indian cloth, already traded to China in the first millennium CE, was in high demand, especially those varieties that were dyed in rich colours and calendered to imitate the gloss of silks.[72] In Japan, Indian cottons were appreciated for their colour and softness. Traditionally, the island had relied on silk textiles for the dress of the elite and cheaper hemp, arrowroot, wisteria and Japanese linden textiles for the poorer classes.[73]

The process of assimilation of Indian cotton textiles within a social and cultural process that we call 'fashion' came to the fore in Europe in the sixteenth to the eighteenth centuries. This does not mean that Indian cottons were unknown to Europeans before that date. Indian calicoes were already prized in the Mediterranean basin by the late medieval period. Venetians and Genoese merchants actively traded with Asia via intermediaries in the Levant who procured for them spices, luxuries such as precious stones and Persian silks, and Indian calicoes.[74] A flourishing cotton industry had also developed in southern Europe, producing fustians and other mix-cottons that were used in place of heavier woollens and to complement lighter woollens. Notwithstanding this, before the foundation of the European East India companies, European markets remained relatively removed from the world of long-distance trade with Asia. Europe was the last link in a system in which European traders and markets were at best peripheral.[75]

Conclusion

The world that Indian cottons clothed was made up of a variety of consumers and trading networks, and was catered for by a variety of specialised areas of production. The space of interaction of Afro-Eurasia was both flexible and fragile at the same time. Cotton textiles were a key commodity not just for consumption but also for the trading of other commodities. India emerged as the motor of this system. I defined this as a 'centrifugal system', a space of exchange dominated by a logic of integration and cooperation rather than competition between different areas. Such a logic was, however, not just present in the trading and consumption of cottons across Eurasia, but also dominated the knowledge of raw cotton and the technologies used to process this fibre.

3 'WOOL GROWING ON WILD TREES': THE GLOBAL REACH OF COTTON

The fourteenth-century English writer and traveller Sir John Mandeville is rarely cited for the trustworthiness of the observations that he gathered during his alleged travels to Asia in the 1320s. In his *Travels* he says to his readers that in India grew 'a wonderful tree which bore tiny lambs on the endes of its branches. These branches were so pliable that they bent down to allow the lambs to feed when they are hungrie.'[1] He was describing a cotton tree, whose illustration came to be one of the wonders of the Orient (Figure 3.1). Europeans knew cotton textiles and by this time had access to raw cotton from the Near East, but few of them had actually seen a cotton boll with their eyes. Europeans were not the only ones to have little familiarity with cotton. Before the sixteenth century hardly anyone in Japan had seen a cotton plant, though by this time the Japanese were avid consumers of cotton textiles. This lack of knowledge was perceived as such a major failure that the sixteenth-century *Chronology of Japanese History* narrates how it was a young man, speaking Chinese and coming from Southeast Asia, who made the first attempt to introduce cotton to Japan when he was swept ashore in a small boat in the summer of the year 799 CE. Tradition maintains that he brought cotton seeds with him. The seeds were washed, soaked and planted in different parts of the country.[2] Yet, they did not grow to become plants. Japan had to wait several centuries until cotton cultivation was finally successfully introduced.

These two stories are particularly poignant for the fact that England and Japan became in the nineteenth and twentieth centuries respectively the two major world producers of cotton textiles. Yet, as late as the eighteenth century, their knowledge of cotton and cotton cultivation were limited. Mandeville was correct in identifying cotton as something quintessentially Indian. By describing cotton bolls in the form of little lambs, he was not just equating the functional use and property of Indian cotton to those of English wool, but suggested also that like the sheep's fleece for Europe, the wealth and riches of India were linked to access to a material that other parts of the world did not have. This

Figure 3.1 A cotton tree as depicted by John Mandeville, featuring sheep instead of cotton bolls.

chapter asks if Mandeville was correct: was it true that the advantage of India in the production of cotton textiles derived from its knowledge of the cotton plant and its early cultivation and commercial use? This chapter argues that in the 'old cotton system' of Afro-Eurasia, access to the local raw material was fundamental to the development of a competitive industry, though this criterion came to be less binding as we move into the early modern period. Secondly, the chapter shows that cotton cultivation and the productive use of this fibre was not a prerogative of India and that the period that I define as the 'first cotton revolution' saw the spread of cotton cultivation to different areas of the world.

The spread of cotton

Scholars have suggested that cotton originated in India and was first cultivated in the Indus Valley in 3200 BCE. Textile fragments found in the *Mohenjo-daro* (the 'Mound of the Dead'), an ancient Indus Valley civilisation *circa* 2600–1900 BCE, include a variety of textiles using cotton from a plant closely related to *Gossypium arboreum*.[3] By the year 600 BCE, cotton started to be traded in Mesopotamia, reaching Europe in the fourth century BCE. Here, the plant did not find a hospitable environment and its cultivation remained limited. Although some cotton cloth reached Rome, it was probably a rare fabric. Several Roman authors mention the existence of a strange material called cotton when talking about the peculiarities of the Near East. Cotton must have appeared to the Roman world as an extraordinary material, not just for its innate qualities of softness and lightness but also for the peculiarity of the trees producing it. Herodotus explains how the troops serving in the Persian King Xerxes' invasion of Greece wore garments made of 'wool growing on wild trees' that was 'surpassing in beauty and quality the wool of sheep'.[4]

Passages like these testify to the limited spread of cotton cultivation in ancient times. The cotton plant was also nearly unknown in China before the beginning of the second millennium CE. Why was this the case? And why did it take so long for cotton cultivation to be transplanted to areas with suitable climatic conditions? The response can be found in the fact that it is not just a matter of transplanting cultivation. The adoption of cotton by a different ecologic environment had to be accompanied by the transmission of sufficient knowledge about its potential uses as well as the conditions in which the plant could prosper. When cotton finally started penetrating the agrarian systems of China, the Middle East and Africa between 800 and 1000 CE, its adoption was accompanied by a transmission of agronomical knowledge. This is a process that Linda Shaffer has defined as 'southernisation', that is to say, the spread of raw materials (including cotton), related processes and technologies from southern Asia to other parts of the Asian continent and, eventually, the entire globe.[5] Such a process depended upon the capacities of receiving areas to learn and put into practice suitable techniques and technologies for the processing of this material.

Cotton had already made some inroads in ancient times and its cultivation probably reached the Persian Gulf, Arabia, Ethiopia, Nubia and Upper Egypt to arrive in Mediterranean regions in pre-Islamic times.[6] By the tenth century it was to be found in several areas of the Islamic world: parts of Anatolia, Persia and Syria were well known for their high-quality cotton in the early Middle Ages. From Asia Minor and North Africa, cotton spread to Greece, Cyprus, the

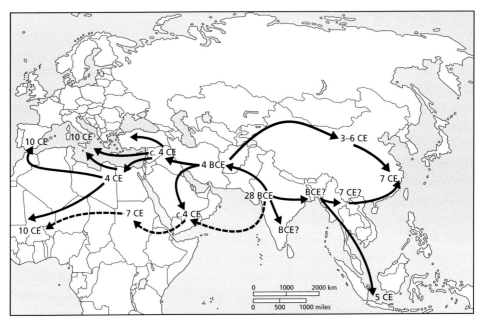

Map 3.1 The spread of cotton cultivation in Afro-Eurasia.

Aegean islands, southern Italy and southern Spain (Map 3.1).[7] These were the only regions of Europe where cotton could be successfully grown before the early modern 'little ice age' made most of the continent climatically unsuitable for its cultivation.[8] Cotton growing also moved eastwards and arrived in Indochina in the first or second century CE and was carried by the Ai-Lao 'barbarians' along the banks of the Irrawaddy River in the fourth century CE. However, cotton cultivation and processing did not spread to China before the seventh century.[9] As it was impossible to grow cotton in the cold environment of Europe, so it was difficult to cultivate it in the tropical climates of Malaya, Borneo and Sumatra.[10]

This chronology suggests that the expansion of Islam might have played a role in the spread of agronomical knowledge between Asia, Africa and Europe. Cotton cultivation reached both sub-Saharan Africa and southern Europe around the tenth century.[11] The spread of cotton eastwards was facilitated by the linking of India to the central Asian silk roads connecting Samarkand in present-day Uzbekistan, Altai and Nainté-Sumë in present-day Mongolia, moving in a direction opposite to the manufactured commodities traded from China to central Asia.[12] In the sixth–seventh century CE cotton reached the area of present-day Turpan in Xingjiang, in central China, although it was initially used simply as an ornamental plant.[13] We know that annual varieties of cotton (*pai-tieh*) were cultivated in this region by the ninth century and that at the end of the Tang period cotton cultivation was widespread in Fujian.[14] There was however a second route through which the perennial variety of the cotton plant (*Gossypium arboreum*) entered China at the end of the first millennium. This was a southern route via Indochina, the Yunnan region of China and the island of Hainan.[15] Via Thailand and Vietnam (where cotton arrived in the seventh century CE), cultivation reached Southeast Asia, central Burma, Cambodia, East Java, Bali, Sumbawa, Buton and the southeastern part of South Sulawesi.[16]

Why did it take so long (several centuries if not even an entire millennium) for cotton to spread across the temperate zones of Afro-Eurasia? Clearly the structuring of strong connections through religion (Islam) and trade (the silk roads) catalysed the spread of agronomical knowledge. Yet there were several barriers. The first was genetic. Probably it was the perennial variety of the cotton plant that was most easily transplanted; this, however, presented important limitations as to how widely cotton could spread, as the annual variety (*Gossypium herbaceum*) had greater potential to mature in colder climates.[17] This was the case for China, where it was only after the development of annual varieties that cotton cultivation spread northwards, becoming an important crop in the Lower Yangzi area in the twelfth century.[18]

The case of the spread of cotton cultivation to Yuan and Ming China shows the existence of another important barrier. Its initial reception did not coincide with the development of cotton processing and manufacturing on any large scale. Cotton, a fibre shorter than ramie or flax, necessitated the retooling of both spinning and weaving, a process that took the best part of a couple of centuries.[19] It was only in the thirteenth century that cotton textile production, as well as cotton cultivation, became two of the most common occupations in rural China. Institutional factors played a key role in the success of cotton as an 'industrial crop'. After some resistance by silk manufacturers, the Chinese government decided to use cotton as a way to collect taxation in kind. By the fourteenth century, the Yuan dynasty collected more than half a million bolts of cotton cloth annually as taxes.[20] An edict of 1365 made cotton growing compulsory for all farmers cultivating over an acre of land.[21] The Mongol regime promoted cotton cultivation also through state-commissioned publications such as the *Fundamentals of Agriculture and Sericulture* (*Nongsang jiyao*) (1273) and by instituting bureaux for cotton cultivation in various provinces.[22]

Cotton cultivation in the early modern world

Which were the characteristics of cotton cultivation in the 'old cotton system'? And did India possess any advantage in the cultivation of this fibre? Probably the most important feature of cotton growing was its smallholding system of production. Throughout Afro-Eurasia, cotton was integrated within the cultivation of other crops in smallholdings, often being of secondary importance to foodstuffs such as rice and grain. Part of the success of cotton derived from the fact that it could be cultivated on land with low agrarian potential. A good example is the Songjiang region, an area south of Shanghai with limited agrarian potential that was one of the first in China to be placed under extensive cotton cultivation. From there, cotton cultivation expanded eastwards towards the Chinese sea and southwards towards the Tai basin.[23] By the middle of the sixteenth century cotton was grown all over the southern province of Guangdong.[24] The success of cotton cultivation was such that in the 1620s in Songjiang more than half of the 130,000 hectares of cultivable land were given over to cotton.[25] In this period in the area of Jiaxing, south of Shanghai, 90 per cent of all land was cultivated with cotton.[26] It was estimated that by the mid eighteenth century 80–90 per cent of all households in Henan and Shantung were engaged in cotton cultivation.[27]

It must be noted that such specialisation in cotton production did not mean the creation of large-scale plantations of the type that appeared in the Americas in the seventeenth century based on the exploitation of unfree labour. The development of monoculture remained linked to household production, though the system became increasingly commercialised over time. A similar system was present in India, although it is difficult to assess the size of the unit of cotton cultivation in the subcontinent. For South India, Prasannan Parthasarathi suggests that two different systems of cotton cultivation coexisted, which he calls 'intensive' and 'extensive'. While intensive cotton cultivation was mostly carried out on rich soil as a monoculture, extensive cultivation was less capital intensive and combined cotton with other crops (grains, dhal, etc.) in order to minimise the risk of harvest failure. The productivity of intensive cultivation was double, if not three times that of extensive cultivation (62.5 pounds per acre against 22.5 in nineteenth-century Coimbatore).[28] According to Parthasarathi, the main factor influencing the choice between intensive and extensive cultivation was not the availability of suitable land but the availability of capital to invest in the more expensive (but more productive) irrigation systems.[29]

There is a clear sense that both in India and in China cotton cultivation became increasingly pervasive. If initially cotton was cultivated on marginal land, with the development of cotton manufacturing, additional areas of reclaimed land were used for this crop, as in the case of Jiangnan in China.[30] Cotton eventually had a transformative effect on the agrarian economies of several parts of Asia. We have better information for China, where cotton growing came to replace hemp cultivation.[31] As productivity of cotton was ten times higher than hemp, it allowed larger quantities of land to be used for the production of cereals.[32] Moreover, cotton growing was less labour-intensive and yielded a surer harvest than silkworm breeding.[33] Cotton also found a space because of changes in the cultivation of other staple crops such as wheat and rice. In the case of rice, the introduction of new varieties with double cropping allowed for the release of further land for cotton cultivation.[34]

Cotton presented a major disadvantage compared to other crops, however: it is hard on soils and tends to quickly deplete the agrarian potential of the soil. This explains why it was later cultivated on frontier land. But there is no proof that this was the case in the pre-1700 period in Eurasia. In China, for instance, cotton cultivation was not based on land claimed from the forests, but on small farms. The integration of cotton with other crops such as rice, barley, beans and other legumes was therefore not just necessary to feed peasant families, but was part of crop rotation, thus avoiding the risk or depleting the land.[35]

The smallholding base of much of cotton cultivation came to shape the entire sector. The initial stages of the processing of the fibre (cleaning it and spinning it) tended to be carried out within peasant households, and especially by women. This created a localisation of the cotton industry that was linked to the availability of raw materials. Yet it also shaped an intricate manufacturing geography, which was mapped on top of an agrarian one. This happened because different areas produced different varieties of cotton. Even if genetically identical, fibres produced in different climatic and terrain conditions varied in quality and length, which meant their suitability for products of different price and value. In India, for instance, Surat cotton was of a good quality but a short staple; Bengal was similar to Surat, but of an even shorter staple; while Madras cotton was deemed to be of the lowest quality.[36] As the names suggest, cotton was cultivated in different parts of the subcontinent and especially in Mysore, on the Coromandel plains and throughout South India in clay-rich dry land.[37] Cotton was also cultivated in many parts of North India: the Mālwa Plateau and the area of Ajmer in Rajasthan, several parts of Gujarat and the surroundings of Allahadad and Awadh in Uttar Pradesh, Agra, Delhi and Multan in present-day Pakistan, as well as Orissa in Bengal.[38]

Similar types of regional specialisations were present in sixteenth- and seventeenth-century Anatolia, where the Mediterranean plains of Adana and Tarsus in southeastern Turkey, the plains between the Menderes rivers in the region of Izmir and the areas of Aydın, Kütahya and Bursa were important areas for cotton cultivation.[39] The 'old cotton system' relied on a variety of different types and qualities of raw cotton, which came to characterise local cloth production from the high-quality muslin down to the cheaper cloths produced with lower-quality raw material. The small-scale cultivation of this fibre made it the perfect raw material for basic industrial processing within the peasant household itself. This was a pattern that characterised not just India, but also China, Anatolia and other parts of Eurasia.

The commercialisation of cotton

I have so far presented the story of cotton as one of diffusion and localisation. First the cultivation of the fibre diffused across most of Asia and Africa and, once established in specific places, it generated local varieties and specialisation of production. Whilst small-scale cultivation seemed to be the general pattern, both the raw material and the finished cloth produced varied from place to place. This is a convincing though simplistic picture that does not consider the increasing commercialisation of the cotton fibre both over short distances (from farm to farm and village to village), long distances (for instance between regions of India or China) and across continents (as in the case of Europe's supplies from the Middle East).

Importation of cotton was a way to supplement local cultivation. Already at the beginning of the sixth century CE raw cotton was traded from India to China, and before 1600 considerable quantities of Chinese cotton from Yunnan reached Burma.[40] Commercialisation of the raw material served to avoid price fluctuations caused by harvest failure and other calamities. An example, both of a calamity and lack of commercialisation, is the great cyclone that struck the Masulipatam region of India in 1633, destroying most of its modest cotton crop. By the following summer cotton prices were up 75 per cent, a crisis that dragged on in the following years.[41]

In less traumatic circumstances, the commercialisation of raw cotton served to expand production beyond the limit of local supplies, releasing land to feed workers engaged in spinning and weaving, and more often also releasing workers from cultivation to specialise in manufacturing. In many ways India did not fare well compared to China. The level of commercialisation of raw cotton in China had no parallel in India or elsewhere in the world. India enjoyed some degree of commercialisation of raw cotton within the subcontinent that helped the emergence of key areas of manufacturing. Much weaker was the position of Southern Europe, a world area that entirely relied on supplies from the Near East, something that hampered the development of a viable cotton industry.

In the Ming period, China developed a truly imperial system of production based on the long-distance trade of raw cotton. As Jiangnan became a key area of cotton textile manufacturing, so the region was in great need of raw materials from elsewhere in the empire. Some cotton arrived from the southern regions of

Map 3.2 Long-distance trade of cotton fibres to Jiangnan in the Ming period.

Fujian and Guangdong. However the bulk of the cotton that 'clothed the empire' reached Jiangnan from the northern provinces of Shandong and Henan, several hundred miles away (Map 3.2).[42] In his 1628 *Nongzheng quanshu* (*Comprehensive Work on Agriculture*) the agronomist Xu Guangqi observed that 'in the north the cotton is cheap while cloth is expensive; in the south the opposite is true. Cotton is therefore shipped to the south, while cloth is shipped to and sold in the north'.[43] This was possible because China had an efficient system of canals that connected the thousands of miles separating the southern parts of the empire from its northern fringes. This greatly helped the emergence of both specialised cotton-growing regions in China and dedicated centres of manufacture.[44]

This relationship between the north and the south of the empire shaped the Chinese cotton industry until the end of the Ming dynasty. Over the course of the seventeenth century the northern regions started specialising in the production of coarser cloth, although the trade of raw cotton between the north and the south of the empire remained important. It was in this period that a new class of merchants emerged in China operating on a par with European merchant entrepreneurs. They bought raw cotton, gave it out to women for spinning and weaving in the countryside and had the resulting cloth dyed in urban workshops.

They finally sold cloth both in China and abroad.[45] Cotton was thus key to the market integration of the Chinese economy, connecting long-distance trade of primary and finished products and supporting commercial networks stretching several thousands of miles.[46] The household remained central to the organisation of production of cotton textile manufacturing, although cotton growing became to a certain degree separated from cotton textile production.

It is more difficult to assess the size and geographic dimension of cotton trade in India. Before the seventeenth century there are few sources attesting the existence of large-scale trade of raw cotton between the major cotton-producing areas of the subcontinent. It is reasonably certain, however, that no cotton entered the subcontinent from other parts of Asia.[47] Coromandel weavers, for instance, relied at least until the second quarter of the seventeenth century on cotton cultivated on the Coromandel plains, with small additional quantities of raw materials coming from Arcot and the Krishna delta.[48] The expansion of production in the region after the 1630s, however, necessitated higher supplies of raw materials. Overland trade of raw cotton from central Deccan to specialised markets near the Godavari delta and the southern delta of the Krishna River developed; cotton being transported from places up to 250 miles away, a trade that expanded in the seventeenth century (Map 3.3).[49] Caravans with 40,000 bullocks transported cotton from the plateau, to be exchanged for salt in the coastal areas. It is estimated that by the late seventeenth century 2.5 million pounds of raw cotton was traded from the Deccan to Coromandel every year.[50] It seems likely that the varieties of cotton that were most commercialised were those of higher quality, worth the high price of transport and the charges of market intermediaries.

Interregional trade of raw cotton was not the only way to provision areas of expanding manufactures. By the seventeenth century, Balasore in Orissa and Cossimbazar in West Bengal were exporting cotton yarn. In the seventeenth and especially in the eighteenth centuries the development of the Bengali cotton manufacturing industry became heavily dependent on cotton imported from central and southern India and spun yard from the Surat area of Gujarat (Map 3.3).[51] While local high-quality cotton was used for the best products, large quantities of imported cotton from western India allowed for the industry to expand.[52]

The pictures of India and China contrast with that of Europe, where cotton cultivation never became anywhere near extensive. Because of climatic conditions, only small ecological niches such as the Mediterranean islands produced cotton.[53] It was, however, rather poor in quality, with the Cypriot varieties being just marginally better than the low-quality cotton produced in southern Spain, Apulia, Calabria and Malta.[54] Higher-quality cotton was imported into Europe

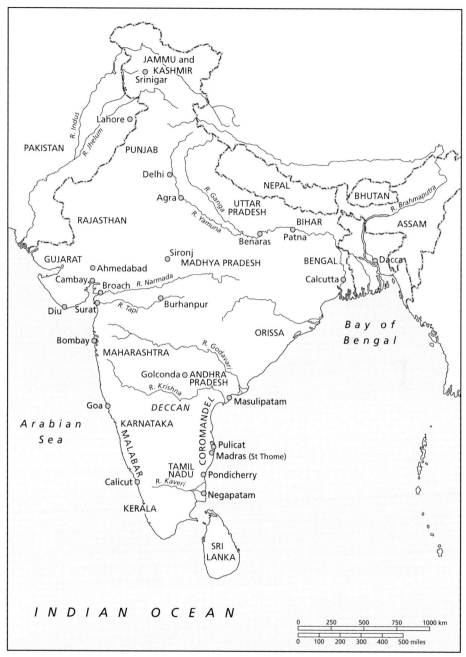

Map 3.3 Regions of India.

Table 3.1 *Import of raw cotton into southern Europe in the thirteenth and fourteenth centuries (Genoa, Venice and Marseilles).*

Port	Region of production	Start of trade
Beginning of the thirteenth century		
Alexandria	Egypt	*c.* 1140
Antakya	Syria	*c.* 1140
	Sicily	*c.* 1140
Beirut	Tripolis (Syria)	1211
Beirut	Jerusalem	
Acre		
Laodicea		1200–50
Jaffa		1200–50
Aleppo	Aleppo	1200–50
Damascus	Caravan from Baghdad–Ephesos–Mecca	1200–50
End of the thirteenth century		
Lajazzo	Lesser Armenia	after 1291
Laiazzo	Karykas and Adera	
	Cyprus	
	Apulia	
	Sicily (from 1140)	
End of the fourteenth century		
Lajazzo	Lesser Armenia	
	Cyprus	
	Crete	
	Syria	(in decline)
	Apulia	
	Egypt	

Sources: Maureen Fennell Mazzaoui, 'The Cotton Industry of Northern Italy in the Late Middle Ages: 1150–1450', *JEH* 32/1 (1972): 262–86; H. Wescher, 'The Beginning of the Cotton Industry in Europe', *Ciba Review* 64 (1948): 2328–33, and 'Cotton Growing and Cotton Trade in the Orient during the Middle Ages', *Ciba Review* 64 (1948): 2334–8.

from the ports of Aleppo and Epiphania in the Middle East, followed by lower qualities from Lesser Armenia, the surroundings of Damascus and from the Syrian coast (Table 3.1).[55] Raw cotton was imported into Europe especially by the merchants of Genoa, Pisa and Venice, three of the so-called Italian maritime republics. Cotton was part of a group of commodities imported by Venice from the Middle East that included pepper and spices, lacca, sugar, pearls, but also silks, *bocasini* (mixed silk and cotton) and indigo.[56] By the beginning of the fourteenth century the commerce in raw cotton had become a major branch of the city's trade and it is estimated that cotton was second only to spices among the commodities traded by Venetian merchants from the Middle East.[57]

Most cotton entering Europe was neither spun nor ginned. In the fifteenth century, for example, only less than 15 per cent of all cotton entering the Italian region of Lombardy was spun cotton, the rest being spun in the Italian countryside.[58] This suggests that Europe, and Italy in particular, already possessed sufficient technological and labour expertise for the processing of what must have been still a relatively new fibre.[59] Spinning and weaving of cotton expanded to other areas of continental Europe, with some areas of France, the Flanders and in particular southern Germany developing flourishing cotton industries in the late fourteenth and fifteenth centuries.[60]

The expanding European cotton industry was however hindered by limited supplies of raw material.[61] Frequent interruptions of trade with the Middle East and increasing demand in Europe pushed up the price of raw cotton.[62] This set the conditions for the future engagement of Europe with raw cotton supplies. Venice, in particular, inaugurated a policy of control over supplies. Although this was never totally successful, it was a first attempt to control production carried out in faraway places. Cyprus became in the fourteenth century a 'colony' of Venice. The island's economy was geared towards the needs of the metropolis: in 1500 Cyprus produced 2,000 tons of cotton a year, reaching 6,000 tons in the 1540s.[63] This 'ecological imperialism' based on the exploitation of natural endowments was to be extended to the New World in the sixteenth century.[64]

Technologies and the creation of cotton cloth

Cotton cultivation diffused throughout Afro-Eurasia in the period between the fourth and the thirteenth century CE. This phase was followed by the intensification of trade in raw cotton across regions, especially in the fourteenth to the seventeenth centuries. Different areas of the world relied on the importation of raw cotton, with differing degrees of success. In India, trade was present but did not determine the path of development of cotton manufacturing in the same way in which it successfully did in China and unsuccessfully did in Europe.

The spread of cotton cultivation was accompanied by the adoption of suitable technologies to transform it from a crop into a finished cloth. Before the mechanisation of the eighteenth century, the transformation of cotton was a relatively simple process from a technological point of view. The majority of the tools and machines used to produce cottons were regionally specialised. The cotton fibre was cleaned by removing the seeds (ginning); it was then disentangled and loosened (bowing) before being spun, and the yarn was then reeled and woven into cloth. Eventually the cloth could be printed or decorated, although in many cases, as in China, cotton was used for padding and therefore was not even spun.[65]

The process of ginning was based on a simple tool for separating cotton from the seeds.[66] This was known as a *chobkin* in India and was also present in pre-Ming China.[67] The rudimentary tool was replaced by a more complex device made up of two wooden rollers that moved in opposite directions with a parallel worm and crank handle. It originated either in South Asia or in the Middle East in the sixth century and came to be known in India as a *carkhī*, becoming widespread in the subcontinent by the twelfth century (Figure 3.2a).[68] Its success lay in the fact that it allowed a man (though more commonly it was a woman) to gin from six to eight pounds of raw cotton a day, four or five times more than a *chobkin*.[69] Hand-operated wood-bar ginning devices were also present in other parts of Eurasia, including Song China, where such a tool is represented in a 1313 *Treatise on Agriculture*.[70] Irfan Habib suggests that this technology diffused from India to China along the southern route through which cotton cultivation had also spread, and thus associates technological and agronomical transmission.[71]

After ginning, cotton was bowed. This process aimed at loosening the fibre and at removing the impurities before spinning. The bow (*naddaf*) might have emerged in the Islamic world between the eleventh and the fourteenth centuries (Figure 3.2b).[72] It is unclear if it developed independently in India (where it was called a *kaman*), or if this technology was transmitted to India by Muslim travellers in the fourteenth century.[73] A similar kind of tool was already present in China in the southern Song, although it is likely that it was improved after cotton cultivation became widespread during the Qin, Yuan and early Ming periods. This tool was eventually transmitted to Japan in the fifteenth century.[74] We also find variations of the same type of bow in Egypt, Russia and central Europe.[75] The bow reached western Europe relatively late on (the fourteenth or early fifteenth century), possibly because most of these early stages of processing were carried out where the raw cotton was cultivated (Figure 3.3).[76]

Archaeological evidence helps us to understand the evolution of spinning. Terracotta spindle whorls have been unearthed in Punjab. They date to the third millennium CE and suggest that spinning might already have been a widespread activity in several parts of India in the Common Era.[77] Spinning is a process shared by cotton, wool, hemp and flax, and it is therefore difficult to determine

(a)

(b)

Figures 3.2 (a and b) Ginning and bowing of cotton in India, 1851. (See also colour plate.)

Figure 3.3 Bowing: technological diffusion (numbers are centuries CE of invention and diffusion). The continous line means a certain connection; the discontinous line means a conjectured connection.

the relationship between the spread of cotton and one of the major technological innovations in the history of textiles: the introduction of the spinning wheel. Spinning wheels vary not just according to the fibre spun but also according to the quality of the yarn produced. Dietmar Kuhn suggests that rudimentary spinning wheels were present in China in the Warring States period (463–221 BCE). The spun yarn would certainly have not been cotton, but it is likely that the search for a tool that could increase productivity was already underway before the period in which cotton arrived in China.[78]

Joseph Needham suggested that the spinning wheel was invented in China and that its use possibly spread to other parts of Asia, including India, though South Asia never adopted the multi-spindle machines that were used in China.[79] Linguistic analysis might, however, suggest otherwise, as the word for spinning wheel (*charkha*) is of Persian origin. Written sources indicate that the spinning wheel was known in the Middle East in *circa* 1260 and that it appeared in northern India in the mid thirteenth century/early fourteenth century and with all probability came from West Asia (Figure 3.4).[80]

According to this interpretation, the spinning wheel was part of a technical (also a wider cultural) and design influence of the Islamic world on Hindu India from the fifteenth to the eighteenth centuries.[81] In South India, an area far less influenced by Islam, the more labour-intensive hand spinning remained common practice well into the Mughal period.[82] Sanskrit sources suggest that the spinning wheel was introduced from India to the Malay peninsula and reached South Sulawesi and Maluku by 1600, though the Philippines received it probably in the following century.[83] The spinning wheel was not successfully introduced in Africa until the colonial period, and both areas of cotton production identified by Colleen Kriger (in the Sahara around Lake Chad and on the Atlantic coast along the Senegal River) continued to use hand spinning (Figure 3.5).[84]

Although spinning was a key activity, it does not seem that technological innovation in this process determined the success of specific world areas in cotton textile production. South India did not readily adopt the spinning wheel, something that might have to do with the quality of warp yarns produced by

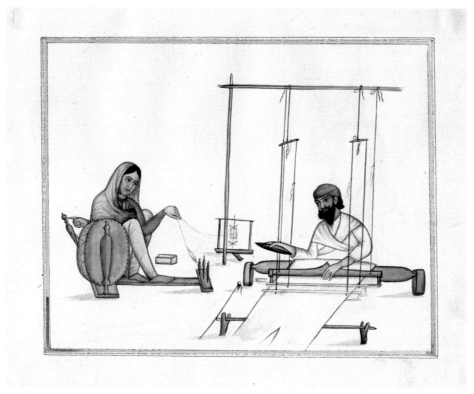

Figure 3.4 Spinning and weaving in India, 1851. (See also colour plate.)

hand spinning. Yet the subcontinent was one of the most important areas of cotton textile manufacturing and trade in the period from the fourteenth century to the eighteenth century. The absence of the spinning wheel in key areas of the Indian subcontinent is in stark contrast with the technological development of

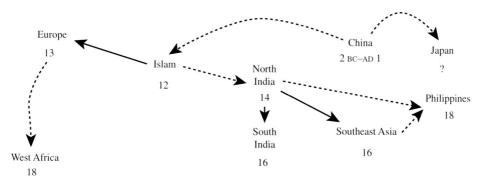

Figure 3.5 The spinning wheel: technological diffusion (numbers are centuries AD of invention/adoption). The continous line means a certain connection; the discontinous line means a conjectured connection.

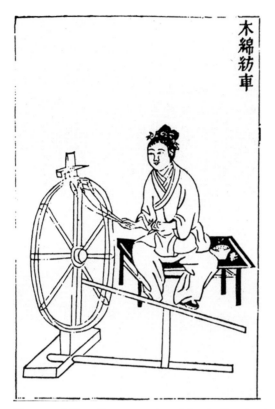

Figure 3.6 Treadle-operated multi-spindle wheel used in China, 1313.

spinning and the doubling of yarn in China. Here, multi-spindle systems (possibly for doubling) were already in place in 1313 (Figure 3.6).[85]

Historians of technology have long discussed why this technology fell into oblivion sometime in the Ming period. Even more complicated is an explanation for why the hydraulic spinning wheels with a capacity to twist 50 kg of yarn per day (Figure 3.7), reminiscent of Richard Arkwright's water frame, remained confined to ramie and were never applied to cotton.[86] These major departures probably found little fertile terrain in which to be put to good use. It is likely that although extremely productive, they were unsuitable for the socio-economic context of textile manufacturing in China, which was based on household production.

The technologies of bowing, reeling, ginning and spinning of cotton suggest the existence of a mutual influence between different areas of Eurasia. There was a slow technological convergence, especially in the preparatory stages (Table 3.2). However, there was no overall 'global' technological paradigm, no best practice

Figure 3.7 Water-powered multiple spinning frame used in China, 1313.

or technological leadership, as each area developed its dedicated technologies, often as a result of specific product specialism.[87]

This was particularly the case with weaving technologies that differed greatly according to the types of cloth produced. In India, different types of looms could be found side by side. The vertical loom was introduced to the subcontinent in the twelfth century and was used to produce textiles or carpets with complex weaving patterns.[88] As for the vertical loom, it is probable that the horizontal loom was introduced to India from Persia in the eleventh century and modified in such a way that weavers could sit in pits, thus alleviating the dryness of the Indian climate.[89] The horizontal loom was used for simpler weaves and probably did not change much before the nineteenth century.[90] Loin looms were present in the northeastern part of the subcontinent, while small and portable backstrap looms (based on mobile body tension) were common in the domestic production of basic kinds of cloth across India (Figure 3.8).[91]

Backstrap looms, which are of common use in India, were instead rare in China until modern times and did not appear in the Middle East until the seventeenth century.[92] Habib suggests that the different speed at which the cultivation of cotton and the diffusion of the bow and spinning wheel happened in Eurasia, especially in the thirteenth and fourteenth centuries, might have created stimuli for the adoption of different weaving technologies. In India, he conjectures, the expansion of 'coarse and ordinary cloth' led to the use of basic looms.[93] As for

Table 3.2 *Spinning in medieval and early modern India, China, the Middle East and Europe.*

	India	China	Middle East	Europe
Spinning – hand	From 3rd millennium BCE. South India continues for all of the 14th century			
Spinning – wheel, 1 spindle	Spinning wheel is adopted from west Asia by the 14th century. Addition of crank handle in the 17th century	A basic spinning wheel for cotton in use in 1270	The spindle wheel was in use in Persia in 1257	Adoption in the 14th century, probably from the Middle East
Spinning – wheel, multi-spindle	Not in use	Multi-spindle wheels are illustrated in 1313. Slow adoption in the following centuries	Not in use	Not in use
Spinning – wheel, advanced	Evidence of spinning wheels powered by water in the 14th century	A hydraulic spinning wheel was said to be in use in the Song period (before 1126)		The U-shaped flyer rotating around the spindle present in 1480

Source: see main text.

spinning, India might have relied on simpler technologies for weaving to those of China, where sophisticated drawlooms were depicted in the 1313 *Nongshu* by Wang Zhen. Drawlooms were also present in India, though their use was probably not as widespread as in China.[94]

In western Africa, too, different looms could be found: the narrow cotton strips dated from 1000 to 1200 CE were woven on a treadle loom that originated in Asia, although in present-day Nigeria, starting from the fifteenth century, cotton textiles were woven through the use of vertical looms probably adapted from raphia looms.[95] In Southeast Asia, backstrap and other tension looms were commonly used for the production of narrow cloth, with treadle looms being introduced only in the eighteenth century from mainland China.[96] It has been argued that the treadle loom, because it allowed weavers' hands to be free and the possibility of two or more heddles, might have contributed to increasing

Figure 3.8 'Weaver Seated at a Loom', *c.* 1800–50. (See also colour plate.)

productivity and with it the competitiveness of Southeast Asian cottons in the seventeenth century.[97]

Before the late eighteenth century textile technology across Eurasia presented some similarities but also important differences. Moreover, textile technology was not at all static, a fact noticed by several historians in recent years in response to a consolidated paradigm that wanted Indian – and more generally Asian – technological development to be characterised by stasis over the long period between 1400 and the arrival of western technology in the nineteenth century.[98] Finally, cotton ginning, spinning and weaving remained relatively simple productive activities. And it was the simplicity of such technologies that allowed cotton production to be easily integrated within household production.

Conclusion

Cotton cultivation spread over the temperate areas of Afro-Eurasia starting in ancient times. It was a slow process of diffusion, which accelerated only after the strengthening of silk road commercial links and the rise of Islam. Both climatic conditions and the relative isolation of medieval Europe made the penetration of cotton and cotton processing limited in the Mediterranean. Technologies seem to have followed a similar path of diffusion, the majority finding their first application in India. The subcontinent enjoyed the advantage of having been the first area of cotton cultivation and manufacturing. Yet this did not mean that India was superior to other areas or that it had unchallenged technological leadership. China, in many ways, was in a better position, having developed in the Ming period a flourishing industry thanks to the wide-ranging trade of raw cotton and finished cloth across the vast expanse of the empire. Similarly, Chinese technologies seemed to have been more developed than those present in other areas, and surely were more advanced than those used in India, though such a finding is subject to disagreement.

Overall, this was a world of 'unexpected similarities', such as the smallholding cultivation of cotton and its association to household and village production. We are left with a question mark: why did India come to enjoy a dominant position in the production and trade of cotton textiles in Asia, Africa and eventually Europe, even though it did not possess either better or more abundant supplies of cotton, nor superior technologies? The next chapter asks if the way of organising production might explain the competitiveness of Indian products, much in the same way that European factory production is deemed to explain the success of European cotton manufacturing since the industrial revolution.

4 THE WORLD'S BEST: COTTON MANUFACTURING AND THE ADVANTAGE OF INDIA

Nineteenth-century European visitors to Panjab in present-day northwest Pakistan bought cheap brush drawings on paper not dissimilar from the drawings still sold in many parts of Asia today. They often naively portray vignettes of everyday life with men and women wearing colourful clothing. This can be seen in a late nineteenth-century drawing (Figure 4.1) that depicts the weaver-saint Kabir (1440–1518) busy at his loom while his wife in the lower part of the drawing spins with a treadle wheel. A musician accompanies their activities, suggesting that Kabir, while weaving, might have been composing one of the poems for which he was famous.

This charming little piece of ephemera has reached us partly because it was collected as a souvenir by John Lockwood Kipling, father of the more famous Rudyard Kipling, while he was director of the Mayo School of Art at Lahore. It is, of course, a late and stylised representation that is not produced to illuminate on textile production or its technologies. Rather, it is a 'scene' and as such it contextualises the characters under one roof, the space we imagine to be a house. It is therefore a good starting point for us to move from textile production as a set of technologies to a set of practices, what is called the organisation of production.

The question this chapter asks is very simple: if the comparative advantage of Indian textile manufacturing cannot be explained in terms of technology, can it be explained by the superior organisation of production? Was cotton production in India carried out in a different way from the rest of the world? Such questions entail an understating of production in India. This is then compared with the organisation of production in other areas of the world, both for cotton and other fibres. This chapter claims that although significant differences are evident across Eurasia, in particular between India and China, spinners and weavers in the subcontinent were not more productive. However, their products were superior for quality, something that I attribute to the high level of textile finishing in South Asia.

Figure 4.1 Late nineteenth-century drawing of Kabir, poet and weaver. (See also colour plate.)

Figure 4.2 Two Indian women winding cotton, early nineteenth century. (See also colour plate.)

Producing cotton textiles in India

In medieval India, spinning and weaving were carried out in areas with easy access to supplies of local cotton. There is sufficient evidence that some of these areas, such as Dhaka for the production of muslin, developed high levels of specialisation thanks to access to higher qualities of local cotton.[1] However, as noted in the previous chapter, the development of long-distance trade loosened the relationship between natural resources and the emergence of specialised production. This was true not just of cotton but also of dyes such as indigo and chay-root red and even lemons for bleaching.[2] Specific locales became important throughout the subcontinent, as in the case of Agra and Ahmedabad for their dyeing in blue and black, while baftas produced in Lahore and Bengal were brought to Broach and Navsari in Gujarat for bleaching.[3] Notwithstanding this specialisation of production, the spinning and winding of cotton remained widespread activities across India, as they were practised by women of all castes who supplied local weavers or sold their spun yarn on the market (Figure 4.2).[4] The yarn was commonly bought and prepared by members of weaving households.[5] Weaving households could have one or more men engaged in textile production on a

Figure 4.3 'Weavers' house at Santipore, the Tantìe at his loom', *c.* 1797.

full-time basis while other members helped by either spinning or by engaging in auxiliary activities (Figure 4.3).[6] The earnings of a helper (or journeyman) could be half those of a weaver, and the earnings of a female spinner probably a sixth.

The position of weavers in the Indian economy is difficult to assess, not just because of differences across regions but also because they were at once independent craftsmen and members of weaving communities or weaving villages.[7] In most cases, a weaver's independence extended not just to the ownership of one or more looms but also over the commodities produced, which he could sell to the highest bidder on free markets.[8] Yet, the Indian weaver belonged to a weaving village and more specifically to the caste system that shaped village life. Whilst apparently enjoying commercial freedom, he was part of a specific social structure. It has been argued that the so-called *jajmānī* system, a caste system widespread in rural manufacturing, was originally oriented towards subsistence production, but that by the sixteenth century it acted as the interface to a commercial world of trade.[9] Moreover, the *jajmānī* should not be seen as a rigid way of organising manufacturing according to strict caste divisions. Individual villages could have weavers from different castes. In Gujarat, for instance, cloth was produced both by servile castes of untouchables and by non-servile groups such as Shundras.[10] The weaving village also provided some insulation against the risk of famine, as the community as a whole would have taken care of its members.[11]

The weaving village had the peculiarity of being a rural structure. There were exceptions to this general rule, with western and northern India producing closer to the main cities and sometimes in urban centres. However, Bengal and the Coromandel coast conformed to the pattern of an industry scattered in the countryside and characterised by small village communities.[12] The census of a sizeable weaving village like Arani on the Coromandel coast in 1772 reveals that out of 246 households, 99 were weaving cloth, 68 were spinning cotton and 40 households belonged to the castes of Lomatties and Chetties, suggesting that they were engaged in mercantile occupations of sorts. Although a rather late survey, it is helpful as it shows the structure of a weaving village and the conspicuous presence of traders as well as producers.[13]

The increasing commercialisation of Indian textile manufacturing was not hindered by its location in villages. It was the village itself that provided the structure through which to commercialise the weaver's products. Within a village, a weaver had three options on how best to dispose of his merchandise. He could simply use its production for subsistence. If the cloth was sold, then this could be done either by the weaver selling it on the open market or by him selling it to a merchant. The relationship between the weaver and a possible buying merchant had two distinctive features: it was based on cash advances (the so-called *dadni* system); and it involved a variety of intermediaries.[14] Om Prakash argues that cash advances were necessary to support the weaving household during the months (up to six) when the cloth was being produced. Advances also reduced the risk of approaching potential buyers directly, especially by those producers in rural areas with limited access to markets, and circumvented the need for weavers to forecast market conditions.[15] The contractual arrangement could be flexible, and it seems that little leeway existed for merchants to enforce contracts, with the result that the weaver could sell his product to someone else and return the advance.[16] This was a risk borne (entirely by the merchant) that could only be avoided by what we would today call social control.[17]

This explains the second important feature of this productive system. The village of Arani, mentioned earlier, boasted a large number of commercial intermediaries. The merchant was not in direct contact with the weaver, as the advance system was mediated both by the village (and its many commercial and social agents) and by other intermediaries who served to smooth the process.[18] 'Export merchants' often relied on 'intermediary merchants' (known in Bengal as *paikars*), who agreed the type of cloth to be produced, the quantity, price and date of delivery. An intermediary might commission an order by relying on a series of other intermediaries within the village itself: there might have been a broker sometimes replacing the intermediary merchant, but at times supplementing him. He could be a weaver within the village who acted for the merchant (or intermediary merchant) and received a small commission of around 1–2 per cent of the price. This figure overlaps with that of the *dadal*, although the latter could be one of the many 'sub-brokers' employed by a gomasta (*gumashta*), who was instead a local agent. Finally there could be a head-weaver (*hoofd wever*) who also acted as a main broker and might employ sometimes up to a hundred weavers.[19]

Thus the structure of village production was neither simple nor led to a direct relationship with trade. Within the network of figures with some stake in the production and commercialisation of cloth we find at least one producer, one merchant, a commercial interface for the producer, one for the merchant, and a *super-partes* figure within the village to mediate different positions (Figure 4.4a). Was this structure based on villages an efficient way to manage the market? This is a difficult question that requires some comparative references. I wish first to compare it with the proto-industrial structure of production for woollens in Europe. Secondly I will compare the efficiency and organisation of production of Indian cotton manufacturing vis-à-vis the other major early modern systems of cotton production and trade, namely China, the Levant and southern Europe.

Textile production in India and Europe

The animated debate of the 1980s and early 1990s on whether Indian (and for that matter Chinese) textile production followed a proto-industrial path remains an open one. The concept of proto-industry was developed by Franklin Mendels in the 1970s for early modern Europe.[20] The parallels with India are difficult to miss in that before modern industrialisation, several manufacturing branches of the European economy were neither static nor confined to urban locations.[21] Growing manufacturing activities were conducted in rural locations that produced not just for subsistence but increasingly for the market. This was particularly the case for the linen and woollen sectors that in several regions of Europe had developed to become large-scale activities. Their industrial organisation was not based on factories but on decentralised production carried out by workers who were part-time agriculturalists who conducted spinning and weaving on the side, to augment their household incomes. A decade of intense study and debate showed the variety of experiences but also the importance of the phenomenon.[22] Two key features should be underlined. First, the proto-industrial regions of Europe were not necessarily those that developed to become

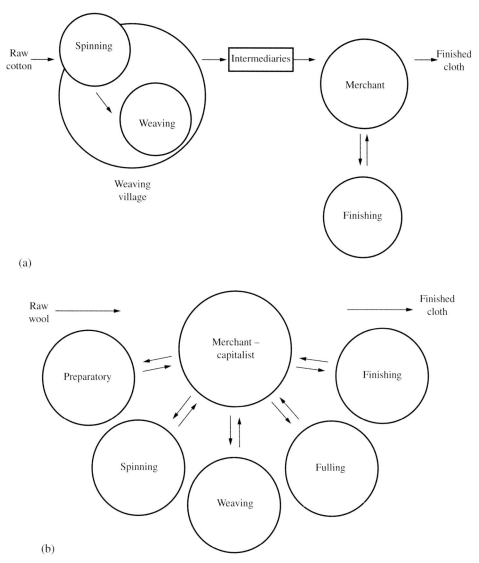

Figure 4.4 (a) (*above*) The organisation of production of the Indian cotton industry; (b) (*below*) The organisation of production of the European woollen industry (West of England).

the industrial regions. This is why proto-industrialisation cannot be represented as the 'first phase of industrialisation'.[23] Second, the production carried out in the countryside was coordinated by merchants (named merchant-capitalists) who were the interface with markets that were often 'distant', or more precisely national and international.[24]

As the proto-industrialisation debate led to continent-wide comparisons, it comes as no surprise that economic historians of Asia started asking similar questions for their own countries and areas.[25] Frank Perlin, in particular, concluded that Indian artisanal textile production was conducted very much along the same lines as the rural textile industry of Europe.[26] There were, however, several important differences that could explain some of the different logics underpinning production in Europe and India. Indian textile production seems to have been characterised by a high level of independence for spinners and weavers. Spinners bought raw materials and sold spun yarn in a free market. Weavers retained ownership of their own looms and raw materials. They also had good bargaining powers in their relationship with the merchants.[27] There might have been limited access to markets, but in India, merchants were not controlling weavers and advances were rarely made in the form of raw materials or tools.[28]

The situation in Europe was different. Here merchants had a much stronger role in controlling production. Weavers and spinners, within what has been defined as a putting-out system, did not own materials or tools.[29] Spinners were often allocated wool or flax (and later raw cotton) to be spun by merchants who paid them piece rates. Looms were often rented by weavers who were also supplied with yarns and asked to produce the cloth at pre-set prices. Compared to their Indian counterparts, European weavers were in a weaker position. Both could work for different merchants, but the ties of the average European weaver to a specific merchant look stronger than those of his counterpart in India (Figures 4.4a and b). Why was this the case? Market conditions in early modern India and Europe were not very different, as both areas experienced an expansion of textile trade and production. What is significantly different, however, is the role played by merchants. In India, merchants interacted with long chains of village intermediaries.[30] The merchant had to find some accommodation with the authorities within the village before being granted access to the weavers.[31] The logic of the weaving village, its stratification according to castes and the complex relationship between weavers and merchants helped the weavers to retain a high degree of independence.[32] The European system is striking instead for the closeness between merchant and weaver and for the fact that their relationship was both unmediated by any social structure (village, parish and neighbourhood) and dealt with either in kind or through credit–debt situations.[33]

What were the economic outcomes of these differences in the context of market expansion? In the long term, while in India the expansion of markets led to *specialisation*, in Europe it led to *concentration*. For example, in India, increases in demand created problems and pressures for weavers. One rational response might have been to increase the scale of production by acquiring more looms and employing waged weavers.[34] But this strategy was not common because looms were simple machines that were relatively inexpensive to acquire, and weavers were rather mobile.[35] Most parts of India followed the path of specialisation of process, of product, and of locale.[36] Already during the Vijayanagara period (1336–1650), different stages of production were carried out by specialised artisans.[37] In the 1670s, European traders reported that in Madras the division of labour was highly refined, both for production and finishing (dyers, wood-block cutting and designing with charcoal on textiles).[38] Specialisation had a geographic dimension: entire villages – much to the astonishment of Europeans – were specialised in the production of commodities for particular markets and were sometimes named after the product they were specialised in.[39] The result was a 'tapestry' of productive clusters, a bewildering variety of products and plural geographical divisions of the industry and its market. This was a system that was centrifugal and in which Indian merchants reassembled products by acting as merchandising agents.[40]

The market expansion and the commercialisation of production in Europe led to very different consequences. Rather than specialisation, concentration was perceived as the best way to manage markets from the viewpoint of merchants. They took the opportunity to create hierarchical relationships with spinners and weavers and maintained clear stakes in the productive processes. Merchants often took an active part in the finishing stages, creating their own dyeing, pressing, calendaring and packing facilities, in contrast to the independence of printers and dyers in India. Eventually, from the late seventeenth century, they realised economies of scale by creating proto-factories. The logic of European merchants was not simply 'capitalist' but, as Sidney Pollard noted many years ago, bureaucratic and managerial as well.[41] The logic of the weaving village in India was instead strongly enmeshed in what one could define as the social structure of production, in which, as Lakshmi Subramanian has observed, textile production and trade were 'a matter of politics, not simply a commercial transaction'.[42] The result was that trade and manufacturing remained practically and conceptually more divided than was generally the case in the West.

The outcome was, for India, what we call Smithian-growth, that is to say economic growth generated by trade and specialisation of a major manufacturing activity, that in turn increase efficiency and productivity, though it might have also led to higher coordination costs and a low level of technological change due to a highly refined division of labour. In Europe, the power of the trading agents led to a different type of system that has more of the features of modern economic growth that appeared in the West; that is to say, growth generated from economies of scale, the imposition of complex and centralised productive structures and the eventual application of mechanical devices to manufacturing, all factors flowing from higher levels of mercantile investment in fixed capital. The European model was also based on remuneration of labour, a payment of wages and more often piece rates, independent of the conditions of agrarian production and the cost of food. The Indian system, based upon the fixed pricing for final products, took into account the conditions of agrarian economies, not just the cost of raw cotton but also the cost of food grains leading to increasing prices for cotton textiles during periods of bad harvests.[43]

The Chinese cotton industry

Paul Bairoch estimated that by the mid eighteenth century Indian manufacturing accounted for a quarter of the world's industrial output and that cotton textile production had the lion share.[44] The Chinese cotton industry was no lesser rival: already by the seventeenth century the empire's production might have been at least as large as the Indian cotton industry and accounted for a quarter of the total value of manufactured goods in the empire. The main difference between these two world areas was that while the Indian cotton industry exported its products widely across the Indian Ocean, China consumed most of its production within its own borders.[45] More than half the entire Chinese cotton production was internally commercialised and cotton textiles were the second largest national commodity in terms of production after food, well ahead of silk, salt and tea.[46]

The agronomical introduction of cotton into China in the eleventh and twelfth centuries was followed by a period of intense expansion of manufacturing in the first fifty years of Mongol domination, starting in 1280.[47] The new government established cotton bureaux in several provinces of the empire in 1289 and made cotton integral to the taxation system in 1296.[48] The empire used cotton to support the needs of its own military and administration.[49] Already in 1365 the cultivation of cotton was made compulsory for all farmers holding over 5 mu of land.[50] Cotton therefore became in just less than a century one of the tools through which the Yuan dynasty shaped the empire's economy: it acted as a form of taxation in kind; it supplied the army and the court; it shaped private demand (leaving the expensive silks for the elite or for export); and it made the peasant household a key unit for production.[51]

'Men plough and women weave' is a typical Chinese saying based on the fact that cotton manufacturing was a subsidiary activity to farming.[52] Within the household, men were in charge of the farming activities while women supplemented family income by spinning and weaving.[53] Spun yarn was widely traded in urban markets or sold to merchants. The 1512 *Songjiang fu zhi* for instance, reported that 'village women go early in the morning to market with cotton yarn, which they exchange for raw cotton, and then return home. The following morning they again leave [the village for the market town] with cotton'.[54] Spinning and weaving could be separate activities. Poor peasants, without the capital for a loom, might concentrate their efforts on spinning cotton on basic spinning wheels, selling a few ounces of yarn every day in order to buy more raw materials and food.[55]

Was cotton production in China also a 'proto-industrial' activity? Opinions differ greatly. There is no evidence that a system of advances of credit on raw materials was in place. Moreover, it remains unclear how production in the home was linked to markets, even if an increase in the commercialisation of production over time is evident.[56] Some historians have noticed a certain parallelism with India, observing that 'in the cloth market [of Ming China] there was a kind of "agency" that monopolised exchange – the *yahang*'.[57] This was a complicated structure of exchange dominated by a series of intermediaries, some of which had powers of feudal origin that structured relationships between producers and merchants. Exchange was based on several layers of tradesmen and middlemen among which were large numbers of cotton merchants linking the north and the south of the empire, travelling merchants and large shops that controlled the collection of cotton textiles from subcontracting shops that, in their turn, coordinated household spinning and weaving.[58] Other historians, however, emphasise how merchants remained extraneous to the production system, thus setting Chinese cotton manufacturing apart from European proto-industries based on the putting-out system.[59]

As in India, Chinese production was linked to the peasant household and to long-distance trade. And similarly to India, the result was an increased specialisation of production, with specific localities becoming well known for their differentiated products. In the 1630s it was said for the prefecture of Jiangnan that 'every village and market town has its own varieties and names' and that 'the list is inexhaustible'.[60] The region's cotton textile production dominated the national markets, as Jiangnan cotton cloth was widely used by urban consumers.[61] It has been estimated that from the seventeenth through to the eighteenth centuries 35–40 per cent of that region's cotton cloth production was exported.[62]

Specialisation, as in the case of India, led to the multiplication of the varieties of cottons available on the market. In sixteenth-century Guangxu, as many as seventy-two varieties of cloth were produced.[63] In Ming Songjiang, more than twenty different varieties of cotton textiles were sold on the market, ranging from the basic cloth used for taxation purposes to fancier varieties including the 'three-shuttle' cloth used for the emperor's underwear.[64] 'Three-shuttle cloth', 'floral cloth', 'silk cloth' and 'eye-brown knit' were high-quality cotton textiles normally woven in complicated patterns. 'Standard cloth', 'T-cloth' and 'mid-loom' cloth were plain or ordinary cloths produced mostly by rural households.[65] Different areas specialised also in the manufacturing of non-competitive varieties of cotton textiles.[66] Variety meant choice for consumers, and a mid-Ming observer reported that cotton had 'spread through the empire', adding that it was 'used a hundred times more than silk and hemp'.[67]

Chinese cotton manufacturing thus shared several of the features of the textile production of India and Europe. Yet the industry possessed two distinctive characteristics. Firstly, the state fostered the growth of cotton cultivation and manufacturing while at the same time regarding it as being at the service of the needs of the state itself. Secondly, the peasant household remained a central unit of production of raw material, spun yarn and finished cloth. Both features might have played against the long-term development of the Chinese cotton industry.

Cotton manufacturing in the Levant and Ottoman Empire

Southern Arabia, the Mesopotamian steppe, North Palestine and Syria all developed cotton cultivation and manufacturing before the eleventh century CE. By the fifteenth century cotton was grown in southern Anatolia and the Aegean coast, and its cultivation extended to the Thessalian plains and Macedonia in the seventeenth and eighteenth centuries (Map 4.1).[68] There were also attempts to imitate the production of cottons imported from India. In Basra, Baghdad, Kirkuk and Mosul cotton manufacturing developed together with silk production.[69] Present-day Syria developed a vast cotton industry in the later Middle Ages.[70] Aleppo, in particular, was an important centre for the manufacturing and trade in cotton textiles in the Middle East. During Ottoman times the area was one of the main suppliers of cotton to the imperial arsenal, and the industry must have been rather large, as is indicated by the existence of brokers, wholesale merchants and a separate guild of bleachers of cloth.[71] By the seventeenth century places such as Gaziantep, near the present-day border of Turkey and Syria, specialised in the production of copies of Indian textiles that were sold both within the empire and to Europe.[72] The fact that such fabrics competed successfully with Indian imports suggests that Ottoman products were well received both by local and international markets.[73]

Cotton textile production in Anatolia expanded under Ottoman rule. During the sixteenth century the city of Manisa in western Anatolia, fifty kilometres from Izmir, became a prosperous centre of cotton textile production.[74] This was one of the two main regions of cotton cultivation and production, the other

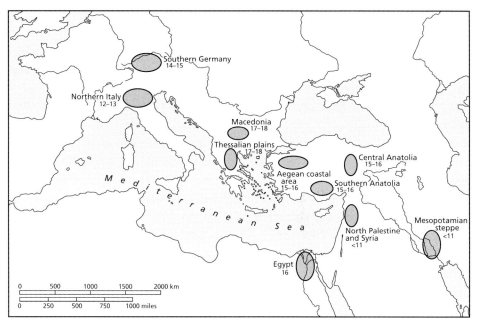

Map 4.1 Main areas of cotton manufacturing in the Levant, Middle East and Europe, eleventh to the eighteenth centuries (numbers are centuries AD when the industry developed).

being the area of Adana, in Çukurova, southern Turkey. Other smaller areas in central Anatolia, such as Erzincan and Malatya, were also important centres of cotton manufacturing.[75] Cotton cultivation developed later in Thessaly, where both linen and cotton cloth production (mostly used for undergarments and for linings) and the production of cotton yarn to be sold to central Europe and the Habsburg Empire flourished in the seventeenth and eighteenth centuries.[76] Central Greece, and espccially the area of Salonica (Thessaloniki), became a major cultivator of raw cotton in the eighteenth century: spun yarn was exported to east and central Europe and locally produced sailcloth was commercialised across the empire.[77] The growing Egyptian cotton industry was instead reliant on imported raw material from Syria, and cotton cultivation and manufacturing expanded greatly after the beginning of Ottoman domination, in 1517. During the following three centuries Egypt, and especially Cairo, became a centre of production of mixed cottons (two-thirds cotton and one-third linen) that were sold to the Red Sea, sub-Saharan Africa and Europe.[78]

Evidence of the organisation of production of the Ottoman cotton industry is hard to come by. Cleaning and spinning were carried out as commercial activities in the areas of cotton production, though only part of the raw material itself was commercialised. Weaving remained a rural occupation, with linkages to the market through 'putting out', especially in the eighteenth century. Wealthy entrepreneurs were active in the finishing stages of dyeing and printing and might have provided capital as well as coordinating the trade of the finished cloth.[79] The later industry of Thessaly was, however, organised very much along the lines of a proto-industrial system, with merchants providing cash advances and trading both in finished cloth and yarn, which they exported to central Europe.[80]

The Ottoman cotton industry had three main markets: most of its products were traded and consumed within the empire. Common cotton cloth (*bez*) was used by ordinary consumers for everyday attire, while more sophisticated cloth made of better-quality yarn was to be found at metropolitan markets and especially in Istanbul, where it complemented silken, woollen and mixed silk and cotton (*kutni*) fabrics.[81] Over time, and especially in the seventeenth and eighteenth centuries, the quantity of printed cottons such as chintzes (*çit*) must have increased substantially when cities such as Manisa, Diyarbékir, Urfa Ayntab and Aleppo came to specialise in printed fabrics.[82]

The second market for the Ottoman cottons consisted of exports to western and eastern Europe, but also to Russia, central Asia, and North and sub-Saharan Africa. Middle Eastern textiles were in high demand in Europe well before Ottoman times. The trade between the Levant and Venice was well under way by 1400 and it included cotton and silken textiles, particularly high-quality goods for the refined markets of Italy and other parts of Europe.[83] Since at least the sixteenth century, textiles from the Levant entered Europe not just through the Mediterranean and Adriatic seas, but also via the Danube into eastern and central Europe. Ottoman power intensified from the early sixteenth century onwards, and by the end of the century several Turkish merchants were active in the great plains of Hungary.[84] Cotton goods and silk yarn were among the most traded commodities. Hungarians could now buy several varieties of cottons for clothing and fabrics. These textiles were either imported from India and Persia or produced in Anatolia, as in the case of *yazma* cloth.[85]

Suraiya Faroqhi observes that the cotton textiles exported from the Ottoman Empire were 'nothing but the tip of the iceberg' when compared to overall production.[86] She refers not just to private demand but also to the needs of the Ottoman administration, which bought quantities of cottons: 150,000 pieces of cotton sailcloth in 1565–6 and 300,000 ells for the arsenal from the recently conquered Cyprus in 1582, just to cite two examples.[87] It is difficult to say how much the demands of the state itself accounted for the overall production of cotton textiles in Anatolia and the empire as a whole, but it is likely that several areas of the empire sold a great part of their products to the central administration.

Cotton manufacturing in medieval and early modern Europe

Cotton textile manufacturing first emerged in Europe in the mid twelfth century.[88] Cotton was part of the expansion of the European economy after the year 1000, when increasing production and renewed commercial links between southern Europe and the Mediterranean basin contributed to an upsurge in the continent's economy.[89] Between 1150 and 1300 the area of northern Italy (the Veneto, Lombardy, Piedmont and Liguria, and later Tuscany) started manufacturing cotton textiles in imitation of the cottons that were imported from Syria and Palestine.[90] The scale of production in Italy far exceeded that of the Spanish cotton textile industry, which had developed in the ninth and tenth centuries after the invasion of the Moors. The southern European cotton industry differed from other areas of Eurasia in relying on raw cotton and spun yarn imported from the Levant by Genoese and Venetian merchants.[91] Such cotton was sold to the cities of mainland northern Italy, such as Milan, Cremona and Pavia, where fustians (mixed linen and cottons) became an important part of their textile industries.[92] These cities were already major areas of production of woollen textiles. Cotton spinning was carried out in their immediate hinterlands, while weaving borrowed the technologies and organisational structures of woollen manufacturing and developed as an urban activity.[93] With a few exceptions, such as the high-quality Milanese products, Italy produced cheap varieties of mixed cottons (mostly fustians) as the quality of spinning did not allow for the production of cotton thread strong enough to serve as warp (Figure 4.5). Only the weft was made of cotton, while the warp was made of flax. Italian 'cottons' were, however, in demand in Spain, France, northern Europe (Basel, Nuremberg, Bohemia, as well as Flanders and England) and were traded beyond Europe, as there is evidence that in the thirteenth and fourteenth centuries they reached North Africa and even Syria.[94] In Europe, the manufacturing of cottons coincided with the introduction of new textiles and garments such as doublets and quilted short jackets (occasionally padded), and they were probably also used for sails.[95]

The success of the northern Italian cotton industry was, however, short-lived. The plague of 1348, the impoverishment of the northern Italian urban economy, international monetary instability and shifting commercial routes have been seen as the main factors in the peninsula's economic decline.[96] By the mid fourteenth century Milanese cotton producers complained about the rising competition from Swiss and southern German towns. Whilst a few years earlier they had been major buyers of Italian cotton cloth, the towns of Bavaria and Switzerland now started buying raw cotton in Venice and undercut Italian producers.[97] The south German city of Ulm became a centre of cotton production in the 1320s, and the German

Figure 4.5 Blue and white linen and cotton towel produced in Italy, *c.* fifteenth century. (See also colour plate.)

cottons found easy markets across Europe. The products of Ulm, but also nearby Biberach and Augsburg, were sold in Flanders, at the fairs of northern France and along the Danube to Austria and Hungary.[98] The industry remained particularly active throughout the fifteenth century, engaging not only in fustian production but also in the imitation of the popular Italian 'bombazines', mixed fabrics with silk warp and cotton weft. By the end of the sixteenth century 700,000 lengths of cotton cloth were bleached every year in Augsburg. In the Swiss towns of Lucerne, Basle and Zurich, too, fustian industry remained buoyant until the seventeenth century.[99]

By the fifteenth century raw cotton started to be imported through the Catalan ports for an expanding Spanish production.[100] Cotton arrived at the port of Marseilles and was sold to Germany and to the new manufacturers of Flanders.[101] The city of Leiden became a producer of fustians in the first half of the seventeenth century. In 1620 a quarter of all the 97,000 pieces of cloth produced in the city were fustians, for a time replacing the production of woollen textiles and camlets as the city's main activity.[102] Small quantities of cotton were imported from Venice into England as early as 1200, and cotton was imported directly from the Levant to Britain from the second decade of the sixteenth century, to be used for quilting, stuffing and yarn for candlewicks.[103] However it was only in the late sixteenth century that the production of cotton goods is first documented in the British Isles. By the mid seventeenth century Lancashire had emerged as an important fustian-producing region. It manufactured the majority of the 40,000 pieces of fustians produced in England every year, mostly by using raw cotton imported from Smyrna and Cyprus.[104]

The competitiveness of Indian cloth

This survey of cotton textile manufacturing in China, the Levant and Europe provokes us to ask whether Indian textiles were relatively successful on international markets because of specific comparative advantages in productivity or because of their organisation of production. It is worth underlining that we are comparing industries that were regional and that only to a certain extent fit within modern state boundaries and divisions. Moreover, the units considered are very different in size. Figures are difficult to come by, but it is clear that in Europe cotton textiles were at best a niche production situated in very specific localities and that they remained marginal for the overall textile industry of the continent until the eighteenth century. In China, the size of the cotton industry was considerable. The government alone consumed as much as 22–30 thousand tons (15–20 million bolts) of cotton in the mid fourteenth century, equivalent to an estimated 225–300 million yards of cloth.[105] In the Ottoman Empire, production was much smaller, as the population was at best one-tenth that of China. Suraiya Faroqhi has estimated that the production of cottons in late sixteenth-century Anatolia might have been between 4.2 and 7 thousand tons, equivalent to 13 to 35 million yards of cloth.[106] This was approximately a fifth to a half of the cloth that was imported from India into the Ottoman Empire via the overland caravan trade at the end of the seventeenth century, and a quantity not much different from the 1.2 million pieces of cloth a year imported into Europe by the VOC and EEIC at their peak in the late seventeenth century.[107]

The limited quantitative evidence available suggests that total production per spinner might have been rather similar in India and China. Ian Wendt calculates that in the late seventeenth century an Indian woman spun 6.5 kg of yarn a month. His figures are not very different to estimates of spinning productivity in China, where a woman apparently produced 6–7 kg of spun yarn a month.[108] Processes of ginning, spinning and weaving were not so different in seventeenth-century Songjiang and South India (Table 4.1).

In China, to produce a cloth three yards long and one yard wide took 2 days for cleaning and ginning the raw cotton (22 to 24 hours of work), 3.6 to 4 days

Table 4.1 *Hours' work to produce a cotton cloth three yards long and one yard wide in seventeenth-century India and China.*

	Songjiang in China[a]	South India[b]
Cleaning and ginning	22–24	17.3–21.7
Spinning	39.6–48	39.2–49
Weaving	11–12	8–10

[a] Calculations based on one bolt (*pi*) of cotton cloth. A bolt could vary in width from 32 to 41 cm and in length from 5.72 to 11.45 m. The average bolt was 7 metres long and 40 cm wide (2.8 sqm). A day's work has been calculated at 11–12 hours.
[b] The type of cloth is a salampuris. A day's work has been calculated at 9–10 hours.
Sources: (India) Ian Christopher Wendt, 'The Social Fabric: Textile Industry and Community in Early Modern South India', unpublished PhD thesis, University of Wisconsin-Madison, 2005, pp. 336–7. (China) Philip C. C. Huang, *The Peasant Family and Rural Development in the Yangzi Delta, 1350–1988* (Stanford University Press, 1990), pp. 46, 84; Francesca Bray, *Technology and Gender: Fabrics and Power in Late Imperial China* (Berkeley: University of California Press, 1997), pp. 181 and 216; Dieter Kuhn, *Science and Civilisation in China*, vol. V, *Chemistry and Chemical Technology. Part IX. Textile Technology: Spinning and Reeling* (Cambridge University Press, 1998), p. 196; Bozhong Li, *Agricultural Development in Jiangnan, 1620–1850* (New York: St Martin's Press, 1998), p. 120; Dixin Xu and Chengming Wu, *Chinese Capitalism, 1522–1840* (London: Macmillan, 2000), pp. 215–16.

work for spinning (39.6 to 48 hours) and 1 day for weaving (11 to 12 hours).[109] For late seventeenth-century South India, figures are very similar, with weaving requiring 1 day (8 to 10 hours), cleaning and ginning just over 2 days (17.3 to 21.7 hours) and spinning around 5 days (39.2 to 49 hours).[110] Both in India and China, the four-day work of a spinner produced enough yarn for one day's work for a weaver. Both economies needed four times as many full-time spinners as weavers.[111]

Within the chain of value-added for the final product, the cultivation and the ginning and spinning of cotton may well have been equivalent activities across different areas of the world, thus suggesting that India may not have enjoyed substantial comparative advantages in any of these basic processes. This is evident if we compare data for late seventeenth-century South India and early nineteenth-century Thessaly (Table 4.2). The percentage of value-added by cleaning, spinning and ginning is more or less the same in these two areas. In India, raw cotton might have actually been a higher percentage of the total value

Table 4.2 *Production, cleaning, ginning and spinning 100 kg of cotton yarn in south India, late seventeenth century, and Thessaly in 1831 (as percentage of value added).*

	South India	Thessaly
Cost of raw cotton	25–32	22
Cleaning and ginning	4–10	12[a]
Spinning	60–63	61[b]
Loss of cotton	n.a.	5

[a] Work of a woman for 31 full working days (3.2 kg per day), plus bowing.
[b] 15.6 weeks, spinning around 2 kg of ginned cotton a week.
Sources: (India) Ian Christopher Wendt, 'The Social Fabric: Textile Industry and Community in Early Modern South India', unpublished PhD thesis, University of Wisconsin-Madison, 2005, pp. 336–7. (Thessaly) David Urquhart, *Turkey and its Resources*, p. 48, cited in Halil Inalcik, 'When and How British Cotton Goods Invaded the Levant Markets', in Huri Islamoğlu-Inan, ed., *The Ottoman Empire and the World Economy* (Cambridge University Press, 1986), p. 378.

of spun yarn, though it should be noted that Thessaly was at its productive peak in the early nineteenth century and that the price of cotton in India was subject to substantial fluctuations.

Let me summarise. It seems from all accounts that there were variations in labour productivity, but that these were relatively small because of the similarity of technological solutions. This world of broad similarities was, however, characterised by different ways in which cotton industries were organised in India, China, the Middle East and Europe (Table 4.3). For example, Europe was different from all other areas: it totally relied on imported raw materials. Other areas ranged from local cotton supplies to buying raw materials far away. In China, the cotton trade between the north and south of the empire (across a distance longer than that separating Acre in Syria from Ulm in Germany) provided a solution that Europe did not have. The fustian manufacturers of Italy and Germany were adversely affected by an endemic lack of raw material. Europe competed against the Levant cotton manufacturing industry for raw cotton.[112] The more the raw cotton market internationalised, the more different areas came to interact and compete to secure raw material.

Across all the Eurasian cotton regions, cleaning, ginning and spinning were female activities, mostly carried out within rural households to complement agricultural production. In India, China and the Levant a substantial percentage of spinning was carried out in households that produced raw cotton, thus linking

Table 4.3 *Comparing cotton manufacturing across the early modern world.*

	India	China	Ottoman Empire	Europe
Raw cotton	Local Increasing commercialization	Local Commercialization north to south	Local Evidence of some trade	Totally imported from the Levant
Cleaning and spinning	Rural and female Commercialised	Rural and female Commercialised	Rural and female(?) Partly commercialized	Rural and female Mostly commercialized
Weaving	Rural village and male	Rural household and initially female	Rural (villages), male State manufactures	Urban through guilds, male
Merchants/proto-industrialisation	Presence of merchants but weak power	Presence of merchants	Presence of some merchants	International trade
Role of the state	Tax on trade and looms High-quality consumption of court	Cotton as tax State consumption of basic cloth Encouragement of industry by Mongols	State consumption of basic cloth (sail, etc.) Control of industry, including production	Privileges to cotton guilds Taxation of trade of raw cotton
Distinctiveness	Stability of key areas of production	Strong rural link	Pressure on raw materials Role of the state	Import of raw material Role of urban production

the cultivation of raw materials and the first steps of its processing. For all three areas, spinning also developed as an activity for market production in which women would buy raw material and sell spun yarn. In Europe, it emerged as a manufacturing activity in the hinterlands of urban weaving centres.[113]

The organisation of weaving varied widely across these areas. In Sung and early Ming China, weaving was a female occupation, becoming a male occupation only in the seventeenth century and thus following a global trend. In China and in India, weaving remained a household activity. China had no equivalent to India's weaving villages. Cotton textile weaving was widespread and by the seventeenth and eighteenth centuries more than half of rural households in the empire had a loom.[114] In the Ottoman Empire, weaving was similarly performed by men, in all probability working in small urban centres but not necessarily under the control of guilds.[115] In Europe, fustian weaving did not develop within the household, but from the very start was performed in urban areas under the rules and guidance of guilds or under the organisation of merchants. Already in 1214 the city of Verona had a guild of cotton producers, as had Padua in 1236, and the city of Parma had a guild of weavers of cotton cloth in 1253.[116]

Cotton textile commercialisation varied widely across the world. The general trend observed in all areas is for cotton to be increasingly part of a market economy coordinated by merchants. The power of such merchants and their function within each industry differed. In India, they basically performed commercial functions; in Europe, merchants – following established patterns in the manufacturing of wool – participated in shaping production. Intermediate positions can be referenced for both China and Anatolia, where merchants took care of the finishing stages of production.

China and the Ottoman Empire also shared similarities when we look at the role of states. In both empires the government itself consumed large quantities of cotton textiles and, in different ways, tried to promote and protect the industry. In India, the court consumed higher-quality textiles and received taxes from trade and loom licences, but did not establish a system of taxation in kind through cotton, as in the case of China. Finally, in Europe, cotton did not feature prominently in the interests of the early modern states that limited themselves to simply taxing the trade of raw materials and finished products.

Each area displayed distinctive features. Europe emerged as a small area of production characterised by a peculiar urban nature and the import of all its raw materials. India relied on established areas of specialisation that continued to expand over centuries. The Chinese cotton production was characterised, instead, by a strong link with the rural economy and the needs of the state, leaving little space for trade beyond the borders of the empire itself.[117] And finally, in the Ottoman Empire cotton production developed under the control of the state.

The distinctiveness of Indian cloth

Early modern India became the key area for production and trade of cotton textiles, but it was probably neither more efficient nor a distinctive model for cotton producers elsewhere to follow. So the question remains: what was distinctive about Indian cloth? And why did they sell so well on global markets? My hypothesis is that the explanation has more to do with the processes of finishing than production and costs of raw materials. Cotton textiles are easily decorated through the mediums of printing, painting or pencilling. Even for the low-price cloths, it was Indian designs and colours that attracted consumers globally in the medieval and early modern periods. Printing, painting and pencilling added value to an otherwise ordinary cloth. India excelled in the finishing of cotton textiles.

Application of resist (waxing the areas to be kept white) and mordant (using chemical agents to fix colours) dyeing were already known in the subcontinent as early as the second millennium BCE.[118] Knowledge about dyeing substances also developed early. Blues and blacks were obtained from *Indigofera*, red from a variety of turmeric plants and mango bark. Colours were not just applied through dyeing but also painting (*kalamkari*) and printing with wooden blocks (*chit*), stamping and *ikat* processes.[119]

Painting and printing were the most common techniques and were to be found in several areas of India, such as Musulipatam, Nizampatam, Golconda, Narasapur, Armagaon and Madras.[120] The technique of cotton printing might have arrived to India from Persia and was already well developed in several parts of the Indian subcontinent by the twelfth century (Figure 4.6). By this time wooden blocks for printing were in use in Gujarat and on the Malabar coast. These were what came to be known as chintzes, from the word *chit*, meaning printing.[121] The third major area of Indian cotton production, the Coromandel coast, specialised in the painting of cottons.[122] The differentiation between printing, painting and pencilling includes a variety of sub-specialisations.[123] In West India and Gujarat, for instance, chintzes were printed with wooden blocks by using one or more of the various techniques that included 'direct printing', 'bleach printing' (bleaching the design on an already dyed cloth), 'mordant printing' (printing with mordants and then bleaching the unmordanted areas) or 'resist printing' (printing a viscous substance, followed by dyeing, followed by the cleansing of the substance). Several Indian sources confirm that

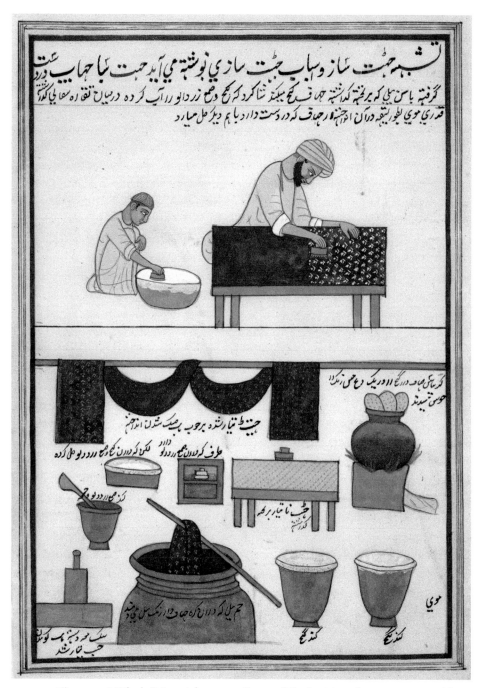

Figure 4.6 'Cloth Printer' from an album of Kashmiri trades, *c.* 1850–60. The inscriptions in Persian are the names of the implements used. (See also colour plate.)

the degree of division of labour in calico printing was highly refined and that the process could involve as many as a dozen separate dye transfers to the cloth.[124]

The suitability of cotton for printing also explains why the processes of printing and painting were adopted in other areas of Asia. In China, woven cotton textiles were at the top end of the market, but dyed and printed fabrics (yaobanbu) produced by stencilling, resist-dyeing and block printing were already popular in late Song times and were patterned with towers and pavilions, human figures and flowers. They catered for the middle market and distinguished themselves from the cheaper varieties of coarse cloth produced for home consumption.[125] Southeast Asia combined two different traditions in textile finishing: ikat and batik. Ikat was based on the weaving of yarn that had previously been dyed by knotting it, thus creating complex patterns through simple weaving, a technique already well developed in the eleventh century. Batik made use instead of wax to prevent the dye from penetrating the cloth. This technique became widespread by the eleventh century, although it is not clear if it originated locally or derived from other parts of Asia.[126] Printing was adopted in Japan only during the Edo period, but names such as bengara(-jima or -gôshi) (the striped or checked cloth from Bengal), santome(-jima) (striped cloth from São Thomé) and matafû(-jima) (striped cloth from Madras) suggest a possible knowledge transfer from the Indian subcontinent.[127]

Different techniques for cotton painting, and even more for printing, diffused from northern India and Persia both eastwards and westwards to the rest of Asia, creating local specialisms. Block printing was used in Mamluk territories in the fourteenth century and by the sixteenth century Indian techniques for painting and printing cloth were also used in Anatolia. According to the French visitor Pierre Belon, in the second half of the sixteenth century Istanbul had several textile printing workshops.[128] Over the seventeenth century printing developed in provincial cities such as Sivas and Tokat thanks to the migration of specialised craftsmen from Persia and India as well as Armenia. The quality of the products, especially those finished outside the capital, might not have been as good as the Indian products, but according to another Frenchman, Pitton de Tournefort, writing in 1717, they were good enough for the Muscovites and Tartars to be 'content with them'.[129]

It is worth noticing, however, that unlike ginning, bowing, spinning and weaving technologies, painting and printing did not spread to either Africa or Europe before the seventeenth century.[130] They remained quintessentially Asian techniques, something that came to characterise Asian cotton textiles in a global trade dominated by India.

Conclusion

This chapter has argued that India's success in cotton textile manufacturing did not go unchallenged. In the period between 1200 and the seventeenth century many parts of Eurasia developed flourishing industries. They borrowed agronomical knowledge on how to cultivate cotton and technical expertise on how to process this raw material from South Asia. However, they developed industries that retained specific organisational features, specialisations of production and linkages both with trade and the state. India enjoyed a clear advantage not so much based on cheap labour or better technologies.

The subcontinent clearly had a longer experience than any other area in the production of cotton textiles, and it relied on a well-organised system of trade. But its most important advantage lay in having mastered the processes of the finishing of cloth to a level that was unmatched by China and the Levant, as well as by Europe. This is what made India capable of selling its products to all other parts of Afro-Eurasia.

PART II

LEARNING AND CONNECTING: MAKING COTTONS GLOBAL, *CIRCA* 1500–1750

When Europeans first disembarked from their ships in India at the very end of the fifteenth century, they were amazed by the profusion of cotton textiles. Just over three centuries later European ships disembarked cargoes of cotton cloth produced in Europe on the same shores of India. What had happened between 1500 and 1800 to radically change the geography of world production and trade? The second part of this book explains this change as a slow but important transition in the position that Europe occupied in global trade and manufacturing. The concentration on a single commodity serves to explain a transformation that was much wider than cotton manufacturing and trade. The central section of the book argues that the early modern period witnessed the emplacement of the conditions for cotton textiles in particular and manufacturing in general to bring the West towards a modern industrial society.

The introduction to this book points out that the 'divergence' of the West has been explained in different ways. From the microperspective of the cotton industry it can be represented as a protracted and cyclical process dependent upon a variety of factors, some endogenous to Europe, but in most cases dependent on the connections that Europe created with other continents. The aim of this section is not to explore a world of 'endless possibilities', and it therefore sidelines what other parts of the world did (or might have done) to create their own modern industries or develop versions of a cotton textile sector to rival India. Europe was a rather improbable candidate to become the new powerhouse of cotton textile production and trade, because the continent had never enjoyed much success in developing a sophisticated cotton textile industry before 1500. Indeed, the striking feature of the textile world at that time was that Europe performed well in wool, linen and even to some degree in silk manufacturing, but was rather backward in spinning, weaving and finishing cotton cloth.

The next four chapters map how backwardness was transformed into primacy via processes of learning about products and techniques, as well as consumers and their tastes. Cotton textiles did not emerge as a key sector of the European economy in the wake of technological innovations in spinning and weaving. This industry developed to become part and parcel of Europe's economy and material culture for a variety of reasons. It took Europeans a great deal of time simply to master the basics of manufacturing and especially to develop high-quality printing. Trade with Asia provided them with the information required to learn about varieties of cottons and the tastes of consumers. There was a great deal of experimentation in supplying varieties of products not just for European consumers but also for international markets.

This multiplicity of factors had a chronology to it that makes the emergence of a cotton industry in Europe both contingent and less revolutionary than the many histories of industrialisation in the West have suggested. Over time cottons became integral to the consuming habits of Europeans and made fortunes for traders and producers. Europe acted like a sponge, absorbing technological and commercial knowledge, acquiring materials and translating and transforming products. This emerged thanks to the connections that the continent established with other parts of the world. Europe's ability to get things from outside its frontiers, sometimes by force and plunder, at other times by scientific investigation or by means of trade, was distinctive. Its ability to combine different factors – inserting cotton fibres from the Americas into a system of exchange for slaves from Africa; the exchange of slaves from Africa for cloth produced in Europe; the cloth produced in Europe thanks to Asian knowledge of printing techniques – to the specific tastes of domestic and foreign customers was remarkable. These triangulations are important not just for their complexity, but also for their truly global scale.

5 THE INDIAN APPRENTICESHIP: EUROPEANS TRADING IN INDIAN COTTONS

Piles of cotton cloth are for sale in this nineteenth-century European painting of everyday life in India. Unlike similar paintings of commercial life on the subcontinent, this image shows the process of opening, measuring and assessing the quality of the wares for sale. A measuring stick is used to check that the length of the cloth is correct. Many pieces are still folded, which suggests that this task might take a while. This painting takes us to the heart of an important problem in the history of trade and exchange: what was the knowledge behind the products being sold? Clearly the purchaser in this picture is taking precautions against being swindled. We also presume that he is informed about the goods that he is buying and that he has already in mind who he might be selling them to in order to make healthy profits.

An early modern European trader (one of the many servants of the East India companies purchasing cottons in India) would have looked less composed and comfortable in carrying out such a task. There are endless reports in the correspondence of the European companies on the frauds that they encountered in India. Cloth frequently fell short in fineness, length and breath. As the French traveller and writer Jean-Baptiste Tavernier explained, a bale of cloth contained up to two hundred pieces 'among which five or six and up to ten pieces . . . may be inserted of less fine quality; thinner, shorter, or narrower than the sample of the bale'.[1] Clearly European traders had to trust samples, but they were often given coarser and thinner goods. Measuring lengths was also problematic as it implied opening each bale supplied. But the problems faced by European traders did not stop there. Unlike many of their Asian competitors, who had been trading in Indian cotton cloth for centuries, the Europeans, at least initially, had little understanding of varieties and markets. Getting to know the business was essential to the success of an entire enterprise and was no simple task. This chapter considers the process by which Europeans came to comprehend cotton textiles. This process of learning about cottons started in India and, through

Figure 5.1 Painting of selling cloth. Company school, *c.* 1860. (See also colour plate.)

trade, developed into attempts to make cottons a viable commodity for sale in Europe, Africa and the Americas.

The trade carried out by the European East India companies was an important factor explaining the relocation of cotton textile manufacturing from India to Europe at the end of the eighteenth century. Central to such a process was knowledge of products and markets that the companies accessed in India in the period between 1600 and the late eighteenth century. Trade is generally represented as the means to accumulate capital for investment in domestic manufacturing. Trade also exposes consumers to new commodities that might later be produced at home. Thus, the East India companies, so often portrayed as impediments for development, were fundamental to Europe's economic growth and transition to an industrial system of production. Moreover, far from being monopolistic entities, they competed with each other to secure supplies of Indian cottons and other Asian commodities, embodying a wider European interstate economic competitiveness in the seventeenth and eighteenth centuries.

Portuguese traders in the Indian Ocean

It was only after the opening of the Cape of Good Hope route, at the end of the fifteenth century, that Europeans reached Asia via a direct sea route. This new artery of trade became the backbone of exchange between India and Europe over the following four centuries. Chinese tea and porcelain, Japanese lacquer and Indian printed and painted cottons arrived for the first time in large quantities in Europe. In exchange for Asian wares, the European chartered companies carried substantial quantities of silver: unable to profitably sell European commodities in Asia, they used the large reserves of silver mined in the Americas from the 1560s onwards to buy commodities in India and China.[2]

How important was the presence of European traders in the Indian Ocean? For Europeans, it was an extension and an intensification of traditional exchange with Asia that circumvented the risks and costs of dealing with intermediaries in central Asia and the Middle East. The trade between Europe and Asia increased steadily and in 1800 it was twenty-five times larger than it had been in 1500.[3] Yet this enormous expansion of the European trade with Asia amounted to only a third of the size of trade with the New World.[4] Some historians are sceptical of the existence of any globalising effect of Eurasian maritime trade before 1800, while others emphasise the qualitative changes in consumption and taste that Asian commodities brought about in Europe.[5]

The arrival of European traders in the Indian Ocean was also welcomed with mixed feelings and justified suspicion by established traders. The first European nation to trade with Asia was Portugal. The discovery of the Cape route had been financed and backed by the Portuguese crown, and regular trade was organised by the Carreira da Índia, the first European chartered company, which served as a model for the later Dutch, English, French, Danish and Swedish companies.[6] The Portuguese and later European companies were both commercial and semi-diplomatic bodies. Unlike the various communities of traders in the Indian Ocean, they were 'corporate' organisations, put together for trade, and not part of long-standing commercial connections.

The Portuguese and Dutch were known as 'barbarians' in Japan and they might have deserved such an appellation, not just because of their uncivilised manners, but also because of their aggressive behaviour both at sea and in the trading ports. The Europeans did not adopt a logic of mercantile cooperation: the Portuguese famously imposed *cartaz*, a racket system for protection of merchants' ships deemed under threat of being robbed and sunk.[7] They also claimed unique rights over key nodes across the Indian Ocean, including Nagasaki, Batavia, Hormuz, Bombay and Cape Town. Here they established 'factories', small semi-territorial enclaves through which trade could be coordinated and local political structures could be infiltrated.

Imported cotton textiles did not immediately become key goods for European consumers. Spices from Southeast Asia, rather than cotton textiles from India, were considered by the Portuguese to be the most desirable commodities for European markets, and the problem of how to pay for Asian commodities soon emerged.[8] Because around the Indian Ocean spices could only be bought in exchange for cotton textiles, it was reported that local traders in Melaka and Java 'want nothing but the cloths of Cambay'.[9] Overall, in the early sixteenth century textiles accounted for less than 1 per cent of the Portuguese exports back to Europe, increasing to 10 per cent in the second half of the century.[10] Surviving artefacts might not be a representative sample, but they show that the type of textiles the Portuguese brought back to Europe were rather idiosyncratic: beautiful coverlets depicting Europeans immersed in hunting scenes with printed and embroidered borders with a strong European influence (Figure 5.2).

Not until the late sixteenth century, and after a decline in the spice trade, did the Portuguese start investing in textiles. By the early seventeenth century expensive taffetas, satins, *semians*, chintz, *percalcos*, *sarja*, salampura and *roupas da seda* (silk cloth), but also middle-range baftas, beatilha, arganizes and berame accounted for over 60 per cent of their trade to Lisbon.[11] The Portuguese also sold cottons within the Indian Ocean. In 1643 they traded over 40,000 textile pieces to Mozambique and Mombasa.[12] There, they competed with those merchants such as the Gujarati banyans who for centuries had controlled trade from India to East Africa and Southeast Asia.

More space for trade was available instead on the markets of West Africa, where already in 1617 the Portuguese sold 15,000 pieces of 'Guinea' cloth through their post at the Castelo de São Jorge da Mina.[13] West Africans were keen consumers not just of Guinea cloth but also of other cottons such as *pano da India*, *caudeis* (a Bengali muslin) and *mantises* (a variety of cotton produced in Gujarat).[14] Portuguese trade also reached the New World and Brazil became an

Figure 5.2 Cotton coverlet embroidered with Tussar thread, produced in India, *c.* 1600. This is an example of a textile produced in India for the Portuguese and representing scenes from the Judgement of Solomon and the story of Judith and Holofernes, as well as hunting scenes with Portuguese. They were produced in Satgaon where the Portuguese were based between 1536 and 1632. (See also colour plate.)

important market for Indian cottons, as did Manila where from the late sixteenth century cotton textiles of Indian origin were exchanged for American silver.[15] This was a new direct trade that integrated Africa, the Americas and the Pacific.

The European East India companies

From the beginning of the seventeenth century the Carreira was joined by the English (EEIC) and Dutch (VOC) East India companies. Later in the century other European East India companies such as the Danish (1616), French (1664) and Swedish (1732) also started trading in Asia. After the decline of the Portuguese presence in the first half of the seventeenth century, the VOC and EEIC became the two most important European traders in Asia and between Asia and Europe. The two companies were rivals, yet their interests and success were quite different. For the VOC, the trade in cotton textiles to Europe was never a primary aim; conversely, by the 1660s the EEIC had become the major trader in Indian cottons to London.[16] Competition in the Indian Ocean (what is called 'country trade') was a different matter, and for the entire seventeenth and the first part of the eighteenth century the VOC remained the dominant European trading company in Asia. It was successful not only in securing strongholds in India, but also in engaging in the remunerative trade in spices and luxury goods with China and Japan. The EEIC dominated the intercontinental side of operations, with cottons becoming a staple product for European markets and for consumers in the Americas and in West Africa.[17]

When the EIC and the VOC began to trade in textiles early in the seventeenth century, quantities were small, although the two companies already specialised in different types of fabrics. The VOC traded cheap Guinea cloth, normally striped, that was probably re-exported to Africa, while the EEIC brought back to Europe baftas and simians. The EEIC was in a position of inferiority, however, as the VOC had access to wider networks of textile procurement thanks to the company's trade in spices in Southeast Asia. The EEIC's specialisation in trade to the western Indian Ocean and back to Europe was not part of a preconceived strategy, but more the result of contingency. In 1612 the company established a factory at Surat, followed a few years later by another in Bombay, and by 1619 it started sending white and striped sashes and chintzes from Ahmedabad back to Europe.[18]

The French had initially resisted the call to participate in the Indian Ocean trade, but were finally convinced that it was best to import Asian commodities directly rather than buying them from either the English or the Dutch.[19] The first Compagnie des Indes Orientales (FEIC) was established in 1664, followed by the Compagnie de la Chine in 1698.[20] The French never achieved a high degree of success in the Indian Ocean trade: overwhelmed with financial difficulties, the FEIC's purchases of cloth were initially very small.[21] Its commercial position was hindered in particular by the fact that the French company had no factory in Bengal, a key area for cotton textile procurement from the early eighteenth century.[22] Nevertheless, the company imported around 100,000 pieces a year of white calicoes and blue and painted muslins at the end of the seventeenth century, rising to 300,000 pieces in the early years of the following century.[23] The only other substantial European trading company in the Indian Ocean was the Danish East India Company, which was established as early as 1616 and which was refounded several times. Its activities could be defined as irregular at best, with several periods in which no ships were sent to Asia.[24] The Danes followed the same practices of the larger European companies, trading heavily in Bengal from a factory in Tramquebar, especially in *pano comprido* and salampores, selling them in Copenhagen but also to Germany and as far as the West Indies.[25]

Knowledge and information: what to buy

The extensive archives of the European East India companies include important materials that have been studied and partly published.[26] They contain page after page of commercial correspondence detailing prices, varieties of commodities and local market conditions. Such documents are not just a mine of information for historians but also testimony to the unique scale of what is effectively the first intercontinental information system. Original letters were sent from London to India and vice versa and copies were kept locally. Everything was carefully noted, counted and reported. Knowledge is power, and the European companies knew that the chance of making profits out of a trade based on voyages lasting several months, if not years, was dependent on a constant and reliable flow of routinised information. A great deal of importance was attached to matching production and purchases in India with knowledge of consumer markets in Europe. A problem that all the European companies faced was how much to buy in India. It was not simply a matter of filling ships to the brim, but of assessing what would sell at advantageous prices. Textiles were initially seen as a subsidiary commodity for imports to Europe and remained so for a considerable period in the history of European trade in Asia.[27] For several decades the quantities remained small, but in the three decades 1680–90 the intercontinental cotton trade boomed and reached a substantial 1.3 million pieces per year (Figure 5.3).[28]

Focus on the Europe-bound trade can, however, be misleading, as the VOC appears a smaller competitor to the EEIC. In reality, during the two centuries of existence of the VOC (1600–1795), the Dutch company sent to Asia more than double the number of ships sent by the EEIC.[29] The difference between these two companies was that the VOC specialised in the intra-Asian trade.[30] On the Europe-bound trade, the EEIC specialised in textiles (in particular cotton textiles) while the VOC imported a wider variety of commodities, including substantial amounts of raw silk and silk cloth. For the EEIC, cottons accounted for more than 50 per cent of their cargoes for most of the seventeenth and eighteenth centuries, compared to less than 30 per cent of the value of commodities traded back to Europe by the VOC (Figure 5.4).[31]

The fact that the EEIC specialised on the import into Europe of Indian cottons vis-à-vis the more varied cargo of the VOC is no indication that textiles had little importance in the Dutch trade with Asia. Quite the opposite. After all, the overall size of the VOC trade was larger than that of the EEIC and the quantities of Asian textiles imported into Europe by the Dutch company were substantial.[32] Moreover, the VOC traded much more widely in cotton textiles in the Indian Ocean than the EEIC did. Figures are difficult to come by, but we have a sense of

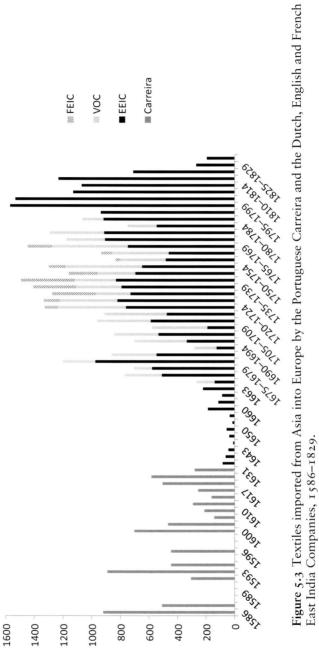

Figure 5.3 Textiles imported from Asia into Europe by the Portuguese Carreira and the Dutch, English and French East India Companies, 1586–1829.

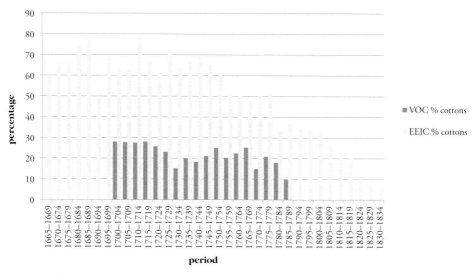

Figure 5.4 Cotton textiles as a percentage of the value of all commodities traded to Europe by the VOC (1700–1789) and the EEIC (1665–1834).

the relative size of the VOC's intra-Asian and European-bound trade for the year 1712–13. The total trade back to Europe was worth 15.6 million guilders, of which just under 4.3 million was in cotton textiles (27 per cent). The intra-Asian trade was worth 14.3 million guilders (7.4 of Indian exports and 6.8 of imports), of which 3.3 million guilders (23 per cent of all intra-Asian trade) was in cotton textiles.[33]

If we sum together the textiles for the European trade and for 'country' trade, the Dutch bought in India larger quantities of cotton textiles than the English did. During the seventeenth century the VOC acquired an acute understanding of cotton textile markets through its engagement in the Southeast Asian spice trade. The English saw themselves disadvantaged in the purchase and sale of cloth in Asia and noted that 'The Hollanders doth take such extraordinary courses in putting out their cloth to the Chineses ... we cannot sell any of ours because it is not so vendible in the country, for they giveth them choice of commodities, that which is fitting for the country, whereof we have little store'.[34] An EEIC's servant in Bantam in the early 1660s could only admit that 'the Dutch's cloth is much better than ours both in length, breadth, and fineness, which causes it generally to be sought after before ours'.[35] Yet the VOC did better in the Indian Ocean than in the trade back to Europe. Moreover, the EEIC suffered from being second to the Dutch in purchasing cloth in India, but it has been argued that the English company's more flexible organisational strategy, which encouraged their servants to follow their own judgement in terms of what to buy and how much money to advance to weavers, was key to the successful development of trade with Europe.[36]

Dealing with variety

The trade between Europe and Asia was complicated by the fact that those in charge of purchasing in India had no clear sense of how well the products might sell in Europe, while those in charge of selling to European metropolitan markets had little understanding of how procurement worked in South Asia. Although these two worlds were in continuous correspondence, the time lag between a letter being sent and a decision being reported back from India to Europe and vice versa took several years. It was therefore paramount for traders to avoid overstocking. The FEIC had its fingers burned in the early days of trade with India in the mid 1680s. It was a victim of bad purchasing choices and 'too large consignments of cotton goods that have been carried out to the present', with the result that some of the commodities made up to 50 per cent losses.[37] This scenario repeated itself in the early 1730s, at the beginning of the expansion of French trade in India, when the company invested heavily in expensive cloth with the result that a factor had to recommend to his colleagues in Bengal not to send any '*marchandise fines*' because 'there are in the depot in Nantes a great deal of this quality of fine cloth that remains unsold'.[38] Similar orders were imparted by the VOC directors to their agents to refrain from buying certain types of cloth and to seek others, in order to avoid large warehouses full of rotting cottons.[39]

These and many other observations by the French, Dutch, English and other European company servants point to the fact that Indian cottons were a complex and varied category of merchandise that included varieties of textiles ranging from cheap Guinea cloth for the African trade to fine and expensive muslin for European elite consumption.[40] The Indian textile industry was segmented and connected by product specialisation from village to village. The profusion of names is truly astonishing, with literally hundreds of varieties being traded at any one time.[41] European East India companies had to cope with endless varieties.[42] One of the FEIC servants concluded that 'All the science of the merchant is restricted to the knowledge of the different types of these cloth'.[43] There was a high risk of stocking unsuitable goods. The EEIC, for instance, traded for the best part of the seventeenth and eighteenth centuries more than fifty different varieties of cloth. Some of them were traded for limited periods as a response to demand in Europe, or because supplies from specific localities in India became abundant

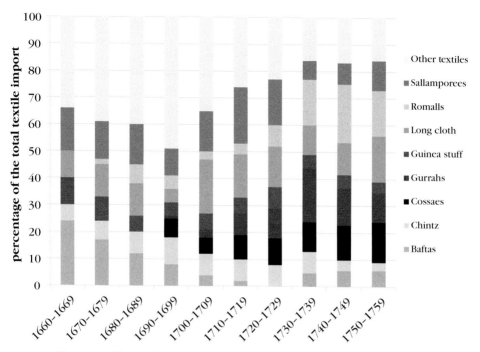

Figure 5.5 Types of cotton textiles imported into Europe by the EEIC, 1660–1759.

and cheap. Figures reveal, however, that the company must have changed its purchasing strategy after the 1690s, when it ran into serious troubles because of financial overexposure and unsuccessful political tactics.[44] It started to focus on a smaller range of varieties that came by the mid eighteenth century to constitute the bulk of the company's trade: baftas, chintzes, cossaes, gurras, Guinea cloth, longcloth, romalls and sallamporees, which together formed from half to five-sixths of imported textiles (Figure 5.5).[45]

A similar strategy was implemented by the VOC. The annual 'eis van retour' (literally, demand of return) included all the items the Heren XVII (the Board of Directors of the VOC) wanted from Asia. Types, quantities and measures are mentioned, though in this case we are dealing with requests rather than what they actually got. These are revealing documents, however, especially for the period after 1683 when orders from India are distinguished by geographic areas. They show how orders included 'quilted cotton blankets', finely painted chintzes, coarse chintzes, printed cotton blankets, mouris, and so on, and include the occasional observation such as 'no longer demanded' or 'to be excused' to mean a shift in demand.[46]

Product failures and customisation

The shift to trading in a smaller selection of textiles should not be seen as a reduction in variety but as the result of a clearer understanding of what would sell in European markets. The 'apprenticeship' of the English and other European East India companies was based on the learning of how cottons would fit within a broader material spectrum of textiles and how to position them next to European linens, woollens and silks. But the East India companies were not passive receivers of goods that they tried to sell as best they could on domestic markets. Their strategy consisted of making new products intelligible to consumers back in Europe by adopting a terminology used in a linen trade already familiar to consumers. They also considered various uses for textiles and decided that white baftas were good for bed and table linen while chintzes, *pintadoes* and calicoes could be suitable for curtains and hangings. They also displayed acute awareness of the importance of colours and designs, often conveying strict recommendations on what had to be purchased in India.[47] This was the case with the VOC servants imparting orders that sarasa cloths had to have 'just one flower and a range of leaf patterns', specifying that 'The quality was to be average and there was to be as much diversity in the lots produced as possible'.[48]

European companies, however, were not immune from failures. In the 1680s the Dutch attempted to expand sales in the Javanese market by commissioning Coromandel weavers to copy Javanese batik, but the final product turned out to be not just of lesser quality but also five times more expensive than local batik.[49] The Indian Ocean trade was also an arena for learning that small differences might render entire cargoes unsellable. This was the experience of the early English traders in the seventeenth century, who were victims of what they defined as a 'great oversight'. They were astonished to find that Malay consumers would not even touch their cloth because it had 'a little narrow white edge, and the upright [correct] Maley cloth must be without it'. The English trader Peter Floris concluded that 'if I had not now found it by experience, I had never believed it, that so small a fault should cause so great an abatement in the price'.[50]

Occasional failure did not deter the European companies from taking serious risks in order to develop new markets. This occurred when the EEIC introduced cotton shirts into what had been an English market dominated by linen shirts. In 1682 the EEIC ordered from their factors in Madras 200,000 ready-made cotton shirts and shifts to 'introduce the using of Callicoe for that purpose in all these Northern parts of the world'.[51] This was one of the EEIC's most ambitious schemes as it meant substantial investments in what turned out to be the largest 'clothing speculation' of the early modern period: one garment for every two adults in London, or 2 per cent of all clothes sold in Britain in a year according to contemporary estimates.[52] It was also a plan with important political ramifications, as it was based on the replacement of linen, which was imported from continental Europe, with cotton imported from India. It was argued that the 'more general... wearing of Callicoes in stead of French Holland, or Flanders Cloth' would have been a 'National Benefit' as Britain would have no longer relied on commodities imported from enemy states.[53] Notwithstanding the carefully crafted justification for embarking on such a vast import, the substitution failed. Consumers rejected cotton shirts and shifts. They were considered 'strongly sewed for the poor people's wear' but also unsuitable because they were made of cotton.[54] Consumers were not yet ready to embrace cotton as a substitute for linen. Even when the company tried to sell off the shirts and shifts at cut prices, most of the stock remained unsold.[55]

The case of ready-made shirts and shifts reveals that the European companies commissioned products that were not part of the classic productive repertoire of Indian producers. As early as the 1620s, Capitaine Ripon noted how in Pulicat the VOC employed weavers and painters who 'do all... works that the Dutch put them to work to'.[56] Indian artisans had already been dealing with customisation for centuries, because they produced specific products for a variety of Asian markets. Surviving artefacts show the flexibility of producers in adapting to the requirements of consumers from thousands of miles away.[57] A region like Gujarat produced cotton textiles for a series of different markets, each of which was characterised by precise product specifications, ranging from productive techniques to exact design, patterns and colours. The relationship between Indian producers and European consumers was, however, rather different from the customisation within the Indian Ocean.[58] There was no direct contact and no possibility of finding out consumer preferences by observing final markets. Yet, European companies had a sound foothold in the consumer markets back home. Customisation was used to reduce the risk assumed in merchandising. The European companies showed an active interest in shaping products and manipulating taste already in the mid seventeenth century. It was as important to present European consumers with something 'exotic' as it was to alter these products to make them suitable to their taste. In 1643 the EEIC directors in London sent letters to the factors in India asking them to change the design to suit English tastes:

> Those [quilts] which thereafter you shall send me we desire may be with more white ground, and the flowers and branch to be in colour in the middle of the quilt as the painter pleases, whereas now most part of your quilts come with red grounds which are not so well accepted here.[59]

British consumers seemed to prefer textiles with light-colour backgrounds, quite different from the deep blue and red backgrounds that had for long been the staple of Gujarati and Coromandel production for both Southeast Asia and the Near East (Figures 5.6 and 5.7).[60] The EEIC actively sought products that could be used together with white and embroidered linens, thereby reinforcing the preference for whiteness that had characterised notions of cleanliness and decorum for several centuries in Europe. Thus, the EEIC unwittingly opened a door for European production of printed cotton to flourish, because the production of cottons with white backgrounds was not favoured by Indian printers and painters. The technique based on the waxing of vast parts of the cloth to remained undyed was expensive. It was much more common, and cheaper, to produce 'white motifs on blue or red backgrounds' rather than 'blue or red motifs on white backgrounds', as the latter would have meant the waxing of most of the cloth. Yet, European printers learned the Indian techniques of waxing and tepid indigo fermentation in the last quarter of the seventeenth century and by the early eighteenth century they were already experimenting with techniques unknown in Asia. The most important of these was the use of cold vats obtained by dissolving indigo in iron sulphate that allowed the printing of blue on a white background.[61] Consumers in Europe did not just remodel products but also shaped the innovative technologies used to produce them.[62]

The East India companies made use of samples and drawings to communicate the specific motifs, pattern and colours of the textiles being demanded.[63] The EEIC, for instance, commissioned palampores with 'large branches for hanging of Roomes'.[64] These were the types of furnishing much in fashion in mid-seventeenth-century Europe, quite different from similar hangings traded from India to other markets in Asia (Figures 5.8 and 5.9).

The palampores commissioned by the EEIC used the motif of the tree of life – deemed to be from Scandinavian mythos and Genesis – probably sent as a pattern from Europe.[65] The tree of life was first exoticised, as most consumers in Europe thought it to be an Asian motif, and was later reintroduced into European design and aesthetic preferences with copies being produced around Europe and especially in the city of Genoa (Figure 5.10).[66]

A great deal of the companies' correspondence was, however, not given to design but to measurements and product specification. This might appear surprising. One seventeenth-century EEIC's dispatch to India specified that cottons 'must be either 13 or 15 yards on a fine calico. Half of fine bunches of four colours, namely, the ground work drawing black, filled up with red and peach blossom color and the twigs or spring green'.[67] This was no trivial matter. Consumers in Europe were used to very precise lengths and imported textiles had

Figure 5.6 An Indian cotton cloth with dark background, which was in demand in Southeast Asia, *c.* 1680–1760.

Figure 5.7 A cotton cloth preferred by Europeans. A woman's chintz jacket, c. 1725, produced on the Coromandel coast for the European market. (See also colour plate.)

to conform to notions of quality and with the regulations imposed by law.[68] The correspondence of the FEIC explains that only certain sizes were easily sold in France and advised factors in India to get hold of those 'types of cloth which we get painted in ordinary chittes for France, because of their [suitable] width', though the French admitted that the cheaper varieties, 'which are hardly wider than these', might be suitable for the less demanding markets made of 'common people as well as for the American islands'.[69] What we read in this correspondence is a language of customisation, but also precision and exactitude in following specifications that were sometimes hard for local producers to implement.

Regulating production

The fact that Indian cloth came in a wide range of varieties and in different standards of quality, length, weaving and finishing made it difficult for the European traders to ensure that supplies were constant and consistent. The limited access that they had to weaving villages and finishing workshops in India was a further hindrance in implementing product customisation and in checking

Figure 5.8 Part of a palampore, bedcover or hanging, produced on the Coromandel coast for the Indonesian Market and found in Sumatra, eighteenth century. (See also colour plate.)

Figure 5.9 A large palampore produced on the Coromandel coast for the European Market, *c.* 1720–40. (See also colour plate.)

that minimum standards of quality were adhered to. This was the complaint of a FEIC servant when in 1704 he observed that several orders of a thousand pieces each were given to middlemen who, in turn, employed 3–4,000 workers each. The final result turned out to be highly unsatisfactory, 'so much so that

Figure 5.10 Block-printed mezzaro inspired by Indian palampores, produced in Genoa, Italy, early nineteenth century. (See also colour plate.)

one will make his piece fine, another will make it thicker [closely woven], others will use a thread which will be round – and which will be of the same quality as the first one even a little finer'. Moreover, he explained, 'The same workers will differ in length – some will give 1 or sometimes 2 fingers more than that ordered, and others will give less.' The French report concluded that 'during the 25 years that we are doing this business we have noticed that it is not possible to have 100 pieces of goods of this country of undoubtedly the same size'.[70]

Similar complaints were voiced by the servants of the EEIC posted at Agra as early as 1617 when they explained that it would have been impossible to provide calicoes two yards broad, as 'all which is sold here is brought from far, where they will be loth to make of any save their ordinary and accustomary sorts and sizes, except they were sure of more buyers of them than ourselves'.[71] It was only with 'continued investment in all places round where weavers inhabit' that, as Thomas Hoskins at Broach reassured the president and council of Surat, 'wee might comply with the quantityes you require of us' with cloths satisfactory 'not only in theire lengths and bredths but also in theire cure and chinting'.[72] Indian weavers had to be convinced that it was worthwhile to implement change to satisfy European requests.

The abundance of complaints might imply that the European companies kept their standards too high. This was surely the case for the EEIC in the seventeenth century. One employee in Surat distressingly wrote to the factory that he could not 'attaine to the quantityes you write for' and explained that 'One great obsticle is our stricnesse and severity to them [the Indian weavers] in keeping them to theire true lengths and bredths; which they would with lesse trouble have been brought to, were it not for other buyers, that stand not upon it so much as wee do'. Competition between companies must have decreased expectations. The Dutch, the same report explained, 'looke neither to thicke nor thin, broad or narrow, if they want not above halfe or three quarters of a yard in length and two or three and a halfe inches in bredth; which makes us thinke some times that they doe it on purpose to weary us out and hinder our buying any'.[73] By the beginning of the following century both the English and the Dutch used a three-tier system of quality for their supplies on the Coromandel, and were keen to negotiate for lower grades at reduced prices.[74] Negotiations were necessary as it was impossible to be sure if the cloth commissioned was going to be delivered in the quantity or quality agreed upon.[75]

The problems encountered by the European companies occurred partly because trade to Europe was a seasonal affair and was based on a precise shipping calendar, with all vessels having to leave India before the end of October in order to avoid the worst of the winter months. The French reported that it was advisable to place orders before the end of May, when prices were low, but the risk of arriving late, or of late delivery, was high.[76] Moreover, this was incompatible with good finishing. Bleaching was a laborious process that entailed both the use of vast quantities of water and good weather to dry the cloth. It was thus an activity that was carried out mainly at the end of the rainy season. This meant that most of the bleaching had to be done in a hurry, leaving little time for the dyers to ensure that the process was completed correctly.[77]

There are repeated requests in the EEIC's correspondence to ensure that all cloth was checked, something that was far from possible. Criticism was also raised over the way in which cloth was stored in warehouses and on board ships. In 1661, for instance, the EEIC's Surat factory was instructed that calicoes had to be specially packed in cotton wool and wax cloth and the bales had to be covered with skins in order to avoid damage.[78] As the problem persisted, three years later

Jeremy Sambrook – the son of Samuel Sambrook, the keeper of the company's Calico warehouse in London – was appointed to supervise the examining and packing of all calicoes.[79]

Improving the quality and ensuring regular delivery of suitable cloth were not easy tasks. The tasks were rendered even more complicated by the fact that access to weavers remained limited and mediated through a series of intermediaries who were presented by the companies' servants as 'perfidious' and dangerous. The latter worried about having 'their throats cut if one reduces the least among from what they demand. They do nothing for anybody unless paid in advance and (even) when thus paid, serve you as badly as they can'.[80] In these circumstances, customisation was difficult to achieve. Similarly, contracts were often broken, leading to frequent occasions in which no cloth was available for purchase at all. It has been argued that the political control of parts of India, especially by the British, in the second half of the eighteenth century allowed the European companies to travel directly and to actively coordinate the textile production, thus achieving better control over the qualities and deliveries of textiles.[81] The company came to coordinate the work of spinners, weavers and finishers, a fact that Indian historians have depicted as part of a trajectory of increasing exploitation of the Indian workforce by European powers.[82]

The gradual shift from independent producers to waged workers employed by European companies has been linked to the decline of the Indian export capacity and an increase in the power of European companies.[83] Historical sources seem to confirm this. Just a decade after Plassey, servants of the FEIC complained about the dominance of the English traders, especially in Bengal, where they were able to source merchandise at prices up to 30 per cent lower than those paid by the French.[84] Yet, when we look at the price of Indian cloth in Europe and the profits of the EEIC, the picture is less clear (Figure 5.11). From the 1660s to at least the 1780s the purchasing price of Indian cottons paid in India by the EEIC for a piece of cloth increased constantly. Although prices paid varied substantially from year to year, over a century they nearly doubled. Part of this increase has been explained by the fact that in the early years of the eighteenth century the EEIC switched procurement from Gujarat and the Malabar coast eastwards to the Coromandel coast and especially to Bengal, where higher-quality textiles were sought.[85] Yet the trend of rising purchasing prices was evident both for textiles purchased that were shipped from Bombay and those shipped from Bengal. This finding is in line with the copious sources complaining about the dearness of cottons purchased in India over the eighteenth century and with recent interpretations that see Indian weavers as fairly well off (at least until later in the eighteenth century) rather than exploited by the European

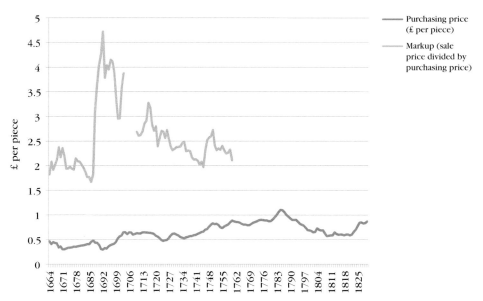

Figure 5.11 Purchasing price and markup of the EEIC on textiles imported from India, 1664–1829.

companies.[86] The EEIC tried to soften the blow by reducing profit margins and expanding quantities traded, something that it might have been forced to do by virtue of increasing competition from cottons produced at home.[87] We might conclude that as consumption expanded in Europe, there was an incentive to replace increasingly expensive Indian cottons with competitively priced products produced in Europe.[88]

There is also sufficient evidence to suggest that while prices increased quality worsened. A French *mémoire* of 1753 on trade in Masulipatam noted that 'these cottons are always getting worse, and this is a continuous process if we compare them to those we got ten years ago from the same places, we find them quite different for quantity as well as for the quality of the yarn that makes the fabric. We look in vain to a remedy for this abuse.'[89] From the late seventeenth century, and in a more acute form from the early decades of the eighteenth century, a tension emerged between European consumers wanting better-quality textiles (by then used for dress) and the stagnant, if not even decreasing, quality of textiles available.[90]

The East India companies were indeed keen to find out how exactly production worked. When in the late 1710s the VOC servants struggled to receive sufficient supplies of good-quality cloth on the Coromandel coast, the company launched an investigation of the inland weaving villages. Responses by the weavers were unenthusiastic to say the least, as business was buoyant and they had no intention of changing their working practices to suit the requirements of the Dutch.[91] The companies did their best to acquire knowledge of the processes of bowing, spinning and weaving – shown in the many eighteenth-century prints and drawings of textile manufacturing in India.[92] However, with the exception of textile printing and painting, there is no clear understanding of how much this acquired knowledge of production processes in India informed the development of a European industry.[93]

Conclusion

During the seventeenth and eighteenth centuries substantial quantities of Indian cottons entered Europe. This early phase of engagement with cotton textiles occurred within a highly competitive but well-developed marketing system should be seen as an integral part of any narrative tracing the economic development of cotton textiles, a narrative that has focused far too narrowly on wage differentials and technological innovation. Europe had to become acquainted with cotton as a commodity before moving into import substitution. This chapter has shown how this was a trade of great potential that took time and learning to realise because communications were difficult, products could be unsuitable and the quality and price of the cloth that reached Europe was not always satisfactory.

What I have defined as an 'Indian apprenticeship' was not just based on learning about merchandising and consumer preferences, but extended to an appreciation of the entire process of production starting with raw materials, passing through spinning, weaving and finishing, and successfully trading finished cloth on domestic and international markets. As we will see in the following chapters, this knowledge took several generations for Europeans to accumulate and was based on a combination of different types of understanding ranging from chemical knowledge to the gathering of botanical information, to the putting in place of complex systems of trade. Different European nations showed differing degrees of success. The English did not necessarily enjoy better access to Indian cottons than the Dutch or the French, yet their imperial markets for the supply of raw materials and for the sale of finished goods provided a favourable context for the development of a local cotton textile industry.

6 NEW CONSUMING HABITS: HOW COTTONS ENTERED EUROPEAN HOUSES AND WARDROBES

There are few surviving examples of everyday garments worn by people in the early modern period. It is paradoxical that we have better indications of the expensive and rare clothes of the elites than the more common forms of apparel worn by millions of people in the past. We are left only with fragmentary evidence of the choices of what have been defined as 'plebeian consumers', a varied but vast category of customers that many historians have identified as central to the expansion of European consumption in the late seventeenth and eighteenth centuries.[1]

Historians are sometimes lucky and find precious evidence in unexpected places. This is the case for the thousands of fabrics now deposited at the London Metropolitan Archive. These are not the types of textiles normally collected by museums. They are in fact to be found literally pinned to the pages of large volumes of records. Each page is the record of a child left in the care of the London Foundling Hospital, an orphanage founded in the 1740s. It lists the date, gender and age as well as the 'marks and clothing of the child', thus suggesting that bodily and sartorial peculiarities were seen both as complementary to and sufficient to denote the identity of a person. The mother or person leaving the child also left a 'token', something distinctive that would allow the identification and the eventual reclamation of a child. These are moving objects, as we know that few of these children were ever reclaimed or survived the harsh conditions of the orphanage.[2]

The female child left to the hospital on the 15 November 1745, age 3 weeks, came from Lambs Conduits Fields, just opposite the hospital, and the token left as a distinctive symbol for the child was a silk ribbon and an entire sleeve (Figure 6.1). This sleeve, together with several hundred other samples of cloth, provides one of the best 'material archives' of everyday textiles worn by people of the lower ranks, often women in difficulty who could not take care of their own children. The sleeve is a striped 'cotton' (a fustian) possibly produced in

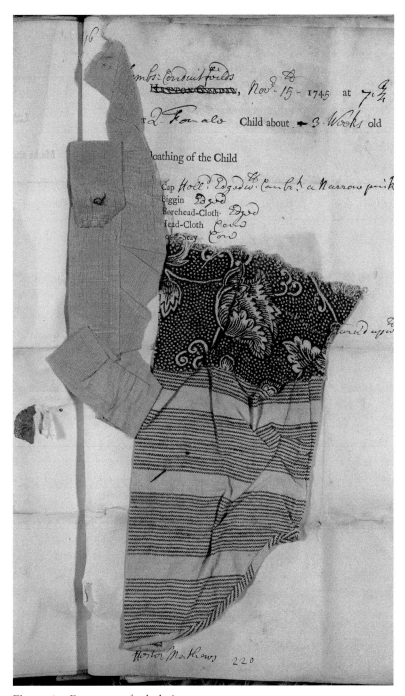

Figure 6.1 Fragment of a baby's garment, 1745.

Lancashire in this period. The purple cuff is instead identified as linen and was a cheap fabric printed in one of many London printworks.[3]

The records of the Foundling Hospital provide a snapshot of the types of fabrics commonly worn in the mid eighteenth century. These cotton textiles are less colourful or sophisticated than the beautiful chintzes and calicoes to be seen in numerous museums. They also provide us with a question: how common was the use of cotton textiles in Europe in this period? Generations of historians have claimed that the importation of Indian cottons into Europe created by the end of the seventeenth century a 'calico craze' for these exotic and cheap textiles, which European consumers found not just desirable but increasingly within their reach. From the mid seventeenth century onwards Indian textiles were imported by the East India companies and their imitations were sought after by consumers not just in England but also in most European countries. But their popularity was not a 'craze', as many contemporaries defined it, but a slow process of 'familiarisation' with a new fabric and a new medium of design and fashion. Exotic Indian cottons did not take Europe by storm: their success was slow and relied as much on a process of familiarisation as on uncertain and unstable competitive relationships with other fabrics of local manufacture. Consumers also made their choices within a precise institutional framework, one in which Indian cottons were banned for most of the period. Smuggling and the breaking of laws were everyday occurrences in the difficult process of securing congruence between what consumers and governments demanded.

A calico craze? The popularity of cotton

The main objection to the notion of a sudden rise in the popularity of Indian textiles among European consumers in the second half of the seventeenth century is that Indian fabrics had reached western Europe well before the setting up of the East India companies. The Portuguese Carreira da Índia was importing significant quantities of Indian cottons in the late sixteenth and early seventeenth centuries, and silks, cottons and other commodities from the Levant were arriving in Marseilles, London and Flanders. When, in 1592, an English privateer captured the Portuguese vessel *Madre de Dios*, its cargo of Indian painted cottons was sold across England, probably enabling Indian cottons to enter into the houses of people of modest means.[4] Eastern and northern Europe and Russia relied instead on supplies traded via the Middle East and Anatolia.[5] 'Red calicoes', named as such because of their red backgrounds, were popular in Russia and could have been either original Indian or Anatolian copies of Gujarati textiles.[6]

There is, however, no overall agreement on the precise chronology of the 'success' of Indian cottons among European consumers. Our understanding has long been dominated by research carried out by K. N. Chaudhuri for the period 1660–1760. He showed the importance of textiles for the overall business of the EEIC and the many millions of pieces of cotton cloth imported yearly from India into the port of London.[7] Chaudhuri's selected time span has created a misleading impression that it was only during the last four decades of the seventeenth century that the trade expanded. More recent research has attempted to evaluate the Asian trade using a longer time scale (see Figure 5.3) and underlined both its slow growth over time and modest share on a world scale.[8] Meanwhile, some historians have concluded that tea, silk, spices and cotton textiles were luxuries within reach of the European elite, but that they had a limited impact on the structure and growth of the early modern European economy.[9]

Historians considering consumption, rather than trade or economic development, make the opposite point by arguing that the commodities imported into Europe from Asia (especially cottons) became significant in cultural terms because they shaped European innovations, imitation and taste.[10] Furthermore, the quantities of cottons traded were not negligible: between 1670 and 1760 the EEIC imported on average 3 yards of cotton cloth per British person per year, not an insignificant quantity compared to the 7–8 yards of cloth estimated to have been consumed in India.[11] These textiles imported by the English and other European East India companies were auctioned in their respective headquarters in London, Lorient or Amsterdam and bought in large quantities by merchants and wholesalers. They were then sold via a variety of tailors, dressmakers, haberdashers, 'cheap clothes' warehouses, either as cloth or ready-made garments. They were purchased by consumers not just in the main centres of trade in France, England and the Netherlands, but also in more remote landlocked localities.[12] Their cheapness has, moreover, long been seen as a key factor behind the competitiveness of Indian cottons vis-à-vis European textiles. There is sufficient evidence that the cottons reaching Europe were not inexpensive: their price ranged from 10 to 30 pence a yard against a 10 to 20 pence for European mixed cotton and linen (Figure 6.2).[13]

Cottons were bought by European consumers for the same reasons they were bought by consumers in most of the known world in the early modern period: namely, because of their desirable properties.[14] Fastness of colour allowed them to be washed and to resist fading when exposed to light.[15] This explains why sellers in Europe were keen to advertise the colours of their Indian cottons. The 1696 catalogue of merchandise sold by an anonymous London merchant mentioned chintz cloth 'cheickered [sic] with a variety of colours, as Red,

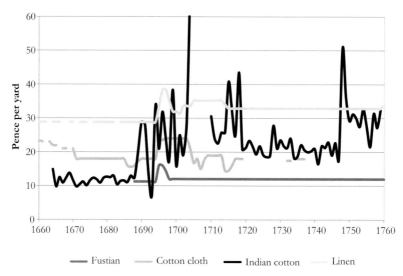

Figure 6.2 Cotton and linen textile prices in London, 1660–1760.

Yellow, Blew and Green...wears very well in anything you shall think fit to use it for'.[16] Silks and woollens could not be as easily washed, while linens (used mostly for undergarments) were washed more regularly but were mainly appreciated for their whiteness. Cottons could be washed without loss of brightness or colour.[17]

Indian cottons were also light fabrics that substituted for more expensive silks and the middle-range light woollens. The shift towards lighter fabrics had already started in Europe when thick woollens produced by using carded weft and warp were replaced with worsted textiles made of long combing wool.[18] These were the famous 'new draperies' that had originated in the Netherlands in the late medieval period. They were produced in Norwich in England from the late sixteenth century and exported to most of Europe and to the Middle East.[19] They were coarser but lighter, and above all, cheaper than traditional woollens.[20]

Indian cottons were initially appreciated also for their 'novelty' and exotic motifs. Like tea, china, chinoiserie, and other Asian goods, the novelty value of calicoes fits the notion of pre-industrial European product innovation. But we should be wary of seeing this process as simple. Beverly Lemire has emphasised the importance of creating new distribution channels and fostering established ones (shops, second hand, peddlers), which allowed the new fabric to reach all consumers, rich and poor alike, while John Styles has underlined how the success of Indian cottons was not necessarily the result of their intrinsic qualities.[21] He follows K. N. Chaudhuri, who observed that the 'expansion in the sale of the East India Company's textile imports from India in the 1670s was deliberately accompanied by an attempt to popularise their use in Europe'.[22] They all seem to agree that the success of Asian cottons could not be taken for granted: European consumers needed aesthetic and tactile training in order for a market for these new commodities to be created.

How long this process took is difficult to say. Lemire argues that Indian cottons achieved popularity as early as the second half of the sixteenth century, when they could be found even in remote Iberian locations.[23] From Spain they reached other parts of Europe. It was to one of his brothers, probably in either Cadiz or Seville, that in 1547 the Florentine merchant Matteo Botti asked: 'send me some stuff from India to adorn beds…such as those cottons (*cotonini dipinti*) painted by printing that are bright and some are blue and some are red'. His letter suggests that this was not the first time that similar cloths were requested. He added in fact that he wished to receive 'other design, and send me bright but pleasing things such as for instance stuff to adorn chests (*cassoni*) or bedroom chests and send as many as you can, though I would like to have ten or twelve of those painted cottons, half blue and half red, but make sure that they are large and beautiful'.[24]

It is difficult to say how common these episodes were. The penetration of cotton cloth into European wardrobes over the course of the seventeenth century was characterised by a steady but unimpressive growth. In the case of England, inventories show that local fustians, rather than imported cottons, become increasingly popular for the lower and middling sorts during the first half of the seventeenth century.[25] Yet, in the seventeenth century fustians not only ranked much lower than omnipresent cloth and canvas but were not as common as linen, kerseys, wool, stuff and russets.[26] This has led John Styles to offer a view that cotton became a truly 'popular' choice only in the second half of the eighteenth century.[27] By then cotton textiles, both imported and home-produced, had become common in most European nations. Amsterdam inventories for the period 1740–82 show how next to Dutch and European woollens, Asian chintzes, muslins and other cottons, but also printed cottons and mixes such as *bont* and cambai cloths, were present in at least a quarter of all households and were consumed down the social ladder.[28] At the eve of the French Revolution nearly 40 per cent of Parisian wage earners' wardrobes included cottons and fustians.[29] Similarly, in Castile the use of cotton expanded over the eighteenth century, although it became more popular than wool or flax only by the beginning of the following century.[30] The import of Indian cottons set off a slow shift of textile consumption in Europe, but the full triumph of cotton had to wait for the end of the *Ancien Régime* and the mechanisation of its production.

How competitive were cottons?

The increasing popularity of cottons can be partly explained by looking at the relationship between these new textiles and established fabrics used by European consumers: linens, woollens and silks. Whilst the 'cultural value' attached to Indian textiles is hard to deny, their impact on the 'textile mix' cannot be reduced simply to the straightforward substitution or replacement of existing fabrics. Cottons also came to influence the ways in which people understood and valued textiles in general.[31] They reshaped, for instance, established ideas of durability and worth. The anonymous author of *The Trade of England Revived* (1681) observed how hard-wearing woollens could last twice as long as a calico and, even when worn out, 'will serve for one use or other afterwards for children'.[32] By contrast, calico did not last long and could hardly be reused. Cottons might have been cheaper, but consumers were not necessarily satisfied with their short lifespan.

The acceptance of Indian calicoes might also have been hindered by the fact that they became more expensive over the eighteenth century. The EEIC's employees in India and London knew well that increases in prices in India had profound consequences on the retail markets in Europe, with consumers shift-ing back to cambricks, lawns and other linens and woollens when cotton prices increased.[33] The companies lamented the high purchasing prices in India and shrinking sales in Europe (Figure 6.2).[34] Indian cottons became increasingly expensive. Import prices and contemporary comments suggest that by the early eighteenth century there were clear incentives to replace Indian cottons with other similar but home-produced wares.[35] Imported cottons remained cheaper than linen, but again the price differential between the two dramatically shrank after 1700. In the first half of the eighteenth century, the period of the prohibition of cotton textiles, high prices – rather than legal zeal – might have hampered the use of Indian chintzes and calicoes in England and mainland Europe. Substitutes of European manufacture were at times cheaper than original Indian cottons. At the end of the seventeenth century an *indienne commune* (a basic Indian printed cotton) cost 4 livres and 14 sous per aune in Paris while a *toile imprimée à Gênes* (a cotton cloth produced in Genoa) could be purchased at 2–3 livres.[36] At the bottom end of the market, mothers leaving their children to the Foundling Hospital might have found a European printed linen or fustian more affordable than a better-quality Indian chintz.

The visible hand of the state

The inroads of Indian cotton textiles into the consuming habits of Europeans generated resistance on the part of linen, woollen and silk producers, who lobbied governments in an attempt to limit the import and wearing of Asian textiles. This differed from other parts of the world, where imports of Indian cottons were considered to be positive for trade and material welfare. In Europe, they came to be seen as damaging at both the economic and the moral level. Dutch, Swedish, French and English moralists all agreed that Eastern luxuries corrupted the moral fibre of society.[37] They lamented that while woollens and silks had 'semiotically marked' rank, printed and painted cotton imitated other fabrics and led to 'disorder and confusion' across the social hierarchy.[38] Whilst for some it was a matter of extreme concern, for others it was the perfect subject for mockery of the 'strange Trollops in Callicoe Gowns', as a 1703 comedy at the London Royal Theatre called such women 'of no Fortune, that have made a good figure in an old Sheet printed black and white'.[39]

Such moral opposition also relied on an economic argumentation. Petitions called cottons 'a torrent of pernicious commodities' as they encouraged consumers to spend more, dissipated national wealth, and reduced employment for poorer artisans.[40] Such imports were paid in bullion (silver) rather than in exchange for domestic exports, generating a negative balance of trade and leading – the most pessimistic argued – to a general impoverishment of national economies. The use of Indian cottons in Europe was concomitant with the formulation of 'mercantilism', a keen interest on the part of governments to promote the political and economic prosperity of their respective nations through a positive balance of trade. Fostering exports while limiting imports was considered to be part of the policies of a state intent on developing and taxing its economy in competition with other states. It was assumed that a nation's capacity to raise taxes (through customs on trade and excise on production), pay for its own armies and protect its borders was first and foremost the result of its prosperous trade.[41] The very foundation of the East India companies was conceived as an act of state manipulation of markets in an attempt to foster and guide trade by conferring privileges and monopolies. It turned out that the interest of traders might not be that of the state, with the companies' actions being limited through the means of restrictions, tariffs and prohibitions when their actions were deemed in opposition to higher national interests or the interests of stronger power groups.[42]

Indian cottons seemed to polarise detractors and supporters. The latter underlined the fact that cottons increased internal and international trade and rejected the argument that they might have been pernicious for the national production of linens and woollens. An anonymous late seventeenth-century English pamphle-teer argued, for instance, that 'the Indian goods are so different in their qualities from the products of our country and the main of our manufacture that it is absolutely impossible that it should ever do them any injury'.[43] Others presented the idea that Indian cottons stimulated the consumption of woollens and other European cloths, for instance in quilts stuffed with wool, or supplemented these textiles as in the case of children's clothing, handkerchiefs and aprons 'in which the Woollen cannot be made useful'.[44] This was the position taken by English and other European companies against the mounting campaigns to ban the import of Indian cottons into Europe. A late seventeenth-century French pamphleteer made the opposite argument when he observed that cottons imported from India gen-erated not just the loss of millions of livres but also the decline of manufactures long established in the country and 'the ruin and desertion of workers' employed in silk, wool and linen manufactures.[45] This was a powerful argument linking a possible loss of national wealth, decline of manufacturing and the 'whimsical choices' of consumers more concerned about sartorial finery than the prosperity of their country.[46]

The debate over imported Asian cloth became the subject of literally hundreds of publications that either supported or condemned their trade and consump-tion. Philosophers, journalists and academics all participated using hyperbolic rhetoric in an attempt to convince not just law-makers but also the general pub-lic that their arguments were valid.[47] In England, debate intensified from the end of the seventeenth century when a literary celebrity like Daniel Defoe wrote either in favour or against the import of Indian cottons, according to whoso-ever paid for his services. This debate 'on paper' served to create unity across varied economic interests. It bridged the divided agendas of the English silk and woollen manufacturers who, although united in opposing cottons, had different interests according to their regional and product specialisation.[48] The tone of the debate suggests that these printed materials provided better reading in one of the many metropolitan coffeehouses than the learned discussions in Parlia-ment. They belonged to a culture of the press in which public opinion promoted political intervention rather than vice versa, and underlined the fact that textiles constituted a fundamental part of the national economy and contributed the bulk of a country's export.[49]

In Europe, Indian cottons also infiltrated trade and consumption and entered into the spheres of political and public debate. Pamphlets, satires and journal articles preceded and informed the passing of a series of laws enacted across Europe between the 1680s and the 1720s for the limitation and later the ban-ning of the import and wearing of Asian cotton and silk cloths. Cottons were prohibited first in France (1686) and later England (part prohibited in 1702 and totally in 1721), Spain (1717), Prussia and elsewhere on the continent.[50] It is difficult for us to understand the animosity that accompanied the passing of these laws. States had long had an active interest in ruling over consumption choices through sumptuary laws; yet what is remarkable is the intensity that the anti-calico feeling assumed outside parliamentary chambers. In London, for instance, the aborted act of 1700 attempting to ban Indian cottons was followed by protests by more than three thousand weavers, who attacked both East India House and the residence of the company's director.[51] The weavers clearly saw Indian cottons and silks as pernicious to their own wellbeing. Violence preceded and followed also the later 1721 act, with several cases of women being stripped naked in the street because they were found wearing forbidden cloth by the crowd. In June 1720, Dorothy Orwell was assaulted in Red Lion Fields in Hoxton, London, by weavers 'who tore, cut, and pull'd off her Gown and Petticoat by Violence, threatened her with vile Language, and left her naked' in the square.[52] In other cases, women found wearing calicoes had acid thrown at their clothing, a bitter act reminiscent of assaults on women wearing fur at the end of the twentieth century.

In England, the banning of cottons was the culmination of a process that had lasted nearly a generation, during which time the rhetoric of the inefficient and iniquitous privileges of the EEIC came to be opposed to the 'wealth of the nation' in the same way in which corrupt Asian fabrics were perceived as detrimental to the prosperity of the national textile economy. Duties increased steadily from the early 1690s; they were first set at 20 per cent and in 1700 at 35 per cent.[53] This was a progressive move towards restricting the use of cottons, ending in the 1721 act that banned the sale and use of all Indian cottons with the exception of muslins and blue-dyed calicoes.[54] *The Weavers Tryumph*, a one-page broadsheet, proclaimed that 'many Thousand poor Souls will most joyfully Commemorate the gladiom [of gladness] Day, and unanimously return Thanks to the King and Parliament, for thus Retreving their Ruined Trade' (Figure 6.3). Yet the victory of the sheep, the woollen cloth and of Britannia as represented in the image was a partial one. The 1721 act sought to hamper the success of cottons not by forbidding their trade from India but by outlawing their sale and consumption domestically. It was clearly a compromise that satisfied national textile producers while preventing the demise of the companies' trade. The English and French East India companies (the Dutch did not ban Asian textiles) could still import Indian cottons, but mostly for re-export to colonial and African markets or for sale in those few European countries in which they were still legal.

Figure 6.3 'The weavers tryumph or an abstract, of the callicoe-act, of parliament', broadsheet, 1722.

Stopping the rise of cottons?

How successful were these legal measures? Did they curtail the penetration of cottons into the wardrobes of common people? Evidence suggests that these laws might have been rather ineffective at stopping consumers from wearing forbidden cloth. In France, the ban of 1686 had to be periodically repeated in the early eighteenth century, with dozens of *arrêts* (rulings) that showed how much the law was generally disregarded.[55] Although these rulings made it clear that the ban extended to all commodities from China and India worn at home or in public (no exception was granted, even to the court in Versailles), the use of imported calicoes and chintzes was nevertheless endemic.[56] One of these *arrêts* of 1705 commented that 'many people still wear clothing made of these [forbidden] fabrics and those called furies, that come from the Indies, or are counterfeited in Holland or within this Kingdom; similarly tailors, seamstresses and upholsterers use these fabrics to produce clothing and furnishings, as they are convinced that because they work for people of high standing, they will not be condemned to the punishments established by these edicts'.[57]

A 1701 estimate put the value of calicoes sold in France at 12 million livres (*c.* £500,000), mostly comprising cloth smuggled by the FEIC or illegally brought in via Amsterdam and London.[58] In England, Defoe – now writing in defence of the woollen interests – complained that prohibitions were ineffective and that calicoes 'being imported by the Dutch' and 'either printed in the Indies or in Holland' were 'clandestinely run on Shore here, in Spite of former Prohibitions'.[59] Governments did their best to keep smuggling under control. In France, large quantities of Asian textiles were imported illegally to Lorient and were sold before they were properly inventoried. The French government decreed that special marks (called *plombs*) had to be used to identify all Asian textiles traded by the FEIC, with the result that Dutch and other traders mastered the art of counterfeiting plombs (Figure 6.4).[60]

There is little evidence that anyone wearing forbidden cloth was fined or prosecuted in England. There were occasional outbursts of violence, with the angry mob attacking ladies dressed in calicoes, but that was confined to the period immediately after the passing of the ban, in 1721. In France, some people were fined, but it seems that the law was upheld only occasionally, as in the case of the embarrassed wife of a councillor of the Rennes parliament, who was surprised 'at eleven o'clock in the morning near the city walls, dressed in calicoes'.[61] In Paris, the *généraux de police* reported 3 legal proceedings against women wearing calicoes in 1721, 11 in 1727, increasing to 63 in 1737.[62] They were found wearing forbidden cottons on their bodices, skirts and more rarely informal wear.[63] These were cottons that came not just from India and the Levant

Figure 6.4 'Plombs' used to identify white cottons and muslin cloth legally imported into France. Although the plombs were regularly changed, they were still easily counterfeited.

but also that were printed in cities like Marseilles, which had dispensation under the 1686 law because of their semi-autonomous juridical status.[64]

Attempts to enforce the law were particularly feeble in the first decades of the eighteenth century. The *inspecteur de manufactures* of the city of Bayonne in the Pyrénées-Atlantiques reported in December 1715 that 'all the prohibited goods that are to be found in the vessels of the Compagnie des Indes are without doubt consumed in France' and that there was an abundance of 'English [cotton] goods that are so prejudicial to the products of France'. He listed the names of the men and women found wearing forbidden cloth: 4 in July, 7 in August, another 7 in September and a further 3 in the following two months. They were found wearing printed and painted gowns and *robes de chambre* of Indian cotton, but also cottons printed in France, in Agen and Bergerac.[65] The Bayonne's public servant was keen to show his zeal in the hope of receiving part of the fine; other colleagues lamented instead that they hardly had any authority at stopping people of higher rank, with the result that also the lower sorts did not respect the law.[66]

Inspectors also seized goods from workshops and artisans' houses, where they found not just forbidden cloth but also tools, colours and mordants to print them. Yet this was an endless fight as the cottons produced in those French cities with special jurisdiction or just across the border in Switzerland found easy customers in France.[67] The availability of cottons seems to have been little affected by their ban. If woollen and silk producers had envisaged that a simple legal act could stop consumers, they were shown to be wrong. The banning of Indian cottons created instead the need to provide similar types of textiles by circumventing the law. What had been intended as a measure to destroy the rising demand for cotton turned out to be one of the key factors transforming this imported product into a domestic one by replacing Indian cottons with printed linens and mix cottons produced in Europe.

Import substitution: from consumption to production

Asian cottons made inroads into the consuming habits of Europeans between the late seventeenth and the early eighteenth centuries. One response was to resist these new products by imposing tariffs and prohibitions. Another was to convince consumers to buy 'substitutes', textiles produced in Europe in imitation of Asian cottons. But why did European textile producers want to rival their Indian counterparts and compete in a sector in which they had little knowledge and experience? Maxine Berg argues that between the end of the seventeenth century and the early decades of the eighteenth century the goods themselves, with their visual and tactile attributes, stimulated desires that in turn produced attempts to replace them with European-made imitations. This process extended well beyond textiles, as so many of the commodities initially imported from Asia, such as porcelain, lacquer and silks, were eventually produced at home. Such commodities were partially adapted to suit European tastes and consumer expectations.[68]

The substitution of locally produced goods for imported commodities was already an established idea in seventeenth-century and eighteenth-century Europe, and was seen as a flexible response to changing consumer preferences. At the beginning of the seventeenth century, James I had supported the attempt to cultivate mulberry trees in England. What turned out to be an unsuccessful project was aimed at developing a national silk industry that could eventually put an end to the substantial imports of raw and woven silk.[69] The same could be said about tapestries and glass, areas of production that the English state nurtured by encouraging the settlement of migrant skilled workers from Flanders and Venice.[70] Mercantilism therefore aimed not just at keeping out foreign goods but also at encouraging their replacement with domestic products. These were the policies devised in France, England and in most of continental Europe through state-supported manufactures, the protection of property rights, privileges over invention and financial rewards for innovation in manufacturing. They gave substantial incentives to product innovation, the acquisition and development of skills and the reinvention and reinterpretation of products. By the late seventeenth century this process had become part of the way in which the manufacture of consumer goods was conceptualised, discussed and practised.[71]

The banning of imported Indian cottons ended up being a protectionist measure that facilitated processes of substitution. As we will see in the following chapters, European calico printers and manufacturers faced enormous problems in developing products that could be competitive not just in terms of price but also style and quality. Their success, however, varied considerably across Europe. The trajectory of cotton production in England and France, for instance, was somewhat different. Whilst in France the 1686 ban might have retarded and in some cases halted the development of domestic calico printing, across the channel the 1702 and 1721 acts created a *cordon sanitaire* in which domestic calico printing could thrive.[72] These divergent outcomes were the result of discernible differences in the legislation banning Indian cottons in the two countries; while Britain allowed printing for export and – after some disagreement – also printing on fustian and mix cottons, France upheld a total ban that included also domestic production.[73] The city of Marseille, a prosperous centre of calico printing before the end of the seventeenth century, saw this manufacturing activity fast decline and later be banned.[74] Those few cities that could continue printing on cotton, as they were semi-autonomous from the French crown, had few legal markets in which to sell their products.[75]

In contrast, British legislation had been rather murky concerning domestic production. The 1721 act allowed for white cloth to be printed domestically but reserved this product for export. The same act, however, left unspecified if the printing on linen and, more importantly, on fustians and other textiles that were partly made of cotton was legal or not. For more than a decade this issue was left dormant, but it became a 'hot topic' in the early 1730s when the production of fustians and other mixed linen-cotton started developing in northwest England. Some woollen and silk manufacturers were keen to have the remit of the 1721 ban extended to include fustians, as they considered these textiles competitors against their woollens, worsteds and silks on foreign markets.[76] Others were more open-minded as they saw the opportunity to invest in a potentially profitable new line of business, complementing their core activities. It was only in 1736 that, after much campaigning by the cotton producers of Manchester and Lancashire, an act (the appropriately named 'Manchester Act') clarified that the production of 'Goods made of Linen Yarn and Cotton Wool manufactured in Great Britain' was legal.[77]

The ambiguity of the English law was perhaps better suited than the inflexible French ban to the setting up of a domestic cotton industry. But it was not simply a matter of escaping the law. The Netherlands never enacted any legislation either prohibiting or restricting the import and wearing of Asian fabrics. Here too, strong lobbies opposing the VOC attempted as early as 1642 to have Asian textiles banned. A generation later, in 1676, the city of Haarlem made a request to the State of Holland to ban cotton and chintzes, 'both white and printed, coloured and painted'.[78] The cloth weavers and merchants of Leiden and the silk producers of Haarlem protested repeatedly from the mid seventeenth century to the mid eighteenth century, arguing not so much for a ban, but for limitations on imports and the promise from the VOC to encourage export of Dutch textiles.[79]

These protests were unsuccessful, suggesting that the commercial interests of the Dutch Republic stood ahead of the manufacturing interests of any of its towns and cities.[80] In the long run, however, this might have been a counterproductive decision: the Dutch, who had been the first to set up calico printing workshops to imitate Indian cloth in the mid seventeenth century, failed to develop a cotton industry. Unlike in France or England, the Dutch printshops remained located in urban areas where salaries were high. They also seem to have been little innovative from a technological point of view, continuing with traditional practices and expanding production, especially in the most popular market. Historians suggest a progressive decrease of quality, so much so that when Oberkampf visited Amsterdam in 1774 he was appalled: 'I would have never thought that they produced such low-quality work as that I have seen, and ten livres more expen-sive than ours'.[81] The relaxation of the ban in England and its repeal in France in 1759 had meant a severe blow for the Dutch calico printing industry.[82] By becoming the trading port of a great part of the cottons passing through Europe, the Netherlands seemed to have undervalued production and the opportunity to create a solid fustian and later cotton textile industry.[83] The 'first modern economy' did not become 'the first industrial economy'.[84]

What were cottons for?

'What were cottons for?', textile historian John Styles has recently asked.[85] This apparently simple question is in fact rather problematic. In Europe, up to the third quarter of the seventeenth century, Asian textiles were used primarily for decorating domestic interiors. The Portuguese had imported cotton furnishing, a practice continued by the Dutch and English companies. Such textiles penetrated into the houses of the middling sorts, together with other exotic goods and fur-nishings such as 'Japan' chests and stands, ivory and Madre pearl Indian tables, cabinets and screens.[86] Painted and printed cotton textiles successfully invaded domestic interiors and were used for the decoration of walls as well as for soft furnishings, pillows and curtains.[87] Large palampores were specifically produced to physically fit European walls and beds. Although they were out of reach for most consumers, they were cheaper than the tapestries or leather coverings com-monly used in wealthy households.[88] They were also often customised to suit the tastes of Europeans by introducing heraldic motifs, or hybrid decorations that included Chinese designs next to Indian flora and fauna or sophisticated Japanese designs (Figure 6.5).

It was only at the end of the seventeenth century that Indian cottons came to be increasingly used for clothing. Samuel Pepys approached Indian cottons cautiously and noted in his diary to have 'bought my wife a chint, that is a painted East India callico for to line her new study', but only 'after many trialls'. Only later did he and his wife acquire calicos for dress. First he was sent 'a token, namely, a very noble parti-coloured Indian gown for my wife' by a certain Mr Creed, probably one of his suppliers. This must have been to Mrs Pepys's taste as in early 1664 he noted that his wife had 'put on her Indian blue gown which is very pretty'.[89] Pepys had already bought himself 'an Indian gown' (banyan) in July 1661, but the dressing of his wife in calico, probably for a gown to be used in public, was another matter.[90] Many must have followed Pepys's example, as flowing *robes de chambre* in either Asian silk or cotton became the fashion of the last decades of the seventeenth century (Figure 6.6).[91]

Figure 6.5 Part of a palampore made of chintz produced on the Coromandel coast of India, possibly for the European market. The unusual design is inspired by a Japanese lacquerware or textile and shows a complex scene with flowers and swallows. (See also colour plate.)

Not everyone approved of Pepys's enthusiasm for cottons. Defoe commented sarcastically about the success of Indian cottons, noticing that they had 'advanced from lying upon their floors to their [consumers] backs, from the footcloth to the petticoat'.[92] Another English commentator observed that 'on a sudden . . . we saw all our women, rich and poor, cloathed in Calico, printed and painted; the gayer and the more tawdry the better'.[93] Even in the period of the ban after 1721, it was not difficult to get one's hands on both Indian furnishing and clothing fabrics with an anonymous petitioner complaining that 'the Running of the said Prohibited Goods is increased to that Degree that we have Dayly great Quantities by Patterns brought to our shopps to Maketh for Linings, besides what we see fresh made up and worne with Linings of ye same sort and used in furniture' (Figure 6.7).[94]

The success of cottons can be explained by the fact that they came in a variety of qualities, types and prices, something that facilitated their integration into the consuming habits of rich and poor: if calicoes were more suitable to middling-class consumers who appreciated light but steady textiles, the lower classes had to content themselves with 'raft' cottons, cheap but strong plain

Homme en robe de Chambre

le Pautre delin. et sculp. cum Priuil. Regis.   ce vende sous les charnier St. Jnocens.

Figure 6.6 'Homme en robe de chambre', etching by Jean Lepautre, Paris, *c.* 1675. Robes de chambre, otherwise called 'banyans' (from the caste of Indian traders) made of Indian cotton or Chinese silk were popular across Europe in the late seventeenth century.

Figure 6.7 Back lining of a stomacher, possibly printed fustian, English, 1740s. (See also colour plate.)

cottons that easily turned yellowish, or ready-made clothes produced in India that were 'strongly sewed for the poor people's wear'.[95] Consumers of modest means had to make do with cheap calicoes such as 'Birom Banies', a striped brown and white variety that was considered to be 'naturally a rotton sort of wear' and for that reason 'fit only to hang up for Curtains either for Beds or Windows'.[96] It was this low-quality market that eventually became important for simple striped or chequered cottons, as well as simple flowered motifs both printed and embroidered, commonly produced in Europe from the second half of the eighteenth century (Figures 6.8 and 6.9).

Slowly people came to adopt cottons into their everyday attire. But how was the use of cotton perceived by consumers? And was cotton the material that brought fashion to the masses, as many historians have argued? John Cary, writing in 1699, commented somewhat disparagingly that 'now few think themselves well dresst till they are made up in calicoes'. He listed practically every item of apparel as made of cotton: 'both men and women, calico shirts, neck cloths, cuffs, pocket-handkerchiefs, for the former, headdresses, nightrolls, hoods, sleeves,

Figure 6.8 'Molly Milton, The Pretty Oyster Woman', hand-coloured mezzotint, London, 1788. At the centre of the image stands an oyster seller gaily dressed with a flat hat, possibly a printed cotton handkerchief, an apron over a quilted petticoat, and a dress with flowered patterns not dissimilar from those produced in Rouen and other European cotton centres in imitation of simple chintzes. (See also colour plate.)

aprons, gowns, petticoats and what not, for the latter, besides India-stockings for both sexes'.[97] Cottons were not necessarily cheap substitutes; but does it mean that cottons became fashionable? Several historians, including myself, have argued that cotton allowed fashion to flourish.[98] Once reserved for the expensive silks of the elites, fashionable consumption came to spread socially thanks to the use of colourful printed cottons that mimicked the design and visual effect of silks at a price that was accessible to a much wider stratum of society: motifs

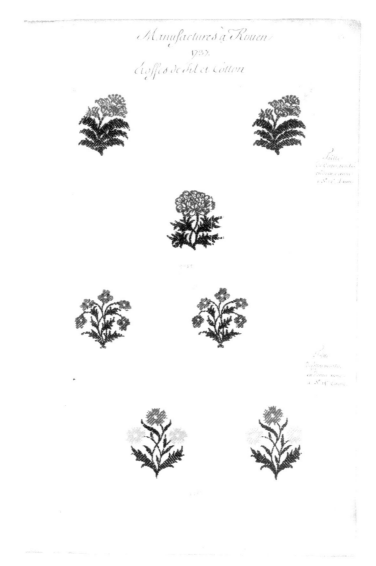

Figure 6.9 'Manufactures à Rouen. 1737. Etoffes de fil et cotton', page from the *Collection d'échantillons d'étoffes du Maréchal de Richelieu*. This page, which was collected for a survey of textile production in France and other European countries, shows a type of cotton linen textile (probably linen cloth embroidered in cotton with flowers) produced at Rouen. The flowered pattern is very similar to those on the dress of the English oyster seller. (See also colour plate.)

that were previously embroidered or delicately woven could be reproduced *ad infinitum* through the medium of printing.[99] *The Laboratory; or, School of Arts* (1757) pointed to the fact that calico patterns were 'for the generality in imitation after the fashions of the flowered silk-manufactory, with only such variations as

Figure 6.10 (*left*) 'Silk Fringe', flowered silk with fly braid; (*right*) 'Flowered Cotton', a printed cotton. Both are textiles from the Foundling Hospital's admission books. The two textiles are visually similar but the one on the left cost a multiple of the cheap printed cotton. Cotton textiles achieved the same kind of naturalistic effect, though not the intensity and shine of colour of silks. (See also colour plate.)

may best answer the nature of the different sorts of works...the principal of which are the whole chints, by which they can imitate the richest silk brocades, with a great variety of beautiful colours: these make the best appearance on an open white ground'.[100] The result was not the same as silk, but it was good enough to please the eye (Figure 6.10). The fact that these textiles were also cheap made the cycle of their replacement quicker. They came to be appreciated not because of their quality, beauty or meaning (as had happened in many societies across the globe), but because one pattern could be quickly replaced by another. This did not happen year by year (as exemplified by Lyons silks in the late seventeenth century), but depended on what was on offer at auctions in major European metropolises after the arrival of the East Asian Company's vessels from India.[101]

Yet we should not see the possible fashionability of cotton textiles as separate from the political and economic debates of the time. Mercantilism, by virtue of supporting the national economy, saw in fashion an important – though improbable – ally.[102] When in the 1680s discussion over a possible ban of Indian fabrics intensified in France, the jurist Goulleau provided an interesting line of argument in defence of imported fabrics. He claimed that these fabrics supported the metropolitan economy and provided good business for a multitude of *marchands merciers*, the Parisian sellers of fashionable goods. Any prohibitions, he said, would have been an injury to the French economy, as these were '*etoffes de mode*'. If they could no longer be legitimately sold, France was likely to lose its primacy in fashion.[103] Fashion was used not just in discourse but was noticed also as a practice. The mid-eighteenth-century economist Jacob Nicolas Moreau had no doubt that the success of cottons was not due to 'their low prices' but to fashion: 'it is fashion, and . . . a certain vanity', he said, 'that makes the women of the lower classes so curious about calicoes. Dressed in light or printed cottons, they think themselves no longer at the same level of women of their social station . . . they think themselves superior to their social condition because ladies of quality too wear calicoes'.[104] Fashion was seen as a powerful force that encouraged consumers to desire cottons in the hope of escaping the sartorial and visual differentiation that signified social hierarchy in pre-modern European societies. Moreau's contemporary, André Morellet, saw the force of fashion unifying rather than dividing social ranks when he noted that 'this fashion makes it preferable to wear Persian dress; if ladies at the court wear it, then everyone wants to own one'. This was an urge that, according to Morellet, did not 'even spare the wives of those manufacturers that most protest against these cotton fabrics'.[105]

What exactly made Indian cottons so attractive to consumers? Once their novelty wore off, European consumers started to be rather opinionated on the designs of Indian cottons. They were keen to have them in patterns that suited their tastes and they seemed to care more about the fastness of colour than the exoticism of their decoration.[106] The overall result was often a hybrid that included original Indian influences, established canons in European textile design and some innovation introduced by the experienced eye of servants of the East India companies.[107] Indian products were 'Europeanised' in the same way in which European copies were 'Indianised': John Holker reported in 1751 to the French government that large quantities of English cottons were smuggled into the kingdom 'which are sold as Indian chintzes'. This was 'because of the special finish they are given and also because the purchasers of this type of English goods have but slight knowledge of them'.[108] Consumers did not care where they came from and in many ways saw them fitting with European dress and decoration. The ultimate success of cotton lay not so much in its fashionability but in its slow but relentless conquering of a variety of garments that were increasingly incorporating what was once an exotic material. This explains why both Indian and European copies of calicoes and chintzes came to be part of the traditional folk dress of Frisian women and came to decorate the capes worn by Provençal ladies (Figure 6.11).[109]

Figure 6.11 Hooded cape in black glazed cotton with Indian floral patterns and cotton linings. Southern France, *c.* 1790. (See also colour plate.)

Conclusion

Indian cottons and later European copies slowly became part of the consuming habits of Europeans over the seventeenth and eighteenth centuries. They came to be used for furnishing and clothing, complementing rather than replacing woollens, worsteds, silks and linens. Cottons contributed to enlarging the choice of available textiles and provided at the same time something new in terms of colour (and sometimes design) that came to be part of notions of fashionability, display and style for larger segments of society. Yet, one must not forget that cotton textiles found only with difficulty a stable market identity, that they were subject to wide price fluctuations, and that they were passionately vituperated and opposed by competing fibres and their powerful economic interests. Consumers only slowly came to like cotton and appreciate its material and semiotic qualities. This happened in a socio-political context in which there was a clear incentive to replace Indian fabrics with domestically produced ones. But the story of cotton was not just about making this product suitable for Europeans. Its strength also lay also in conquering international markets; in becoming the first truly global commodity thanks to European trade.

7 FROM ASIA TO AMERICA: COTTONS IN THE ATLANTIC WORLD

African Woman is a large canvas by the seventeenth-century Dutch artist Albert Eckhout. Together with its matching picture, *African Man*, it can now be seen at the National Museum in Copenhagen. The title of this picture is deceptive as it suggests that the scene is set in Africa. The painting is instead a view of Brazil in 1641. Eckhout made a name for himself during his stay in Brazil between 1637 and 1644 as one of the main painters of the luxuriant plenty of the New World. The child is holding corn, the woman a Congolese basket with citrus fruit. Both are wearing jewellery and the woman also wears a large hat, possibly African, and has a Dutch clay pipe tightened into her waist-dress.[1] We are presented with an idealised view of slavery; one of the many Africans transported to Latin America to produce the new 'plantation exotics' that Europe was starting to appreciate, namely sugar, coffee, cocoa and tobacco. There were no cotton plantations at this time in Brazil, although cotton, in the shape of a cloth, appears as prominently in this picture as it does in the painting of her male counterpart. The African woman is wearing a striped cotton cloth, the male a chequered one. These manufactured products are neither from the New World nor from Africa, but in all probability are examples of the checks and stripes imported by European traders from western India. In this painting Asia, Africa and the Americas are brought together by European trade of produce, manufactured goods and people.

This chapter reflects on how and why in the seventeenth and eighteenth centuries cotton textiles came to be used across the globe, well beyond the borders of Afro-Eurasia, within which they had been traded for centuries. In the hands of European traders, Indian cottons became globalised: they reached the most remote parts of the known world and were among the first commodities traded to the many places in the Americas and the Pacific that had entered for the first time into contact with Eurasia in this period. As the world became increasingly connected during the period that historians have called the early modern phase of

Figure 7.1 *African Woman* by Albert Eckhout (Brazil, 1641). (See also colour plate.)

globalisation, cottons came to be one of the most visible signs of such economic and cultural integration.[2]

Why was cotton, among all commodities, a material that came to be appreciated by people around the world? And in what ways is such a success linked to wider forces such as slavery and intercontinental trade? Europe became the new 'pedlar' of world trade, integrating the Indian and the Atlantic oceans through the medium of cotton. As the commercial world globalised, the position of Europe strengthened. But Europe did not become simply the carrier of other people's goods: a century after Eckhout's picture, an African slave in Brazil would have most probably worn cloth woven in Manchester or Rouen or printed in Alsace or Lancashire. This chapter explains why Europe shifted from trade to manufacturing and started replacing Indian cottons with products of its own making.

Selling cottons to Africa

In the 'old cotton system', cotton textiles percolated from their manufacturing core in India across Afro-Eurasia. They reached East and West Africa, the Middle East and Europe, with trade continuing to pass through the hands of many intermediaries. The arrival of the European East Indian companies in India changed the mode of exchange, allowing for direct maritime trade from Asia to Europe and the Atlantic. No Asian trader ventured beyond the Cape of Good Hope to create a new world of trade that was then effectively monopolised by Europeans. What might look like an extension of the trading world of the Indian Ocean was in reality a restructuring of the entire system of trade on a scale that eventually generated profound consequences for the world economy. It was not industrialisation that brought about this new global system, but vice versa.

It would, however, be incorrect to consider the East India companies' trading to Asia as separate from the European trading ventures to Africa and the Americas. From the very beginning of the European trade in Asia, it was appreciated that cottons had the potential to be a major commodity not just in the intra-Asian trade or for consumers back in Europe, but also on the markets of Africa, the Americas and the Middle East. By the 1580s the Portuguese were already trading Indian cottons to North Africa and the Levant.[3] In West Africa, they started selling low-quality textiles that they purchased in Gujarat, Sindh and Cambay and that they exchanged mostly for slaves. Profits were high: an Indian cloth length sufficient to buy a slave in West Africa might cost 20 cruzados, but the same slave could be sold for five times as much in Brazil and eight times as much on Caribbean and Mexican markets.[4] Cottons in Southeast Asia were a medium of exchange used for purchasing spices; in West Africa, they became a medium of exchange for the purchase of slaves.

The African taste for 'exotic' textiles included not just Indian cottons. Portuguese traders had entered the West African markets just decades after exploration brought the first European vessels to the area in the second half of the fifteenth century. They started selling English and Flemish linens and woollens in exchange for gold and ivory.[5] Asian cloth came to supplement and expand this European trade. By the second half of the sixteenth century Europeans carried cloth both from Europe and from India to West Africa. The Portuguese were now joined by British, Dutch and French traders. Textiles formed the bulk of an increasing trade: in the closing decades of the seventeenth century, the Gold Coast of Africa imported 20,000 metres of European and Asian cloth a year, which complemented an intracontinental trade in cloth estimated at 5–10,000 metres, much of it from Benin (see Map 9.1).[6]

Trade to Africa was organised through state-sponsored or state-chartered companies: the Dutch West Indies Company (established in 1621), the English Royal African Company (incorporated in 1660 and replacing the EEIC and the previous Guinea Company), and the French Compagnie du Sénégal (1673) and the later Compagnie de Guinée (1684). Indian cottons were an important commodity. In the mid seventeenth century they accounted for a third of all commodities sold by the EEIC in Guinea.[7] A ship like the *Royal James and Henry*, a 300-ton 24-gunner, sailed with a crew of sixty men from England in September 1660, arriving in West Africa on the 21 December (and later in Madras in early July 1661). Its cargo, worth just over £10,000, was composed of linen and rugs (50%), iron (8%), but also narrow baftas, Guinea stuff, nicannees, tapseil and gingham and a variety of other Indian cloth.[8] Indian Guinea cloth and other textiles became even more popular in the eighteenth century, especially in the Gold Coast and the Bight of Biafra.[9] Between 1699 and 1800 cloth accounted for 68 per cent of all commodities exported from England to Africa, 40 per cent of which came from India.[10] The same could be said for the Dutch trade: already in 1595 metals and textiles formed half of the cargo sent to West Africa, with textiles increasing to 60 per cent of all commodities by the mid 1640s.[11] By the early eighteenth century Indian cottons such as chintzes, Guineas and nicannees formed the bulk of the Dutch trade.[12] The popularity of Indian cloth in eighteenth-century Nigeria was such that one of the most common varieties of cotton textiles was called 'George', probably from Fort St George in Madras, where it was purchased.[13]

How important was such trade of European and Indian cloth to Africa? The best figures available are those of the British trade to West Africa.[14] Throughout the eighteenth century two-thirds of all British exports to Africa were textiles.

The trade developed in line with the overall expansion of British foreign trade, the African trade being worth *circa* £100,000 a year from the late seventeenth century to the early 1720s, doubling over the next three decades and then growing exponentially to reach over £1 million a year at the end of the century. Woollens of British production accounted for the majority of the textiles exported to Africa in the early eighteenth century, declining in importance as Indian cottons came to be in demand. In the 1740s, at the peak of their popularity, Asian cottons accounted for up to 60 per cent of all textiles exported to Africa. Similarly, textiles constituted from half to three-quarters of the commodities sold by French traders in Africa in the 1770s and 1780s.[15] In the early 1770s, the French trade of Indian textiles to West Africa was worth 1.4 million livres (£60,000) a year and accounted for 37 per cent of the entire cargo (or 63% of all traded textiles).[16] Indian textiles – especially from Coromandel – continued to make the lion's share (up to 50%) of all commodities traded by the French over the following decade and up to the revolutionary period.[17]

Africa was the ground for a second type of 'cotton apprenticeship', this time by British and other European traders selling cottons to African markets. As they learned about buying cotton and merchandising varieties in India, they also learned how to make cotton a global commodity by selling it on the African market in exchange for slaves. In a well-known plate from Chambon, *Le Commerce de l'Amérique* (Figure 7.2), a European slave trader wearing full dress and hat (something quite inappropriate for the local climate) is visually opposed to naked African slaves. In reality, the West African population was dressed in bright cottons and in a variety of other European and locally woven textiles. The myth of African nakedness – a sign of lack of civility – was reinforced by a process of cultural unclothing of the enslaved African. A representation like this denies that cloth itself was a key commodity that Europeans sold in exchange for slaves.

African buyers were not just clothed but also quite sophisticated in their tastes.[18] West African consumers had been used to purchasing Indian cottons for centuries and had precise ideas about the types of cloth they wanted and the prices they were willing to pay.[19] European traders soon learned that it was not the painted calicoes that were in demand in West Africa but the simpler geometric patterns of stripes and checks.[20] They also realised that Africans preferred bright colours: in 1660 two bales of blue and black perpetuana sent by the EEIC to Guinea found no purchaser in West Africa, as the locals wanted more colourful textiles. The result was that the bales were sent from Guinea all the way to Bantam.[21] African demand for Asian and European textiles also changed from place to place. The EEIC did its best to meet this shifting demand: in 1661 it sent several pieces of gingham and other cottons to Guinea with instructions

Figure 7.2 'Marché d'esclaves', plate from M. Chambon, *Le Commerce de l'Amérique par Marseille* (Avignon, 1764).

that small samples of the most popular types had to be sent to Madras with information about the quantities needed.[22] In other cases, the European traders cautiously tested the market in Africa, introducing new products, as in the case of the Galinhas area in present-day Sierra Leone, where they started the use of chequered cotton cloth, something that was not part of the local consuming habits.[23]

Europeans also learned that the African trade could be integrated within a wider space of exchange that encompassed the entire Atlantic. This was a 'triangular trade' in which raw materials (mostly dyes and raw cotton) were traded from the Americas to Europe, where they served to manufacture and print cotton textiles. Such textiles were sold on international markets, becoming a key commodity in the trade to Africa. Here they were used to buy additional raw materials (for instance, gum used for the process of printing on cotton) and in particular slaves, which were transported to the Americas and employed in plantation cultivation.[24] Many have argued that the triangular trade brought resources, markets and profit for Europe. The commercial logic that underpinned it was as important for the development of the cotton industry in Europe as it was for the setting up of a plantation system in the Americas.

The triangular trade came to change the position of Africa in world trade, and its domestic manufacturing. West Africa and the Atlantic might have become central to international trade, but it is incorrect to emphasise this increasing connectedness of the early modern world (part of a story of globalisation) as older connections, such as trans-Saharan trade links, were disrupted or discontinued. Frederick Cooper sees this new position of Africa as 'damaging and destroying' the articulated trading systems of the Indian Ocean and the Sahara desert.[25] Africanists have also debated the relationship between the intensification of trade and its consequences on local production in West Africa. They disagree on both the relative importance of textiles traded by Europeans and on whether such textiles, which were exchanged for slaves in Africa, caused a decline of the local African textile industry. Marion Johnson, for instance, points out that the quantities of imported textiles suggest this was not just a niche trade catering for luxury consumption, but that the woollens, linens and in particular cottons bought by African consumers from European traders were used for everyday purposes. David Eltis is less optimistic when he claims that 'only a small proportion of Africans could have been wearing imported cloth'.[26] The 9.5 million yards of cloth imported by Europeans into West Africa in the 1780s provided no more than 0.4 yards per person.[27] Notwithstanding disagreement on the relevance of imports, Eltis and Johnson agree that there is little evidence of a decline of the African weaving industry in the eighteenth century. Johnson goes as far as to suggest that European trade might have provided an opportunity to expand the exchange of African textiles from textile-producing areas to other parts of the continent.[28] This position, supported more recently by Colleen Kriger, is however disputed by Joseph Inikori, who sees European trade as a barrier to the economic development of western Africa in that it increased the availability of cheap imported textiles and decreased human capital as a result of slavery.[29]

The cotton trade to the Americas

Africa was neither the largest nor the most promising of markets for Indian and European cottons and other textiles. In the seventeenth and eighteenth centuries, large quantities of cheap cotton cloth were sold to the West Indies plantations and to Latin American markets.[30] It has been estimated that only a third to a half of the cottons traded by the Portuguese was sold in the Iberian, Mediterranean and West African markets, the rest being traded to Brazil and Spanish America. Profits were healthy: in the seventeenth century, a canequin bought for 1 or 2 cruzados in India would sell at 6 or 7 in Brazil.

The trade to Spanish America relied on the annual fleets sent from Seville and Cadiz. These were major entrepôts for the textile trade from Flanders, the Low Countries and Belgium.[31] Asian as well as European goods were then sold at trade fairs in Cartagena de Indias, Portobelo and Veracruz. From there, a capillary system of merchants transported cottons and other commodities to the markets of Mexico and the Andean highlands, where they were sold by travelling salespeople or through shopkeepers.[32]

The Latin American market was divided into two broad categories: higher-quality imported goods and cheaper local products.[33] The local production was mostly organised on a household system or through larger textile workshops (called *obrajes*) that produced woollens. In the household, cotton fibres were spun to produce basic white cotton textiles for shirting and other domestic uses (Figure 7.3).[34] These locally produced textiles were commonly found next to more expensive European products from Italy, France, Spain and the Low Countries.[35] Cottons could be imported from India via Europe or, by the early eighteenth century, they could be European imitations of Indian cottons such as the *Ruán florete*, literally 'flowered Rouen cotton', a type of printed cotton cloth produced in the French city.[36] But Latin America had another access route to Asian textiles: Indian cottons, as well as Chinese silks and semi-precious stones from Southeast Asia, found their way to Mexico via the Pacific Manila–Acapulco route that was opened across the Spanish Empire in the 1570s. This was the case, for instance, of chintzes known in Mexico as *indianilla*, fabrics from India influenced both by European chinoiserie and by Chinese silken textiles that were particularly fashionable among the plebeian classes in late seventeenth- and early eighteenth-century Spanish America.[37]

Figure 7.3 *De Chino, e India, Genizara* by Francisco Clapera (Mexico, *c.* 1780). The woman is spinning the cotton fibre from a basket with which the child is playing. The entire family wears white cotton cloth, possibly the result of household production. (See also colour plate.)

Latin America enjoyed high levels of consumption of all sorts of commodities imported via the Atlantic and the Pacific, both from Europe and Asia, in exchange for its abundant reserves of precious metals, silver in particular. Visitors were impressed by the variety of dress worn by the various ethnic groups in Mexico and South American countries. Already in the seventeenth century the colonial authorities of Brazil were concerned with the sartorial magnificence and 'the superfluity of elegance used in the dress of the female slaves of that State'.[38] The Spaniard Artemio de Valle-Arizpe reported that in eighteenth-century Mexico City 'ordinarily worn is a silk skirt or printed calico decorated with bands of gold and silver, with brightly coloured ribboned belts'.[39] Another contemporary in Veracruz claimed that 'the most wretched black woman wears her underskirt of good embroidered muslin'.[40] The Spanish crown was anxious about this abundance of goods, although it also saw the potential to increase Spanish production of cottons and other textiles, which would bring additional revenues through taxation.[41]

Two sources provide substantial information about the high level of textile consumption in Latin America: the so-called 'casta paintings' and inventories. Casta paintings (representing the ethnic mix of the Latin American popula-tion) depict men, women and children wearing a variety of high-quality brightly coloured chintzes and calicoes.[42] The Latin American market was very different from the African one, as it preferred floral motifs on gowns, bodices and banyans (Figure 7.4). Probate inventories tell us that the majority of textiles that were worth recording were imported. Cottons were commonly used in menswear, as confirmed in the paintings. The testament of the wealthy *capitán* Juan Moyano de Aguilar (1686) from Mendoza in Argentina reveals a profusion of fabrics and garments in his wardrobe, including a jacket (*jubón*) of white cotton.[43] In eighteenth-century Brazil, the consumption of textiles was also very high: the inventory of Manoel de Miranda Fraga (1746) mentions a variety of linens, woollens, silks as well as cottons. The cottons included locally produced textiles (probably of lower quality), canequin (imported from India) and other imported varieties.[44]

The British North American colonies were also good consumers of cotton textiles. An older literature emphasised the reliance of colonial households on homespun yarn and locally produced cloth. The reality is that fabrics (especially clothing fabrics) were bought from Europe, as households had neither the textile-making equipment nor the fibre supplies to produce sophisticated weaves.[45] Already in the 1640s, fabrics arriving in Boston included cottons, fustians and calicoes, suggesting that both Asian and European varieties were for sale.[46] By the 1730s, North America imported not just Indian cloth and European imitations but also nankeen cloth from China.[47] The American market was a 'free market',

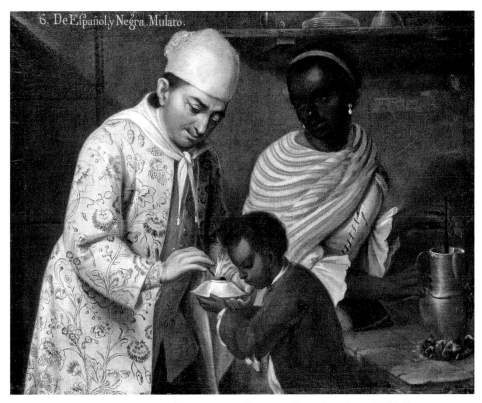

Figure 7.4 *De Español y Negra, Mulato*, attributed to José de Alcíbar
(*c.* 1760). The man is wearing a very elaborate banyan made of printed cotton
probably from India. The woman is instead wearing what might be a striped
cotton shawl. (See also colour plate.)

that is to say, there were no restrictions on the consumption of cottons similar to
those passed in Europe. To a certain extent, cottons consumption was promoted
by the European mother countries (England and France), as it helped to sell
the Indian cottons forbidden at home, it supported a growing European cotton
industry, and it created revenue in the form of trade duties.[48]

Merchants' correspondence shows the increasing importance of cotton textiles
in their trade of 'blue', 'India', 'negro' as well as printed and painted varieties,
which were exported from England to the American colonies in large quantities.[49]
The samples of calicoes and Indian pieces traded by David Barclay of London to
James Alexander of New York in 1726 give us an idea of the types of cottons sent
from London to the American colonies in the early eighteenth century, including
some early European mixed cotton-linen printed with indigo (Figure 7.5). The
trade of cottons to the Americas developed through established merchant networks that sold British woollens, new draperies and linens. London merchant

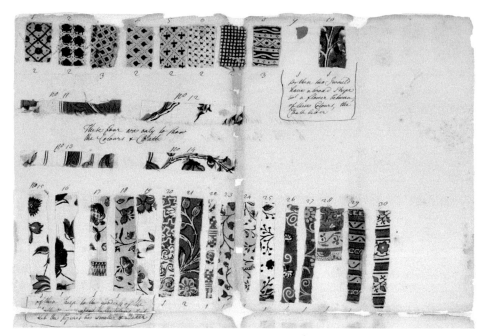

Figure 7.5 Textiles ordered by James Alexander of New York from David Barclay of London, 1726. (See also colour plate.)

houses had agents in North America that dealt with local merchants. During the century this commercial network expanded greatly, relying on complex credit structures but also on a precise appreciation of market preferences, with correspondence indicating exactly the types of cottons that were required, the design and the colours that would sell, as in the case of James Alexander's correspondence.[50]

Robert DuPlessis's analysis of inventories shows that cotton penetrated into the wardrobes of colonists in both French and British possessions in North America and the Caribbean. It was said that cottons were particularly suitable for the West Indies. In a 1704 petition, British traders claimed that in Jamaica, 'being situated in a hot climate, much of the clothing of the inhabitants is stained calicoes, which being light and cheap and capable of often washing contributes very much to the keeping them clean and in health'.[51] In continental North America, too, consumers came to favour white and coloured cottons instead of heavy woollens.[52] A series of inventories for Quebec for the period 1666–1756 shows how cottons were used for different clothing items such as *bonnets de nuit* (night's caps), *mouchoirs* (handkerchiefs), *mouchoirs de col* (neckerchiefs), as well as *jupons* (petticoats), *tabliers* (aprons) and *capes* (cloaks).[53]

Perhaps even more than in Europe, cottons came to be part of the everyday textiles used by consumers in the warm climates of the Caribbean, but also in areas as varied as New France, Pennsylvania, South Carolina and Louisiana. As in the case of Europe, cotton textiles' popularity increased in the first three decades of the eighteenth century, not in spite of but because of their higher price compared to linens. Robert DuPlessis shows how the increasingly prosperous colonists actively sought more refined and expensive products. Imported cotton textiles, both from Asia and from Europe, became an important new category within a material culture that had traditionally been dominated by fine woollens imported from England and homespun coarse woollens and linens.[54] By the 1760s and 1770s, consumers in the American colonies were provided not just with velvets, satins, damasks and taffetas, but also with a variety of printed and painted cottons used for dress, the upholstering of beds, chairs and sofas, the furnishing of festoon and canopy beds as well as for window curtains.[55]

Re-export substitution

In what ways was the expansion of the cotton trade in the Atlantic connected to the development of cotton manufacturing in Europe? The importance of finding consumers for European cotton textiles beyond the continent's borders has been seen since Eric Williams's 1944 *Capitalism & Slavery* as an important condition for the development of a European cotton industry.[56] Williams's influential explanation was centred on the role played by human capital, the labour of African slaves in the Americas, in the production of raw cotton for the European mills. More recent explanations have instead put a great deal of emphasis on the European trade to Africa, which allowed for the purchase of slaves in exchange for manufactured goods. The stimulus for European textile (and in particular cotton) manufacturing came not only from access to cheaper raw material supplies but also from the export of textiles. Several European countries were in the process of substituting European for Indian cottons. However, without the stimulus provided by foreign markets, the import substitution on domestic markets of Indian cottons with home products might have not been able to support the long-term development of European cotton textile production.[57]

Eighteenth-century English, French and to a certain extent Dutch traders started exporting cottons and fustians produced in Lancashire, Rouen or Holland instead of re-exporting cottons that they purchased in India. This is a so-called 're-export substitution'. The size of foreign markets was indeed quite large. West Africa accounted throughout the eighteenth century for 5–8 per cent of the overall English trade and 2.5 per cent of the French trade.[58] This might not have been as large a market as one might expect, but, as we have seen, it was dominated by textiles. Textiles had a lesser role in the West Indian and

North American colonial markets, but the size of these American markets was substantial. English trade to the West Indies and North America was throughout the eighteenth century ten times as large as the West African trade. In the early part of the century, it was the West Indies that took the lion's share of this trade. By the end of the century (and in conjunction with the economic decline of much of the West Indies) the newly independent United States imported nearly 60 million pounds worth of English merchandise, three times as much as the value of the entire trade from India into England.[59]

The cotton trade to West Africa, the West Indies and the American colonies was composed of three different varieties. It could be the simple re-export of Indian striped and checked cloth and other calicoes and chintzes; it could be the export of cottons (normally mixed linen and cottons) produced in Europe in imitation of Indian products; or – in between these two categories – it could be the export of cottons imported white from India and printed (very often with stripes and other simple motifs) in one of the many European printworks.

The re-export of Indian textiles to non-European countries was an important share of the EICs' trade.[60] In the case of the EEIC, by the last decade of the eighteenth century, a quarter of all cottons imported from India into the port of London found their way to African consumers. It is more difficult to estimate the share of Indian imports that were re-exported to North America and the West Indies, but surviving artefacts and a variety of historical sources suggest very high levels of consumption of Indian cottons in those two markets. Two points are worth highlighting. First, the fact that the so-called triangular trade that connected European traders and producers, West African consumers and slaves, and the American plantations should be extended to include India. This was a four-sided system (what I would define as a 'diamond-shape system') that extended over the Atlantic and the Indian Oceans and that through the medium of cotton connected the differing interests of the EICs, Atlantic trades and European manufacturers.

The Atlantic and the Indian Ocean trade were not separate. The interests of the EICs were not divergent from those of British and other European exporting merchants. Second, it is worth highlighting that the export of Indian cottons and of European substitutes developed hand in hand. This is visible in the case of the trade of cottons to West Africa by British merchants. Even after the mechanisation of cotton textile production in England in the last quarter of the eighteenth century, the trade of Indian and of English-produced cottons followed a similar path and these commodities were subject to the same kinds of trade fluctuations throughout the eighteenth century (Figure 7.6).

In the following decades this relationship between the Asia-bound trade and the Atlantic cotton trade came to change, with British cottons becoming far more traded than Indian goods, both to Africa and to the Americas. By

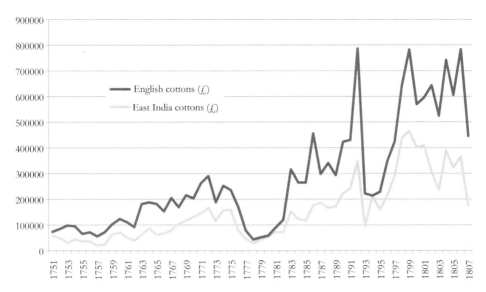

Figure 7.6 Indian and English cotton textiles exported to West Africa, 1751–1807.

1827–30, 6.9 million yards of English-made cottons were sold to Africa compared to just 2.8 million yards of East Indian cottons. A decade later, in 1841–50, England exported twenty times as much cotton cloth to West Africa as Indian cloth.[61] However, it is worth highlighting the fact that in the key phase of the expansion of the British cotton industry in the late eighteenth century, Indian cottons played an important (indeed, an increasingly important) part in international trade and in linking the Indian and the Atlantic Ocean trade. Cotton did not become a global commodity because its production was mechanised and industrialised; on the contrary, it became mechanised and industrialised thanks to the fact that it was a global commodity. This is a principle that is valid not just for Britain. The late eighteenth-century French scholar of the Coromandel trade, Legoux de Flaixs observed a strong connection between India, Africa and the Americas when he remarked upon the fact that the demand for cotton textiles in the West Indies supported production in India to such an extent that 'if the colonies in the Antilles cease to buy slaves, one can say without doubt, that this article will decline'.[62] Perhaps de Flaix exaggerated this dependence of western India on the Atlantic trade, but quantities confirm that this was an important component of trade for the Coromandel coast, with six million pieces of Indian-blue *guinées* being exported to the Atlantic between 1672 and 1791.[63]

The shift from Indian to European cloth started in the 1740s and 1750s and was fostered by the expansion of the African and later American markets.

Figure 7.7 Exports of English printed cottons and linens by geographical area, 1765–1800.

Over the period 1765 to 1800, from 70 to 85 per cent of all English printed cottons and linens were exported to either Africa or North America (Figure 7.7). The Atlantic effectively created a market for textiles that could supplement Indian varieties. Large and expanding markets fostered cost-reducing and quality-raising innovations: it pushed up the productive capacity of the industry and served as an 'apprenticeship' for the successful engagement of England in the European and North American markets in the later part of the eighteenth century.[64]

Import substitution and re-export substitution were paths for the development of a European cotton industry based on the spinning, weaving and finishing of mixed cotton and linen, and later pure cottons. There is, however, a further important path to substitution of imported Indian cottons. Indian cloth was used as a semi-finished commodity on which to perform the high value-added operations of finishing mostly through printing and to a lesser extent painting. Contrary to the notion of a calico craze based upon finished and exotic calicoes, it was white Indian cotton textiles (sossaes, gurras and sallamporees) that dominated imports of the EEIC, accounting for at least half of their cotton trade.[65] The same can be said about the import of Indian cottons by the FEIC, for which white cotton cloth and muslin constituted three-quarters of all fabrics imported into France from India between 1720 and 1770.[66]

These textiles were used as plain cloth on which English but also Dutch, French, German, Spanish and Italian calico printers printed an increasing variety of designs and colours. Whilst pursuing their own financial interests, the European East India companies also fostered the establishment of European calico printing. This was an emerging branch of the European cotton industry, which for most of the eighteenth century remained more important than cotton spinning and weaving. The calico printing industry would not have achieved the same levels of output had it confined itself simply to the printing of European linens or mixes of linen and cotton, as both did not take dyes as well as pure cottons.[67] White cloths from India therefore became key commodities not for European consumers, but for European manufacturers, who increasingly specialised in their finishing. This was the 'Indo-European' cloth (woven in India and printed in Europe) that was sold to consumers in Europe, Africa and the Americas. Africa provided in exchange not just slaves to cultivate cotton in the Americas but also the dyes and gum needed in dyeing and printing processes carried out by expanding textile printing in Europe.[68]

Two issues remain unanswered, however. First, how exactly did trade foster production in either England or France? And second, how is it possible that both European and Indian products were winners in international markets during this period? The response to these questions makes us consider the micro-processes that link production and trade in specific localities – Manchester in England and Rouen in France – that emerged as new poles of European cotton manufacturing in the eighteenth century. But it also leads us to consider exactly what type of cloth was imported from India and in what ways Indian piece-goods became intermediate goods for a new European calico printing industry.

Poles of European cotton manufacturing

One of the limitations of a global approach is that, by necessity, it needs to generalise. Therefore labels such as Europe, Africa or North America are used as large markers of space and are often confused with their present-day meaning. The literature on contemporary globalisation has the same problem when it presents China or India as uniform units, thus putting together futuristic Shanghai and remote villages in inner China. This is even more of a problem for the early modern period, when the majority of localities forming a nation or geographic area were not involved either in national or in global trade. As connections did not link homogeneously every part of the world, so economic and productive changes were not visible through the entire system or even across whole nations. The British industrial revolution was a regional affair located first in the central northern part of England.[69] Yet, this does not mean that the local and the global should be seen in opposition. This book argues that what happened in Lancashire in the second half of the eighteenth century did have global causes as it had global consequences. The local and the global should be seen as part of one process.[70]

It was the region around Manchester, not England or the United Kingdom, that emerged as a supplier of cottons, especially to the West African market. Cotton textile production in Manchester developed from the 1710s but remained mostly a small-scale industry for national markets at least until the mid 1730s. Manchester was no bigger than a small market town in the early part of the century, but it had two important characteristics. First, its hinterland had developed from the late sixteenth century as a place of production for fustians. Second, and perhaps more importantly, the port of Liverpool, one of the largest European slave trade ports, was located only a few miles away.[71] Trade and manufacturing combined. The case of Thomas Hibbert exemplifies this. He was a member of a prominent Manchester cotton manufacturing family. He became a slave factor in Kingston, Jamaica in 1734 and was later founder of one of the largest London West Indian houses.[72] A further two major cotton manufacturers in Lancashire, Sir William Fazackerly and Samuel Touchet, were both members of the Company of Merchants Trading to Africa.[73] In the case of Touchet, he was a trader in Liverpool active in trade to Africa and the West Indies, a cotton checks producer in Manchester, and one of the main financial backers of Lewis Paul and John Wyatt's first (failed) attempt to construct a cotton spinning machine.[74]

The birth of the Manchester cotton industry was neither revolutionary nor particularly illustrious, as later narratives of Britain's industrialisation have implied. The town specialised in the production of cheap cotton mixes such as the striped cottons called *annabasses* (a type of cloth also produced in Nantes, France), not the richly decorated calicoes and chintzes that were, especially in the early eighteenth century, either imported from India or produced in small printworks around London and in other major European cities. Manchester 'cottons' (a misleading appellative, as they were mixed linen and cotton) were aimed at replacing the cheaper textiles from Surat and Gujarat on the African and American markets.[75] John Holker, the Englishman turned spy for the French government, observed in his 1750/1 report to the French government that the production of Manchester textiles was fast increasing and commented that the output of Lancashire was 'so large that scarcely a week goes by without a thousand rolls being sold and sent to London unbleached'.[76]

In what is one of the finest collections of textile samples for the period, Holker included checks for furniture and dress, hooping (similar to checks but of linen), ticking (for linings), chereyderys (silk warp and cotton weft), fustians, cotton and Manchester velvets, grandurelles (cotton-linen for the colonies), nankeens, dimities, silk velvets, jeans, handkerchiefs, chintzes, messinets (with silk stripes) and woollens of different quality.[77] Although the report implied that the majority of such textiles were produced in Lancashire, it was clear that the higher-quality chintzes were printed in London. The majority of 'cottons' from Manchester were mixed linen and cotton with dyed cotton yarns being woven as the weft of stripes and checks. Microscopic analysis shows that the pure cotton cloths (cotton and Manchester velvets) were produced by doubling the warp, thus creating a more resistant yarn and also a heavier cloth than Indian cottons.[78]

Holker was not the only person to notice the progress of Manchester cotton manufacturing. *The Laboratory; or, School of the Arts* (1757) commented on the many manufactories set up in Manchester 'for the weaving of thread-cotton, in which they so well succeeded, that now they are hardly distinguishable from a fine calico'.[79] This was an exaggeration; although Lancashire produced goods 'in all the widths used for the calico fabrics from India', as late as the 1760s, Manchester cottons were no competitors in quality for Indian cloth.[80] A merchant of Liverpool reported to the Treasury in 1765 that English textiles such as 'checks & other goods made in Manchester in imitation of East India goods' were an important part of cargoes to Africa, but only 'when the latter [Indian cloths] are at a high price or not to be got', adding that the Manchester producers had still a great deal to improve as 'some they cannot imitate & their imitation of many kinds is but indifferent'.[81] Manchester seems to have done well when the EEIC was unable to supply sufficient quantities, this being the case in particular in the mid century when the African trade was expanding at a faster rate than the Asian trade.[82] In 1769, for instance, the wholesalers John Coghlan and Messrs Bostock & Bainbridge of London, suppliers of 'the Merchants Adventurers to Africa with East India piece-goods', complained to the Treasury that they had been 'totally rendered incapable of fitting out several ships which they intended immediately for the Coast of Africa' because the EEIC had no cloth to sell. They hinted at the fact that 'many other Species of the Manufactures of Great Britain would accompany the export of the Chelloes now wanted for the African Trade', probably suggesting that their competitors would have done good business by selling Manchester cloth instead of an Indian one.[83]

Manchester's cotton production boomed in the 1750s when quantities increased and the overall quality of production seemed to have risen. From the mid century the so-called 'Manchester linen checks' became a significant part of the region's production, accounting from 48 to 86 per cent of all exported cottons between 1750 and 1774.[84] These products were of sufficient quality to find a market in West Africa, as suggested by the fact that Thomas Melvin, the British governor of Cape Coast Castle, was confident that Manchester goods could replace Indian cottons in Africa and be traded in exchange for indigo.[85]

Again according to John Holker, Manchester calicos were mostly for export, not just to the Americas and Africa but also to France, where they were 'sold as Indian chintzes because of the special finish they are given'.[86] Holker might have somewhat exaggerated his claims, as several reports indicate that printing in Lancashire was still far from perfect and that, before the late 1770s, the production of cheap stripes and checks continued to account for the majority of the trade to West Africa and the West Indies.

Yet, the slow substitution of Indian cloth for the African and American markets had a twofold effect. Firstly, it allowed production to expand quantitatively. By 1788, when the application of new technologies was just starting to have an impact on the size of the industry, it was estimated that the manufacture of textiles to be traded to Africa relied on a fixed capital of £0.3 million and gave work to up to 180,000 people. The trade to Africa was worth £200,000 a year, to which an additional £300,000 worth of cottons were sent to the West Indies.[87] The products themselves had changed. After having specialised in cheaper checks and stripes, Lancashire shifted its production to higher-quality products (increasingly made of cotton weft and warp) that allowed the region to expand trade to the more sophisticated markets of North America.

Lancashire was not the only area in Europe that developed a cotton industry to cater for the African and Atlantic markets. In France, production developed in several parts of the country and especially in Nantes, Rouen, Dieppe (Figure 7.8), Marseilles, Limoges, Paris and Bordeaux, as well as Colmar and Mulhouse that were at the time outside the kingdom's borders.[88] They produced Indiennes (printed or painted with flowers), toiles (unprinted or printed), checks, printed handkerchiefs and curtains, the two latter varieties being a speciality of the city of Rouen.[89] The African trade was central to cotton production in the cities of Rennes and Nantes, where, as for Manchester, the influence of the slave trade was clear. Laurencin, Montaudouin, Michelin, Thiercelin (1719), Dutertre & Bainville (1727), the Grande Manufacture (1729) and the Langevin Mill (1759) in Nantes, but also the cotton mill by Pinczon Du Sel des Monts in Rennes (1742) were financed by slave traders and organised through shares. Cottons such as *anabas* (with blue and white stripes), the *Indiennes*, *garras* and *calencas* (multicoloured calicoes) and the rougher *baffetas*, *guinées*, *nicanneas* and salampuris were among the most common products.[90]

By the 1750s the Dutertre & Bainville and the Langevin mills produced *garras*, *guinées*, *calencas* 'peintes à l'anglaise jusq'à 8 et 18 couleurs', *siamoises* and blue toiles for Spain and the Spanish colonies, as well as 'indienne perses', suggesting that their market was expanding and differentiating.[91] Yet the progress of the cotton-producing and calico-printing industries in France remained slow, at least until the repeal of the anti-calico law, in 1759.[92] And still in 1789, the cotton

Figure 7.8 Indiennes produced at Dieppe, 1783. (See also colour plate.)

industry was the smallest of all the textile industries, including silk.[93] A major exception was the city of Rouen, in the north of France, that started integrating its production of linens with mixed linen-cottons and *siamoise* as early as the 1690s, developing in the following decade the production of fustians, basins and cotton handkerchiefs.[94] As for Rennes and Nantes, so Rouen was strongly linked to the African trade. From the 1730s, Rouen came to combine the production of heavy brocaded *chinés* and *lancés* with cheaper and lighter mixed linen and cotton, in particular stripes, checks, blue *guinées* and *toiles peintes* (often counterfeits of Indian textiles) for West African markets (Figure 7.9).[95] The city's production increased from just over 80,000 pieces of cotton in 1730 to over 435,000 pieces in 1743.[96] In the second half of the eighteenth century, France exported from Rouen 750,000 livres worth of goods to Africa a year, a third of which consisted of cottons.[97]

Figure 7.9 Typical checks traded to Africa that were seized in Rouen, produced by a Tocqueville manufacturer, 1785. (See also colour plate.)

It has been recently argued by Parthasarathi – following Montgomery and Chassagne – that the Rouen cotton industry developed later than in Manchester.[98] There is sufficient evidence to show that this was the case. The products of Rouen were not as good as those produced in Manchester, though they might have been cheaper. African consumers were also not easily conned by the Rouen copies and preferred the real Indian cloth. A *mémoire* of 1783 says that the Rouen producers went to such extremes to pass off their 'counterfeit' as Indiennes that they scented their products to make them smell as well as look like Indian cloth.[99] Over time and as the industry grew, the quality of production seemed to have improved: the trade of cottons from Rouen and Havre was worth 2 million livres (*c.* £85,000) in 1784, and the city of Rouen alone produced in 1786 nearly 150,000 pieces of printed calicoes.[100]

Parthasarathi also argues that the French cotton – and the Rouen *siamoise* production in particular – followed a different path compared to the development of cotton in England: the French cottons were heavier, with only the weft being made of cotton in order to respect the regulations imposed by the Parlement of Rouen. Parthasarathi concludes that Rouen, much more than Manchester, was on the way to replacing Indian pure cotton cloth.[101] There is limited material evidence (the cloth itself) to allow for a straightforward comparison.[102] Statistical and documentary evidence, however, suggests that earlier in the eighteenth century production in France was probably carried out on a smaller scale than in England, though by the 1760s France had developed a thriving calico-printing industry on a par with England. Parthasarathi is correct when he says that *siamoise*, of which Rouen was the main producer, was heavier than Indian cottons and checks (Figure 7.10). France, however, produced a variety of other (cheaper and lighter) 'cottons' in which the proportion of linen and cotton yarns did not vary substantially from English products.

To complicate things further, it is difficult to relate a story of increasing domestic production for foreign markets with one of direct substitution of Asian textiles or the achievement of textiles increasingly made of cotton rather than cotton-linen mixes. This is the case because the supply of raw materials seems to have changed the relative percentage of cotton and linen used from year to year. In England, Samuel Touchet complained in 1751 of the high cost of cotton and that 'the high Price of Cotton has obliged them [the Manchester producers] to use coarse Linen instead of it'; some cottons were 'made use of 7/8 Parts Linen' and 'Another Species, which used to be made all of Cotton one Way, was now made not above 1/4 Part Cotton; and in another Species, 1/4 Part less Cotton was used than formerly'.[103] Moreover, the heaviness of textiles was not just dependent on the materials and the final use of the cloth, but also on the quality of the yarn. The advantage of Manchester was far from clear, with another witness reporting on the same date that 'the *French* and the *Dutch* work up this Cotton much in the same manner as the Manchester Manufacturers do' and that they enjoyed good access to raw materials as well as the cheap labour of spinners in their countries, in Switzerland and in Germany.[104]

Both England and France used the Atlantic (African and North American) markets for cotton as a way not just to sell imported Indian cloth but also the products of a new sector, such as the European cotton industry, that slowly emerged in specific localities that had commercial and capital links with the Atlantic trade and the slave trade in particular. Critics of this 'Atlantic explanation' point to the fact that the African trade was very modest and that continental Europe remained a key market both for France and England. Moreover, before the spread of the use of the water frame in the 1770s, African consumers were

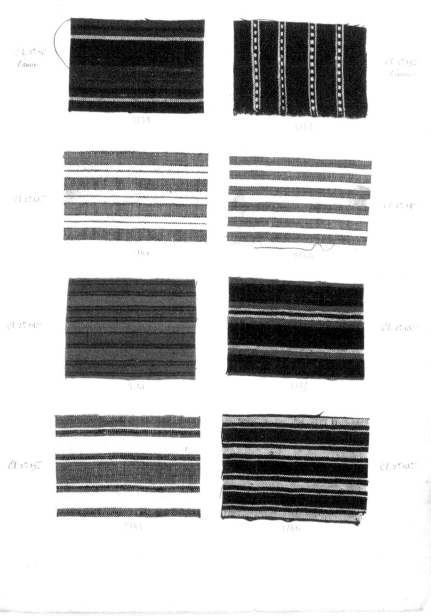

Figure 7.10 'Manufactures à Rouen. 1737. Siamoiserie', from the *Collection d'échantillons d'étoffes du Maréchal de Richelieu*. Collected for a survey of textile production in France and other European countries, this page shows a type of cotton-silk textile produced at Rouen. (See also colour plate.)

more likely to receive mixed cottons than pure cotton cloth. It might therefore be correct to say that the African trade was 'never an essential precondition to the industrial revolution', as concluded by Boulle,[105] though it might have been an important condition for the industrial development of specific areas starting with relatively unsophisticated commodities.

Conclusion

The upsurge in the trade in cotton textiles into the Atlantic economy was not a simple expansion of the system of circulation of such textiles centred on the Indian Ocean. European traders developed substantial new links with West Africa and with both Latin and North America. The volume of textiles traded, especially in the seventeenth and early part of the eighteenth century, might have not been as large as some historians have suggested, but it was important in activating trade and exchange of other primary and finished goods as well as slaves. Two points have been underlined in this chapter. First, it is myopic to see Atlantic trades as separable from the operation of the East India companies in Asia. The triangular trade was strongly linked to the logistics of European trade in Asia. West Africa and the Americas entered into a process of globalisation of trade through the construction of a new global web of connections formed by the trade of new as well as old commodities.

Second, Europe came to be the linchpin of this emerging system not because of its economic or manufacturing superiority but by way of the enterprise and capacities of its traders to operate on multiple markets and act as connectors between the old world of Eurasia and the new world of the Americas. This chapter has also shown the connection between the structuring and development of trade under what historians have defined as early modern proto-globalisation and the emergence of new industries in Europe. Cotton manufacturing in Europe developed as a supplementary and complementary type of manufacturing for international markets. Manchester, Rouen and Nantes emerged during the period from 1700 to the 1770s as key areas for manufacturing cotton textiles. Europe began its engagement with the production of this new commodity not through spinning and weaving but by developing a printing and finishing industry that integrated trades in white cotton cloth from Asia, domestic manufacturing and the sale of cheap finished products on international markets.

8 LEARNING AND SUBSTITUTING: PRINTING COTTON TEXTILES IN EUROPE

The celebrated toile 'Les Travaux de la manufacture' by the French calico printer Christophe-Philippe Oberkampf shows a series of vignettes of his printworks in Jouy-en-Josas in the year 1783 (Figure 8.1). Craftsmanship and industrial organisation are woven together in a design that is at the same time a narrative of industrial achievement and the demonstration of the unparalleled quality of European printed textiles. This artefact needs deciphering, however. This is a printed cotton cloth that an Indian artisan would have recognised, but found at the same time very puzzling. He might have guessed that the cloth itself was Indian, but he would have been surprised by the printing motifs, which are very different from the floral and animal designs commonly used in India. An Indian artisan would have also been quite surprised to find that this cloth was neither painted nor resist-dyed (by waxing the cloth), but was printed with madder red, a technique not used in India. The scene, clearly borrowed from an etching, was also alien to Indian craftsmanship as it did not make use of a wooden-block technique but used copper plates not dissimilar from those deployed for printing on paper. Although the cloth was woven in India, this was surely neither an Indian cloth nor a counterfeit or imitation. This was something new: a European printed cotton.

The newness of this product should also be put in context. If we step back in time, to the end of the seventeenth century, we find that European travellers to India were surprised by printed textiles, something that they had not seen produced in Europe. The Englishman John Ovington, during his travels to Surat in 1689, noted how 'In some things the artists of India out-do all the ingenuity of Europe, namely, the painting of chintes or callicoes, which in Europe cannot be paralleled, either in their brightness and life of colour or in their continuance upon the cloth'.[1] Like Ovington, many other Europeans were impressed by the bright colours of Indian cottons and admired the precision of their design.[2] A couple of generations later, in the mid eighteenth century, Ovington's statement was out of date. Europe had learned how to print cottons, although many still

Figure 8.1 'Les Travaux de la manufacture', toile produced by Oberkampf (1783). Vignettes represent the process of production of toiles by Oberkampf in his printworks in Jouy-en-Josas. (See also colour plate.)

raised doubts that this was an industry that had a future. The Guilds of Paris, for instance, declared in 1758 (at the eve of the revocation of the ban on Asian cottons in France) that 'The project of establishing in France manufactures for the printing of calicoes and other cloth is a chimerical one'. They no longer thought that the problem lay in the superior quality of the Indian cloth, but that it resided in the fact that 'cotton printing in France . . . is a third more expensive than in

India'.[3] A quarter of a century later, no one would have doubted that France could compete with India in printing cottons as, by this date, the calico-printing industry was an industrial activity that produced cloths such as the Oberkampf's toile.

'Les Travaux de la manufacture' is, however, a very opaque object, perhaps even misleading, as it proclaims itself to be something new and distinctively European. It does not reveal to us how recent and still tentative this textile manufacturing branch was in Europe. More importantly, it is silent on how and how much Europe's success in textile printing was heavily dependent on Asian skills and knowledge. This chapter considers what kind of 'useful and reliable knowledge' European producers borrowed from India and the Middle East in the course of the late seventeenth and eighteenth centuries. Knowledge has been at the centre of recent attention as one of the key factors explaining the divergence of Europe, or to be more precise, the path of industrial development that characterised the continent from the eighteenth century onwards.[4] Joel Mokyr has argued that knowledge creation and accumulation was an integral feature of western society and that in many ways it distinguished Europe's path of development from other world regions.[5] This chapter extends Mokyr's argument to include the contribution of knowledge from outside Europe.[6] It was the knowledge of printing on cloth borrowed from India and the Ottoman Empire that became the 'launch pad' for the development of a new calico-printing sector in Europe.

Weaving and printing

Europe and Asia specialised in the production of different fibres. Europe had abundant supplies of wool and produced woollen textiles, while Asia – and India in particular – concentrated in the cultivation of cotton and the manufacturing of cotton cloth.[7] This specialisation created not just different 'spheres' of textile production and consumption in Eurasia, but also had profound repercussions on the way in which the design of textiles evolved. In Europe, woollens but also silks and velvets were patterned on the loom and their designs were the result of complex methods of weaving and finishing. European textile producers could dye both yarn and cloth pieces, but had little familiarity with printing on textiles, with the exception of some linen printing performed in fourteenth-century Germany.[8] The patterning of textiles in Europe relied mainly on weaving and embroidery (Figure 8.2, white boxes), while in India it was based on printing, painting and various types of dyeing (Figure 8.2, darker boxes).[9]

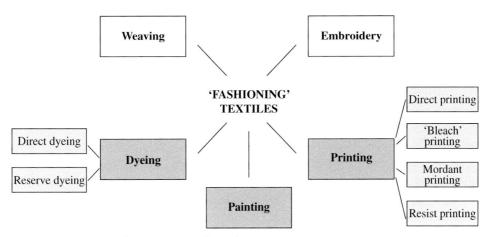

Figure 8.2 The patterning of textiles in Eurasia.

The difference between these two broad processes (printing and painting for India, and embroidering – but most commonly – weaving for Europe) was important: while printing was a flexible process based on the articulation of dyes and mordants, patterning through weaving was more costly and less adaptable. To set up a loom was an expensive activity that could take months for the most complex weaves (Figure 8.3). Any change in textile design was costly as it implied resetting looms. Printing was labour-intensive but at the same time extremely flexible, as the simple change of dye or mordant could create enormous variations in the colours printed on to the cloth (Figures 8.4 and 8.5).

Knowledge of printing had spread from India to China and Japan and to Iran and the Ottoman Empire before the sixteenth century, and reached Russia, Ukraine and eastern Europe in the early seventeenth century.[10] Yet, before the second half of the seventeenth century it did not reach the rest of Europe. The continent had little knowledge not just of the techniques of printing and painting but also of fast colours and mordants. In the sixteenth century, European textile producers attempted to imitate Indian textiles by painting linen with oil and watercolours or by printing simple motifs.[11] The contrast with Indian products could not be greater: European textiles were printed in one colour and did not use mordants (and therefore could not be washed) (Figure 8.6).

Learning from India

Promoters of a European cotton industry could only look to Asia for knowledge and information about productive processes as well as types of cotton products.

Figure 8.3 'A Weaver' by Jan van Vliet, published by Cornelis Danckerts in 1635. This print shows the complexity of weaving a cloth and creating a design through the medium of weaving.

In reality, any search for information about manufacturing in Asia, and in India in particular, was far from easy. Alexandre Legout de Flaix concluded his early nineteenth-century study of the Coromandel coast with the thought that it was surprising that after three centuries of contact, Europeans had 'ideas so little precise as on the methods and practices of the arts of these [Indian] people'.[12] Europeans had access to products but much less access to the technologies used in their production in Asia. This was true not just for textile production but also for the making of Chinese porcelain and Japanese lacquerware.[13] Many historians have argued that because access to manufacturing in Asia was limited, the European imitation of Asian commodities did not rely on original technologies. This hypothesis does not explain the rise of calico printing in Europe.

There were, however, several problems in transferring knowledge. Dr Helenus Scott, a surgeon in the service of the EEIC in Bombay, wrote to Sir Joseph Banks, then president of the Royal Society, that 'It is extremely difficult to learn the arts of the Indians ..., for father to son exercises the same trade and the punishment of being excluded from the caste or doing anything injurious to its

Figure 8.4 'Malabar de caste Cavari qui peint sur toile'. Calico printer from the Malabar coast of India, mid nineteenth century.

interests is so dreadful that it is often impossible to find an inducement to make them communicate any thing'.[14] It also seems unlikely that Europeans could rely on any codified knowledge. Texts such as *Mir'āt ul Istelah* by Anand Ram Mukhlis, an eighteenth-century lexicon with entries on dyeing and tie-dyeing, or the *Nuskha Khulāsatul Majarrebāt* (transcribed *c.* 1766), an anonymous medical treatise that described seventy-seven operations for making forty-eight colours and shades, were never in the public domain.[15] Even if there does not seem to have been any degree of secrecy exercised by the Indian craftsmen, calico printing remained in the eyes of Europeans an unintelligible process. The lack of printed recipes was a major problem as quantification and precision were keys to the successful replication of printing and dyeing.

The learning of printing and painting was easier as Europeans had more access to the finishing stages than to spinning and weaving. The finishing of

Figure 8.5 'Peintre sur toile'. Calico painter, probably from the Malabar coast of India, eighteenth century. (See also colour plate.)

Figure 8.6 Fragment of a European printed cotton, *c.* 1660–1700. This early European printed textile lacks the beauty of colour of an Indian textile. Such textiles were also often inferior to the copies of Indian textiles produced in Iran and Anatolia. (See also colour plate.)

cloth was often carried out in urban workshops rather than in more secluded weaving communities. The VOC, for instance, acquired direct experience of cloth finishing in the Coromandel coast, as they directly employed a group of native calico painters.[16] The FEIC was similarly involved in knowledge transfer through the action of three Frenchmen who between the last quarter of the seventeenth century and the mid eighteenth century seem to have played a key role in gathering 'useful and reliable knowledge' on a variety of productive techniques for the dyeing, printing and painting on cloth in India.[17] Between 1678 and 1680, Georges Roques compiled a detailed analysis of the production of textiles in Ahmedabad, Burhanpur and Sironj. The FEIC's Lieutenant Antoine Georges Nicolas de Beaulieu was the author of a second manuscript probably compiled in 1734.[18] And finally, a third document was produced as a series of letters by Père Coeurdoux, a missionary of the Society of Jesus who lived in India between 1742 and 1747.[19]

In 1966 the Roques manuscript was unearthed at the Archives de la Bibliothèque Nationale de France.[20] Although Roques's account includes several parts on matters not related to textiles, it has been studied mostly for cotton printing and dyeing.[21] Roques believed that it could 'only be a good thing to know how these people set about applying the colours to their cotton cloths' and invoked the very concept of 'useful knowledge' when he said that 'Everyone can see for himself how useful this would be when he envisages what the possibilities could be for our cotton, linen and hemp cloth'.[22] Roques was partially continuing a 'commercial' tradition intent on providing information about quality control, competitors, seasons of production and the system of orders.[23] However, his manuscript includes an in-depth explanation of the processes of dyeing and printing as performed in Ahmedabad, and it is a key source of knowledge on how mordant block printing was carried out in eighteenth-century India.[24]

The Beaulieu manuscript, written in 1734, is perhaps the most successful of these accounts on Indian calico printing.[25] It has been suggested that Beaulieu had been asked by the well-known chemist Charles-François de Cisternay Du Fay to pursue the study of cotton printing in India. Du Fay was not only the official inspector of dye works and mines and *inspecteur* of the Parisian botanical gardens, but also one of the most famous chemists of his time.[26] It could be the case that a thorough analysis of the process became possible thanks to Du Fay's precise instructions based on observation and evidence. Unlike previous accounts, the Beaulieu manuscript concentrates entirely on the production of chintzes in Pondicherry. It also follows a 'scientific' style of analysing the productive process based on the description of each productive stage after which

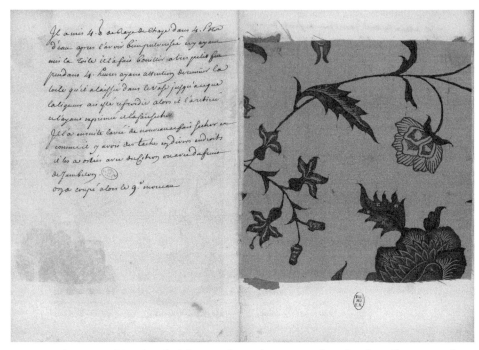

Figure 8.7 *Manière de fabriquer les toiles peintes dans l'Inde, telle que M. de Beaulieu, capitaine de vaisseau l'a fait exécuter devant lui à Pondichéry* (1734). Stage 9. (See also colour plate.)

a piece of cloth was taken and attached to the manuscript (Figure 8.7).[27] It was not just the thoroughness of Beaulieu's analysis that makes the account so important. It also appears that the manuscript was widely circulated in Europe. It is consulted by Chevalier de Querelles for the writing of his *Traité sur les toiles peintes* (1760) and by the Basle calico printer Jean Ryhiner for his 1766 *Matériaux pour la coloration des étoffes*.[28] In both cases, the authors argued that Beaulieu had produced a reliable account of printing that, when properly followed, allowed European producers to achieve results comparable to those obtained in India.

More than any of the previous observers, it was the Jesuit Coeurdoux who was aware of the importance of Indian knowledge and the contribution that his letters might make to the development of European calico printing. He thought that 'knowledge is to be acquired here which, if transmitted to Europe, would possibly contribute to the progress of science or to the perfection of art'.[29] Coeurdoux, like Beaulieu and Roques before him, strongly believed in the value of Indian knowledge of calico printing; their mission, he believed, was to codify the processes of production into clear descriptions that could be subsequently replicated in Europe. This faith in the 'usefulness' of the knowledge that was being carried back to Europe needs, however, to be questioned. There is no proof that attempts to learn the 'secrets' of Indian cotton printing, especially in the 1730s and 1740s, meant that Europeans were either unable to replicate fast colours before that date, or that they constitute a fundamental knowledge transfer from India to Europe. Knowledge transfer of cotton-printing techniques relied, in fact, not just on information gathered in India but also on the technical know-how of artisans in the Ottoman Empire and especially in southern Anatolia, an area that had developed over the previous centuries a flourishing cotton-printing industry.

The role of Armenian artisans

Recent scholarship on knowledge transfer has underlined the importance of tacit knowledge, those skills and practices that can only with difficulty be codified or conveyed in written form.[30] The very limit of the attempts by Roques, Beaulieu and Coeurdoux to convey knowledge on specific productive processes lay not just in their relative inexperience and imprecision, but also in the difficulty of reproducing knowledge that had been codified through description. We can describe how to drive a car, but it is actually easier to learn it by training under the supervision of a skilled driver. This happens because it is difficult, if not impossible, to convey in words a great deal of the knowledge used in complex as well as simple processes. Europeans learned the 'art' of calico printing not just through indirect (codified) knowledge from India, but also through the transmission of workshop practices from the Near East.[31] Such practices were embodied in skilled workmen, especially Armenian calico printers who, by moving to Europe and setting up calico printshops, carried with them their know-how.[32]

In the sixteenth century the Ottoman Empire had developed a thriving calico-printing industry producing imitations of the most popular Indian cloths in the sixteenth century. By the seventeenth century textile printing had developed in Istanbul thanks to Indian practices. In 1634 Evliya Tchélébi reported that there were in Istanbul twenty-five workshops that employed 150 workers who specialised in the production of chintzes using Indian fast-dye processes. These workshops were owned by Armenians from Tokat and Sivas in northwestern Anatolia.[33] They produced cottons with red flowers, trees, snakes and peacocks and a variety of other printed fabrics often listed in seventeenth-century Ottoman inventories.[34] European, and especially French consumers were well acquainted with these cotton fabrics printed in the Ottoman Empire. The city of Marseille was in the seventeenth and eighteenth centuries one of the principal importers of printed cottons from the Ottoman Empire. Some of this cloth probably originated in India or in Iran (the so-called *Persiennes*), but the majority was printed in the Ottoman Empire, not just in Istanbul but also in places such as Diyarbékir in southern Anatolia or Aleppo in northern Syria. Diyarbékir produced *chafarcanis* (a red or purple chintz with white flowers), probably an imitation of the jafracani produced in Sironj and Ahmedabad in India, while Aleppo specialised in a variety of blue cotton cloth called *ajamis*. These cottons were traded across the empire and large quantities were exported to France and Spain, where they were frequently imitated (Figure 8.8).[35]

Armenians were key to the printing of cottons in several parts of the Ottoman Empire, probably having learnt the process in Iran.[36] They sold cotton cloths printed in Diyarbékir and other nearby centres such as Malatia and Celebi to France, the Near East and eastern Europe. They also traded the 'original' goods produced in Gujarat to Iran, Bantam and Manilla.[37] Their wide-ranging trade relied on the commercial and financial services provided by the Armenian mercantile communities present in Europe and Asia. After the destruction of Julfa in 1605, Armenian traders migrated to Mesopotamia, India, Indonesia, but also to Venice, Livorno and Amsterdam, acquiring prominent positions in the trade of silk and dyes in Europe.[38]

Recent studies on Marseille, Genoa and Amsterdam suggest that the early development of cotton printing in these European cities heavily relied on the presence of Armenian workmen. In 1672 it was two Armenians who set up the first workshop in Marseille for the 'painting of calicoes as done in the Levant and Persia', in partnership with two local businessmen.[39] A few years later, in 1678, an Armenian from Celebi established a calico printing shop at Amersfoort in the Netherlands in association with two merchants of Amsterdam.[40] Calico printing was introduced in the Italian city of Genoa in 1690 by an Armenian workman who was granted the monopoly of the activity for ten years.[41] In all these cities, Armenians were employed to 'draw and colour or dye all kinds of East Indian cottons, which has never before … been practiced'.[42] The places where skilled Armenian workmen decided to set up calico printshops were European cities such as Genoa, Livorno, Marseille, Nantes, Le Havre and Amsterdam, which were already part of extensive Armenian finance and trade networks.[43]

Figure 8.8 'Toilles de Cotton … Marseille 1736 … Indiennes ou Guinées'. This page from the *Collection d'échantillons d'étoffes du Maréchal de Richelieu* shows a variety of cotton textiles printed in Marseilles, ranging from imitations of Indian textiles to imitations of Ottoman cottons. (See also colour plate.)

The development of calico printing in Europe

The set of skills introduced into Europe by Armenian artisans started a process of 'cross-fertilisation' of a group of European centres of calico printing that in turn generated further knowledge of the productive processes across the continent. Central to this spreading of technical knowledge was the high mobility of specialised workers and entrepreneurs in the sector.[44] A calico-printing business was opened in Rome in 1677 by two merchants, possibly from Marseille. French printers were also to be found in Berlin in 1686 and Geneva in 1688.[45] The industry emerged in the proximity of London thanks to the expertise of foreign workmen, mostly French, who had been employed in similar establishments in the Netherlands.[46] The international dimension in which these skilled artisans operated continued over the eighteenth century, with improved technologies spreading from centre to centre thanks to skilled artisans. In the 1750s the Swiss printer Johann Heinrich Streiff of Glarus, for instance, having heard of a new blue printing process, relied on the Genevese colourist Fazy to teach his workmen the process. In just a few years Glarus became well known for its blue-on-white prints and the Streiff family continued innovating by being in touch with key dyers and colourists in Europe.[47] The city of Rouen – that as we have seen in the previous chapter became a centre of cotton manufacturing – also developed as a centre of calico printing. In 1772, Jean-Michel Haussmann of Colmar, Alsace established in Rouen a *fabrique* specialised in the printing of gold and silver colours, processes that he had probably learned during his training as a chemist in Augsburg. Another technician who settled down in Rouen was François Forestier, who had previously worked for Oberkampf at Jouy-en-Josas. Experts came from Germany, Holland and Switzerland to 'perfect' design, copper engraving and colouring processes.[48]

It was the mobility of skilled workers and entrepreneurs that enabled the printing industry to acquire a truly European size.[49] In England, William Sherwin of West Ham near London took out a patent in 1676 'for invention of a new and speedy way for producing broad calico, which being the only true way of the East India printing and stayning such kind of goods'.[50] The Ryhiners, the famous family of calico printers, were originally from Holland and moved to Basle in the late seventeenth century. From Basle, calico printing spread to Mulhouse and Neuchâtel (1716). In France, during the long ban lasting from 1689 to 1759, production was instead confined to those cities that enjoyed autonomous jurisdiction, such as Marseille, with it developing later in centres such as the Arsenal in Paris (1746), Angers (1753), Rouen (1755) and Nantes (1758).[51]

The development of calico printing in Europe started in full only in the 1740s. Before that date, even the most developed printing works in Marseille that made use of advanced Anatolian techniques could only manufacture products of low quality, such as blue Guinea cloth and other cheap textiles printed in just two colours.[52] In the 1740s, however, the sector both expanded and increased the quality of its production. Holland had the largest concentration of printshops, counting over a hundred firms, ninety of which were in Amsterdam and its immediate surroundings.[53] Yet it was the dynamic calico-printing industries of Switzerland and England that took over the innovative role of Holland in the second half of the eighteenth century. Competition by Swiss, Habsburg and British printers was already evident in the 1720s. In 1728 it was pointed out that Swiss printed cottons were stronger, cheaper and more beautiful than Dutch ones.[54] A decade later, in the late 1730s, Spain too was fast developing its own calico-printing industry, based in Barcelona.[55]

Differently from India, calico printing in Europe developed as an industrial activity. It was not based on small workshops employing a few artisans, but on large undertakings of hundreds of workers. In the late 1750s the Fabrique-Neuve at Neuchâtel in Switzerland employed more than 300 workers.[56] The famous printworks at Orange in Provence employed more than 500 men and women (Figure 8.9).[57] When Buytendruk, the largest printworks in Amsterdam, was sold in the 1770s, it was worth 225,000 guilders (more than £20,000) and had seventy-six printing tables.[58] In the 1780s and 1790s the average size of printworks increased even more. Baron, Sallé & Cie in Beauvais, France, had more than 800 workers in 1778, and Dollfus & Cie, in Alsace, more than 700 in 1788.[59] At the turn of the nineteenth century the Fabrique-Neuve in Neuchâtel had doubled in size and gave work to over 600 workers, and in 1805 Oberkampf at Jouy employed 1,300 people.[60]

Productivity was high. It was estimated that twenty workers and six boys could produce 640 pieces per annum, suggesting that division of labour was not uncommon.[61] Yet printworks did not rely on unskilled labour. The entire process of production relied instead on highly skilled workers: specialised designers, drawers, colourists, painters, printers, folders, measurers and so forth, several of whom were women. Quality and precision was paramount, as entire lengths of cloth could be wasted because of single imperfections.

The industrial scale achieved by calico printing can also be seen in the value of printworks. The average manufacturing business in England in the 1780s was insured for a value between £300 and £500, with the largest woollen mill in Leeds being insured at £4,900. Yet just among the London calico printers in the period 1755 and 1790, ten businesses had insurances at a value more than £5,000, with Thomas Watson of Lambertt being insured at £9,750. In 1766 the calico printshops at Wesserling in Alsace had a capital invested of 400,000 livres (c. £17,000) and in 1781 the fixed capital of Oberkampf's printshop in

Figure 8.9 *Manufacture de tissu d'indienne des frères Wetter: atelier des ouvrières* by Joseph Gabriel Maria Rosetti (1764). This is one of four views of the calico-printing factory in Orange showing the large size of the premises and the considerable number of workers employed. (See also colour plate.)

Jouy was valued at £14,000.[62] The scale of investment often required business partnerships. The relatively small-scale partnership to set up a printshop at the Ververspad in Amsterdam in 1769, between two merchants and a printer, was based on a capital of 4,500 guilders, fabrics worth 9,000 guilders and the premises belonging to the printer himself.[63] High sums were therefore needed

Figure 8.10 *The Factory at Jouy* by Jean-Baptiste Huet (1807), showing the large size of the printworks, which included several buildings and also a great deal of land. (See also colour plate.)

not so much as running capital but for the investment in buildings, canals, water mills and the land needed to dry cloth (Figure 8.10).[64]

Reinterpreting global colours

The development of a European cotton-printing industry was not just based on knowledge of Asian processes of production; it also involved experimentation with mordants and dyes, especially from the Americas, and the development of new technologies for printing. This was particularly the case with two basic colours: madder or Turkey red, and indigo blue. Such colouring agents had long been used for the dyeing of Asian cottons, but also European woollens and linens, and were among the most globally traded commodities during the early modern period. Red was produced from a variety of substances, such as kermes, cochineal, madder, brazilwood, sappanwood and lac, which were widely traded, especially from the Americas to Europe. Since the Middle Ages, sappanwood reached Europe from as far away as Thailand and Subawa, and its trade was later monopolised by the VOC.[65] Cochineal was widely exported from the New World, both to Europe and Asia, and the profitable indigo trade was in the hands of Armenian traders based in Gujarat, much to the annoyance of the European East Indian companies.[66] Alum was imported from the Middle East and the isle of Chios before the discovery of European deposits at Tolfa near Rome.

The exploitation of knowledge and world commodities was sometimes hindered by cultural and institutional factors. Indigo was cultivated in several areas of Asia, with Gujarat being one of the major world suppliers until the eighteenth century. Here indigo was harvested and transformed into small blocks of pulverised substance that were exported to Baghdad and Aleppo and from there to Europe. Indigo was a luxury dye that allowed the production of deeper shades of blue than those obtained by the European-grown woad. For woad growers, the potential competition from indigo was already considered to be a threat by the sixteenth century. Its use, for instance, was banned in France from 1598 until 1737. In Britain, indigo was denounced as the 'food of the devil' and its use was allowed only in conjunction with woad.[67] It was only in the eighteenth century and in response to an unprecedented demand for dyes from a rising European industry that resistance to the use of indigo declined. As for cotton, starting in the seventeenth century and developing in particular in the eighteenth century, indigo plantations became a major feature of the West Indies economy, which supplied large quantities of the dye at increasingly cheaper prices (Figure 8.11).[68]

Early European printed cottons were therefore the result of Asian knowledge, dyes imported from both Asia and the Americas, and plain cotton textiles and design models borrowed from India. The knowledge and material borrowing of Europe from Asia and the Americas produced an overall reinterpretation of the very processes of decoration of a cloth. Two factors must be underlined. First, the fact that these changes preceded the classic 'cotton revolution' in spinning and weaving of the late eighteenth century. In many cases, printing was a stage in the development of a European cotton industry, as key centres of printing later became cotton manufacturing areas. Second, the overall reinterpretation of Asian knowledge was in many cases fostered by state-sponsored bodies such as academies, government *bureaux*, but also privileges, patents and copyright protection, all areas that historians consider part of the institutional forces influencing economic development in Europe in the eighteenth century.

Some of the technological innovations were the result of the specific preferences of European consumers. It was mentioned how Europeans preferred 'blue designs on white backgrounds' to the more common Indian 'white designs on blue backgrounds'.[69] The Indian technique for the production of 'blue cloth' was a so-called indigo resist-dyeing process based on tepid indigo fermentation at 115 degrees Fahrenheit that European printers mastered between the end of the seventeenth century and the first decade of the eighteenth century. This was

Figure 8.11 'Indigotoire', French, second half of the eighteenth century.

unsuitable for achieving a 'blue on white' design, however, as it meant the wax-ing of most of the cloth.[70] The European innovation was the introduction of the use of cold vats (or *cuve à froid*) obtained by dissolving indigo in iron sul-phate (*couperose*). This process, originally invented in England in 1734, quickly replaced the hot fermentation of indigo, which damaged the reserve (those parts that were waxed to remain undyed).[71] Two further innovations characterise the European use of indigo. Wax printing was probably first adopted in the late seventeenth century and allowed for substantial labour savings compared to the traditional techniques of painting (with a brush) or pencilling (with a small wooden tool) wax on the cloth, as done in India and other parts of Asia. Finally, another innovation was the discovery of a method for printing indigo – rather than dyeing it – by using potash, quicklime and orpiment. This technique, called 'English blue', suggesting that it originated in England, allowed printing in several colours, something that was immediately recognised as an advantage over Indian producers.[72]

The re-elaboration of Asian knowledge and its innovation to serve new purposes was the result of practical experimentation as much as theoretical analysis. In Marseille, for instance, cotton printing and dyeing emerged from the knowledge transfer embodied in Armenian workmen.[73] By the 1720s, however, the city became receptive to a new wave of innovations, this time from northern Europe. The *blue d'Angleterre* (locally known as *blue au pinceau*) was introduced to Marseille by an English workman employed by the Swiss-born entrepreneur Wetter in 1744, just ten years after its invention.[74] The mobility of 'experts' and the promptness of adoption of these new productive processes in the numerous calico-printing centres of Europe are remarkable. Calico printing fits the definition of 'open technique', a technological space of innovation that is not dominated by secrecy but is based on a freer flux of information and knowledge carried by networks of specialised workmen across an entire continent.[75] The professionalisation of colour makers and colourists, as well as the constant participation of technicians and entrepreneurs in discussions over calico printing and dyeing, were key elements that created a self-sustaining relationship between human capital and innovation.

A similar process of innovation can be seen in printing and dyeing in red. Madder was a colouring agent cheaper than American cochineal and it produced better colours than bark dyes. Anatolia had long been specialised in dyeing with madder, a process that was known as 'Turkey red'. Early attempts at producing Turkey red were made in the Netherlands in the 1670s and in Switzerland in the 1680s.[76] Results must have been poor in the 1740s, as France still imported 5–6,000 bales of red cloth from the Levant each year and even sent part of its home production of cottons and woollens to be dyed in Turkey. Further attempts were made to set up madder-red dye houses in Europe by bringing dyers from the Levant to France.[77] The real breakthrough seems to have been achieved by the Frenchman Jean-Claude Flachat, a traveller, entrepreneur and innovator who successfully replicated Middle Eastern dyeing and printing techniques on cottons, linens and fustians.[78] Flachat spent several years in the Levant and returned to France in 1756, where he set up a Turkey-red dye works at St Chamond, not far from Lyon. He employed a Turkish master dyer, two dyers from Adrianople, two tinsmiths from Constantinople, a Persian spinner, a Smyrna thrummer and two Armenian vitriol makers.[79] Flachat was not just a careful observer of productive processes and market opportunities. He combined an in-depth understanding of the great variety of productive specialisations with business acumen, thus becoming one of the earliest *manufacturiers-innovateurs* of eighteenth-century textiles manufacturing.[80] Flachat's innovations did not remain a secret. Johann Zeller of Zurich opened the first Turkey-red dye house in Switzerland in the early 1760s after spending some years working in Nîmes.[81] John Holker set up the first 'Adrianople' dye house in Rouen in the 1760s and was in all probability the source of information about madder-red dyeing in England.[82]

From art to industry

The process of printing also came to differ significantly from original Indian practices. European printers had two problems to solve: first, how to make printing quicker and therefore cheaper; and second, how to improve the quality of the printed cloth. These two issues were addressed not by improving the skills of workers or the knowledge of the productive processes, but through the application of mechanical devices, namely the invention of copper plates and roller printing. Why did Europe invest in the invention of new technologies when it was relatively inexperienced in the basic techniques of dyeing and printing on cotton? Printing, rather than painting, was consciously seen as a way for Europe to compete with Indian products. The calico printer Ryhiner commented in 1766 that printing was the only possibility for developing cottons in Europe 'because the use of painting . . . demands a greater degree of skills and is much slower, which means that even granted all things equal we could never adopt their [Indian] methods, for we lack skilled craftsmen and could not keep the maintenance costs so low'.[83] Europe had extensive experience in both printing and engraving on paper, techniques that had been perfected to reproduce paintings in the form of etchings and popular prints. Printing on textiles underwent a series of major technical changes in the second half of the eighteenth century, all of which were closely tied to the technology of artistic production on paper.[84]

A first major innovation was the use of copper plates instead of the traditional wooden blocks, and was first applied by Francis Nixon of Drumcondra, near Dublin, in 1754.[85] The use of copper plates partially responded to a technological issue: they allowed higher-quality printing on linen that in some cases might have constituted the majority of production for European printworks. Secondly, by using copper plates larger than the normal 10 by 5 inch wooden block, they allowed fast colour printing of large motifs (Figure 8.12). These had been prefigured in seventeenth-century silk handkerchiefs (though not with fast colours) and followed an established European visual tradition based on a representational language already used on paper. The toile, as French chintzes

Figure 8.12 Linen and cotton cloth printed from engraved copper plates and wood blocks and painted blue by Robert Jones & Co., Old Ford, Middlesex, England, 1769. Robert Jones was one of the major English calico printers. When he sold his business, in 1780, the printworks occupied 67 acres and the assets included 200 copper plates and 2,000 blocks and prints. (See also colour plate.)

were known, came to be the standard for a new European product. Oberkampf, who started calico printing with copper plates only in 1773, became perhaps the best-known producer of toiles in Europe (Figure 8.1).[86] The process quickly spread not just to the rest of France but also to England, Germany and Switzerland.[87] The success of copperplate printing was so great that in the 1770s the English East India Company was already thinking of a scheme 'for exporting to India Metal Plates and Machines for working them, Blocks, and other Utensils used in the Business of [calico] Printing'.[88]

The search for higher-quality printing was accompanied by attempts to increase productivity through the adoption of machinery for printing. A wooden printing roller was used in Moravia in the late 1720s and a three-colour roller press was invented in England in 1743.[89] However, it was only in 1783 that Thomas Bell, who worked at Livesey, Hargreaves Hall & Co. in Preston, England, patented a method of printing from engraved cylinders. Two years later he was printing in six colours.[90] Roller printing must have appeared revolutionary compared with Indian painting: according to Beaulieu, it took an Indian craftsman two weeks to paint a calico seven metres long; by contrast, it was calculated that in 1851 the average calico printwork could print 6 pieces (equal to 168 yards, at 28 yards a piece) per day, and machine printing allowed the printing of between 200 and 500 pieces a day (5,600–14,000 yards), an increase of productivity of 30 to 80 times.[91] Production boomed. In 1750, the total British production of printed cottons was estimated at 50,000 pieces; in 1796, it was 1 million; and in 1830, 8.6 million pieces.[92] The European calico-printing industry came to be even more capital intensive with the adoption of copperplate and rotary printing. Capital was necessary for the designs: it is estimated that a design by a distinguished artist such as Huet (who worked for many of Oberkampf's toiles) might cost up to 1,500–2,000 francs (c. £60–80).[93] Although productivity of a roller was at least twenty times higher than that of a wooden block, profits could only be made by printing on a large scale, as each roller cost more than £7 to carve.[94]

Science and the state

The transformation and reinterpretation of calico printing cannot be set apart from wider changes in other parts of the economy, or from the cultural and institutional context of eighteenth-century Europe. Research on colouring processes was not limited to textiles. Josiah Wedgwood, one of eighteenth-century Europe's best-known entrepreneurs and innovators, spent several years of his life experimenting with colours on ceramics.[95] Scientific research – either aimed at theoretical analysis or as a methodology of experimentation – became an important catalyst for European innovation. European scientists were interested not only in 'how' productive processes took place, but also in 'why' such processes followed precise scientific rules. Already in the 1730s, the concept of fastness for colours became part of the realm of precise measurement and scientific investigation. The French chemist Du Fay systematically tested all known dyes, providing a general scale of fastness. This in turn allowed Berthollet to provide the first chemical explanation of mordants.[96]

Knowledge circulated through both scientific and practice-based writings. Books were written on how to grow madder; on the use of indigo, mordants and other colouring substances; on recipes for dyeing, and so on. An area of particular importance in colouring and dyeing was the European engagement with Linnean ideas of the ordering, categorising and classifying of substances.[97] From Linnaeus' *Species plantarum* first published in 1753 to the publication of *Prodromous* by the French botanist Augustin Pyramus de Candolle in the early nineteenth century (where forty-three different varieties of madder were carefully listed), the knowledge of dyeing agents increased dramatically.[98] The circulation of research in print facilitated a process of testing and verification. The chemist Jean Hellot's *Théorie chimique de la teinture des étoffes*, the result of a visit to Persia in 1737, was originally published in the *Mémoires de l'Académie des Sciences* in 1740–1. Although Hellot's theories were based mostly on a mechanical understanding of chemical processes (rather than on chemical reactions), his book – as many other *mémoires* – acted as a way of storing relevant information that could eventually be disseminated, verified or disproved. These constituted the foundations on which Pierre-Joseph Macquer and Le Pileur d'Apligny were able to codify knowledge on dyeing in the second half of the eighteenth century.[99]

The epistemological basis of textile printing did not grow simply thanks to the interest of famous chemists. The economic significance of textiles made research a matter of strategic importance for economic as well as political reasons at local and national levels.[100] The protagonists of textile-printing research in France (such as Du Fay, Jean Hellot and Pierre-Joseph Macquer) were connected to the hierarchies of the public administration.[101] Jean Hellot, for instance, was drawn into the study of colours (especially kermes) not only by being the pupil of Du Fay, but also thanks to the support of the French Académie des Sciences. In England, Robert Boyle and Robert Hooke were among the many scientists who presented their findings on permanent colours at meetings of the Royal Society.[102]

European states had a keen interest in technical and scientific development, often financially supporting projects of knowledge accumulation and transfer.

This a characteristic distinctive of Europe that can be traced in the copious documentation left by administrative bodies dealing with trade and commerce, or by the many societies for arts and manufactures that mushroomed in Europe in the eighteenth century.[103] In England, for instance, Richard Williams received a government grant of £2,000 in the 1780s for his processes of dyeing with cochineal; Dr Warwick was rewarded for having invented the so-called 'Warwick green' using aluminium potash; the well-known chemist Bancroft was granted a patent in 1785 for his results on orange and yellow colours, enjoying exclusive rights to sell the dye until 1799.[104]

Textile production was also an arena of intense international competition: spying, copying and attempts to produce better and cheaper goods were common tactics in what we can define as the 'economic warfare' between European governments.[105] The Englishman John Holker, who, as we have seen earlier, acted as a spy on behalf of the French government, in 1761 sent the Rouen manufacturer Godinot four samples of English indigo-dyed cotton yarn, which could be bought at lower prices than similar yarn from Rouen.[106] States also controlled the quality of their own production, imposing quality standards through a system of marks and plombs (as used in France) or by training inspectors to 'discern when they [printers] print with false Colours' – a system in place in England.[107] The action of the state extended to protect and foster the sector. In continental Europe, it was not uncommon for printworks to obtain royal patronage. This form of patronage can be seen in the case of the Silesian printworks set up in the late 1750s, or the privileges received by the Genevese printer Duplantier, owner of printworks near Frankfurt, who in 1741 established cotton printing in Berlin under royal privilege.[108] In other cases, states used fiscal tools to support emerging industries. Thanks to the ban on imported Indian cottons, calico printing developed in most of Europe protected from extra-European competition.[109]

Conclusion

The linkage between scientists, the state and businessmen was a strong nexus for the emergence of calico printing in Europe, and can be viewed as a distinctive characteristic of a so-called 'industrial enlightenment', to use Joel Mokyr's expression.[110] Yet, the enlargement of the epistemic base – the very knowledge of the processes – was not just the expression of a culture privileging scientific enquiry. It was the interplay between knowledge transfer, the circulation of such knowledge through skilled workmen, the action of the state and the contribution of scientific analysis and experimentation that allowed calico printing to develop in Europe. None of these elements were unique to Europe, but their combination perhaps was. This is a point recently emphasised by Tirthankar Roy when he observes that 'Industrialisation cannot automatically follow from knowledge of more productive techniques alone, but also requires favourable factor endowments, efficient markets, and appropriate institutions'.[111] The distinctiveness of European scientific and technical knowledge in the eighteenth century remains a subject of debate. Rather than asking in what ways Europe was unique or on a superior trajectory, this chapter has shown that Europe was a relatively backward region in terms of printing on cloth and made use of the knowledge coming from outside its own borders.

PART III

THE SECOND COTTON REVOLUTION: A CENTRIPETAL SYSTEM, *CIRCA* 1750–2000

The final part of this book enters well-trodden terrain – that starting in the mid eighteenth century and normally classified as the period of European industrialisation. This is the time of cotton par excellence, and a vast literature explains how cotton was integral to the industrialisation of Europe. Most of these industrial histories have little space for the many topics that we have encountered so far and neglect to mention that at the time that Richard Arkwright, the putative inventor of one of the most revolutionary cotton spinning machines, perfected his device in the north of England in the 1770s, the Indian cotton industry was still the undisputed world leader.

The previous chapters have elaborated and explained how Europe caught up with cotton textile manufacturing in Asia. The final part of this book enquires into why Europe did not become just another area among many producing cottons. I argue that under the label of an 'industrial revolution' there was a reconfiguration of the global economy. The first step of the restructuring of manufacturing and trade involved raw materials. Chapter 9 shows how Europe developed a new and dynamic industry on the back of supplies of raw materials totally coming from another continent. This was unprecedented. Millions of slaves were transported from Africa to the Americas to cultivate cotton and other produce for western markets. This was a coercive system that foresaw the 'industrial' path that cotton textile production came to assume in Europe, creating a global division of labour for the first 'modern' industry.

Something extremely important certainly happened in Europe and technological innovation was indeed central to the story, but the reasons why such innovation emerged first in Europe (or to be more precise, in England) must be considered in relation to the positions of Indian and Chinese cottons. I argue that innovations in spinning and weaving were aimed not only at increasing productivity but also at quality, in order to manufacture a type of cloth that was not necessarily cheaper but that was of a quality produced on the subcontinent of India. In this sense, innovations in spinning and weaving are represented here as a continuation of a trajectory that started with printing and that then proceeded to replace not just the final stages of production but also the intermediate good (plain cotton cloth) previously imported from India into Europe. Chapter 10 argues that incentives to industrialise might have been stronger in specific parts of the world by comparing the European and Chinese trajectories for technological and organisational innovation in cotton manufacturing.

Cotton textile production had long been an Asian specialism. Why Europe retooled itself in order to compete in a relatively unknown sector still remains subject to debate. What exactly was the attraction of cottons to Europeans? We need to assess not just the industrial but also the ecologic potential of cotton. In Chapter 11, I return to cotton as a raw material but also as an industrial input. I put forward the argument that cotton became revolutionary not simply via the application of machinery, but because machinery and cotton *together* allowed for a tremendous expansion of production. This could have not been achieved by any other natural fibre. The revolution in manufacturing was a 'wave of cotton', not a 'wave of gadgets' (to use Ashton's famous expression). If machinery were applied (as eventually it was) to wool or linen, the results would have been much more modest because the elasticity of supply for raw cotton remained very high. From the beginning of the nineteenth century, the United States became the prime source of raw material for Europe's cotton industries. Better access to American fibres became key to the success of the British industry vis-à-vis its French and Spanish rivals.

The book concludes with a depiction of a new global industry, a 'restructured' system that united different areas of the world by way of connections to raw materials, products and technologies. The new system contained a clearly defined core set in Europe and North America. The West produced enormous quantities of manufactured commodities that sold on world markets in exchange for raw materials and primary products. Factories in Lancashire, Catalonia, Alsace or Massachusetts produced cotton textiles in European and western ways and designs. Power (imperialism and colonialism), but also the power of ideas and concepts such as modernity and liberalism, played an integral part in setting and maintaining a privileged position for the West. The system was 'centripetal' as it operated to consolidate and sustain comparative advantages for the western core.

9 COTTON, SLAVERY AND PLANTATIONS IN THE NEW WORLD

The early eighteenth-century traveller and writer Francis Moore commented enthusiastically about the village organisation of the Pholey people living in the Gambian inland of West Africa. 'They are very industrious and frugal', Moore wrote of this tribe, 'and raise much more Corn and Cotton than they consume, which they sell at reasonable Rates'.[1] He had no doubt that they were 'the greatest Planters in the Country'. To the eyes of an eighteenth-century European, they approximated civility as, he explained, 'their towns are surrounded with palisadoes, within which they have plantations of cotton, and on the outside of this fence they sow their Indian corn' (Figure 9.1).[2] Moore's cotton and corn plantations were not organised on slave labour. Quite the opposite: the Pholey town and plantation represent an idealised vision of cotton cultivation in uncontaminated Africa. Moore continued by explaining that their 'kindness' was such that 'if they know of one of them made a Slave, all the Pholeys will redeem him'.[3] The image of a plantation economy served to represent the virtue of a perfectly organised community able to redeem its members even from slavery.

This chapter starts with an idealised opposite of what cotton production had become already by the time when, in 1738, Moore published the first edition of his *Travels into the Inland Parts of Africa*. Readers would have not failed to notice the irony of Moore's description of free Africans cultivating cotton to be sold to Europeans. An increasing share of the world's cotton was cultivated in the Americas by African slaves rather than in Africa by free labour. Yet, this image allows us to ask why this was the case: why was the raw cotton used for the production of textiles in Europe produced by slave labour, and why did it come from the Americas? Was it not possible for cotton to be cultivated in Africa in exchange for foreign goods? This chapter considers how plantations came into existence and why by the eighteenth century the needs of Europeans were starting to have ecologic, commercial and economic repercussions worldwide.

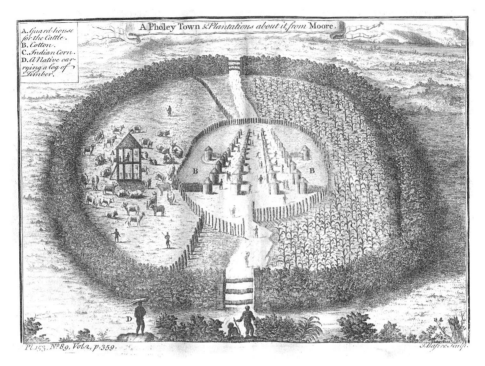

Figure 9.1 'A Pholey Town & Plantation', from Francis Moore, *Travels into the Inland Parts of Africa* (1738).

Why America?

Since its medieval start, the European cotton industry had suffered from an endemic lack of raw cotton. Cotton supplies from the Levant, the Mediterranean islands and later the Balkans were expensive and at the mercy of frequent political and commercial disputes. By the early decades of the eighteenth century, Levant cotton had become inadequate even to satisfy the demand of a small but growing European cotton industry. Cotton prices were subject to fluctuations, depending on harvest conditions in the Middle East and the competing demand from the cotton manufacturing industries of Anatolia and Syria.

There was a clear interest on the part of European manufacturers, projectors and traders to find new and abundant supplies of raw cotton. What the market could not provide could be had by creating one's dedicated production. By the seventeenth century this was not a new concept, as cultivation by means of plantation slavery was a well-developed practice for the production of sugar and other tropical produce. In the case of sugar, the plantation system had already been promoted by Europeans in the Mediterranean islands in the eleventh

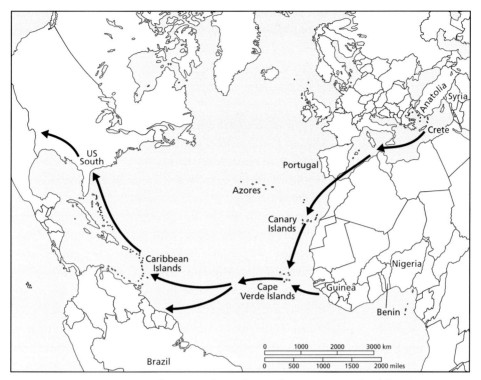

Map 9.1 Cotton cultivation: from the Mediterranean to the Atlantic.

century, extending to the islands of the Atlantic coast of Africa in the fifteenth century and to the Americas in the following century. Produce could be grown in large quantities by finding cultivable land in areas with favourable climatic conditions. Several European states (Venice in the early Mediterranean phase, and later Spain and Portugal) granted land rights and made legal the use of enslaved labour.[4]

Crete and Cyprus never developed plantation slavery for cotton, while the Canaries and the Azores were unsuitable for its cultivation. It was the islands of Cabo Verde, Sao Tiago and Fogo that became the first cotton proto-plantations under the Portuguese. By the mid sixteenth century, slaves were employed in cultivating raw cotton, its cleaning and spinning and its weaving into cloth (Map 9.1).[5] The peculiarity of these 'plantation households', as they came to be known, was that cultivation was complemented by the manufacturing of different kinds of *panos* (cloths), which were sold both to West Africa and to the New World.[6] These plantations were not yet units specialised only in the growing of raw cotton, but continued the traditional integration between cultivation and manufacturing. Yet, they made the idea of expanding cotton production on the African continent seem realistic. By the seventeenth century, Dutch reports underlined how on the coast of West Africa cotton could 'be found everywhere, and a large quantity could be had if the Negroes did not use it themselves for weaving of cloth of various qualities'.[7] Europeans had little doubt that with some encouragement, Africans could be convinced to sell large quantities of raw cotton.[8]

The idea that the cultivation of all sorts of plants was possible in tropical climates – a trope that historian Philip Curtin calls the 'myth of tropical abundance' – had particular currency in early modern Europe. It was matched by the belief that abundant resources in the overseas regions of the world could remedy the scarcities that Europeans encountered at home.[9] As John Richards put it, early modern Europeans began to see 'unending natural abundance in an enlarged world as the source of wealth, profit, and material comfort'.[10] At the end of the seventeenth century the English Royal African Company started contemplating a plan for setting up plantations in Africa. Yet, notwithstanding the repeated promise that cotton was 'cheap and in great plenty', a couple of decades later there was still no sign of any cotton cultivation.[11] As for sugar, attempts to develop plantations in Africa were fraught with problems, the first of which was that the land with low salinity suitable for cotton cultivation was in the interior and not on the more easily accessible coast of West Africa.[12] Moreover, English, Dutch and Danish reports commented on the difficulties of transforming subsistence production, as practised in village communities, into a market-based system.[13]

Europeans were in no position to impose a large-scale slave plantation system in Africa also due to the many diseases that decimated them in just a few weeks after landing.[14] Coastal areas were good trading partners for the exchange of European and Asian commodities for slaves, but this human capacity could be more fruitfully employed elsewhere where land was easy to deforest and the local population easy to coerce. The Portuguese started using the labour of enslaved African captives in the Americas in the sixteenth century when they established Rio as the entrepôt of the trade with Angola.[15] The development of sugar plantations in Brazil in the second half of the sixteenth century showed a change in European thought from simple plundering to the more calculated exploitation of the New World.[16] In the sixteenth century, Europeans started mining large quantities of silver from Potosí, but also started using the natural resources of the New World. The ecologic exchange of plants and animals between Eurasia and the Americas defined by Alfred Crosby as 'Columbian exchange' gave way to what the same author termed 'ecologic imperialism'.[17] Several staples of European consumption came to invade the ecosystem of the Americas, altering landscapes and environments for the large-scale production of produce such as sugar, coffee, cocoa, rice and eventually cotton. In the Americas, the so-called 'European expansion' created a settler society of Europeans that killed off, drove away or at best subordinated the indigenous people. The settlers claimed the land for the cultivation of produce needed in Europe.[18]

The concept of ecologic imperialism has had great fortune, but it is in many ways problematic when applied to cotton. Cotton was a fibre well known in the Americas before the arrival of the Europeans.[19] It is even unclear if the cotton plantations that Europeans came to develop in the West Indies made use of a domesticated variety of American cotton or relied instead on Asian or African seeds. Moreover, cotton was not an immediate success. Small quantities of cotton from New Spain reached Europe in the late 1560s, and some Brazilian cotton early in the following century, but before the 1620s hardly any American cotton was cultivated to be exported to Europe.[20] Cotton cultivation was first practised in Barbados in the 1620s, spreading to the Bahamas islands in the 1630s.[21] Over the following half a century, cotton made inroads into most of the West Indies, with its cultivation being first practised in Jamaica in the 1670s. Eventually cotton cultivation reached mainland North America, arriving in Virginia in the late 1640s and South Carolina in the mid 1660s.[22]

Why was cotton cultivation taken up so late in the Americas? A possible response might be found in the fact that before the mid seventeenth century cotton was not in high demand in Europe. The European cotton industries that had developed in northern Italy, southern Germany and the Flanders were still suffering from the turmoil caused by the Thirty Years' War. Indian cottons had not yet kicked in to push production in England and France. This market-led explanation finds, however, a counter-example in sugar and other tropical produce, crops that were able to create their own market in Europe.[23] Cotton might have found a barrier also due to the fact that other commodities enjoyed a boom and hefty returns on investment. An indication that this might be the case comes from the fact that cotton – as in the case of Barbados in the 1630s and 1640s – developed only when the price of tobacco declined suddenly from over 25d to under 5d per pound in less than a decade following the introduction of Chesapeake cultivation.[24] Decreasing profits from other produce made it convenient to diversify production and include small quantities of cotton in what one might call a plantation's portfolio. Results were not prodigious. With the exception of St Thomas, where, in the early 1690s, 81 out of the 101 plantations on the island cultivated cotton, the growing of this fibre remained small, accounting for 2 to 4 per cent of the value of plantation exports at the end of the seventeenth century.[25] In this early phase of ecologic imperialism, the tropical exuberance of the Americas might have worked against cotton. Differently from other crops, cotton cultivation was labour-intensive and did not enjoy substantial economies

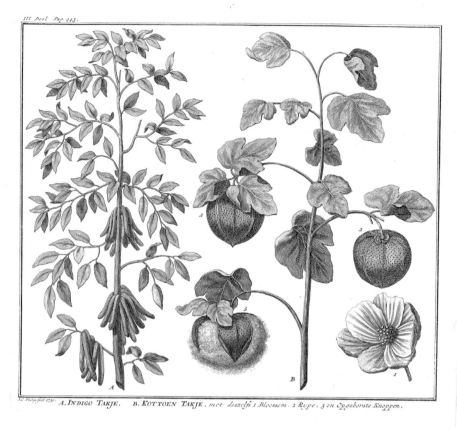

Figure 9.2 'Indigo and Cotton Plants', from a print by I. C. Philips reproduced in a Dutch publication of 1730.

of scale.[26] The cultivation of tobacco and sugar had instead larger economies of scale that were easy to achieve in a period of great land abundance.[27]

Cotton cultivation also had a much shorter history in terms of European botanical and agronomical knowledge compared, for instance, with sugar. Images of the cotton plant and basic information on its growing were included in several recounts of voyages to different parts of the world. More detailed analyses started to appear in botanical treaties from the second half of the seventeenth century, often together with disquisitions on the indigo plant (Figure 9.2).[28] It is, however, unclear how much these and other printed materials were of use to potential planters or if instead practical experimentation with seeds might have proved more fruitful. Again, information is scant, although the case of the American colony of Georgia shows that the botanical and the experimental might have gone hand in hand. It was through the colony's experimental garden that the Trustees of the State of Georgia promoted cotton cultivation in the 1730s. In the following decades would-be planters looked to the West Indies, the Mediterranean and the Levant to gather knowledge on cotton seeds and instruction on how to cultivate the crop and gin the raw material.[29] Practical experimentation continued and half a century later Georgia planters attempted to improve the quality of their cotton by importing seeds from the Caribbean (and possibly from Brazil). Similarly, in the Mississippi valley, French settlers experimented with Sea Island cotton varieties in the 1720s and after several unsuccessful attempts they imported seeds from Siam.[30] Cotton seeds imported by the Dutch from Siam were also planted in the Caribbean island of Saba, producing a particularly good type of cotton.[31]

Fred Knight argues that in the West Indies the European colonists' understanding of how to cultivate cotton might have been supplemented by the tacit agrarian knowledge of a small group of Amerindian workers who came to settle on Barbados.[32] Scholars have also questioned the easy equation that long saw slavery as the cheapest form of unskilled labour. The emergence of rice plantations in the Americas is now deemed to be dependent on the practices and knowledge of enslaved cultivators from Africa.[33] There is no evidence that this was the case for African labour working on cotton plantations, although it is likely that some of the slave workers had previous experience of cotton cultivation in Africa.[34]

Knowledge of how to cultivate cotton, the different strands of the fibre, and the optimal conditions for its growing and processing remain elusive topics also because of the different climatic conditions of the various islands of the West Indies. A great deal of what Londa Schiebinger calls 'colonial bioprospecting' was carried out to assess the potential of different locations.[35] Exploration and settlement went hand in hand with the assessment of the potential to support commercial agriculture.[36] One such report 'respecting the culture of Cotton' in Bermuda underlined that the 'discouragement the planter meets with, arises from the great difficulty of defending his trees from the violence of high winds, which carry the spray of the sea quite across the Island, in such quantities as often times to injure and sometimes to destroy whatever vegitables [sic] are in its way'.[37] What one needed to know was exactly what type of cotton was most suitable for cultivation. Cotton seeds themselves probably circulated from island to island with contemporaneous cultivation of different varieties such as 'Common Jamaica', 'Brown Bearded', 'Kidney or Brazilian', 'Nankeen' and the superior 'Sea Island'.[38] As for other crops, knowledge of cultivation moved together with people. In 1733 a Swiss called Peter Purry introduced West Indian cotton seeds into South Carolina and a year later Samuel Auspurger, another Swiss, introduced them into Georgia.[39] As for other crops, this 'hand-to-hand' transmission was by the eighteenth century supplemented by an extensive (though repetitious) literature on cotton cultivation readily available in print.[40]

Cotton cultivation in the Americas developed late and in the shadows of other more remunerative crops. Had its cultivation developed a century earlier, most of the American crop would have found its way to Cadiz and southern Europe rather than the port of Liverpool and northern Europe. Cotton emerged in conjunction with Britain's increasing power in the Caribbean. This had been since the early sixteenth century an area of Spanish influence and later Dutch expansion. However, in the half a century between the 1620s and the 1660s, Britain occupied several key islands of the West Indies. The Treaty of Breda of 1667 secured Antigua, Montserrat and St Kitts for Britain, leaving only France as a possible competitor for the control of the Sea Islands and North America.[41]

In the late seventeenth century it was sugar, not cotton, that was the driver for the occupation of an increasing amount of land. Cotton came only slowly to be considered as part of the advantages of settlement in the West Indies. The Englishman Thomas Dalby in his *An Historical Account of the Rise and Growth of the West-India Collonies* (1690) was one of the first to make a clear case for cotton, which he recognised as 'a Commodity of great Value' and a 'mighty Advantage to the Common-wealth' costing up to a third less than similar fibres 'Imported . . . from Forreign parts'.[42] Yet it was not until well into the eighteenth century that cotton became a significant commodity for European trade. By the middle of the century, when European demand for raw cotton started booming, Britain had consolidated even further its position in the West Indies and North America. The capture of Guadalupe in 1759 and the substantial territorial gains following the end of the Seven Years' War, in 1763, advanced the power of Britain in the Americas.[43] Political power meant considerable economic returns, as the 1760s inaugurated a long period in which Britain was able to expand trade, replace expensive raw materials with cheaper substitutes, draw on the demand of prosperous trade partners and exclude competitors in strategic key areas of the world.[44] By the 1790s the global reach of British power and trade had expanded dramatically and the West Indies were a small but important part of Britain's imperial ambitions.[45]

It is easy to exaggerate the success of Britain at shouldering other European countries away from an area of great agrarian potential. British political domination did not necessarily mean that merchants of other nationalities were excluded from business. Cotton grown in British territories was an enumerated commodity and therefore had be to transported in British ships and sold via English ports. This was, however, not a problem as both smuggling and re-export were ripe. Cotton was re-exported out of England duty-free, a measure to encourage the profits of plantations but seen as highly unfair by British cotton manufacturers.[46]

Yet, the political control of areas of cultivation allowed for the implementation of a series of economic measures that encouraged the expansion of cotton. This was illustrated by the granting of a substantial export bounty to cotton, which was passed in 1744 by the colonial legislature of South Carolina and repealed only a quarter of a century later.[47] Parliament in Westminster legislated not only on the trade, production and use of finished cloth, but also showed an increasing interest in aiding the supply of raw materials for an expanding British industry.

Why plantation slavery?

The Americas became in the course of the eighteenth century an important reservoir for cotton cultivation. Yet this does not explain why cotton came to be associated with plantations and slavery. Marx famously saw the slave cotton plantation as a 'category of the greatest importance' and he explained that 'slavery is just as much the pivot of bourgeois industry as machinery, credits, etc. Without slavery you have no cotton; without cotton you have no modern industry.'[48] Today, historians tend to see a less straightforward relationship between slavery and industrialisation, with Barbara Solow arguing that slavery 'did not cause the Industrial Revolution, but played an active role in its pattern and timing'.[49] It is hard to deny the success of slave plantations in the production of raw cotton for an expanding European textile industry. In 1803, less than 8 per cent of the cotton used in Britain came from areas where the crop was cultivated by peasant-holders, the remainder coming from the New World where slaves cultivated cotton on the plantations of Louisiana, Brazil and Suriname.[50]

How did a plantation work? Douglas North, Fogel and Engerman, Gavin Wright and others have unearthed a great deal of material on the structure, organisation, management and productivity of nineteenth-century US cotton plantations.[51] Much less is known about the working of cotton plantations in the West Indies. The nearest we get to a model plantation is the well-known print published in Coltellini's *Il gazzettiere americano* (1763), Chambon's *Le Commerce de l'Amérique par Marseille* (1764) and in Griselini's *Dizionario delle arti* (1768–78) and reproduced in several other publications across Europe, including the *Encyclopédie* (Figure 9.3).[52] The plantation life and the work of slaves are here represented diachronically. A slave picks the cotton from a cotton tree on the left (no. 2), while another slave cleans the cotton (no. 3). Further cleaning takes place under a shed (no. 4), probably by a female slave using a tool similar to a charka. The cotton is then baled (no. 5) with the help of a slave wetting the cotton. The image shows some cotton bales (no. 7) ready to be transported by one of the ships stationed near the plantation (no. 8).

Figure 9.3 'Coton' (plate VIII), from *Le Commerce de l'Amérique par Marseille* (1764).

Before the introduction of lithography and later photography, the labour of slaves in cotton plantations was rarely represented. The medium of photography allowed for the proliferation of representations of plantation life in the US South after the mid nineteenth century, but the majority of such representations lack distinctiveness, concentrating mostly on the picking of cotton. This happens because it is difficult to convey in one image an agrarian process. Chambon's image obviates to such a problem by narrating actions in different times and by showing the progression of the commodity from the tree to the ship transporting it to Europe.

Both Chambon's image and later prints and photographic representations of plantation life point to the fact that what was captured was quintessentially an agrarian unit of production. Apart from ginning and packing, there was no processing activity associated with cotton in a plantation. This was different from other types of plantations, where, as in the case of sugar or indigo production, cultivation was followed by a certain amount of processing such as boiling, refining, and so on. Moreover, over time plantations became specialised with slaves and later labourers depending on the provision of food and manufactured goods traded in exchange for cotton. This allowed for the plantation to be insulated from the performance of other crops, especially foodstuffs. In India, periods of famine were accompanied by substantial decreases in cotton production, with cultivators switching from cotton to rice in moments of food crisis, but this was not the case for plantations in the Americas.[53]

A second important feature of the plantation economy was that it allowed for the first time specialisation of labour on a truly global scale. Whilst in Asia, raw cotton was cultivated by peasant households (often integrating cultivation, processing, spinning and weaving), the growing European cotton industry created a system of provisioning of raw material that was geographically removed from areas of manufacturing. With cotton plantations, Europe's competitive advantage definitively shifted away from agriculture to manufacturing.[54] For the first time a large-scale industry was borne out of a 'commodity chain' that spanned different continents, with European capital and power firmly in charge of its coordination.

The ecologic imperialism that Europe implemented in the Americas could only work with substantial labour inputs. Plantations were therefore the outcome of a specific balance between land, labour and capital. The abundance of land, compared to labour and capital, led to the creation of large-scale units of production. This was an extensive system of agrarian production in which only part of a plantation was cultivated at any one time. Crops were rotated and cultivated on new land, thus avoiding diminishing returns. Neither the productive specialisation nor the geographic articulation of cotton cultivation and processing explain, however, why plantations came to be reliant on the exploitation of slave labour. Studies on US cotton plantations in the nineteenth century agree that the organisation of labour under slavery might have accounted for part of the efficiency of the productive system.[55] But the choice between slave plantations vis-à-vis peasant household production or free-labour plantations was not a straightforward one, especially when we consider cotton cultivation in the seventeenth and eighteenth centuries.

Cotton production came to rely on slave cultivation not out of rational calculations on its efficiency, but because it followed a model already adopted by sugar, cocoa, coffee and tobacco cultivation. Moreover, as Gemery and Hogendorn point out, the West Indies plantations could have not relied on a full stream of free peasants from Europe or elsewhere. Mercantile philosophies, especially strong in England, saw losses of population at home as detrimental, creating a chronic lack of labour in the New World. Few also could afford the expensive cost of the passage to the Americas (£5–6). Those who crossed the Atlantic could do so by becoming indenture labourers (paying over the years for the cost of the passage), but the more familiar climates of the northern colonies offered better prospects, especially of survival. All of this made the growing of tropical produce well beyond the capacity of local European settlers.[56]

A second set of issues explaining the choice of slave labour relates instead to contemporary perceptions. There is little evidence that slave owners had any precise notions of the profitableness of the system of labour that they adopted. This is partially due to the fact that slavery is more similar to a capital purchase on the part of plantation owners than it is to the retribution of labour. There was an estimate of the so-called 'payback' period, that is to say the number of years' work in which the original cost of a slave was recovered. Yet these calculations had to take into account that, because slaves could be easily sold, they possessed also a 'liquidation value' and more generally an 'investment potential' absent in other forms of labour. Finally, slaves also had a 'non-pecuniary value': they were a display of wealth and power in a colonial society that sometimes extended into physical and moral exploitation such as concubinage with female slaves.[57]

The rise and decline of West Indian cotton

One of the problems that cotton faced was that of being too cheap. Unlike the finished commodities or raw materials that were imported from Asia, or much of the tropical produce, dyeing substances and exotic woods that found their way from the Americas to Europe, raw cotton was a bulky commodity that was cheap to buy but expensive to transport. This is one of the reasons

Figure 9.4 'Bagging Cotton' (in Jamaica) by William Berryman, early nineteenth century.

why the East India companies saw little profit in trading raw cotton from India to Europe when they could fill their ships with more valuable finished cloth. A commentator writing in the 1680s observed that this was a problem also for the cotton imported from the Americas: 'were it not that by screws and engines they can make a great deal (of raw cotton) lie in a small room', he said, 'the freight would be so chargeable, that it would not be worth bringing hither raw'.[58] Ginned cotton was packed into sacks by slaves that pressed it with their feet and a stick (Figure 9.4). The sacks had to be kept wet in order to avoid the cotton expanding in volume.[59] Screws powered by horses pressed the cotton so hard 'as to make the timbers of the ship crack'.[60] Still, packing and transport made cotton 20 per cent more expensive in Europe than in the West Indies.[61]

The advantage of America was that the journey of cotton to Europe was shorter and cheaper than a similar journey from Asia or even the coast of Africa. This made transport economically viable, though cotton had still to compete for space against sugar, cocoa, tobacco and other exotic produce. Had the Americas manufactured finished commodities, in all probability cotton would have found little space on ships' holds. Yet until the mid eighteenth century the importation of cotton from the Americas into Europe remained a small affair. Its production had ups and downs, giving way to other crops when it was more remunerative to do so. The value of imported cotton from Jamaica and Barbados was a mere £14,700 in 1686 and just over £25,000 in 1701.[62] As late as the 1730s, the French possession of St Dominque produced less than 300 tons of cotton a year.[63]

The rise of American cotton can be narrated through two subsequent phases of expansion, the first in the 1760s and 1770s (that coincided with the growth in the European production of mix cottons such as fustians) and the second from the 1780s onwards (accompanying instead the mechanisation of the European cotton industry). Suriname is a good example of an area for which decreasing returns from sugar encouraged the cultivation of other crops. Cotton started to be cultivated in the 1730s and by the 1760s the area produced 500–600 bales a year, increasing to more than 3,000 bales in the 1780s and 1790s.[64] The period between the 1780s and the 1800s was one of great economic dynamism, especially in the British West Indies. In islands such as St Kitts, Dominica, Barbados and Jamaica, cotton was central in attracting people and capital as well as in activating backward links in the provision of supplies, slaves, transport facilities and credit (Map 9.2).[65]

This was a period of great prosperity throughout the Caribbean. Visitors were impressed by the high living standards of the white population. Most of them wore, as in the case of Bermuda, Indian and European cotton fabrics such as chintzes, doorguzzees, China and Persia taffeta, 'Bombay stuff', gingham, niccannes, chillaes, and so on.[66] In cotton-producing islands, we can imagine that imported cloth was integrated into the consumption of local varieties. The rather idyllic views of life in Santo Domingo by Augustin Brunias show natives and free slaves wearing a variety of cotton and linen clothing that could be either imported from Europe or from Asia (via Europe) or locally produced in imitation of European and Indian stripes and checks (Figure 9.5). This was the case of *paliacates*, woven kerchieves produced in the area of Sarvapalli near Pulicat in India at least since the early seventeenth century, not dissimilar to those represented in Brunias's painting. In the second half of the eighteenth century these *foulards* were extremely popular in the French West Indies. Legoux de Flaix discussed the potential of this merchandise by saying that 'In Peru, Mexico, and

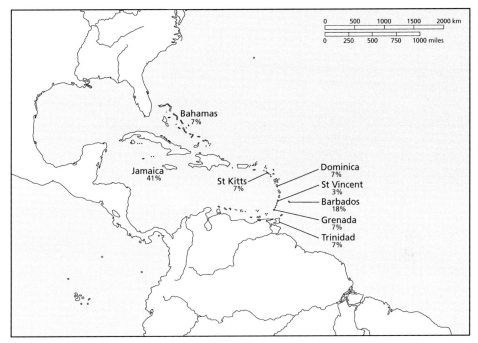

Map 9.2 Cotton-producing islands in the British Caribbean (and percentage of total production in 1800).

the different parts of the West Indies, from the European creoles to the chetive black slave, or the elegant mulatto woman, all love to cover their heads with a Pulicat kerchiefs'.[67]

The end of the eighteenth century was also a moment of population expansion. The intensification of land usage was the result of appealing profits that encouraged people to settle there. In places such as the Bahamas, where cotton cultivation started relatively late, the expansion of that crop was also accelerated by the arrival of 1,600 loyalists from Georgia, South Carolina and New York, who brought with them 5,700 slaves and free blacks.[68] Schemes incentivising settlement were common also in the Spanish and French dominions. In the period between 1783 and 1797, the Spanish island of Trinidad attracted several hundred French settlers thanks to a *cédula de población*, an invitation to settle on the island through the granting of land and tax exemptions. They deforested 85,000 acres of land and created 500 new plantations, most of which were cultivated with cotton.[69]

The low cost of setting up a cotton plantation allowed for the crop to expand fast when European demand increased in the last quarter of the eighteenth century. For some of the West Indian islands, the expansion of cotton cultivation

Figure 9.5 *At the Linen Market in Santo Domingo* by Augustin Brunias
c. 1775. Natives and free blacks are wearing white and striped
cottons and linens, imported from either Europe or India. (See also
colour plate.)

was sensational: St Domingue had produced just 200 bales a year in the early
1730s but by the late 1780s it produced nearly 30,000 bales.[70] The success of
cotton, however, created as many opportunities as problems for the West Indies.
An industry that was going to clothe the world could hardly depend on the
cultivation of raw materials in a few tiny islands of the Caribbean.[71] Production
could not keep up with demand and manufacturers in Britain were worried
about the cost of cotton: in the 1770s, cotton sold at under 20 US cents a pound;
in the 1790s it was traded at 34 cents.[72] By this date, several harvest failures
made the situation critical. Many cotton plantation owners decided to leave the
island of Bahamas and migrated to Georgia.[73] In 1800, cotton cultivation in
Trinidad had nearly completely disappeared.[74]

By the early 1810s the British West Indies had lost their role in feeding the
British cotton industry. In 1812, fourteen islands produced 2,400 tons of cotton,
a third of what they had produced a decade earlier and a mere 15 per cent of
all cotton used by the British industry and less than one per cent of the value

of sugar, rum, coffee and other miscellaneous West Indian produce.[75] The West Indies became a major example of land exhaustion due to global demand for commercial crops. Intensive cultivation had depleted the productive potential of these islands in just over a generation. The 'slash and burn' method had finally run out of land. Remedies were sought, but it was too late. In the Bahamas, planters tried to improve yields by planting short-staple Persian next to long-staple American varieties of cotton, but with little success. The Crooked Islands, where at one point 3,000 acres of land had been cultivated with cotton, by the early years of the nineteenth century were a spectre of their former self: Daniel MacKinnen looked at what had been prosperous cotton plantations 'but which from the failure of crops were now abandoned, and had become covered with a luxuriant growth of indigenous shrubs and plants'.[76] Colquhoun explained how several islands were now deserted and were unlikely to be cultivated again.[77] The decline of West Indian cotton coincided, however, with the emergence of a new world area of cotton production, an area with a productive potential as enormous as its territory: the southern states of the United States.

'King cotton': the century of US cotton production

It is tempting to explain the rise of cotton cultivation in the southern United States simply by relating it to the ecologic *empasse* of the West Indies. In 1791 US cotton production was practically non-existent. Ten years later, in 1801, the US exported as much cotton to England as the entire British West Indies. In 1811, the US sold 43.9 thousand tons of cotton to England, 56 per cent of all cotton used by British mills.[78] The rise of what came to be known as 'king cotton' continued for the entire first half of the nineteenth century, providing by the early 1860s more than 4 million bales of cotton a year to the fastest-growing industry in human history.[79] Yet the nineteenth-century success of US cotton begs the question of why it took it so long for cotton cultivation to expand in mainland North America.

Cotton cultivation was introduced to North America in the early seventeenth century but, unlike indigo, tobacco or rice, it did not become a successful commercial crop. Before the independence of the North American colonies, cotton cultivation was seen as potentially pernicious to the sale of English woollens as it would have encouraged home spinning. Some cultivation was practised, especially in Virginia and the Carolinas, but the output was cotton 'of a coarse kind' suitable only for the manufacture of low-quality textiles.[80] The break-away from the mother country recast the manufacturing future of the new-born United

States: under what has become known as the 'homespun ideology', any raw fibre was seen as good if its spinning and weaving could replace textiles imported from Britain.[81] The potential of cotton for home spinning might explain why in the last quarter of the eighteenth century attempts were made to expand its cultivation and improve the quality of the fibre. In 1775 the Assembly of Virginia, for instance, legislated that 'all persons having proper land ought to cultivate and raise a quantity of flax, hemp and cotton sufficient not only for the use of his own family, but to spare to others on moderate terms'.[82] In the following years, cotton became increasingly important for the production of clothing as traditional supplies of English woollens, linens and fustians came to a halt.[83]

Home consumption of raw cotton was important, but it can hardly explain the scale that cotton cultivation came to assume in the US. As had happened in the West Indies more than half a century earlier, the expansion of cotton cultivation in the US in the 1790s coincided with a sharp drop in the price of several staple commodities such as tobacco, rice and indigo caused by glutted markets.[84] Yet, cotton cultivation was not necessarily remunerative. The short-staple variety of cotton grown in the US could not be ginned with traditional ginning machines. Even by using slave labour, it was not worthwhile collecting the cotton from the fields.[85]

The introduction of a new ginning machine by Eli Whitney in 1794 was as revolutionary for cotton growing as Arkwright's machines were for cotton manufacturing.[86] Whitney's saw-gin was a remedy for the labour intensity of cleaning green-seed cotton. This variety of cotton, which was common in the American South, was different from the Eurasian brown-seed varieties and could not be effectively ginned with a traditional roller system. Several inventors before Whitney had attempted to provide (but only to a limited degree succeeded) a technological solution. Whitney perfected a system based on a cylinder filled with wire teeth (Figure 9.6).[87] The raw cotton was drawn into the cylinder, releasing only the fibre but not the seed.[88] It substantially lowered the amount of labour necessary to cleaning cotton. It was said that while before 1794 it took a day to clean a pound of cotton, with Whitney's machine 'one negro could produce fifty pounds of clean cotton a day'.[89]

The mechanisation of cotton cleaning and ginning only partially explain the expansion of cotton cultivation in the US. The short-staple cotton variety originally imported from the West Indies was not just of low quality and difficult to clean, but also had little resistance to the harsher North American continental climate. Eliza Lucas Pinckney, a pioneer of large-scale indigo cultivation in South Carolina in the mid eighteenth century, complained about a June frost in 1741 that 'cut out ... the Cotton, Guiney corn, and most of the ginger planted here'.[90]

THE FIRST COTTON-GIN.—DRAWN BY WILLIAM L. SHEPPARD.—[SEE PAGE 814.]

Figure 9.6 'The First Cotton Gin', from *Harper's Weekly*, 18 December 1869.

It was only with the breeding of a new variety of cotton, *Gossypium hirsutum*, that a new family of cotton fibres now called 'Upland' cotton was introduced to America. This was a more resistant plant that could tolerate some frost and grew on saline soil. It also yielded greater quantities of long-staple lint, thus making mechaniscd cleaning easier. But it was in particular its resistance to frost that allowed cultivation to expand in Mississippi and in western Tennessee, areas in which previous varieties of cotton could not be grown.[91]

There is a further important difference between the West Indies cotton plantations and those of the US South. Cotton cultivation in the West Indies remained geographically confined by the use of virgin land. By contrast, the expanding cotton plantations in the US relied on a vast territory that was far from uninhabited, however (Map 9.3).

The creation of the cotton states of Mississippi in 1817 and Alabama two years later had profound ecological and social consequences. Land was indeed deforested, canals built and the landscape transformed (Figure 9.7). But this was a region populated by American natives, who were often dispossessed of their land by force. The Chattahoochee and Mississippi rivers were Native American

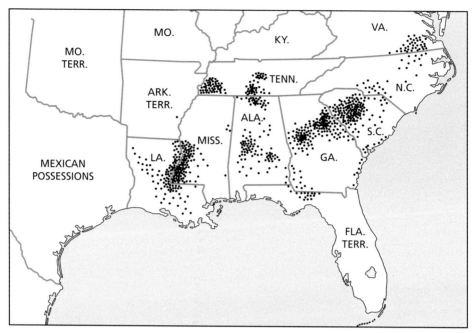

Map 9.3 Cotton cultivation in the US South between 1826 and 1833 (in thousand bales on average a year per dot).

Figure 9.7 *Cotton Plantation* by Charles Giroux, *c.* 1850s–60s. (See also colour plate.)

lands and it is estimated that a hundred villages accommodated a population of at least 30,000 people. The impact of cotton was devastating on the social fabric of Indian life. Many Indians were left with no choice other than to become seasonal labourers (especially women) or itinerant peddlers in the new towns and plantations.[92]

The expansion of cotton production also meant the displacement of the slave population. In 1790, before cotton became an important cash crop, more than 50 per cent of slaves were concentrated in Maryland and Virginia. In the 1790s, the American South had fewer than 700,000 slaves and Mississippi no more than 3,000. A generation later, in the 1830s and 1840s, they had become the bedrock of slavery. Already by 1830, Mississippi had 66,000 slaves and the slave population in the entire US South reached 4 million in 1850.[93] As the US production of raw cotton jumped from 334,000 bales in 1820 to 1.35 million in 1840 and to 2.4 million in 1850, Alabama, Mississippi and Louisiana produced more than half of the crop.[94] It is estimated that 850,000 slaves, especially younger and stronger ones, had to leave their communities in Virginia, Maryland, Delaware, South Carolina and Kentucky as they were sold for work on the cotton frontier.[95] This was a 'new slavery', a regime that, notwithstanding the idealised representations, was characterised by harsher working conditions. Slaves were mostly employed in gangs in turning forests into farms as the cotton frontier expanded (Figure 9.8).[96]

These continental cotton plantations created through deforestation were also different from those of the West Indies in terms of specialisation. There cotton was cultivated in small pockets of land, often mixed with other crops.[97] In the American South, there was little space for small producers. One commentator is said to have seen 'many a workman's lodging at the North [of the US], and in England too, where there was double the amount of luxury that I ever saw in a regular cotton-planter's house on plantations of three cabins'.[98] Small-scale production simply could not compete with monoculture carried out through intensive exploitation of land and labour. According to one historian, these were 'the most intensely commercialised farms in the world'.[99] Whilst the cotton gin allowed the intensification of processing, increasing demand from the English mills generated pressure on land and labour. Cotton plantations became 'industrialised'.

In the old slave states, slaves had lived in families and had the right to keep dogs (useful for hunting), chickens and ducks. They cultivated kitchen gardens, often being able to sell their produce on the open market. They had Sundays off and sometimes even Saturday afternoons. By contrast, the South was 'a little Hell', as one of the slaves transported to work on a Georgia plantation would recount. Slaves were denied all rights and subjected to the worst

Figure 9.8 'A Cotton Plantation on the Mississippi' (1884).

exploitation.[100] The intensification of cultivation led to longer working hours, division of labour and specialisation of work. In the cold season, slaves had to repair fences, fell trees and clear and manure the soil as soon as frost ended. Cotton planting was followed by midsummer thinning of cotton (a labour-intensive operation of straightening the plants) and chopping weeds. From mid August, cotton was harvested. This was an intense time when a high percentage of slaves fell sick. This relentless toiling did not abate even in December, when, the third picking concluded, cotton had to be processed.[101]

What is distinctive of nineteenth-century US cotton production is not just its incredible expansion or its 'industrial intensity', but the fact that the majority of the crop was exported. Cotton was transported in large shipments down rivers to major cotton markets such as Charleston or Savannah in Georgia, where buyers acting on behalf of English and European mills made offers for the different qualities of cotton through the mediation of a 'cotton factor', who received from 4 to 12 per cent of the value of the cotton sold (Figure 9.9).[102] With the exception of the period of the American Civil War, throughout the nineteenth century export accounted for more than half of the US cotton crop.

The US had nearly limitless supplies of land, abundant labour, and well-developed infrastructures and credit networks that made the cotton trade

SCENE ON THE LEVEE, AT NEW ORLEANS.

Figure 9.9 'Scene of the Levee, at New Orleans', from *Ballou's Pictorial* (1855).

flourish. From the late eighteenth century, southern US cotton began to be shipped to New England by New York merchants.[103] These merchants acted as the interface for international markets and especially with the United Kingdom.[104] This has been defined as a neo-colonial system in which the industrial development of the northern part of the US as well as that of Europe was fostered by international specialisation of labour.[105]

Conclusion

It is worthwhile to return to the image with which this chapter started. The Pholey town and plantation presented the idea of integration between the growing of cotton, its processing and transformation into cloth and the cultivation of other crops. This was a common occurrence, not just in Africa but in most of the early modern world. The rise of the plantation system in the Americas proposed a very different model. This was not based on community production slowly opening up to the opportunities of exchange and trade; it was a specialised productive system that was created by trade and exchange. It was also a unit of production that had little connection with its own locality apart from the exploitation of land: it used labour from Africa, capital from Europe and exported its entire production. Plantations privileged monoculture, becoming disentangled not just from the world of manufacturing but also from the variations of other crops. Through the plantation system, Europeans secured staple supplies of key crops that over time were provided at increasingly cheaper prices. Cotton emerged as part of such crops only late, but its production increased dramatically when the needs of industrialising Europe made it necessary.

10 COMPETING WITH INDIA: COTTON AND EUROPEAN INDUSTRIALISATION

The text above reads: 'Arkwright of England struggled with making a machine to spin a cotton yarn for several years, which made his family impoverished. Seeing him wasting money without success, driven by the anger, his wife broke a scale model. Arkwright got so mad at her that he kicked her out of the house. After that event, he successfully invented the machine and made fortunes on it.'[1]

In 1793 a select committee of the British House of Commons reported that British consumption of Indian cotton textiles was 'reduced almost to nothing'. It was claimed that shops around the country offered 'British muslins for sale, equal in appearance, [and] of more elegant patterns, than those of India, for one-fourth or perhaps more than one-third less in price'.[2] How was it possible that Britain was now producing cottons that were cheaper and even better in quality than those of their Asian counterparts? The classic response is that an 'industrial revolution' swept Britain, changing the way in which production was carried out. Central to industrialisation was the application of a string of techno-logical inventions that include John Kay's flying shuttle (1733), John Wyatt and Lewis Paul's roller spinning machine (1738), James Hargreaves's spinning jenny (1765; patented 1770), Richard Arkwright's water frame (1767; patented 1769), Samuel Crompton's spinning mule (1779) and Edmund Cartwright's power loom (1785).[3]

Generations of popular and academic accounts explained Britain's industrial transition as the outcome of the inventive 'genius' of a series of great 'men', cel-ebrated with statues, prints, poems and museum exhibits from Victorian times onwards.[4] Their stories of creative aptitude and entrepreneurial mastership gave body and soul to otherwise abstract economic processes. They provided human agency and at the same time positioned technological innovation as the cen-trepiece of modern industrial capitalism. With them technologies moved from being pure tools for the reconfiguration of the productive and economic system of Europe to the very reasons why the continent became first industrial and then wealthy. The appeal of such stories soon achieved transcultural significance. In

Meiji, Japan, Richard Arkwright was deemed to be worthy of inclusion (along with Thomas Carlyle, American customs and European dress) among the most important things to know about the West (Figure 10.1). Here, Arkwright's rise to prominence is suitably contextualised in a familial scene in which the threat posed by rioting workers intent on destroying his machine becomes his wife's neglectful behaviour. By showing Arkwright's irate reaction and the consequent ejection of his wife (duly sent back to her parents), the machine becomes the centrepiece of the story.

More or less in the same years in which this print was produced for Japanese consumption, a British author concluded that it was the spinning jenny and power loom that had 'conquered the native weavers' of India, adding that 'the Arkwright machinery indeed seemed to defy all opposition'.[5] He then proceeded to cite verbatim the 1793 Select Committee passage, confirming that in the space of just a few years at the end of the eighteenth century, British cottons became globally competitive. Explanations like these and the idiosyncratic narrative of the contemporaneous Japanese print set technological innovation as central to the rise of a British cotton industry.[6] This chapter aims to 'unpack' this established wisdom in three ways. First, we need to reassess the importance of technological innovation and how much it really explains about the rise of European (and specifically British) cotton textiles. Capital-intensive mechanised industrial production might seem to us ineluctable, but in the context of the manufacturing world described so far, it is was less than predictable. Second, we need to explain the genesis of technological innovation; not just how an 'industrial' system of production came into being, but also why. This is the subject of a rich discourse and explanations. And finally, and as a corollary to the previous point, we need to address the possible reasons why northwestern Europe was the first part of the world to successfully make the transition into an industrial society.

Industrialisation and the historiography of manufacturing

That something remarkable happened to cotton textile manufacturing in the British Isles at the end of the eighteenth century is beyond doubt. Cotton textile production increased tenfold between 1770 and 1790 and tenfold again in the following dozen years. In 1770, the export of English-produced cottons was 4 per cent of that of wool textiles (£200,000 worth compared to £5 million for wool). By 1802, cottons' exports had surpassed those of woollens, and two years later they reached the value of £10 million. With rates of growth estimated at 9 per cent a year between 1770 and 1801 and 6 per cent in the following thirty years, British cotton textile manufacturing grew as fast as the Chinese

Figure 10.1 Sir Richard Arkwright, inventor of the spinning machine, second half of the nineteenth century.

and Indian economies of today.[7] These performances have made cotton textile manufacturing the most important sector in narratives of British and European industrialisation.[8] Key to the expansion of cotton textile manufacturing was a decrease in the cost of production. In the fifty years between 1780 and 1830 the production cost of a yard of calico cloth fell by 83 per cent and that of a yard of muslin by 76 per cent.[9]

That technological innovation was part and parcel of this momentous change is also beyond doubt.[10] Yet two points are worth emphasising: first, technologies might have been necessary but are far from sufficient in explaining the context and ways in which cotton production came to be the cornerstone of an industrial sector; and second, and most importantly, technological applications were sought after and encouraged across Europe but their aim was not just to improve productivity.[11] The quality of production was key for both governments and entrepreneurs as competitiveness was also a function of excellence in manufacturing. The overall result was that technologies changed the way in which production was carried out, dramatically increased levels of output, but also reshaped products and their qualities, as we will see for cotton.

The British industrial revolution is perhaps one of the most prolific topics for discussion among historians and has produced an astounding amount of literature.[12] For more than a century discussions on industrialisation were based on explanations endogenous to Britain and suggested that technologies themselves were the cause of economic change. Global history has provided a good corrective to the notion of a 'British' industrial revolution by considering what happened in the British Isles vis-à-vis other parts of Europe and the rest of the world. Through comparisons and by unearthing important world connections and entanglements, the story of a transition to modern economic growth transcends the narrow borders of Britain and the straightjacket of industrialisation. Factors ranging from ecological resources to institutional frameworks are today more central to explanations of divergence (rather than industrialisation) than technologies per se.[13] But even the discussion of technological innovation – still central to the understanding of manufacturing – has dismissed the idea that technologies explain macro-economic changes and see them instead as tools through which economic development was created. Yet this leaves us with an even more urgent need to understand why and how new technologies came to change manufacturing in one area of the world (and not others) and the ways this outcome might have been related to global forces.[14]

The changes in production experienced in northwestern Europe at the end of the eighteenth century are explained in different ways. One might generalise to identify two broad positions: those economic historians who emphasise the

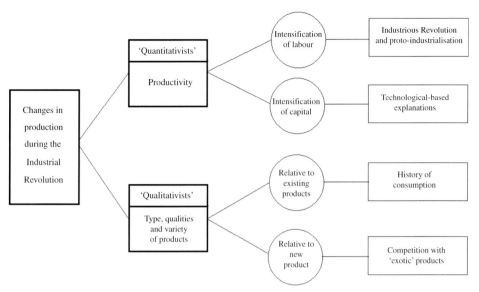

Figure 10.2 Explanations of changes in cotton textile production during the Industrial Revolution.

quantitative changes in production (that I call 'quantitativists'); and those who underline instead the qualitative nature of such changes (that I call 'qualitativists') (Figure 10.2). It is worth pointing to the fact that these are not alternative positions and that the economic changes that we ascribe to the 'industrial revolution' had both important qualitative and quantitative dimensions. Yet, 'quantitativists' point to the fact that the invention and application of new technologies and new ways to organise production are aimed at (and explained by) gains in productivity. Technologies allow the production of the same length of cloth by using fewer inputs in terms of capital, materials and labour. This means that it will cost less to produce the same quantity of output, thus increasing competitiveness on domestic and international markets. 'Qualitativists' highlight instead how a great deal of technological and organisational innovation, while increasing output, also provides new and better products. They claim that competitiveness is not just a price war but includes capacities to match (and surpass) the quality of what other producers have to offer consumers.[15]

Productivity gains can be achieved by intensifying the contributions of individual (or all) factors of production.[16] The intensification of labour means that more work, but more importantly more efficient work, can achieve better results and decrease production costs. This is a 'labour-intensive' type of industrial development that was indeed present not just in Europe but also across the early modern world in what have been defined as proto-industrialisation and in Jan de Vries's concept, an 'industrious revolution'.[17] A second route to increased productivity is 'capital-intensive', that is to say, based on more efficient applications of technologies and organisation of production, often requiring substantial outlays in terms of R&D and the purchase and maintenance of machinery. Needless to say, process and product innovation were often intrinsically linked.[18]

The literature dealing with technological and organisational innovation aimed at increasing productivity during the classic period of the industrial revolution is too vast to summarise here. It has positioned machines and inventions at the forefront of debates over rates of growth, genesis of invention, technical capabilities, and so on. These interpretations remain the orthodoxy of much economic history of industrialisation. Yet, in more recent years historians, especially those influenced by the paradigm of a 'consumer revolution', have questioned these narratives, addressing instead the change brought about by the industrial revolution in terms of how many new commodities and how much more stuff it made available to consumers. They have shifted the attention from processes of production to markets. A second approach – that will find a more extensive treatment here – has connected changes in manufacturing in Europe to the influence of Asian products. In a nutshell, it argues that if Europe wanted to develop a viable cotton industry, it had to produce at prices and qualities that were comparable to those offered by Indian and Chinese producers.[19]

Industrious paths: Europe and China

In mid-eighteenth-century Europe, it was far from certain that technological innovation would lead the way towards productivity or qualitative improvements in cotton manufacturing.[20] In France, for instance, it was claimed that 'the spinning needed for the production of calicoes spreads work to the countryside, and gives employment to a number of people who are not engaged in agriculture; it fills slack times that the seasons and the bad weather provide to cultivators, gives employment to women and children, and gives them the means to support themselves or to improve their conditions'.[21] This *mémoire* on cotton production in Alsace in the early 1750s reminds us that part of the cotton textile sector had already mechanised and industrialised: while the printing of calicoes was based on *fabriques rassemblées* (centralised production), the *mémoire* argues that this could promote *fabriques disperses* (decentralised production) through spinning and weaving in the countryside.[22]

Contemporary economists and commentators saw cotton as a natural extension to other fibres, especially linen. In early eighteenth-century England, cotton spinning and weaving were carried out mostly in the countryside. As for wool and linen, imported cotton was integrated within agrarian work.[23] This is why many saw cotton as a way to increase rural employment. In 1739, a report to the French government positively commented upon the fact that cotton carding, spinning and reeling gave work to 900 people in the countryside near Nîmes while another 250 workers spun raw cotton from Martinique and St Dominigue in the local paupers' hospital.[24]

As we have seen in previous chapters, the cotton yarn and cloth that were produced were not only of low quality but were far more expensive than products imported from India. By the mid eighteenth century, Europeans could rival India in printing, but their expanding system of spinning and weaving produced only cheaper varieties of cotton-linen cloth such as those sold to the West African markets. Machinery was not yet perceived as a viable alternative to labour, either to increase productivity or quality. Many thought that notwithstanding the higher costs of production of Europe vis-à-vis India, it was skills rather than machinery that would provide a solution (Figure 10.3). A French project of 1752 put forward the idea of using Indian workmen to learn superior skills in the spinning, weaving and finishing of cotton cloth, as it was explained that 'only the eye and practice can instruct the men in this works'.[25] Nothing came of this proposal, as was the case for a similar initiative by the Portuguese crown. In 1750, the Portuguese crown attempted to attract weavers from San Thomé in Chennai to establish the manufacturing of chintzes in Portugal. However the project was a non-starter as it was observed that among Indian workmen, 'there is a great reluctance to leave their homeland, to which especially contributes the caste-differences which they always observe among each other'.[26]

These were no isolated episodes. The largest initiative of acquisition of human capital from India was carried out in 1784 by the French under the coordination of the *intendant du commerce* Jacques-Marie-Jérôme Michau de Montaran, who organised for fifty skilled artisans from the Coromandel coast to relocate to France.[27] They arrived in Thieux (a couple of miles from today's Charles de Gaulle Airport) in October 1785 (Figure 10.4). Among them were twelve weavers, twenty-five spinners, a dyer and nine other helpers. The project was funded by the French government and was aimed at training local apprentices in the practices of spinning and weaving adopted by the Indian workmen. Results were disastrous, to say the least. The sickly and insubordinate Indians managed to produce cloth worth 12,000 livres against a cost of 41,000 livres spent to support them. None of the apprentices completed their term and the Indian artisans were sent back to the Coromandel at the end of 1787.[28]

These examples point to the fact that well into the second half of the eighteenth century cotton textile manufacturing in Europe expanded along rural and artisanal lines. The *mémoire* cited earlier for Alsace, for instance, explained how

Figure 10.3 'Coton' (plate IX), from *Le Commerce de l'Amérique par Marseille* (1764). Spinning is portrayed as an activity based on skills, thus visualising the gesture of a hand next to a machine for reeling.

cotton was given out, to be spun or purchased by women at the weekly Wednesday market in a way not dissimilar to what was happening in the Yangzi delta of China in the same period. A comparison between Europe and China is particularly appropriate, as Kenneth Pomeranz and others have debated why European cotton production mechanised and industrialised while China's did not.

Figure 10.4 'Tisserands qui mouillent le coton filé avec de l'eau pure et qui le pétrissent' ('Weavers who wet spun cotton yarn with pure water and who comb it'), *c.* 1780. This drawing, contemporary to the Montaran attempt to settle an Indian colony in France, shows the interest on the part of Europeans to learn how spinning and weaving were performed in India. It focuses on a little-known process that was unfamiliar to European spinners.

In Europe, fustian manufacturing became a proto-industrial activity developing strong links with national and international markets.[29] Spinning and weaving gave work in the countryside to vast numbers of women and men, who sold their products on the market (often through merchants), supplementing their earnings from agrarian occupations. Such earnings were spent on purchasing a variety of commodities, many of which were cotton textiles. In fact, people became quite willing to work more in order to have more money to spend on goods. Jan de Vries refers to this an 'industrious revolution', the expansion of production that is mediated by commercial incentives, relies on exchange and specialisation of production and fosters Smithian growth.[30]

Some of the conditions described by de Vries for Europe can also be found in the most commercialised areas of China. Although historians debate whether it is appropriate to talk about an industrious revolution in the case of Ming and early Qing China, there is sufficient evidence that specialisation of production and intensification of labour in rural households accompanied the expansion of cotton textile manufacturing in seventeenth- and eighteenth-century China.[31] Similar conditions seemed, however, to have produced different outcomes. Whilst de Vries claims that in Europe an industrious revolution 'preceded and prepared

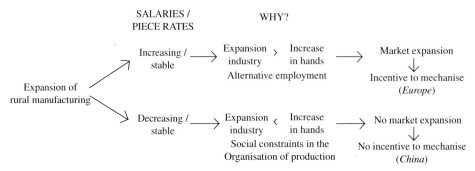

Figure 10.5 European 'industrious revolution' and Chinese 'commercial involution'.

the way for the Industrial Revolution', Bin Wong is adamant that in China an industrial revolution did not follow a possible industrious revolution.[32] In both cases one might expect labour to become increasingly scarce and more expensive as people opted for leisure rather than work. The difference between China and Europe is that China was characterised by a higher elasticity of labour supply (due to its enormous and increasing population) and that women, often relegated to the household, had few employment opportunities beyond domestic spinning and weaving.[33] In Europe, by contrast, earnings remained high (as the labour supply was not as elastic), possibly because a wider set of work opportunities were available, especially to women. Whilst Europe took the path of an industrious revolution in which more work expanded consumption and consequently extended the market, for China, Philip Huang talks about an 'involutionary commercialisation' in which market opportunities led to a diminishing marginal productivity, that is, for every additional hour of labour, the amount of product would diminish (Figure 10.5).[34] Whilst Europe developed a 'positive feedback' system, China seemed to have taken a 'negative feedback system' in which more work produced exploitation and poverty rather than consumption and prosperity.

These are hotly debated issues that it would be impossible to convey here in a nuanced way.[35] What is central, however, is that market expansion in Europe (people consuming more) created the context for product innovation (and linked with lags to process innovation). In China, by contrast, due to the fact that the expansion of the market was barely able to counteract demographic growth, consumers were not just increasingly poor but often regressing to self-production. This might partially explain why China moved away from rather than towards technological innovation and adoption. The Chinese treadle-operated three-spindle wheel used for cotton was never upgraded to a 32-spindle water-powered machine used already in the early fourteenth century for spinning hemp, a machine that, as Mark Elvin argues, bears uncanny resemblances with Arkwright's invention.[36]

The parallelism between Yuan, Ming and Qing China and early modern Europe is useful as it shows that technological invention per se is not sufficient to explain the rise of cotton textiles in Europe. The contrasting histories of China failing to diffuse an effective technology and Europe developing and putting to profit a similar technological solution (though nearly five centuries later) requires us to analyse the specific conditions that made China different from Europe. First, the household remained the main unit of production in China: based on kinship, family ties and a gendered division of labour, the Chinese household was both a mode of production and a social institution that justified manufacturing according to socio-cultural values as well as economic rationales.[37] The fact that by 1860 *circa* 45 per cent of all Chinese households wove cloth is indicative of the importance of how the domestic system shaped production. Kuhn concludes that the reason why large spinning machines did not diffuse in Ming China is that manufacturing remained centred on small units of production that required small spinning wheels operated by wives and daughters.[38] Water-powered hemp-spinning machines might have been technologically feasible also for cotton and economically more efficient than spinning wheels, but for the Chinese they were socially and culturally unacceptable and alien to how production was organised.

A second characteristic seems also to distinguish China from Europe: of all households spinning and weaving cotton in China in 1860, 80 per cent also cultivated substantial shares of the raw materials that they used.[39] The absence of an agrarian linkage in Europe between the cultivation and processing of textile fibres, particularly for cotton, allowed for an easier transition *away* from the rural household as a unit of production. There are always serious social and political costs to any major reconfiguration of modes of production. In Europe, for cotton these were minimal, not just because cotton was a new (and in many ways supplementary) material and product, but also because it had very limited linkages with the agrarian structure of cultivation. By the very virtue of being cultivated in a remote (and removed) location, cotton did not submit itself to the classic rules that connected agrarian production and rural textile manufacturing.

Competing with India: productivity

How and why an 'advanced organic economy' (based on wide commercialisation, intensification of handicraft labour and the use of organic energy resources) such as industrious Europe became an 'industrial inorganic economy' (based on industrial production and the use of inorganic energy resources) remains a puzzling and elusive problem for an economic history now becoming global in its aspirations.[40] It is not just a matter of shifting production to a higher plateau (in fact several times higher than traditional systems) but also a change in the way in which the entire economic system and its social underpinning functioned. One needs to consider the incentives that people had to create, foster and support change that are technological but also institutional, organisational, political and cultural. Incentives towards change are effective in a society that either (a) believes that what it is trying to achieve will be possible in the not too remote future (in time), or (b) that it is aware that others have already achieved it (in space).

A great deal of the literature has privileged the analysis of incentives 'in time' by creating chronological (and sometimes teleological) narratives of economic growth, development and modernisation. These narratives were often 'absolute' in the sense that they resolved themselves within the confines of Europe (and more often Britain), explaining what kind of incentives and processes were in operation and how these progressed over time. In effect, they treat the history of European economic development through technological change as normal and rational and ask why other areas of the world did not do the same.[41] Over the years, David Washbrook has been critical of the idea that industrial development should be treated as the yardstick through which to measure comparative economic performances at a global level. He criticises in particular the idea that India and other parts of the world should have followed the same (industrial) path of economic development to that of Europe.[42] Washbrook and other historians point to the fact that there was no specific reason why a prosperous and expanding Indian economy – a world leader in the production of cotton textiles – should have embarked on a search for new productive techniques. For a very long time, India's handicraft economy hardly appeared to need an industrial revolution.[43]

The opposite was true of Europe, where a cotton industry developed in a context of intense international competition and a clear sense of inferiority compared to Indian producers. The terms of the debate on how best – and even more importantly, if it was desirable – to develop cotton textile production in Europe were explicitly 'global'. For example, the textile producers and traders of Rouen – France's leading cotton centre in the mid eighteenth century – wrote a frank report underlining the weaknesses of the country's cotton industry compared to its Indian competitors. They evaluated the cost of some basic varieties of cottons produced in India and in France, and concluded that garats were on average 70 per cent more expensive in France, Guinea cloth was 30 to

40 per cent more, and even the basic baftas produced in Rouen were 20 per cent more expensive than those imported from India.[44] They proceeded to show that the cost of raw materials was high (over 40 per cent of the total cost of production compared to less than 25 per cent in India), and that the remainder of the cost was equally divided between spinning (roughly a quarter of the cost) and weaving.[45] If little could be done to obtain cheaper raw materials, then the only solution was to reduce the costs of manufacturing. They commented upon the role of the low wages of Indian craftsmen, explaining that 'these people do not have either luxury or ambition, and above all they are satisfied with rice for their diet'.[46] A similar argument was made in Britain when the petitioners for the ban on Asian cottons attributed the success of this imported cloth not to its beauty or fashionability but to the fact that it was produced by workers paid two pence a day and therefore was extremely cheap compared to any other British-produced cloth.[47]

The cost of labour for cotton textile production in Europe and India has been a thriving field for debate in recent years, with historians either confirming eighteenth-century views that Indian labour was cheap because living standards were low, or supporting a more optimistic view suggesting instead that real wages in India were not that different from those in Europe.[48] Focusing on labour can, however, be misleading because incentives towards creating labour-saving machines cannot offer a complete explanation for their development and diffusion. There is also little point in trying to resolve the explanation of technological transformation through a series of incentives without paying due attention to the context in which such inventions took place. Economic historians have underlined how successful technologies require suitable factor endowments and institutions that are conducive, as well as efficient factor and commodity markets.[49] Others have also pointed to the randomness of processes of technological innovation that do not respond to the logic of supply and demand.[50] There were long lags in development and diffusion. For instance, the power loom proved suitable only for coarser cloths until the 1840s, and only after the middle of the century did it come to be widely adopted for the weaving of higher-quality products.[51]

Socio-cultural contextualisation supplements human agency in explanatory models of technological innovation. These types of interpretations go back to the long-established tropes of the 'invention' and the 'inventor', though modern versions consider the wider realm of local and national 'cultures of invention' that are often both compared and connected to other world areas. This is the type of approach recently embraced by Joel Mokyr in his concept of an 'industrial enlightenment'. Mokyr claims the specificity of the cultural and intellectual milieu of eighteenth-century Britain in producing an unprecedented critical mass of inventors, scientists or simple technicians and underlines the linkages between inventors and entrepreneurs, as in the case of Peel supporting Hargreaves or earlier Touchet financing Wyatt and Paul. Mokyr draws on research on the character of institutions, scientific investigation and the cultural background of eighteenth-century Europe to argue for a particularly intense creation of 'useful and reliable knowledge' that found important economic applications.[52]

Although this socio-cultural contextualisation of knowledge production and its translation into economically useful applications is a welcome addition to debates over economic development, it presents two sets of problems. First, it tends to construct a case for traditional European British exceptionalism. Furthermore, it suggests that a set of cultural characteristics conducive to economic growth had evolved in the British Isles and that these characteristics were weaker in continental Europe or even weaker in India and China.[53] Such comparative conclusions are the subject of an ongoing discourse. Parthasarathi, for instance, maintains that the evolution of beliefs, cultures and clusters of institutions for the long-run accumulation of useful and reliable knowledge promoting technological innovation in the Indian subcontinent might have had similar features to that of Europe.[54] Second, by defending a claim for peculiarly British 'differences', the argument sidelines the profound connections between knowledge accumulation and experimentation in Europe and other parts of the world. We have seen in Chapter 8 the connections between the rise of calico printing in Europe and India, and further research has pointed to Europe's borrowing from Asia in the area of botany, medicine and ceramics manufacturing.[55]

The rise of a European industrial society was the result of a comparative understanding of the position of Europe in world markets and the admission of its relative backwardness evident for a long time in spinning, weaving and the printing of cottons. Moreover, it depended on the commerce, knowledge transfers and trade in raw material that came into existence between Europe and other parts of the world: a global dimension for the context of the rise of the cotton textile industry in the West.

Cotton and the Indian road to quality

Concerns over the productivity and competitiveness of European cotton textile manufacturing in the second half of the eighteenth century were of secondary importance compared to issues of quality. It was clear that for many decades both European consumers and potential customers in the Americas and Africa preferred Indian to European cotton textiles. It was not difficult to understand why: with the exception of some small manufacturing of pure cotton handkerchiefs in areas of Switzerland and Germany, the majority of European cotton production were mixes of cotton and linen (fustians) that were neither as soft nor as pure as cottons, nor did they take dyes as well. The problem was that before 1770 European hand and early machine spinning could not produce cotton yarn strong enough to be used as warps.[56] European producers had 'bastardised' the meaning of what a 'European' cotton textile might be by printing on white Indian cloth (as well as on linens and fustians), but this early form of import substitution was partial and limited.

There was a great deal of experimentation in response to this problem, and many failures. A report to the French government dated 1779 sadly observed that 'many manufactures of muslin that were established in the past have closed down because of the low quality of spinning. We have without success attempted to support them by using yarn imported from India together with French yarn; low count yarn with high count yarn; yarn of different quality and thickness that produced anything but imperfect results.'[57] The difficulty of creating cotton yarn of sufficient tensile strength was caused by the fact that it had to be of a constant thickness, something that Europeans did not seem to be able to achieve as easily as Indian spinners. That a mechanical device was seen as a possible response to improving the quality of yarn might come as a surprise when so much of the literature implies lower quality standards for machine-produced products.[58] Yet one of the achievements of the technologies invented in the classic period of the industrial revolution was that while they improved productivity, they also increased quality. This was the case for the many spinning machines, but also eventually for power looms (and the application of Jacquard punched cards), as well as machines for carding, finishing and ribbing of cloth.[59]

The search for more efficient forms of manufacturing was often connected to the improvement of quality. One of the many projects for developing cotton manufacturing in France, in this case the production of muslins in Nancy, made explicit the link between a relative concept of quality (measured against Indian products) and mechanical application when it explained that the aim of the venture was 'to produce yarn from which we can make muslin and *baptistes* comparable to the most beautiful [textiles] that come from the Indies, and that no mechanical device has been able to produce until today'.[60]

The argument that European mechanisation was strongly influenced by attempts to rival Indian products has been restored recently by Maxine Berg and Prasannan Parthasarathi. They propose quality and variety of production as key guiding principles for the development of an industry that from its early beginnings attempted to become competitive in global markets.[61] This is in line with trade theory that predicts an initiating stage of import substitution or

Figure 10.6 Richard Arkwright's water frame, *c.* 1775; a machine probably used in Arkwright's Cromford Mill at Matlock Bath in Derbyshire, England.

export competition, though it has to be later sustained by an expanding range of products. Contemporary sources made a similar kind of argument. For instance, Dorning Rasbotham, signing himself as 'the friend of the poor', observed as early as 1780 that in England 'the cotton manufacture is now almost a *new trade*. The fabrick, the quality of the goods we make, is amazingly *changed*. How many *new kinds of cloth* are made, in very great quantities, which could *not possibly*, have *been made*, at least in any quantity, or so cheap as to sell, without *machines*?'[62] He correctly pointed to the fact that a result of mechanisation had been an expansion of types of cottons manufactured in Europe: low-quality fustians soon gave way not just to hard-wearing pure cottons but also to more refined fabrics for clothing and furnishing and high-quality muslin.

The very story of Arkwright, the inventor of the water frame, is representative of this transition (Figure 10.6). His machine allowed yarn to be spun for warping, thus making it possible and economical to produce pure cottons. This explains why in 1774 Arkwright was keen to campaign for a repeal of the 1721 act that forbade the production and consumption of pure cottons in Britain, claiming that his machine now allowed for 'Goods so made wholly of Cotton' that were 'superior in Quality to the present Species of Cotton Goods made with Linen Yarn Warps'.[63]

Recent research by Knick Harley underlines how quality and cheapness went hand in hand: between the 1760s and the 1820s it was the price of fine yarn (100 counts twist) that declined more markedly than other (coarser) varieties. Machinery, while allowing for the spinning of all types of yarns at much cheaper prices than with a simple spinning wheel, was particularly cost-effective for the fine types of yarn and for the more expensive yarn used for warps.[64] The result was that in Britain it became particularly economical to produce the fine textiles (the most famous of which are muslin) that were in high demand in international markets.

If one follows the logic of quality, then the disjuncture between the history of calico printing and that of the mechanisation of spinning and weaving becomes less significant. The search for a quality to match Indian products persisted over long stretches of the eighteenth century, starting with the finishing stages (that were high value-added if not in terms of basic functions, then surely in terms of the visual appeal of the products) and continued with attempts to replace white Indian cottons (printed in Europe) with cloth spun and woven locally.[65] The miraculous spinning machines should therefore be seen as the final 'stage' of a process of development that began with the finishing end of production, a process that had already started before the end of the seventeenth century and which was most deeply influenced by Asian products and technologies. Taking the longer view of the history of cotton textiles allows us to appreciate not just the global nature of these processes, but also the incremental character of an industrial transition that is only partly to be explained by spinning and weaving technologies.

Comparing England and India

Although the earliest spinning machines (such as the jenny) were small enough to fit into domestic and proto-industrial settings, the invention of more complex technologies created the need to centralise production. Spinning in many ways followed the path that printing had foreshadowed a couple of generations earlier. In some cases, the capital necessary to set up large factories came from calico printers themselves. Fustian manufacturers and merchant-entrepreneurs were also keen to expand their activities by investing in new and costly cotton machinery and by building entirely new establishments.[66] Mechanisation was costly to achieve. At a time when production in India remained based on light looms and inexpensive spinning wheels, in Europe the increasing complexity of machines adopted to spin, weave and finish cottons was matched by the size of investments required. Already in the late 1780s (when the industry experienced its first crisis), it was observed that bankruptcies had become major destabilising events. At that time buildings and machinery in the British cotton industry were worth £2 million. Ten years later, at the turn of the century the industry's assets were estimated at £5 million and in 1830 at £15 million.[67]

The human scale of industry really impressed contemporaries even more than the machinery. The meaning of work in the English cotton mills was strikingly different to craft production. Visitors were amazed and horrified by the cotton factories employing hundreds and sometimes thousands of men, women and children, who lived in squalid conditions in sprawling urban conurbations that functioned as dormitories.[68] By 1841, Manchester had 128 cotton mills, twelve of which employed more than 500 workers each, the largest giving work to 1,300 people.[69] Looking at one of the cotton mills in Manchester, the American Benjamin Silliman claimed to regret 'the physical, and, more than all, the moral evils which they produce', but he was not 'disposed to join those who rail at manufactures without informing us how we can do without them'.[70] Concerns were raised over the conditions of workers, especially women and children living in the expanding industrial towns.[71]

If Indian cotton production had been based on weaving villages forming a mosaic of product specialisations with concentrations in certain areas of the subcontinent, the distinctiveness of the new European cotton industry was its incredible concentration. Already in 1811 more than 650 mills were active in a radius of 50 miles from the town of Bolton. Thirty years later, 70 per cent of the 1,105 cotton mills in Britain were located in Lancashire. In 1815, Manchester's 90 cotton mills gave work to 11,000 workers, a number that increased three-fold over the following quarter of a century.[72] Cotton took over an entire local economy, with more than a third of the Lancashire population finding work in the cotton industry between 1800 and 1840.[73] The application of steam power in the 1830s to replace water-powered machinery increased even more the concentration of cotton manufacturing in just a handful of localities in Lancashire. By 1838, Manchester, Oldham, Bury, Rochdale and Whalley had more than a hundred cotton factories each and accounted for nearly half of Britain's cotton production.[74]

Never before in the history of humankind had such a confined area produced for such a vast number of consumers across the world. Global production no longer depended on the number of workers, on millions of spinners and weavers busy manufacturing cloth with relatively simple tools. Industrial output became proportional to the power of machines not the number of hands employed (see Table 12.1 below). In England, the cotton mills never came to employ the millions of workers as cotton production did in India and China. Its rhythms of

Figure 2.1 Cotton textile fragment excavated in Old Fustat, fourteenth century.

Figure 2.2 Cotton cloth produced in Gujarat and traded to the Sulawesi islands, *c.* 1340.

Figure 2.4 Ceremonial hanging with a hunting scene, late seventeenth/eighteenth century.

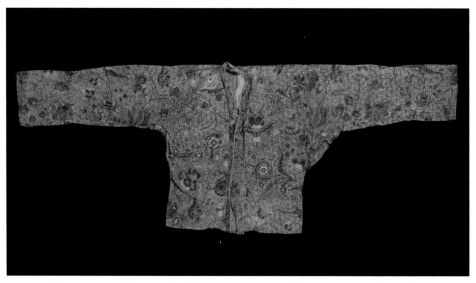

Figure 2.5 Jacket produced on the Coromandel coast, late eighteenth century, and tailored into a jacket in Sumatra.

Figure 2.6 Rai Surjan Hada, the ruler of Ranthambhor, northwest India, submitting to the Mughal emperor Akbar (r. 1556–1605) in 1569. This scene from the *Akbarnama* (*Book of Akbar*) was designed by the Mughal court artist Mukund and painted by Shankar. It shows the profusion of textiles used by the court.

Figure 2.7 Page from an album of sketches of costumes of south India, *c*. 1842.

(a)

(b)

Figures 3.2 (a and b) Ginning and bowing of cotton in India, 1851.

Figure 3.4 Spinning and weaving in India, 1851.

Figure 3.8 'Weaver Seated at a Loom', *c.* 1800–50.

Figure 4.1 Late nineteenth-century drawing of Kabir, poet and weaver.

Figure 4.2 Two Indian women winding cotton, early nineteenth century.

Figure 4.5 Blue and white linen and cotton towel produced in Italy, *c*. fifteenth century.

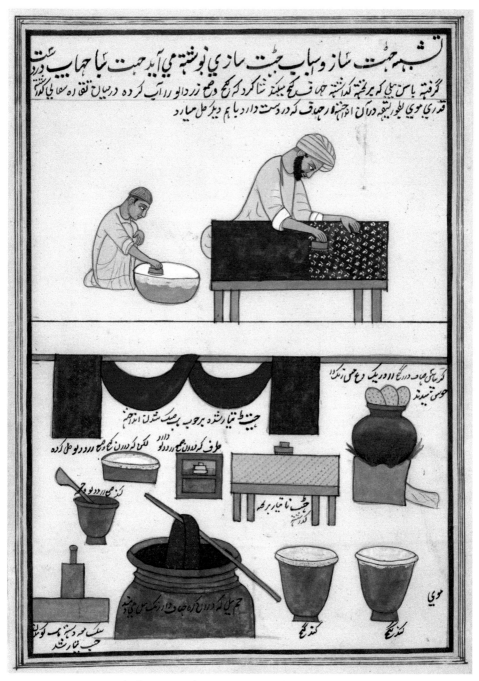

Figure 4.6 'Cloth Printer' from an album of Kashmiri trades, *c.* 1850–60. The inscriptions in Persian are the names of the implements used.

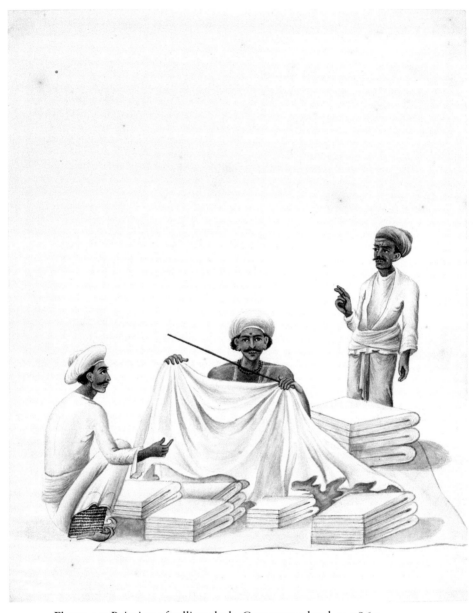

Figure 5.1 Painting of selling cloth. Company school, *c.* 1860.

Figure 5.2 Cotton coverlet embroidered with Tussar thread, produced in India, *c.* 1600. This is an example of a textile produced in India for the Portuguese and representing scenes from the Judgement of Solomon and the story of Judith and Holofernes, as well as hunting scenes with Portuguese. They were produced in Satgaon where the Portuguese were based between 1536 and 1632.

Figure 5.7 A cotton cloth preferred by Europeans. A woman's chintz jacket, *c.* 1725, produced on the Coromandel coast for the European market.

Figure 5.8 Part of a palampore, bedcover or hanging, produced on the Coromandel coast for the Indonesian Market and found in Sumatra, eighteenth century.

Figure 5.9 A large palampore produced on the Coromandel coast for the European Market, *c.* 1720–40.

Figure 5.10 Block-printed mezzaro inspired by Indian palampores, produced in Genoa, Italy, early nineteenth century.

Figure 6.5 Part of a palampore made of chintz produced on the Coromandel coast of India, possibly for the European market. The unusual design is inspired by a Japanese lacquerware or textile and shows a complex scene with flowers and swallows.

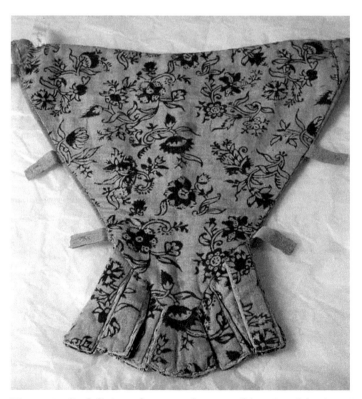

Figure 6.7 Back lining of a stomacher, possibly printed fustian, English, 1740s.

MOLLY MILTON, the PRETTY OYSTER WOMAN.

Figure 6.8 'Molly Milton, The Pretty Oyster Woman', hand-coloured mezzotint, London, 1788. At the centre of the image stands an oyster seller gaily dressed with a flat hat, possibly a printed cotton handkerchief, an apron over a quilted petticoat, and a dress with flowered patterns not dissimilar from those produced in Rouen and other European cotton centres in imitation of simple chintzes.

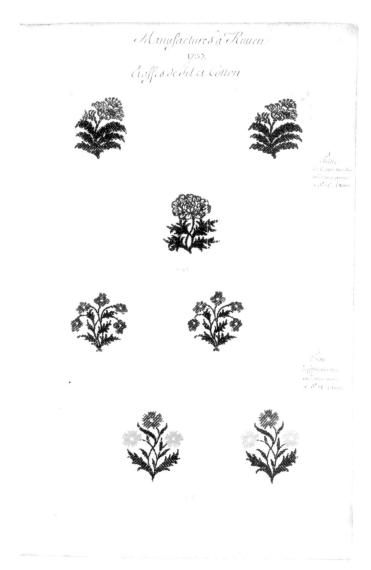

Figure 6.9 'Manufactures à Rouen. 1737. Etoffes de fil et cotton', page from the *Collection d'échantillons d'étoffes du Maréchal de Richelieu*. This page, which was collected for a survey of textile production in France and other European countries, shows a type of cotton linen textile (probably linen cloth embroidered in cotton with flowers) produced at Rouen. The flowered pattern is very similar to those on the dress of the English oyster seller.

Figure 6.10 (*left*) 'Silk Fringe', flowered silk with fly braid; (*right*) 'Flowered Cotton', a printed cotton. Both are textiles from the Foundling Hospital's admission books. The two textiles are visually similar but the one on the left cost a multiple of the cheap printed cotton. Cotton textiles achieved the same kind of naturalistic effect, though not the intensity and shine of colour of silks.

Figure 6.11 Hooded cape in black glazed cotton with Indian floral patterns and cotton linings. Southern France, *c.* 1790.

Figure 7.1 *African Woman* by Albert Eckhout (Brazil, 1641).

Figure 7.3 *De Chino, e India, Genizara* by Francisco Clapera (Mexico, *c.* 1780). The woman is spinning the cotton fibre from a basket with which the child is playing. The entire family wears white cotton cloth, possibly the result of household production.

Figure 7.4 *De Español y Negra, Mulato*, attributed to José de Alcíbar (c. 1760). The man is wearing a very elaborate banyan made of printed cotton probably from India. The woman is instead wearing what might be a striped cotton shawl.

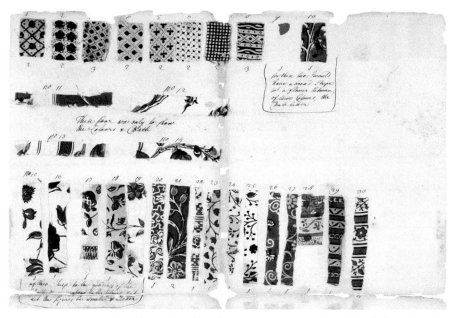

Figure 7.5 Textiles ordered by James Alexander of New York from David Barclay of London, 1726.

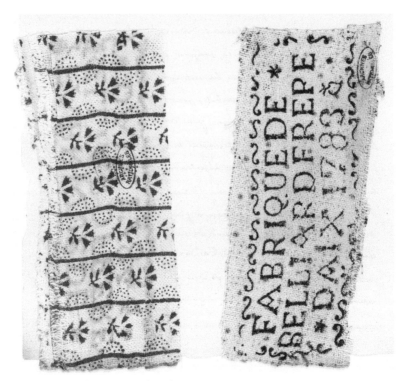

Figure 7.8 Indiennes produced at Dieppe, 1783.

Figure 7.9 Typical checks traded to Africa that were seized in Rouen, produced by a Tocqueville manufacturer, 1785.

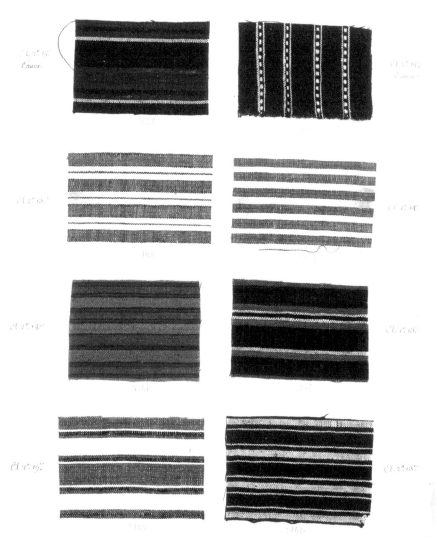

Figure 7.10 'Manufactures à Rouen. 1737. Siamoiserie', from the *Collection d'échantillons d'étoffes du Maréchal de Richelieu*. Collected for a survey of textile production in France and other European countries, this page shows a type of cotton-silk textile produced at Rouen.

Figure 8.1 'Les Travaux de la manufacture', toile produced by Oberkampf (1783). Vignettes represent the process of production of toiles by Oberkampf in his printworks in Jouy-en-Josas.

Figure 8.5 'Peintre sur toile'. Calico painter, probably from the Malabar coast of India, eighteenth century.

Figure 8.6 Fragment of a European printed cotton, *c.* 1660–1700. This early European printed textile lacks the beauty of colour of an Indian textile. Such textiles were also often inferior to the copies of Indian textiles produced in Iran and Anatolia.

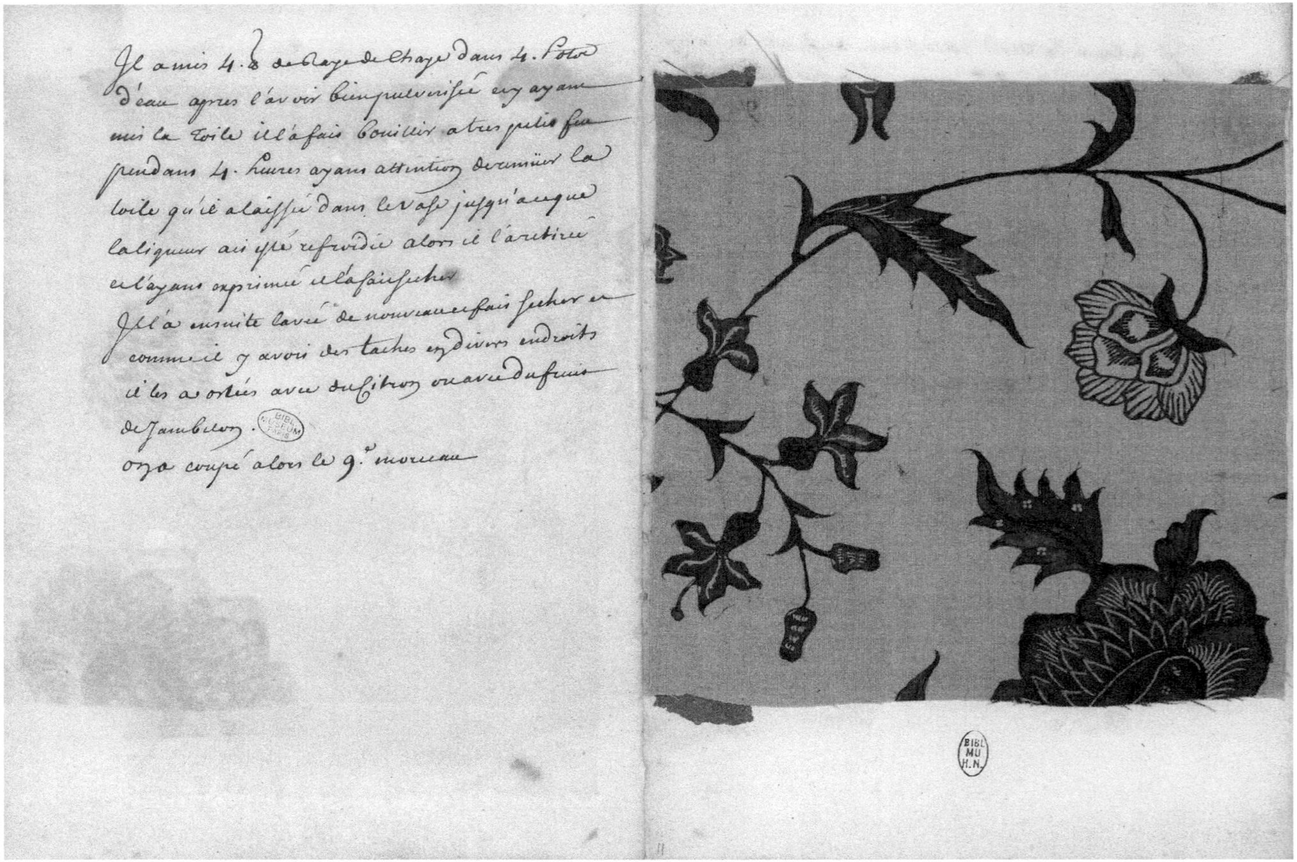

Figure 8.7 *Manière de fabriquer les toiles peintes dans l'Inde, telle que M. de Beaulieu, capitaine de vaisseau l'a fait exécuter devant lui à Pondichéry* (1734). Stage 9.

Figure 8.8 'Toilles de Cotton...Marseille 1736...Indiennes ou Guinées'. This page from the *Collection d'échantillons d'étoffes du Maréchal de Richelieu* shows a variety of cotton textiles printed in Marseille, ranging from imitations of Indian textiles to imitations of Ottoman cottons.

Figure 8.9 *Manufacture de tissu d'indienne des frères Wetter: atelier des ouvrières* by Joseph Gabriel Maria Rosetti (1764). This is one of four views of the calico-printing factory in Orange showing the large size of the premises and the considerable number of workers employed.

Figure 8.10 *The Factory at Jouy* by Jean-Baptiste Huet (1807), showing the large size of the printworks, which included several buildings and also a great deal of land.

Figure 8.12 Linen and cotton cloth printed from engraved copper plates and wood blocks and painted blue by Robert Jones & Co., Old Ford, Middlesex, England, 1769. Robert Jones was one of the major English calico printers. When he sold his business, in 1780, the printworks occupied 67 acres and the assets included 200 copper plates and 2,000 blocks and prints.

Figure 9.5 *At the Linen Market in Santo Domingo* by Augustin Brunias, *c.* 1775. Natives and free blacks are wearing white and striped cottons and linens, imported from either Europe or India.

Figure 9.7 *Cotton Plantation* by Charles Giroux, *c.* 1850s–60s.

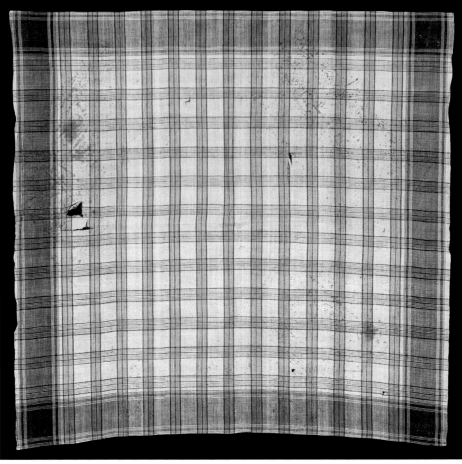

Figure 13.1 Cotton bandana with plaid of maroon and white, produced in India and probably worn in the United States, nineteenth century.

work were no longer determined by seasons or harvest conditions. British mills demanded and received enormous and stable supplies of raw cotton, whereas in India, failures of the monsoon affected the cotton supply and at times brought production to a halt.[75] For centuries, spinning had been dependent on the humidity in the air, which affected productivity according to place and season. Even calico printing, that in Europe most approximated an industrial system before the mid eighteenth century, was a seasonal activity, with little production being carried out in winter as good printing and painting could only be achieved in mild temperatures.[76] The incessant pace of factories are instead well known from early nineteenth-century parliamentary debates and the denunciations of the likes of Engels and Marx that convey also the truly new nature of industrial work: the continuity of production, the repetitiveness of actions and the constant flux of products created.

Two prints, just over fifty years apart, capture the nature of industrial change (Figures 10.7 and 10.8). One represents an Indian weaver intent at producing a cloth using a traditional pit loom. Although we must be aware of the artistic licence of this well-known print by Pierre Sonnerat dated 1782, it shows the simplicity of the tools of production and the individuality of work (though he might have been aided by a helper). By contrast, the 1840 print of Swainson Birley Cotton Mill in Lancashire represents a scene dominated by bulky machines contained in a large structure (in fact, a state-of-the-art building with cast-iron columns) in which the power is not that of the arms of a weaver but of the mechanical force provided by water and steam through a complex system of pulleys. Women now frequently supervise the work of machines in a process that is collective and organised according to pre-established rules.

Factories brought strict regulation of labour practices: rules on working hours, on expected productivity, on breaks and conduct. This signalled a distancing from any informal organisation based on familial practices and on the integration of manufacturing and other domestic activities. At the same time, regulation restructured established gendered notions of labour through a universal and pervasive deskilling of work.[77] This brought standardisation: the late eighteenth- and nineteenth-century cotton factories inaugurated a notion of production based on predictability and consistency over time. Unlike a putting-out system, the cloth's pattern, its finishing and quality were not left to the decision of individual producers.[78] The product of one factory might be indistinguishable from that of another (in fact the convergence of technological adoption helped this process) in a way quite dissimilar from the idiosyncratic production of individual Indian weavers that caused so much trouble for the European trading companies.

Pl. 22.   Voyage aux Indes et à la Chine, Tom. I. Pag. 105.

P. Sonnerat pinx.   Poisson Sc.

TISSERAN

Figure 10.7 Indian weaver from Pierre Sonnerat's *Voyage aux Indes Orientales et à la Chine* (1782). Although idealising the work of a weaver, it shows a lonely craftsman in charge of his own time and the making of the cloth.

Standardisation of working practices and of methods of manufacturing were finalised to achieve high levels of productivity. The factory distanced itself from division of labour based on skills (the female spinner and the male weaver; the different types of woven cloth, etc.) and geographical specialisation (with weaving villages specialising in particular types of cloth). It subsumed all processes within an integrated vision of manufacturing that was no longer dependent on the roles of head weavers, brokers and other middlemen, which characterised cotton textile production in India and China. In a factory, all activities were carried out within the confines of a single multi-storey building, with the physical

Figure 10.8 'View of Swainson Birley Cotton Mill' (1834). This is one of five prints from drawings by Thomas Allom representing a cotton mill near Preston in Lancashire, England. It shows both men and women amid large looms that set the pace and the type of production.

making of products taking place from floor to floor often starting on the top level and proceeding downwards as machinery became heavier (and therefore could not be located on high floors), ending with finished cloth ready to be packed and shipped out (Figure 10.9).[79]

In calico printing – an activity that became increasingly integrated within the overall process of cotton manufacturing – the application of roller printers was expensive and therefore was efficient only on large runs. Today, 300 yards to a colouring – the standard used until the end of the nineteenth century – is not necessarily considered a large-scale production, but this was a multiple of what was produced in one design or colour by an Indian artisan with a simple wooden block or even in Europe itself in the mid eighteenth century (Figures 10.10 and 10.11).

The American traveller Nathaniel Carter visiting cotton-printing establishments in the northwest of England commented that 'The process is simple and expeditious. Thousands of yards are printed in a day, with very little manual labour. The cloth passes through rollers, which are moved by steam and which feed themselves, taking the colouring matter from a trough beneath'.[80] Such an industrial system did not just produce large quantities of one design (relying

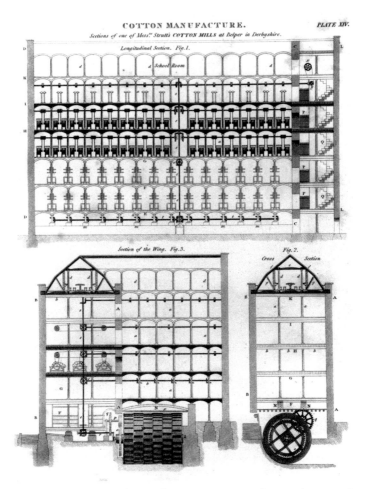

Figure 10.9 Sections of one of Strutt's cotton mills at Belper, Derbyshire, from Rees's *Cyclopaedia* (1819). This factory was initially built in 1789 and used Arkwright's water-frame machines ('F' in illustration, with carding machines above). A schoolroom was situated on the top floor. The building is still standing.

clearly on the size of the market on which to sell the final product) but several designs at the same time. It is difficult to say how many designs an Indian or Ottoman printer might have produced, but an average European cotton factory printed several hundred patterns at any one time.[81]

Indian artisans had operated for centuries within an aesthetic vocabulary that was the result of consolidated practices, access to specific skills and negotiations with middlemen and traders in the attempt to interpret the tastes of distant markets. Within the industrial system of Europe, design became the specialised

Figure 10.10 'Dye House', from the *New and Universal Dictionary of Arts and Sciences* by John Barrow, 1754. This print, eighty years earlier than the print room at Swainson Birley, shows how manual work was still central to printing and dying, with technologies limited to basic equipment such as wooden and brick vats.

Figure 10.11 'View of the print room at Swainson Birley Cotton Mill', 1834. This is one of five prints from drawings by Thomas Allom representing a cotton mill near Preston in Lancashire. It shows the centrality of roller printing technology and the high volumes of production.

work of an artist-engraver, not the artisan-worker.[82] The case of design and printing is an example of the logic dominating an industrial system of production. Business success was no longer determined by a distinctive set of skills or one's reputation, as it might have been for an Indian or eighteenth-century European craftsman. It was instead the protection of rights to exploit one's means of production and products that provided competitive advantages. In the case of calico printing, this was achieved through the protection of design itself with campaigns, first in England and then in France, to secure the right to safeguard design for a certain amount of time (three or six months).[83] This made it possible for those who had invested in the creation and marketing of new patterns to legally retain the right to exploit them against all those imitators who could otherwise steal them 'through a [shop] window, without cutting out a pane of glass', as one contemporary put it.[84] The protection of 'invention' – either in the form of design or machinery – became a distinctive feature of a regime of clear property rights.[85]

Such rights were not given forever: as a design was protected for a few months, most technological innovations were patented for a period of seven years, after which they could be used freely. Yet the setting of a temporal framework for exploitation ensured that new inventions would replace existing ones even before their 'expiry date'. There is a temporal dimension to industrial capitalism that is difficult to convey. Even without falling into the cliché of static pre-industrial practices, mechanised industrial production encapsulated unprecedented dynamism: factories were described as mushrooming overnight, products were constantly changing, workers were shifting in and out of jobs. This became an unstable world for entrepreneurs, workers and consumers alike, but a world, however, in which the future would be one of growth and development in the West and deindustrialisation in Asia.

Britain and continental Europe

Throughout most of the eighteenth century and even well into the 1780s the cotton textile outputs of France and Spain were not quantitatively very different from the English.[86] In 1784, for instance, Barcelona manufactured more printed calicoes than the entire British Isles.[87] The industry had developed thanks to French capital; several important establishments appeared from the late 1730s onwards, such as the famous Esteve Canals founded in 1738.[88] By the mid 1750s there were at least twenty cotton manufactures in Barcelona, all of which had *privilegios* (royal privileges), initially selling to internal markets and in the

Mediterranean and after the mid-century expanding their business to the Spanish Empire in Latin America.[89] France, too, as we have seen, had a prosperous cotton industry selling to African markets, and its calico-printing industry could sometime rival its English counterpart.[90]

Cotton textile industries evolved more slowly in other European countries. In Portugal, textile manufacturers started producing cottons in the 1780s by using raw cotton from Brazil, having banned the import of British cotton textiles.[91] In Italy, from the 1760s onwards attempts were made to replace the import of French and Swiss fustians in cities such as Rome and Milan.[92] Similar initiatives were taken in Germany and central Europe, where the Habsburg monarchy encouraged both the printing and manufacturing of cottons for internal consumption and export to the Near East and Latin America.[93]

Technological innovation played against European continental cotton manufacturing, however. The French cotton industry developed slowly during the 1770s and 1780s, at a time when the English industry boomed.[94] By the time of the Anglo-French treaty of commerce of 1786 (the so-called Eden Treaty), Britain was confident that its cotton industry was far more competitive than the French, noticing that as far as cottons were concerned, 'there is nothing to be apprehended from a Competition with the French Manufacturers in these Articles'.[95] Three years later, at the eve of the French Revolution, France had 900 jennies compared to a staggering 20,000 in Britain.[96]

Anglo–French comparisons have been the hobby horse of economic historians, with many arguing that obsolete *Ancien Régime* French economic rules, lack of entrepreneurialism (especially among the wealthy classes) and cheap labour discouraged industrialisation and the adoption of new capital-intensive forms of machinery and organisations of production. Yet, when we look at the wider picture, France does not appear to be as different from England as it has been argued. The Gallic country seemed to have too many inventors rather than a lack of mechanical genius. Similarly to inventors in Britain, several of them claimed to have invented machinery that would produce not just more but better quality yarn: this was the case of the cleric Père Perronié of Lyon, who claimed to have invented a machine to spin several strands of yarn of the same thickness; of an *inspecteur des manufactures* of Nîmes; of a clock-maker of Aubusson; of a Spaniard living in Lyon; or of the '*moulin à filer le cotton*' invented in 1756 by a certain Lafau of Lyon that Holker himself certified as properly working.[97]

Results were perhaps not as encouraging as in Britain.[98] This was a fact observed at the time and that partially explains why the French state was keen to spy, copy and steal the latest English technological inventions in textile manufacturing.[99] It also sent administrators and adventurers to Britain on fact-finding missions to collect precious information on the productivity of cotton mills, the cost of spinning and the size of manufacturing.[100] France received (and welcomed) an endless flux of English workmen, who claimed to be the carriers of new technologies for the processing of cotton. These included John and James Milne from Manchester, who arrived in France in 1779 and asked half a million livres (eventually they contented themselves with 60,000 livres) for a variation on the Hargreaves machine; or Henry Sykes, who probably arrived in France in 1792 and established the first hydraulic spinning mill. Others, such as the Scotsman John MacWilliam, did not claim technological knowledge, but sold their technical expertise.[101] In fact, the number of English inventors and skilled workers arriving in France was so high that a senior French civil servant complained about 'the multitude of Englishmen who came to our country to propose the erection of mechanical devices for carding and spinning cotton', adding that 'we have too easily believed them and the majority of them deceived us, because our machines do not produce anything near the results promised'.[102]

By the late 1780s the difficulty of developing mechanised production had become coupled with political uncertainty, first in France and in the following decade across continental Europe. Whilst during the period 1792 to 1815 England enjoyed economic prosperity, continental Europe experienced instead great political turmoil and economic upheavals. The French economy suffered first from the revolutionary and terror periods and later from Napoleon's expensive imperial projects. In the midst of such upheavals, the French cotton manufacturing and printing industries were almost wiped out. Flanders, Holland and Germany also suffered the loss of major international markets for their linens, cottons and woollens, such as those of Latin America, which was blockaded by the English.[103]

For a long time historians have explained industrialisation as the process by which European countries and later extra-European nations (the United States, Japan and eventually India) first came to adopt industry and mechanised production. This is a diffusionist model of the British industrial revolution that has been criticised, not least because there seems to be little point in repeating what someone else has already done. It should be also underlined that it was difficult to repeat Britain's economic performances simply because of the advantage that Albion had acquired by virtue of being the 'first mover'. Attempts to develop mechanised spinning in continental Europe, for example, ran into trouble when the final product had to compete against British yarn and cloth. This was the case for France, where it was only under the protection of the 1806 ban on the import of British yarn that mechanised spinning developed.[104] Conversely, when Portugal lifted the ban on the import of British products with the Tratado de

Comércio e Navegação of 1810, its cotton industry entered a phase of decline. Unable to compete with British products, export dropped dramatically and by the 1840s Portugal imported ten times more cloth from Britain than the cloth it exported.[105] The same happened in Ireland, where by 1830 the local cotton industry had been wiped out by the competition of Lancashire mills.[106]

Conclusion

Mechanisation and industrialisation remain important elements of a narrative of economic growth based on cotton. Rather than explaining the rise of mechanised and industrialised production in Europe as a story of wilful achievement, this chapter has underlined the weaknesses that made technological innovation an essential tool for Europe to compete in what was a new economic sector. Competitiveness was identified in terms of productivity and quality and was measured against Indian production and finished products. I have also underlined how the adoption of new technologies was not unavoidable, as there was nothing to suggest that India or other parts of the world were on the way to adopting machines similar to Europe's. The European reconfiguration of cotton manufacturing entirely changed the meaning of production and the role of the producer. It changed the relationship between labour, capital and land, creating an industry that was totally removed from agrarian practices, domestic labour and craftsmanship. These are aspects worth underlining as much as technological invention itself. Finally, we are left with the problem of 'why England first'; a thorny issue that has been here explained not so much in terms of Britain being *exceptional*, but more in terms of Britain being *extreme* in some of the characteristics that existed elsewhere in Europe and other parts of the world.

11 'THE WOLF IN SHEEP'S CLOTHING': THE POTENTIAL OF COTTON

Aesop's wolf in sheep's clothing is a well-known fable of a wolf that having disguised herself in the fleece of one of her prey, 'whole flocks destroys'.[1] Aesop tells a story of deception and devastation that ultimately ends with the wolf being brought to justice. Aesop's tale had great resonance among early modern Europeans, for whom a sheep's fleece was more than a captivating prop for a moral fairy tale. The entire European woollen industry depended on the sheep's fleece, and an eighteenth-century British commentator observed that 'every wilful attempt to supplant or debase it, is an act of treason against the State'.[2] In this story the wolf – cotton – degraded the rules that dominated the moral economy of pre-industrial Europe, opening the doors for an unprecedented growth that extended way beyond the limits that fibres such as wool, flax, hemp and silk had long imposed on the industrial development of the West.

Yet there is one important difference between the story of cotton and that of the wolf. Unlike Aesop's wolf, the ascendancy of western cotton textiles was not halted. The industry displayed a vitality that no creature – however mythical – could possibly embody. Cotton, a fibre that in the mid eighteenth century accounted for a tiny percentage of Europe's textile production, by the early decades of the following century became the most important textile in the West, characterised by new mechanised and urbanised structures of production. Historically, no other area had ever so radically changed its manufacturing economy, transforming a previously minor sector into the largest of its industries. In Britain, where cotton had accounted for just 2.6 per cent of value added in industry in 1770, by 1831 it had reached 22.4 per cent.[3] Over the seventy years classically defined as 'the industrial revolution' (1760–1830), cotton production had increased at rates at least double that of other sectors of the British economy, especially in the 1780s following the introduction of innovative machinery in spinning.[4]

The Wolf in Sheeps Clothing. 23

A subtile Wolfe, more safty to betray,
In a sheepes Clothing does himselfe aray ,
And unexpected now whole flocks destroys,
Till a kind halter ends his stoln joys .

Morall

The zealous Cheat has wrought the land more woe,
Than bare fac'd villainie coud ever doe ,

Figure 11.1 'The Wolf in Sheep's Clothing', from *Aesop's Fables* (1703).

This chapter asks two questions: why was cotton and not another fibre to create such momentous change; and secondly, why did such change happen first in England and not somewhere else in Europe or outside Europe? I put forward the argument that the potential for mechanisation was embodied in the fibre and for a time – possibly the best of half a century – only in the cotton fibre. I call this the 'ecological potential' of the cotton fibre, a factor in industrialisation that has received little attention.[5] Yet, this potential was not unrestrained. The space given to cotton as a new fibre in Europe differed noticeably from state to state. I argue here that the specific political economy of textiles (mostly the complex relationship between cotton and the established

European fibres – namely wool and flax) created a set of conditions for cotton to find inroads into the British manufacturing economy. The chapter concludes by addressing the issue of supplies of raw materials in a period of enormous demand by showing how elastic supplies of raw cotton from the Americas came again to favour the British Isles.

A woollen industrial revolution

In 1751 a committee of the House of Commons concluded that cotton was 'only a temporary Thing'.[6] Cotton was seen as a cheap substitute for flax, which was becoming increasingly expensive. Cotton turned out, however, to be a permanent feature of most European economies and a major cause of momentous industrial change. In Britain between 1785 and 1830, cotton textile production expanded thirtyfold. The workforce employed in this industry was as large as 800,000 already in 1806. Thanks to cotton, small villages such as Bolton, Oldham and Manchester had by the 1820s grown to become large industrial towns. This was just the beginning, as the industry doubled in size in the 1820s and again in the 1830s. By the 1840s several continental European countries boasted similar rates of expansion in their cotton industries.

The elasticity of raw material supplies from the Americas allowed the industry to develop at a uniquely rapid rate without substantial real price increases for raw cotton fibres.[7] Cotton was not a free good. It was produced by a complex system for the exploitation of labour and land. Both these factors were, however, external to Europe. It is this specific feature that explains a great deal of the success of cotton. But how successful were cotton and the cotton industry in general? There are two ways to respond to this question: one might either present figures of what happened or elaborate upon a counterfactual world in which cotton did not exist at all or in which it was not produced in the Americas but in Europe. Counterfactual scenarios allow us to assess what I call the 'potential' of cotton fibres.

Let us consider a counterfactual world in which the industrial revolution was based on woollen textiles rather than cottons. What could the situation have been in 1820 if cotton was not available but consumers desired to purchase a volume of woollen cloth equivalent to the cotton textiles sold in that year?[8] How many million acres of land would have been necessary to feed a sufficient number of sheep to produce enough wool to replace cotton? In 1820, 11.8 million acres of land would have been needed to feed 38.2 million sheep to produce 136 million pounds of woollen yarn (Table 11.1). This implies more than doubling the number of sheep and using 62 per cent of all British cultivable land for their

Table 11.1 *British 'ghost acreages' for replacing cotton with wool, 1780–1850.*

| | Raw cotton | Land | | Sheep | |
	Imported into Britain (in million lb)	Million of 'ghost acreages' required to obtain an amount of wool yarn equivalent to imported cotton yarn	Percentage of UK agricultural area to be given to sheep pasture	Million of animals necessary to produce an equivalent amount of wool	Extra percentage necessary to substitute wool for cotton
1780	7	0.5	3	1.8	*10*
1790	31	2.4	13	7.8	*35*
1800	56	4.3	24	14.2	*53*
1810	132	10.3	54	33.4	*125*
1820	151	11.8	62	38.2	*153*
1830	238	18.6	84	60.3	*240*
1840	576	45.0	204	145.8	*600*
1850	663	51.8	235	167.8	*600*

Notes: Calculations based on the assumption that each acre of land can sustain 4.5 sheep and that the average production of wool per sheep is 3.95 pounds per year (and that therefore each acre of land 'produces' 17.25 pounds of wool a year). Estimates by the author in italics.
Sources: Giorgio Riello, 'Counting Sheep: A Global Perspective on Wool, 1800–2000', in Giovanni Luigi Fontana and Gérard Gayot, eds., *Wool: Products and Markets, 13th–20th Century* (Padua: Cleup, 2004), pp. 103–31 and table 9.1; Peter J. Bowden, 'Wool Supply and the Woollen Industry', *EHR* 9/1 (1956): 45 and 48; Kenneth Pomeranz, *The Great Divergence: Europe, China, and the Making of the Modern World Economy* (Princeton University Press, 2000), p. 277.

pasture. Twenty years later, in 1850, Britain would have needed 167 million sheep (six times as many sheep as it actually had) and more than double of all its total land to produce enough cloth. There would have been no space for either people or factories. Even when we scale up these calculations at a European level, the figures remain impressive. In 1850, Europe would have had to find space for double the number of sheep that the continent had (*c.* 183 million) just to produce enough woollen cloth for Britain to replace cotton production.[9]

Prospects for developing wool textile production at any sustained level in the long term were limited. Development based on woollen textiles could only happen slowly and by relying on external sources of supply for wool. There is a substantial difference between an animal and a vegetable fibre. To produce a pound of animal fibre requires an input of energy way in excess of the energy required to produce the same weight of vegetable fibre. Animals, acting as secondary energy converters, dissipate a high percentage of energy in the process.[10] Wool requires roughly twelve times more land than cotton to produce a unit of fibre. In these terms, the European drive to develop cotton textile production had much less to do with taste and consumer desires than the fact that in order to clothe an increasing population the solution was to switch from a high energy-intensive fibre (wool) to a low energy-intensive fibre (cotton).

A similar kind of ecological explanation has been adopted to explain the industrial revolution as a shift in the energy system from an organic economy (based on wood, wind and animal power) to an inorganic economy (based on coal and steam).[11] These shifts to coal and cotton helped to solve what Paolo Malanima calls the 'environmental resistance to growth' in Europe.[12] Given its demographic expansion, Europe simply had to find the resources to feed and clothe its population.

The problem with these types of counterfactual histories is that they tend to miss factors operating on a global scale. For example, cotton allowed the West not only to clothe its increasing share of the population but also to sell large quantities of textiles to the world. The staple European textile product, woollens, characterised by high cost of production, high profits per yard and relatively small quantities traded, was unsuitable to satisfy popular markets across the globe. Cottons, instead, with their lower cost of production, low profits per yard and higher quantities traded, had extraordinary potential for global trade. This difference between cottons and woollens had been evident throughout the seventeenth and eighteenth centuries, when the success of Asian cottons in Europe and the Atlantic was not matched by a similar success of woollens on Asian markets. Moreover, Europe's concentration on woollen textiles would have created an unprecedented and unsustainable pressure to switch arable to pastoral land. The impact on the existing agrarian economy of western Europe could have been profound. As late as the 1840s, more than 90 per cent of all wool used in European textile manufacturing was produced within the continent, even as the vast interior of Australia and the less hospitable African Cape were becoming major sources of wool for European woollen and worsted production.

Counterfactually, the great plains of North America might have sustained vast flocks of sheep.[13] This is an appealing but improbable scenario. Sheep flocks were introduced to New England in the late seventeenth century and merino breed sheep in the early nineteenth century, but the quantity of the wool produced remained low.[14] The cold American winters were not conducive to sheep. Moreover, in the early nineteenth century the great plains of the United States were not yet settled by westerners. The number of both sheep and cattle remained limited until the adoption of iron and barbed wire in the 1860s and 1870s substantially decreased the cost of fencing, allowing for better monitoring

Table 11.2 *Decennial increase in raw material production: cotton and wool, 1800–1900 (percentage per decade).*

	American cotton	Australian wool
1801–10	77	–
1811–20	97	–
1821–30	94	–
1831–40	67	–
1841–50	52	127
1851–60	37	111
1861–70	4 (US Civil War)	102
1871–80	133	48
1881–90	66	60
1891–1900	20	–26

Sources: Giorgio Riello, 'Counting Sheep: A Global Perspective on Wool, 1800–2000', in Giovanni Luigi Fontana and Gérard Gayot, eds., *Wool: Products and Markets, 13th–20th Century* (Padua: Cleup, 2004), pp. 103–31; Barbara Gaye Jaquay, 'The Caribbean Cotton Production: An Historical Geography of the Region's Mysterious Crop', unpublished PhD thesis, Texas A&M University, 1997, pp. 99–100.

of animals and for an improvement in selective breeding.[15] This, together with the 1862 Homestead Settlement Act, expanded cattle in the area from Montana and North Dakota in the north and from Oklahoma and east Texas in the south.[16] It was, however, a late territorial expansion and still in the 1880s the sheep and goat population of North America was just over 45 million, compared to more than 120 million in Europe.[17] By contrast, southern states facing the Atlantic, where cotton cultivation expanded in the early decades of the nineteenth century, had been colonised for centuries.

Australia enjoyed real natural advantages for the breeding of sheep. Its enormous untapped natural resources of grassland could be used for the extensive breeding of relatively inefficient converters of grass to wool. Climatic and labour conditions explain why wool became a comparative advantage for Australia.[18] From the introduction of merino wool from South Africa in 1797, Australian production of raw wool grew rapidly, especially in the thirty years between 1840 and 1870, and serviced the restoration of the wool textile industry in Europe.[19] But the rate of growth decelerated after 1871 because sheep are not only inefficient energy converters, but by acting as additional converters over the natural world (photosynthesis), their energy per unit of time is low (Table 11.2). This means that elasticity of supply in the physical production of most vegetable fibres is

Table 11.3 *European 'ghost acreages' for replacing cotton with linen, 1830–80.*

	Cotton	Land		Labour	
	Estimated European cotton cloth production (in million yards)	Thousands of 'ghost acreages' to obtain an amount of linen equivalent to cotton cloth	Percentage of the European agricultural land to be given to flax cultivation	Thousands of 'ghost cultivators' employed in growing flax	Percentage of the agrarian population of Europe to be employed in flax cultivation
1830	1,094	*1,553*	0.4	*621*	*1.3*
1840	1,993	*2,830*	0.7	*1,132*	*2.2*
1850	2,814	*4,001*	0.9	*1,600*	*2.9*
1860	5,208	*7,395*	1.6	*2,958*	*4.5*
1870	5,300	*7,526*	1.5	*3,010*	*5.0*
1880	7,178	*10,192*	1.9	*4,077*	*6.3*

Notes: Calculations based on 3 yards of cotton cloth per pound of cotton. Average cultivation of 2.5 acres of flax per person for a total production of around 600 pounds of flax a year. One pound of flax produced in the early nineteenth century 1.75 yards of linen cloth and that 1 pound of raw cotton produced between 2.82 and 3.50 yards of cotton yarn on average. Estimates by the author are in italics.
Sources: Elizabeth B. Schumpeter, *English Overseas Trade Statistics, 1697–1808* (Oxford: Clarendon Press, 1960), table 16; Michael G. Mullhall, *The Dictionary of Statistics*, 4th edn (London: Routledge, 1909), pp. 7, 156 and 280; Barbara Gaye Jaquay, 'The Caribbean Cotton Production: An Historical Geography of the Region's Mysterious Crop', unpublished PhD thesis, Texas A&M University, 1997, p. 88.

higher than that of an animal fibre. Supplies of raw cotton could increase much faster and for a much longer period than supplies of raw wool.

A linen revolution

Let us now imagine a world in which Europe opted to expand its linen production instead of relying on cottons. In many ways, this is a more realistic counterfactual than one based on wool, because European cotton textile manufacturing emerged from the production of textile mixes of flax and cotton (fustians). Moreover, the material properties of light, printed cottons were similar to those of plain and printed linens. The counterfactual argument is ostensibly realistic (Table 11.3).[20]

In 1880, when the European cotton industry operated on a massive scale, to replace cotton with linen would have led to a relocation of less than 2 per cent (10 million acres) of the continent's arable land to flax cultivation. This is not an unimaginable scenario. By mid century, Russia was already producing

Figure 11.2 'Common method of beetling, scutching and hackling the flax' (1791).

huge quantities of flax, with more than 3 million acres of land given to the cultivation of the crop.[21] Furthermore, this counterfactual reveals that before the mid nineteenth century only a very small percentage of the agrarian population would have been used for flax cultivation. Since most flax was produced in Russia where neither land nor agrarian labour were scarce, the possibility of an expansion of European textile production based on linen does not seem improbable.

But why didn't Russia become a world supplier of flax in the same way in which the Americas became for cotton and Australia for wool? The explanation is to be found not so much in the cultivation of flax, but in its processing. The processing of flax required an enormous input of labour (Figure 11.2). Linen production had given work to substantial numbers of households in many proto-industrial areas of Europe because of its labour intensity. The productive process was relatively simple. It was cumbersome but suitable for the employment of the poorer classes, who were employed to weed and crop flax and also to break, scrutch, twist, shake, beat, 'hackle' (remove residual tow, gum and resin) and supervise the 'retting' or putrefaction of the fibre.[22] Some technological improvements diffused, such as the introduction of chloride processes for bleaching as first performed in Ireland in the 1760s, but until the second half of the nineteenth century, the linen industry remained extremely labour-intensive. It was only with the introduction of the chemical processing of the fibre that a great deal of labour could be released.

Yet, and notwithstanding its labour intensity, the linen industry expanded enormously over the seventeenth and eighteenth centuries.[23] In England, the total consumption of linen nearly doubled over the half a century between 1730 and 1780.[24] Irish and later Scottish linen production boomed.[25] The sector was at the core of European proto-industrialisation, with key areas of the continent developing household linen processing, spinning and weaving for sale to distant markets.[26] Before the revolution in cotton came a linen proto-industrial revolution: entire households were engaged in linen manufacturing, with linen itself becoming one of the main items of consumer expenditure during the period that Jan de Vries has defined as an 'industrious revolution'.[27] Nevertheless, there were signs that the intensification of work (both in cultivation and processing of the material) ran into diminishing returns when spinners' wages increased substantially over the seventeenth and eighteenth centuries.[28] The story of linen is one of labour intensification and a path of Smithian growth based on trade along which it might have continued but for its particular position in the political economy of European textile production and commerce.[29]

Cotton in Europe

Our final counterfactual is a world in which climate and soils allowed for cotton to be cultivated anywhere on earth. Since we have better quantitative data for Britain than other European nations, I will focus on the British Isles and posit local cotton cultivation which would – *ceteris paribus* – be feasible because of the 25 per cent price differential caused by the cost of shipping and taxation between the Americas and Britain. Table 11.4 simply takes the quantities of cotton that were imported into Britain and calculates their potential impact on British agriculture. In 1820, *circa* 1.3 million acres of arable land would have been needed in Britain to produce 151 million pounds of cotton. The numbers imply that 7.1 per cent of the British cultivable land had to be relocated to cotton cultivation. If cultivation had been spread throughout Europe, it would have taken just 0.4 per cent of the total European arable land. Twenty years

Table 11.4 *Labour and land impact of the cotton imported into Britain,* *1780–1850.*

	Raw cotton		Land	
	Million pounds imported into Britain	Thousands of workers employed to cultivate cotton in the Americas and Levant	Thousands of acres of land for the cultivation of cotton in the Americas and Levant	Percentage of Britain's agricultural area to be given to cotton cultivation
1780	7	58	62	0.3
1790	31	258	277	1.5
1800	56	337	500	2.7
1810	132	528	1,179	6.6
1820	151	539	1,348	7.1
1830	238	850	2,125	10.6
1840	576	1,704	5,142	23.4
1850	663	1,894	5,919	26.9

Sources: Michael G. Mullhall, *The Dictionary of Statistics*, 4th edn (London: Routledge, 1909), pp. 7–9, 157; Kenneth Pomeranz, *The Great Divergence: China, Europe and the Making of the Modern World Economy* (Princeton University Press, 2000), pp. 276 and 315; Elizabeth B. Schumpeter, *English Overseas Trade Statistics, 1697–1808* (Oxford: Clarendon Press, 1960), table 16; Barbara Gaye Jaquay, 'The Caribbean Cotton Production: An Historical Geography of the Region's Mysterious Crop', unpublished PhD Thesis, Texas A&M University, 1997, p. 88; David Eltis, *Economic Growth and the Ending of the Transatlantic Slave Trade* (Oxford University Press, 1989), p. 189.

later, the production of 663 million pounds of cotton would have occupied a quarter of all arable land in England, or just under 2 per cent of the continent's cultivable land.[30]

These are counterfactual figures as cotton could not be grown in Europe, but they reveal that cotton production is not very land-intensive. If the climate and soils allowed its cultivation in Europe, the Americas would have probably never developed cotton cultivation. However, our counterfactual scenario should also consider labour. I have taken 250 pounds of cotton to be the average production per slave in the Americas in 1810 and factored in changing output per slave over the period considered.[31] These figures neglect technological improvements (for instance, Whitney's gin) and therefore probably overestimate the number of slaves employed in cotton cultivation. However, this counterfactual is useful as it shows the scale of labour involved.[32] In 1850, Britain would have basically needed slightly fewer than 2 million people (possibly labourers as slavery disappeared from Europe in the eighteenth century) out of a total population of *circa*

28 million to cultivate cotton.[33] Considering that Britain consumed half of all the cotton entering Europe at this time, up to 4 million cultivators (*c.* 8 per cent of the continent's agricultural population) would have been needed among the European peasantry to provide the continent with enough raw material to feed this growing industry.[34]

These figures are hypothetical, because even in a scenario in which cotton was a European crop, at a certain point it would have become more efficient to import cotton from somewhere else. The overall message is that the scale of production would have severely affected the European agrarian system, leading not so much to the need for more land, but for more hands to plant, grow, collect and process raw cotton. The transition of Europe from an agrarian to an industrial society could only have been slower, restricted as it would have been by the limited availability of land and labour.

The political economy of textiles

Counterfactuals provide a good idea of the scale of possible change. Yet historical change is conditioned by contingent factors. I focus here on the pressures created by existing interests in textile manufacturing in Europe. We have already seen how the woollen and silk lobbies fought against Asian cottons in the early eighteenth century. Strong anti-cotton coalitions were present in many European countries when their states perceived that the new material and commodity disrupted and destabilised traditional patterns of textile production and trade based on woollens and linens. Yet, notwithstanding a widespread anxiety towards cottons, Europeans did not display a uniformity of political and economic responses to the new fibre. Instead we observe disparity in the conditions in different countries that led to variations in incentives to engage with the cotton fibre. More than for any other European country, the political and economic situation concerning textile production and consumption in the British Isles created incentives to engage with a new and foreign fibre such as cotton. The peculiarity of the British Isles is that it excelled in the production and trade of woollens, but its success with the domestic production of linens was limited. This was not the case in most of continental Europe, where woollen and linen production went hand in hand. One might take France, Britain's arch-rival in the eighteenth century, as an example, to observe a great disparity between the two nations (Table 11.5). The British production of woollens was nearly double that of France, but its production of linens was not even half.[35] This marked difference is reflected in the British balance of trade throughout the eighteenth century, when woollens were the country's most

Table 11.5 *Estimated value of the production of woollens and linens in France and Britain, c. 1790 (in million pounds sterling).*

	France	Britain
Woollens	10.25	19
Linens	12.75	5.5–6

Notes: £1 is equivalent to 23 French livres.
Sources: Guillaume Daudin, *Commerce et prospérité. La France au XVIIIe siècle* (Paris: Presses de l'Université Paris-Sorbonne, 2005), esp. pp. 439 and 445; Giorgio Riello, 'The Ecology of Cotton in the Eighteenth Century: Possibilities and Potentials', unpublished paper, October 2005, available at www2.lse.ac.uk/economicHistory/Research/GEHN/GEHNPDF/RielloPadua.pdf

important export and linens its most important import. British woollen exports were worth in the region of £6.3 million in 1790 and accounted for more than a third of all English exports (and even more in the early part of the century).[36] At the same time in England, more than half of its linen consumption was imported.[37]

Woollens were the motor of eighteenth-century British industry. The scale of production in Wiltshire, Norfolk and the West Riding of Yorkshire was staggering in relation to the relatively small population of the British Isles.[38] But what made wool pivotal to the British economy was exports. Defoe famously put it in lyrical terms that 'all the World wears it [wool], all the World desires it, and all the world envies us the Glory and Advantage of it'.[39] It was patently untrue (as it happened, the British had failed to sell woollens in Asia), though this was the commodity on which, as another contemporary shrewdly observed, 'the Prosperity of the British Empire depends'.[40] British woollens had enormous and increasing success in continental Europe, the Middle East and the Atlantic before, during and after the rise of cotton textiles.[41]

The import of linens into England was equally unusual. No other early modern European economy was so reliant on cloth coming from outside its borders.[42] Yet, this eccentric combination of imported linens and exported woollens made perfect sense in terms of Ricardian comparative advantages. Through trade, Britain relied heavily on vegetable fibres (hemp and flax) for domestic consumption and on an animal fibre for the export of wool textiles (woollens, worsteds, mixes and new draperies). This was a rational choice. The kingdom clothed its population with cheaper linen and exported more expensive woollen textiles. It specialised in the production of energy-intensive woollens but did not misallocate them in clothing its own people. This might appear a rather twisted logic and in fact it was not something that was planned. Woollens and linens are not interchangeable and there was no predetermined rationale in *wanting* to export woollens and import linens. It simply happened that differently from most of the continental European countries where sheep breeding and flax cultivation could be found side by side, England was the land of the golden fleece but had a rather unsuitable climate for growing flax. This geographical situation might, however, have been conducive to keeping a door open to opportunities offered by cotton.

In the early part of the eighteenth century it had become clear that – to cite Defoe once again – 'No People in Europe wear and consume so great a quantity of linen...as the English do'.[43] At the same time, however, it was equally evident that most, and surely the best, of such linen came from Germany, France, Russia and the Dutch Republic.[44] The problem was not necessarily one of balance of trade but economic dependence on politically hostile countries. The establishment of the Boards of Trustees to regulate the industry in Ireland in 1711 and in Scotland in 1727 can be read as steps towards strengthening domestic linen production within the United Kingdom.[45] Political reasons were also important in that the expansion of linen production in Ireland and Scotland in the first half of the eighteenth century placated potential disorder across the Irish Sea and realigned the economic interests of a recently incorporated Scottish kingdom within Britain.[46]

Scotland and Ireland provided only a temporary respite. Notwithstanding English attempts to control Irish production, Irish linen started to compete with woollens in domestic and imperial markets. By the 1740s linen prices were spiralling; in 1763, linen yarn was 40 per cent more expensive than it had been in 1751.[47] The Seven Years' War had effectively destroyed established commercial links between the Silesian linen industry and the rest of Europe.[48] As prices in England increased so the total import of continental linen fell from an average of 30 million yards (for the period 1730–55) to less than 19 million yards in the early 1760s.[49] By 1765 the import of linen into England had fallen below early eighteenth-century levels.[50]

England had all the reasons to play the colonial card at home by securing linen supplies from its peripheries and subordinated territories. Cotton and linen interacted through mixes such as fustians, and one might be prompted to read the rise of cotton as a reaction to increasing linen prices and the outcome of

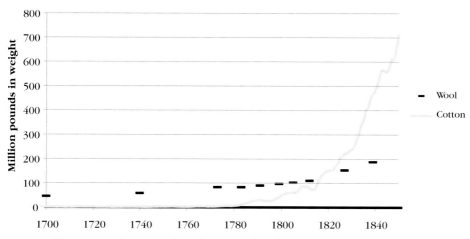

Figure 11.3 Consumption of raw wool and cotton in Britain, 1700–1850.

a more confident intercontinental English imperial project.[51] Conditions conducive to a trajectory towards cotton textiles on the back of linen presented several drawbacks, however. Linen was an unsuitable textile for large-scale production and was characterised by close connections with the agrarian economy and with multi-activity in the countryside. There was the danger of translating these characterisations on to cotton and, in particular, on to fustian. Linen, for instance, was seen as the easiest and most straightforward way of 'employing the poor' as it required little capital and, especially for the production of cheaper varieties, little skill.[52]

The traditional and established status of the golden fleece, so often publicised in seventeenth- and eighteenth-century Britain, might have become a further obstacle for the development of cotton textiles in the United Kingdom.[53] There is an innate tendency to read the story of cotton as one of decline for woollens. In reality, cotton emerged as a real challenge late in the century, when the dynamism of cotton manufacturing, characterised by innovation and staggering rates of growth, made the woollen industry look seriously backward.[54] However, as late as 1796, William Marshall had no doubt that 'the coat of the sheep [was] of the first importance' for the British economy.[55] Just five years later, cottons had displaced woollens as the most important British export commodity, a position that woollens had held for the best part of half a millennium.

But can we read the rise of cotton as facilitated by problems internal to woollen production? The British cotton industry emerged as a switch from woollens to cottons that allowed incredible growth to be achieved over such a very short span of time. Figure 11.3 shows that the British woollen industry had a distinctive dynamism of its own, doubling in size between 1700 and the 1770s, and doubling again in the following fifty years. The British cotton industry was insignificant compared to woollens until the 1780s, it grew rapidly until the end of the Napoleonic wars and expanded at miraculous rates over the next quarter of a century. This graph is a rough approximation because it simply maps the consumption of raw materials without considering the different quantities of yarn and cloth produced by wool and cotton, but also the increasing share of mixed cotton-wool textiles that appeared on the market in the early nineteenth century.[56]

Pat Hudson has warned against reading the British wool textile sector's performances through the yardstick of cotton, which overshadows the growth of the sector. A possible decline of British woollens was already being announced by merchants and manufacturers in the 1730s and 1740s, as they became increasingly worried about the long-term prospects for the industry.[57] Whilst they had established commercial links across the Atlantic, they faced serious competition from France, Germany and Italy, countries that were increasingly successful in selling woollens to European and Middle Eastern markets.[58] British textile producers appeared over-anxious. The half a century between 1730 and 1780 was the period of maximum splendour for the British woollen industry, and as late as the early 1770s the value of woollen manufactures was from two to three times larger than all other textiles produced in Britain.[59]

There was no involution of woollen manufacturing in Britain, or in any other European country, until well into the second half of the nineteenth century. However, in relative terms, the performances of this sector turned out to be mediocre. Estimates indicate that at the beginning of the nineteenth century British per capita consumption of woollen textiles was more than double the levels at the end of the seventeenth century, notwithstanding the enormous demographic increase. However, after the 1770s the industry grew less impressively and the contribution of woollens to the overall textile production of the British Isles fell from 60 per cent of net value-added in 1770 to 34 per cent in 1821, at a time when the contribution of textiles to GDP increased from 9 to 14 per cent.[60]

Instead of blaming the British woollen sector for not having performed as well as cotton, one might ask if it could have performed better. The response to this question takes us to two important factors: one is genetic and the other market-based. It was not just a problem of securing better supplies, but also of producing the right kind of wool. The period of relative crisis of woollen production coincided with what Hartwell defined as a 'revolution in wool' consisting of the lengthening and coarsening of British fleeces.[61] A new breed of sheep, heavier and stronger, was preferred as it produced higher quantities of mutton in a period of high meat prices and increasing population.[62] The 'golden fleece' was not always suitable for producing the lighter and higher-quality woollens that the market wanted.

This 'genetic' story might be convincing from a British point of view, but it is less so when we use a wider lens. Abundant supplies of high-quality wool were available from Spain and by the 1830s also from Australasia.[63] Yet at a global level, by 1900 the value of wool textile production was less than a third that of cottons and possibly only one tenth in yardage. Demand, rather than supply, might have been a real barrier to wool. As we will see, consumers around the world did not want to consume more woollens. They preferred cottons. This was a trend that became evident when cotton manufacturing mechanised and industrialised but it was already emerging in the mid eighteenth century, when European merchants in the Atlantic saw cotton as an opportunity to expand business.[64] The woollen industry did not disappear but continued to expand in niche markets and especially in mixed fabric (wool and cotton in particular).[65]

Patterns of supply: securing cotton in the age of industrialisation

So far I have focused on the enormously superior ecologic potential of cotton and on a political economy and structure of textile production that led to the adoption of cotton by English and later European manufacturers. Yet, the story of cotton might have been one of unrealised potential if supplies of cheap raw materials had failed to reach the factories of Europe. The nearly 'miraculous' story of cotton is one instead of enormous elasticity of supply as captured by the analysis of the price paid for this raw material. Figure 11.4 shows the price of different varieties of raw cotton reaching Europe from the Middle East and the Americas.[66] It reveals an intriguing story that can be divided into three periods.

During the half a century between the 1720s and the European mechanisation of the sector in the 1770s, the price of raw cotton paid by European manufacturers increased substantially, possibly doubled. This is not surprising if we think that fustian manufacturing expanded in several parts of Europe, especially in the 1730s and 1740s, creating high demand for cotton. The upward price trend might explain two phenomena. Firstly, attempts were made to secure larger supplies of raw cotton, especially from the West Indies. This started before the 1770s and continued until the end of the century. Secondly, and much in contrast to supporters of the idea that mechanisation was a rational response to high wages, one might argue that technological innovation was a way to reduce the cost of production in manufacturing at a time in which the cost of raw materials was rapidly increasing.

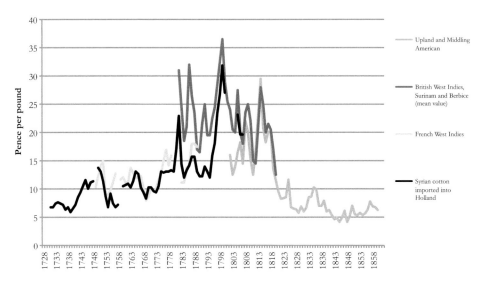

Figure 11.4 Price of raw cotton from the West Indies, the US South and Syria, 1728–1860.

During the period of industrialisation from the 1770s to the 1810s, the price of raw cotton sky-rocketed, reaching a peak in *circa* 1800, the moment of maximum growth for the British cotton industry. This second period was one not just of high prices for cotton due to high demand from an expanding industry but also of high price volatility caused by the fact that supply struggled to catch up with demand and that it was a period of blockades and embargoes. Different European nations competed to secure supplies of cotton from the Americas and the Middle East. It was also a period of uncertainty, with critics foreseeing an imminent crisis for an industry that had developed incredibly fast (especially in England) but that seemed to be 'running out of steam'.

A collapse of the European cotton industry was not an impossible scenario, if the upward price trend of raw cotton continued. Our final period, the half a century between the 1810s and the American Civil War of 1861–5, shows instead a reversal of a long-lasting price trend. This was a period of falling cotton prices and one dominated by the production of US plantations. The quantity of cotton produced in the American South increased by 6.6 per cent per annum between 1800 and 1860 while its price fell by 0.5 per cent per annum during the same period, this trend becoming particularly intense after 1815.[67] By 1840 the price of raw cotton was not just lower than what it had been a century earlier, but supplies were much more abundant and the quality of the fibre much higher. This was an American 'plantation revolution' on a par with the European industrial revolution. What both had in common was the role played by raw cotton.

Let me step back to the eighteenth century, as I wish to show that both in bad and later good times the opportunities offered by the cotton fibre were quite different among the European nations that potentially could develop a local cotton-manufacturing industry. Traditionally, the European fustian industry had been supplied with cotton by the Middle East. Yet, the early eighteenth-century English cotton industry located in Manchester and its surroundings relied on cotton coming from the Americas. Until the 1780s, the West Indies supplied Manchester fustian and cotton producers with 60 to 80 per cent of their raw material, the remainder coming from the Levant.

France, too, pursued a similar strategy, with St Domingue and the other French possessions in the West Indies fast developing cotton cultivation. Supplies were fairly abundant in the 1760s and 1770s. In 1770 St Domingue, Guadalupe and Martinique produced nearly 6 million pounds of raw cotton, compared to a production of just over 3.5 million pounds in Granada, Jamaica and Dominica, part of the British West Indies.[68] Over the next two decades, however, France lost much ground. At its peak of production in 1789–90, St Domingue's 705 cotton plantations produced 6.3 million pounds of raw cotton a year.[69] Overall, the French West Indies produced around 10 million pounds of raw cotton compared with 12.7 million for the British West Indies.[70] Unable to secure a better stronghold in the West Indies, France forged instead extensive commercial links with Anatolia, in particular with the port of Izmir.[71] The rising French cotton industry relied on raw cotton supplies exchanged for woollens produced in the south of France and exported to Anatolia and the Middle East.[72]

Spain, too, was in no better position to secure steady supplies of raw cotton from the Americas, even if it had extensive possessions. Since the late 1730s, Spain had developed a cotton-manufacturing industry centred in Barcelona. Similarly to France, the Spanish cotton industry looked for cotton supplies from the Mediterranean (spun yarn from Malta) and the Middle East. Differently from France, however, the Spanish central and colonial government did not incentivise cotton cultivation in the Spanish dominions until the 1760s. James Thomson argues that Spain's imperial trading network was marred by inefficient rules. For example, all cotton had to pass through Cadiz, rather than being shipped directly to Barcelona, and was transported in an unginned form.[73] The Spanish imperial supplies of raw cotton provide a good counter-example to the British story, as they display a systematic failure to foster and shape the trade of raw cotton through mercantilist economic policies designed to retain the majority of the raw material for the use of domestic manufacturing industry.[74]

There is some indication that before the late 1780s, England did marginally better than France and Spain in securing supplies of cotton from the Americas. The strategy pursued by France was based much more on a traditional pattern of colonial exchange than it was on a complex multilateral system that connected human capital, financial investment, political dominance, raw material supplies and demand for finished products within an area of political influence, as was the case for Britain.[75] Why was it so important to develop American cotton production? Supplies from the Middle East might have been less elastic than those from the Americas. In 1790, the price of a pound of cotton in Cairo was four times what it had been a century earlier.[76] In 1780, the price of Cypriot and Syrian cotton sold in Amsterdam was three times more expensive compared to similar varieties sold in the 1720s.[77] Moreover, Middle Eastern cotton was of a staple shorter than American cotton. Although it was cheaper, it has been argued that it was also quite unsuitable for mechanised processing. It was the longer American varieties of cotton that allowed the application of Arkwright's water frame and Crompton's mule. England's American cotton supplies turned out to be a major factor promoting the adoption of mechanical innovation in cotton textile manufacturing.[78]

France's lack of raw cotton from the Americas became even more problematic in the 1790s, a most important decade for the take-off of European cotton manufacturing and one of very high raw cotton prices. During the immediate aftermath of the French Revolution and under the duress of a continental blockade in the Napoleonic period, French producers found it difficult to obtain sufficient raw cotton supplies.[79] The port of Bordeaux was closed for several years and cotton could only reach the mills of Lille via Antwerp. The situation became even worse after 1810, when the hostilities with Russia prevented Ottoman cotton reaching France.[80] Some cotton started to arrive from Brazil, but the situation was so dire that Napoleon encouraged the cultivation of cotton in Provence, an experiment that ultimately failed because of the unsuitable climate of the region.[81]

It would, however, be a mistake to see England as triumphing in an imperial plan in which political domination secured uncontested ecological and manufacturing advantages. The West Indies was an important source of raw cotton, but only until the end of the eighteenth century. Even in Britain, the problem of raw material supply became a highly debated topic in the late 1780s and 1790s.[82] The cotton industry was growing at such a pace that a House of Commons committee in 1789 reopened the old idea of cultivating cotton in West Africa.[83] Environmental degradation and the need to expand production brought Brazilian and later US cotton to the fore in the first half of the nineteenth century (Figure 11.5).

Brazil was between the late 1780s and the late 1820s a major supplier of cotton to Europe and to England in particular. When the area of Maranhão in northwest Brazil first developed cotton cultivation in 1760, both France and

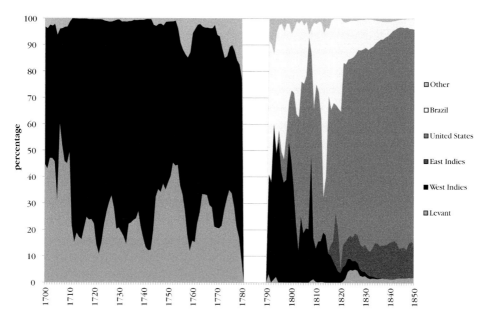

Figure 11.5 Raw cotton imported into Britain by geographic area, 1700–80 and 1791–1850.

Britain became good customers. In the 1780s and throughout the 1790s, Brazilian cotton production expanded, becoming a major crop in Pernambuco.[84] By this time, however, Britain absorbed most of the raw cotton exported from Brazil.[85] Political rather than economic factors further played against France: when in 1808 Napoleon invaded the Iberian peninsula and the Portuguese royal family escaped to Brazil, France was effectively cut off from Brazilian cotton supplies as Brazil's major ports were opened to trade to anti-French coalition countries.[86] Brazil came to be an important ally for the British cotton industry when in the early 1810s supplies of American cotton were impeded because of the war between the United States and the former mother country.[87]

The War of 1812 was, however, a moment of major reconfiguration of cotton production on a global scale that eventually led to a marked decrease of the price of this industrial input. Cotton cultivation expanded in the American South following the rise of a US cotton industry (a false start, as it soon became apparent) and the depression of the indigo and later tobacco markets.[88] The rise of US cotton was dramatic: in 1850, cotton alone accounted for half of the $135 million (c. £20 million) worth of US exports.[89] How did this happen? And why did cotton become so cheap? The availability of land and labour were major factors in the expansion of cotton cultivation, but they alone do not explain why prices declined between two-thirds to three-fourths over just one generation. Increasing productivity of labour and land and decreasing costs of transport are key to understanding the falling price of raw cotton over the first half of the nineteenth century.[90]

It has been estimated that over the period 1800 to 1860 the average amount of Upland cotton picked by a slave in a day might have increased up to four times.[91] A calculation of working hours shows that the number of hours worked in slave plantations was inferior to those worked in British textile mills but exceeded those of farmers and peasants in Europe. Fogel supports the idea that gang labour might have been responsible for high labour productivity. Contemporaries such as Frederick Law Olmsted observed how gangs moved 'across the fields in parallel lines, with a considerable degree of precision' and underlined the nearly military organisation of such a regime of labour.[92] Work was based on the principle of maximum efficiency, with the more able hands setting the pace for everyone else to follow. This allowed plantations adopting a gang system to produce up to 40 per cent more than either farms run on free labour or slave plantations with no gang labour. It was the product per worker that planters were eager to maximise, and, as Douglas North points out, already in the pre-civil war period planters were experimenting with 'scientific management of labour' to increase productivity.[93]

Ecologic factors have also been identified as being central to increasing productivity of both land and labour. It has been suggested that the two early varieties of cotton, *Gossypium barbadense*, Sea Island cotton popular in Georgia, South Carolina and Florida, and *Gossypium hirsutum*, Upland cotton popular instead in Mississippi and North Carolina, were replaced by a new Mexican variety of *Gossypium hirsutum* that was first introduced in the US in 1820 and that became increasingly common (especially as hybrids) in the 1820s and early 1830s. This was a new type of cotton that allowed higher yields and, more importantly, was easier to pick and process, thus increasing substantially the productivity of labour.[94]

More efficient labour and a better type of raw material might have contributed to a decrease of the cost of cotton production. However, the price paid for cotton by manufacturers in Europe depended also on freight rates. Technological innovation once again played a major role, as the freight rates from New Orleans to Liverpool declined more than 60 per cent and from New York to Liverpool about 70 per cent over the thirty years 1820–50.[95] Part of the decrease derived from savings in the transport from the plantations to major shipping ports such as New Orleans when steamboat technology was introduced on the Mississippi River in 1811.[96] Considerable savings were also achieved in the packing of cotton bales. At the end of the eighteenth century a cubic foot weighed 12.5 pounds, but thanks to steam presses by the 1840s the density of a cubic foot reached 25 pounds.[97]

The nation that took advantage more than any other from the fall of the price of American cotton was Britain. The Lancashire mills found suitable supplies first from Brazil and then from Mississippi and the Carolinas. Although the US was proud of its political independence, before the country industrialised and expanded territorially, in the second half of the nineteenth century, its economy remained strongly linked to that of the former mother country. After warfare between the US and Britain came to an end in 1815, a 'special relationship' between the two countries emerged that lasted for more than a generation. Over a third of US imports came from the UK and the latter received more than half of the US's exports, the bulk of which was raw cotton.[98] Direct access to raw materials provided enormous advantages for the British cotton industry vis-à-vis the French, German, Spanish and other European continental industries.

Eventually, US cotton came to triumph globally. In 1816–20 the exports of raw cotton from the United States accounted for 39 per cent of the world market, rising to 63 per cent in 1836–40. In the 1850s, US cotton accounted for three-quarters of all cotton used in British mills, 90 per cent of the cotton used in France, 60 per cent of the German and 92 per cent of the Russian.[99] By 1860, at the pinnacle of pre-civil war productivity, two-thirds of the world's cotton and more than three-quarters of all the cotton traded was grown in the United States.[100]

Imperial ambitions: Indian raw cotton

The strong links between American (especially US) cotton cultivation and European (especially British) cotton manufacturing were viewed with a certain degree of anxiety on both sides of the Atlantic. The power of American cotton became apparent with the crisis caused by the interruption of trade during the American Civil War of 1861–5, when only small quantities of US cotton reached Europe. Between 1861 and 1868 no fewer than 338 English cotton mills closed down.[101] This was a major catastrophe that many had foreseen. In the late 1840s the British protectionist George Frederick Young had boasted that 'we have given the monopoly of supply of the raw material for our staple manufacture to our most jealous manufacturing rivals', namely the US, and had argued that Britain had to develop cotton cultivation within its own dominions 'in India and the West Indies, by the retention of a moderate differential duty'.[102]

Young's position was shared by manufacturers and politicians alike. Cotton cultivation was encouraged in several parts of the British Empire, from British Guyana to the Natal area of South Africa, to New South Wales and Victoria, and to a lesser extent in British-controlled Egypt.[103] But it was India that was seen as the area within the British Empire to have the highest potential to develop extensive cotton production. As early as 1817, the Philadelphian former loyalist turned promoter of American manufacturing Tench Coxe foresaw the decline of cotton cultivation in the American South.[104] In a not so distant future, he explained, a reduction in the cost of transport and the diffusion of efficient ginning machines would make it possible for the cotton of Africa, India and other parts of the world to be sold in Great Britain. He saw India as the most promising location for the cultivation of raw cotton, and indicated that it was already economical to send cotton to Canton. Luckily for US cotton, insurance, commission and freight charges increased the price of Indian raw cotton sold in Britain by a staggering 80 per cent.[105]

Indian cotton never triumphed globally as Coxe had foreseen, much to the disappointment of British manufacturers, EEIC's servants and British imperial administrators.[106] Attempts to assess the potential for cultivation in India to supply British markets had started already at the end of the eighteenth century. The Polish-born scientist Pantaleon Hove spent two years in Gujarat in northwestern India in 1786 and 1787 surveying cotton plantations and leaving a detailed report and copious correspondence on the topic.[107] His observations, which circulated among the scientific community in Britain, were of great interest to the EEIC, as it saw the potential profit to be gained from the trade of raw cotton from India to Europe. Results were disappointing, however. One commentator concluded a couple of years later that 'notwithstanding what was expected from that respectable body', the EEIC had 'not hitherto imported one ounce of the fine cotton wool fit for our [British] manufactures'.[108]

In the late 1790s further attempts were made to cultivate cotton for export by a Malabar spice farm owner and by the naturalist William Roxburgh, but without commercial success.[109] The cost of transport remained a major barrier against a viable trade of Indian raw cotton to Europe. Moreover, at a time during which the cost both of West Indian and Middle Eastern cotton was high (c. 1780–1810), the price of Indian cotton was equally high due to the Chinese demand for this raw material to supply its expanding cotton industry.[110] Finally, Indian raw cotton shared many of the characteristics that Christophe Aubin observed for Middle Eastern cotton when in 1812 he was sent by a Glasgow merchant house to assess the potential for business in Smyrna. The Smyrna cotton was 'pleasing [to] the eye' but was of a short staple and had insufficient strength for mechanical processing. Its ginning and cleaning were equally difficult. Early attempts to introduce Whitney's saw-gin by the EEIC to speed up cotton cleaning failed dramatically. Packing too – on which the cost of freight depended – was problematic, although the adoption of the so-called 'geometric cotton screw' in 1818 seemed to provide an efficient and less labour-intensive way to press cotton.[111] Paraphrasing what the EEIC had observed in India, Aubin concluded that 'under present circumstances this article would leave a heavy loss on sending it to England'.[112]

In the following twenty years further attempts were made to produce cotton in India. It also became increasingly clear that the type of cotton needed was long-fibre Upland cotton as cultivated in the United States rather than the short-staple Indian variety. An attempt by the Agricultural Society of India to cultivate American cotton in Bengal in the early 1830s ended in failure, as did a later attempt to establish American cotton in Coimbatore by Robert Wight, head of the Agri-Horticultural Society gardens of Madras.[113] When the EEIC declared in 1840 that it had 'succeeded in converting India from a manufacturing country into a country exporting raw materials', it forgot to mention a key commodity such as cotton.[114] The company's business in the trade of Indian textiles had given way to other commodities, but it was indigo and raw silk, not cotton, that constituted the bulk of their trade to England in the 1820s and 1830s.[115]

Further attempts were however made to introduce the long-staple American Upland cotton to India. This was part of a wider range of initiatives for the transplanting of West Indian produce, including sugar, to Asia.[116] In the early 1840s, the EEIC convinced American farmers to settle in the Bombay presidency and provided them with land and labour. This attempt was also a failure and within a year the Americans complained that their actions were being undermined by the Company, that they had been given false information concerning the nature of the soil, and that they lacked funding.[117] They encountered endemic infrastructural problems with transportation and irrigation, land taxation and an unsuitable hot and dry climate for the cultivation of Upland cotton.[118]

The limits of this early Upland cotton trial were fully considered in subsequent attempts in the 1850s and 1860s promoted by the Manchester Commercial Association, the Manchester Chamber of Commerce and the British Cotton Supply Association.[119] They lobbied Parliament and convinced the British government in India to undertake extensive deforestation and public works for the construction of railway links, roads and canals (Figure 11.6).[120] The *Cotton Supply Reporter*, the journal of the Manchester Cotton Supply Association, claimed in the 1861 issue that 'The sun never sets upon the cotton soil of British territory!...During every hour of the day the sun is

Figure 11.6 'Cotton bales lying at the Bombay terminus of the Great Indian Peninsula Railway ready for shipment to England', from *History of Indian Railways* (1862).

shining upon vast cotton fields within our own dominions, which lie neglected awaiting only the fostering hand of British capital and labour to teem with plentiful and permanent supplies'.[121] The tentacle of British power and capital over an expanding empire was seen as key to the economic prosperity of the mother country. Yet the rhetoric remained stronger than reality: the Lancashire merchant took Indian cotton only when supplies of better quality fibre could not be obtained from America.[122] Cotton lay behind both the triumph of England's industry and the failure to create an imperial system to replace a market one.

Conclusion

Cotton is representative of what could be achieved from the successful manipulation of resources, markets and natural endowments that lay outside the borders of one continent. This chapter has shown the potential of cotton to transform European economies to a level and intensity that no other textile possessed. But it has also highlighted how potential gains are guided by specific circumstances in which some countries more than others enjoyed incentives to restructure their manufacturing systems. Within Europe, Britain presented a peculiar relationship between woollens and linens and was better placed than any other country to receive abundant supplies of raw cotton.

12 GLOBAL OUTCOMES: THE WEST AND THE NEW COTTON SYSTEM

A room full of men, most of them wearing sombre-coloured suits, hats and ties, captures the capitalist world of the nineteenth century. In 1872 the famous painter Degas visited his maternal family in New Orleans, the world's busiest cotton trading port, and painted one of the offices of the local cotton exchange (Figure 12.1). The artist's brother appears as the man leaning against the window and his uncle as the older man cleaning his glasses. The homage to Degas' family does not detract, however, from the precision of observation: at the centre of the composition dealers are inspecting the quality of cotton; on the right, a busy clerk and his helper are scribbling on large books. This is not the world of the plantation, nor that of a factory and not even the buzzing port of New Orleans, much represented in early photography in the second half of the nineteenth century. Degas takes us instead into the confined space of an office where bureaucracy and expertise embody business. A scene like this would not have been different from scenes of the cotton exchange of Liverpool or the sorting office of Mumbai. We would have found western men dressed in black and wearing hats carrying out similar activities. Degas captures the essence of capitalism: it is not the world of the ocean or the adventurous merchant, but that of the bureaucrat recording figures, assessing information and checking commodities. From a room in New Orleans, decisions could be taken that had global repercussions. Behind the veneer of a carefully constructed sense of boredom, Degas reveals the true nature of nineteenth-century global capitalism in which cotton became king.

What kind of world did cotton create? I have so far emphasised the importance of technological innovation and supplies of a critical raw material behind the growth of a global industry that became larger than any that had preceded it. The scale of production and the transformation that it wrought were truly astonishing. Europe benefitted most by organising production and controlling supplies of raw materials. But central to the success of Britain and the West was their ability to sell cotton goods across the globe. This was no simple task

Figure 12.1 *Le Bureau de coton à la Nouvelle Orleans en 1873* by Edgar Degas.

as it necessitated the establishment of complex structures of trade, distribution, finance and insurance, as well as the capacity to please consumers from many cultures with widely different tastes. The success of the West in making their cotton textiles into a global product went hand in hand with their increasing influence and imperial presence in different areas of the world and their capacity to dictate market structures and even influence tastes in dress and furnishing.[1] In this book I have defined this system as 'centripetal', that is, a system of trade, exchange and power in the service of a 'core' that exploited resources, that made and controlled new technologies and that dominated markets to the detriment of Asian merchandise. For up to two centuries, benefits from this transformed and relocated global industry accrued overwhelmingly to the West and perpetuated economic divergence between the West and 'the Rest'.[2]

The global trade of cotton

Cotton textiles became in the nineteenth century one of the main features of a commercial process that today we call globalisation. It is, however, incorrect to think that cotton textiles became a global industry because production was relocated to the west of Eurasia. As the previous chapters have argued, the opposite is 'more' true: cotton fibres and cotton textiles were already global commodities before their process of production was mechanised. What had originally been an Indian Ocean space for exchange, by the seventeenth century came to include Europe, Africa and the Americas. It also extended into the Pacific, with the Manila to Acapulco route becoming a further important route for cottons to reach the Americas. By the 1760s one could find fine Cambay cloth, Madras handkerchiefs and high-quality Bengali cottons in New Spain.[3]

Industrialisation in Europe extended and strengthened extant commercial networks. Cottons became in the age of industrialisation the most traded of consumer goods in the world. Such cotton textiles were now not those of India but the piece-goods produced in Lancashire and the Clyde valley and later in other industrial regions of continental Europe and North America. Part of the success of western producers lay not just in the superiority of their machinery but also in their capacity to use existing networks of exchange that allowed for the sale of their products worldwide. The scale of manufacture of the industrial age needed new and expanding markets in order to avoid a surplus of production. In turn, the monster-like factories of the industrial West, fed by the ceaseless labour of thousands of workers, were also fed with spectacular quantities of raw materials. They produced millions of yards of fabrics that now literally clothed the world.

The nineteenth century saw a realignment and reconfiguration of textile production and trade on a global scale. If one takes a snapshot of the global trade in textile fibres in 1913, just before the great upheavals of the First World War, a truly remarkable scene can be observed. The value of cotton production was more than double that of all other fibres put together. The world geography of trade of cotton, wool and silk was even more surprising. Western Europe's import of cotton fibres accounted for 85 per cent of all imported cotton in the world, the remainder being imported by Russia and Japan. Cotton might have been exceptional in quantitative terms, but reflected a world trade in organic materials in which 91 per cent of wool also found its way to Europe. A similar picture could be painted for silk, although in this case North America shared Asian supplies of raw silk with Europe. The only region of the world to be a net importer of all textile fibres (silk, wool and cotton) was Europe. The rest of the world had become specialised in providing this continent with different inputs: the Americas (the US in particular) were its main suppliers of raw cotton; Australia of wool; while raw silk reached Europe both from mainland Asia and from Japan.[4]

The world of textile production and consumption created in the nineteenth century was truly global. Europe was a machine that absorbed raw materials and churned out consumer goods in exchange for further raw materials.[5] The

extension and reliance on material supplied from outside the continent's borders was such that when the flow that fed the European textile mills stopped –
as indeed it almost did during the cotton famine of the 1860s caused by the
American Civil War – factories came to a standstill. This is why Europe, by
means of imperialism, force and liberal free trade doctrines, used its economic
and political power to ensure the constancy of supplies and the openness of
world markets to European manufactured products. Cotton came to be representative of a wider range of commodities that included tea, tobacco, coffee
and opium among the many articles of trade resulting from intensive agricul-
tures organised by the West across the globe to feed its own people and its own
factories.[6]

Cotton and cotton textiles were, however, also exceptional in the global capitalism of the nineteenth century. In contrast to other primary products and raw
materials, the bulk of the world's raw cotton was cultivated in North America.
Only a quarter of the cotton used in Europe arrived from the non-industrialised
areas of the world, against an average of 90 per cent for other imported industrial inputs.[7] That changed in the twentieth century with the expansion of cotton
cultivation in Africa and later China, India, Pakistan, Brazil, Uzbekistan and
Turkmenistan.[8] But the story of nineteenth-century cotton might appear exceptional also in terms of the trade of finished cloth. Just limiting our observation
to Britain, at the turn of the twentieth century, two-thirds of its entire output
was sold to underdeveloped areas of the world, which contrasts with about a
one-third average for the rest of the British industrial production.[9] Because of its
quantitative relevance, one might say that cotton textiles were among the most
important commodities for the global expansion of markets in the nineteenth
century. Without cotton, the story of industrial capitalism would have been
much less global. The trade in cotton cloth constituted the backbone of world
trade. At the centre of it was Europe, whose trade in cotton increased eightfold
over the century, first enveloping European and American markets and after
mid-century rapidly expanding towards Asian and African markets. Thanks to
the trade of cottons, in the seventy years between 1800 and 1870 the European
exports to Asia increased more than twenty times.[10]

One European country that assumed a hegemonic role in the strategy for the
intensification of global trade was Britain. The industrial prosperity of Albion
was clearly linked to the development of commercial relations. The economy of
a small island became several times bigger than the needs of its own people. As
Douglas Farnie observed, 'The external functions fulfilled by the [British cotton]
industry became more significant than its domestic functions'.[11] Already in the
final years of the eighteenth century, the productive system that had developed in
the British Isles could be said to be 'leaning forward' to a global dimension. This
went hand in hand with the dominant position that Britain had acquired in world

politics and trade over the course of the eighteenth century and especially after the Seven Years' War. An efficient fiscal-military state ensured the protection of trade through the world's best and most expensive navy. Wars with its European neighbours, not just in Europe but also in the Americas and Asia, created what was later formalised into the British Empire.[12]

The potentially traumatic loss of the North American colonies in the 1770s turned out to be for Britain not as detrimental as imagined. Britain's global trade remained well ahead of all other continental European countries for the entire eighteenth century. The failure of France to develop strong commercial ties with North America in the 1780s (a critical moment for the development of the cotton industry and one of relative weakness for the British after the Peace of Paris of 1783) further favoured Britain.[13] By the end of the Napoleonic wars, the gap between British and French trade was immense: in 1816 the export of British cotton textiles and yarn was worth three times as much as total French export.[14] The French were correctly worried about the fact that the revolution and war had disrupted international commercial links to such an extent that they had 'given an immense benefit to the English', not just in North America but also in the expanding Latin American markets.[15]

The trade of English cottons thrived. The cheap blue, India, 'negro' as well as printed and painted cottons that were exported from England to the American colonies in the mid eighteenth century were replaced by more sophisticated varieties as consumers' expectations increased.[16] Merchants in Manchester and the north of England became increasingly proactive in marketing their own wares through representatives based in North America, cutting out not just the London middlemen who had controlled the Atlantic woollen and linen trades in the second half of the eighteenth century, but also French competitors, who were unable to get a clear sense of what North American consumers sought.[17] Latin America, too, was an important market for the English cotton mills. In 1820 Britain exported 56 million yards of cotton cloth to Latin America, and twenty years later a staggering 279 million yards. This was ten yards per person, an indicator of the receptiveness of Latin America to imported textiles.[18] The small Spanish industry could satisfy only a fraction of the colonial demand, often being little competition against British products.[19]

The British economy was therefore 'unique' not just because it was the first to industrialise and mechanise but also because, more than any other western economy, it relied on an extensive global web of markets, trade and political power that made it the first modern 'export-oriented economy'. Cottons were key to this process: the value of the cotton textiles exported increased a hundredfold, passing from a mere third of a million pounds sterling in 1780 to £30.7 million in 1825. With growth rates for British cotton exports of more than 12 per cent

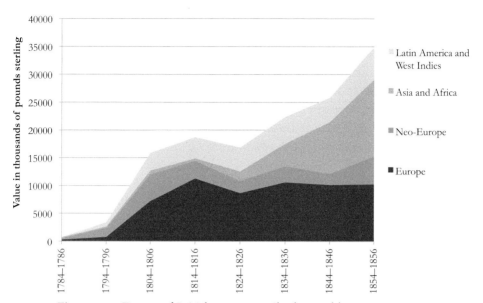

Figure 12.2 Export of British cotton textiles by world area, 1784–1856.

a year over the period 1783 to 1814 and up to 60 per cent of total production being exported, cottons made of Britain the first 'roaring tiger' two centuries before China acquired that position.[20] By mid-century, cotton's preponderance in the UK export economy was unmissable: in 1851, nearly 60 per cent of all cotton production was exported, accounting for two-fifths of all merchandise sold abroad.[21] A similar picture could be drawn at continental level. Throughout the nineteenth century – in a period in which most western countries diversified their economies – cottons were at least a quarter of all exports. In 1913, the British textile export accounted for 38 per cent of all exports, with cotton textile manufacturing remaining the most important manufacturing export sector not just in Britain but in all major European countries.[22] The nineteenth century was truly a century of cloth.

Asian markets and finance

The global success of industrially produced European cottons was in reality the result of two successive waves: the first, stretching over the sixty years between the 1760s and the 1820s, was a phase of sale expansion in western and Atlantic markets, Europe first but also North and Latin America; the second phase starting in the 1820s saw sales of European cloth to Asian markets increased substantially (Figure 12.2). British cottons substituted products that had previously been produced in India and elsewhere in Asia. This chronology is in line with recent calculations of industrial productivity that show that British cottons became globally competitive only in the 1820s and started gaining substantial markets over the course of the following decade.[23]

British products had already made inroads into Asian markets at the turn of the nineteenth century. In 1800 a report by the Commercial Resident in Dacca, John Taylor, to the British Board of Trade already emphasised the pressures caused to the local cotton industry by British products.[24] The Scotswoman Maria Graham, on opening a bale of cloth in a Bombay bazaar in 1808, claimed to be 'surprised to find at least half of its contents of British manufacture, and such articles were much cheaper than those of equal fineness from Bengal and Madras . . . yet still it seems strange, that cotton carried to England, manufactured, and returned to this country, should undersell the fabrics of India, where labour is so cheap. But I believe this is owing partly to the uncertainty and difficulty of carriage here, although the use of machinery at home must be the main cause'.[25] By 1813 English chintzes – often imitations of Masulipatnam and Coromandel textiles but now cheaper than Indian products – were to be found also on the Persian market.[26] However, British products did not become competitive overnight against Indian yarn and cloth. The process took the best part of twenty years. First, it was British yarn that started to displace Indian yarn after 1810. By the late 1820s the price of English yarn was half of that produced by an Indian spinner.[27] After yarn, English cloth too started to be imported into the subcontinent. The amount of British cotton goods exported to India increased from under 1 million yards in 1814 to a staggering 51 million by 1830.[28] The inroads made by British cloth could be seen not just in the main urban markets of the subcontinent but also in remote regions of the interior. Reginald Heber, travelling to Bengal in 1824–5, was astonished to find British cotton goods for sale in Ajmer in the heart of Rājputāna and on the markets of Mārwār, a relatively isolated area where few westerners had previously ventured.[29]

The Indian cotton industry was not the only one to feel the competition of European products. In the first decades of the nineteenth century, European industrially manufactured cottons could be found in the Syrian market.[30] Bright, light and durable English cotton textiles had an immediate appeal in the Middle East. In 1814 the Levant Company wrote that 'The desire for British goods which has been manifested by the subjects of the Porte of every description opens a door to an extension of our trade of the highest importance to this nation. The quantities of these articles consumed in Turkey even under the difficulties opposed to them have far exceeded our calculation, and we have every reason to believe if those obstructions are removed, the demand will be prodigious.'[31] Indeed, demand turned out to be both prodigious and profitable for European manufacturers. Twenty years later, in 1833, the Scottish diplomat and writer David Urquhart concluded that in Turkish markets 'the preference [is] now transferred from Indian to Birmingham muslins, from Golconda to Glasgow chintzes, from Damascus to Sheffield steel, from Cashmere shawls to English broad cloth'.[32] A cornucopia of British and European products flooded the Ottoman Empire, especially after 1840, with the amount of imported cloth increasing tenfold between the 1840s and 1910.[33]

The success of British and to a smaller extent continental products was due to their low prices and to the ability of European merchants to organise distribution, assess markets and convince colonial and friendly governments to enact a series of laws aimed at reducing duties and cut down on bureaucracy. This was easier to achieve in those places in which European presence and power was direct, but, as in the case of the Ottoman Empire, the political and economic pressure of the West could also be exercised indirectly. Whilst the rhetoric of the nineteenth century – in particular after 1846 – was one of free trade and liberalisation of global markets, the reality was that only strong industrial economies like those of Britain, continental Europe and later the United States could reap the benefits of reducing trade barriers and competition across products.

Clearly European goods – and cottons most specifically – came to disrupt established commercial networks. Yet they did not necessarily cause a decline in local, regional and intraregional trade, as one might expect. The intra-Asian trade, for instance, remained larger than the trade with Europe well into the second half of the nineteenth century. One might say that the success of European products relied on the fact that they could find easy markets thanks to the wide-ranging trading system that had developed in the Indian Ocean since the early centuries of the second millennium. In the nineteenth century, European goods came to replace and supplement Asian products in intra-Asian markets. Cottons, in particular, were essential for the purchase of opium in India, which was to be sold in China in exchange for tea, which was sold back in Europe.[34] As Indian cloth had been the medium of barter through which all other commodities could be traded in the early modern Indian Ocean, in the nineteenth century British cloth came to assume a similar function.

The centripetal nature of the system of production, trade and exchange created in the nineteenth century and developed over the following century put Europe at its core and ensured the prosperity of the West vis-à-vis the relative deindustrialisation and underdevelopment of other areas of the world. The advantages provided by technological innovation, industrialisation and increasing productivity were translated in commercial terms into the shaping of a system of exchange heavily reliant on European products, capital and entrepreneurship. The importance of trade was not limited to high returns on investment or on the expansion of national industrial structures: it also stimulated backward linkages to other parts of a country's manufacturing economy, in particular iron, coal and the mechanical industry; it facilitated the building of internal infrastructures in shipping and engineering, and enabled the development of insurance and financial intermediaries.[35] This was specifically the case for Britain, where cotton textiles paid for the import of a variety of produce and raw materials and foodstuffs.[36] England acted also as the main point of control for the supply of cotton to other European countries. The British economy was not just the first to industrialise but also the first to diversify into the tertiary sector, selling its products and services to the entire world.

The global causes of deindustrialisation

> I was widowed when I was twenty-two years old. I had given birth to only three daughters...I began to spin yarn on *asana* and *charkha* ... [basic instruments] The weavers would come to my doorstep to buy the yarn thus spun...and they would immediately advance as much cash money as I wanted. As a result we did not have any anxiety about food and clothing...In this fashion I got three daughters married...Now for over three years, the mother and daughter-in-law are facing ricelessness again. Not only have the weavers stopped coming to my doorstep to buy my yarn, even when I send it to the *hat* [market place] they will not buy at one-fourth of the former price. I am completely at a loss to understand how this has come to pass. I have made inquiries and have learned that the weavers are using English yarn now being extensively imported...When I examined the yarn I indeed found it better than mine.[37]

This often cited passage is the voice of a poor Bengali widow and is dated 1828. It is well known because it shows the personal consequences of a large-scale process that this woman could not control and could hardly understand. We have a sense of the immediacy of the problem and a reflection that combines past opportunities and present challenges caused by the selling of yarn produced with technologies that this Bengali spinner did not even know about. Her testimony serves also to create a visual counterpoint with the confident world of the cotton trader in New Orleans, in which the gender dimension seems to add to the gulf of the economic divergence of different areas of the world.

At the same time, the Bengali spinner prompts us to ask if industrial cottons produced in the West and traded to India, China, Turkey, Africa and other traditional cotton-producing centres of the world truly precipitated and sustained the decline of local manufacturing capacity. The Bengali spinner might have had better luck at finding out about the causes of her problems than historians who seem instead to disagree on the destiny of the Indian cotton industry in the nineteenth century. It seems that spinning and weaving in India were already in crisis before the arrival of European textiles and perhaps even before the arrival of European traders.[38] This is the position supported by Sanjay Subrahmanyam in what he calls 'de-industrialisation before de-industrialisation'.[39] He argues that decline in spinning and weaving on the Coromandel coast of India was already apparent by the late seventeenth century, when cotton manufacturing was losing competitiveness on Asian and African markets. The political weakness of the Mughal state not only opened the subcontinent to the penetration of the English and other European companies, but also undermined the future of its most prosperous industry.[40] Politics and economy were, according to Mukherjee – in an argument further developed by both Om Prakash and Lakshmi Surbramanian – linked in a downward spiral. However, these scholars claim that it was the exogenous interference of the European EICs that had deleterious effects on the structure of production for individual arangs and weaving villages. The European companies also bypassed established distribution networks based on bazaars and local merchants, thereby diminishing the positive externalities of manufacturing on the economy at large.[41]

These interpretations refuse the idea of a sudden decline of markets caused by external forces in favour of a longer 'declinism' that marries economy and politics.[42] Similar interpretations have been proposed for the Ottoman Empire, where, it has been noticed, centres of cotton weaving like Aleppo were already in decline in the eighteenth century, independently of European interference. In a reversal of fortunes, the Ottoman Empire – that for the best part of a couple of centuries had supplied both Indian cottons and locally produced copies of Indian calicoes to Europe – by the 1750s started importing cottons: cotton stockings produced in Europe made their first appearance in Ottoman wardrobes in the 1750s.[43] The arrival of British products in the 1820s and 1830s might have been the last blow, but the causes for concern, so to say, were already visible a couple of generations earlier.[44]

Marxist and postcolonial positions cannot be more in disagreement with 'declinist' interpretations that suggest the slow erosion of competitiveness. Marx himself took the case of India as emblematic of the worst excesses of western capitalism when he repeated Lord Bentinck's (the governor-general of India) famous statement that the misery to be seen among the artisans of the subcontinent 'hardly finds a parallel in the history of commerce. The bones of the cotton weavers are bleaching the plains of India' (Figure 12.3).[45] We might think that Marx tried the emotional card to convince his readers. Yet, the more restrained

Figure 12.3 'King Cotton of Manchester'. The image of the bones of the cotton weavers of India came to assume such currency that it was used by Nazi propaganda against Britain in 1943.

proceedings of the British House of Commons reported already in 1840 that 'the decay and destruction of Surat, of Dacca, of Murshidabad and other places where native manufactures had been carried on, was too painful a fact to dwell upon'.[46]

But what exactly did cause the decline of Indian cotton manufacturing? Postcolonial historiography of India had underlined how the nineteenth-century globalisation fostered by Europe devitalised and possibly destroyed traditional craft industries. One might see, however, an explanatory shift away from the idea that colonialism and imperialism were the main causes of the economic decline of India to interpretations that emphasise instead the role of European industrialisation or of Indian and Chinese failure to adapt.[47] The two are of course difficult to disentangle, as European products found their way into Indian markets not just because of their lower prices but also thanks to colonial regulations and duties that persistently favoured the mother country. Under British rule, in 1810 the rates of duties on goods carried by foreign ships to and from Bengal were doubled while British goods were given preferential treatment with low duties. A reshape of the duty system in 1859 established a 10 per cent duty on

British cotton yarn and cloth that was reduced to 5 per cent three years later thanks to the lobbying of Lancashire cotton manufacturers.[48]

The wage differential that had made Indian cottons competitive against European products in the eighteenth century had been by the 1830s and 1840s completely deleted by the productivity gains of European machines. By the mid nineteenth century it was observed that the products of Vizagapatnam were 'incapable of competing with cheaper cloth from the English market' and that the trade of Cuddalore piece-goods to Sumatra had been 'almost superseded by piece-goods of European manufacture'.[49] British yarn and cotton pieces rivalled the higher-quality goods produced in India and at the same time glutted international markets, such as Java and Persia, that had previously been supplied by India.[50]

Recent interpretations have been less categorical about the extent of economic decline and have underlined instead how the Indian economy, and in particular its textile production, saw a great degree of continuity. Tirthankar Roy supports the idea that only part of the Indian economy was negatively affected by the arrival of cheap industrially produced goods. Sections of the artisanal economy of the subcontinent benefited instead by the widening of markets and increasing access to raw materials. Indian artisans did not succumb *tout court* to foreign (European) competition but 'adapted' to the new situation by cutting costs, relocating, sharing knowledge and information and, Roy argues, by strengthening social capital.[51] There were also areas of the Indian manufacturing economy that remained protected from competition, such as the design-intensive and skilled handloom weaving.[52] This type of interpretation attributes agency to Indian producers and highlights how late nineteenth-century Indian industrialisation only partially followed a European model, maintaining, for instance, a strong handloom weaving sector. It is in stark contrast with analyses that instead emphasise the lack of efficiency and the low productivity of labour in cotton textiles manufacturing in a country characterised by an endemic inefficiency pervading the productive system at the end of the nineteenth century.[53]

The relative decline of Indian cotton manufacturing in the nineteenth century should also be contextualised within what we now call the 'great divergence'. Rather than an exception, India's economic involution embodies a wider trend that saw the economic prosperity of Asia diminish over the century. There is, however, a tendency to exaggerate the scale of the 'rise of the West' and the 'decline of Asia'. In 1830, for instance, total British imports were just 4–5 per cent of Indian cotton manufacturing.[54] Similarly, the size of cotton manufacturing in Europe was much smaller than in India up to the 1830s (Table 12.1).

In the 1820s the British cotton industry was half (and possibly only a third) in size compared to cotton manufacturing in the subcontinent. Twenty years

Table 12.1 Estimates of the number of cotton weavers and cloth output in four areas of the world in the 1820s and 1840s.

	Number of weavers (in thousand employed)		Cloth output (in thousand tons)		Cloth output per worker (in kg)		Output ratio (India = 100)	
	1820s	1840s	1820s	1840s	1820s	1840s	1820s	1840s
India	1,100–1,800	1,800	194–393	237–324	176–213	132–180	100	100
Ottoman Empire	65	62	11–14	8–12	175–213	132–180	3–7.5	2.5–4.6
Britain	126	123	92–116	304–370	730–920	2,471–3,008	c. 30–47	c. 116–127
France	–	–	11.9	36–49	–	–	3–6	14–19

Data: India (1820); Ottoman Empire (1820–2); Britain (1820–1); France (1815–24); 1840s: India (1850); Ottoman Empire (1840–22); Britain (1840); France (1845–54). Estimates for total British output based on 40–50% export and 4–5 yards of cloth per kg.

Sources: Alice Amsden, *The Rise of 'The Rest': Challenges to the West from Late-Industrializing Economies* (Oxford University Press, 2001), pp. 34–6; B. R. Mitchell, *International Historical Statistics: Europe* (New York: Stockton Press, 1970), pp. 376, 428; B. R. Mitchell and Phyllis Deane, *Abstract of British Historical Statistics* (Cambridge University Press, 1962), p. 356; François Crouzet, *Britain Ascendant: Comparative Studies in Franco-British Economic History* (Cambridge University Press, 1990), p. 251.

later things had changed, with British production surpassing that of India. These figures reveal also that the competition was between India and Britain, with important cotton textile producers like the modern French cotton industry and the long-established Ottoman one being relatively small in size.[55] Yet trajectories were different. Whilst cotton textile production was declining in the Ottoman Empire and possibly already in India, it was booming in Britain and France.[56]

The problems faced by India and Turkey were not limited to the competition of European piece-goods. The subcontinent also shared with the Middle East the pressure of an increasing European demand for raw materials. In the case of the Ottoman Empire, Parthasarathi has argued that because of the high demand for raw materials for the expanding European industry, there was an incentive to move away from the production of finished cloth towards the trade in raw cotton and spun yarn. This was evident in Cairo and Bursa, though it is uncertain if this was a general trend across the empire.[57] At the end of the eighteenth century, Cairo had 12,000 workers employed in eighteen different branches of textile production, but half a century later this industry had collapsed.[58]

Neither the power of politics (colonialism) nor the realignment of markets (due to western industrialisation) can fully explain the complex economic trajectories of the cotton industries of Asia. Both the Indian and Ottoman industries entered a phase of decline. Turkish production of spun yarn, for instance, fell from 11,500 tons per year in 1820–2 to just 300 tons a year in 1870–2, with the production of cotton cloth in the empire declining by at least one-half between 1820 and 1910.[59] Yet, as İnalcık has argued, the reason for such a decline might be found in different parts of the economy at different times. The initial decline caused by the replacement of local with imported yarn was followed by the replacement of Indian imports by British goods. Finally, and most importantly, European goods imported into rural inland markets replaced the cheaper and coarser varieties of cotton goods previously manufactured locally.[60] This argument, which has been recently revised by Pamuk and Williamson, suggests that the impact of European industrial goods might have been different according to the markets considered.[61] The import of European yarn and cloth increased dramatically, but it did not always displace local production. Imported yarn, for instance, was suitable for markets that were price-sensitive, but locally hand-spun yarn was preferred where high quality was a priority. Hand-spun yarn was used both for industrial weaving and hand weaving and the finishing of cloth was carried out with factory-made dyes, thus making it difficult to maintain a neat opposition between industrial versus craft or imported versus domestic.[62]

The distinction between craft production and modern industry was even more untenable in the case of India, where from the 1870s onwards Parsi capital financed the setting up of factory production in Bombay with machinery imported from England, an industry that soon came to supply yarn and cotton cloth to international markets such as China and East Africa.[63] Mechanised production also supplied yarn to the local handloom weaving industry. The finishing of Indian cloth was affected by western technologies, too, with synthetic dyes replacing natural ones in the second half of the nineteenth century.[64] Yet the conceptual relegation of Indian production to craft as opposed to the mechanised manufacturing of cheap products in the West was the unforeseen result of campaigns by English design reformers such as Owen Jones, Forbes Watson and Purdon Clarke (Figure 12.4).[65] Although they argued in defence of hand weaving and non-mechanised production (and condemned British industrial goods as horrific from a design point of view), their campaigns could be said to unwillingly contribute to the exoticisation of non-European production and its eventual demotion to the margin of the world of manufacturing. Even the *swadeshi* ('own country') movement of the early twentieth century, by arguing for economic self-sufficiency from Britain, fell into the trap of creating antagonism against mechanised production in which the resistance against British products was equated to the acceptance of rural domestic production.[66]

Changing products and global taste

Was it just price, material quality or the pressures for free trade that made European cottons so successful across the globe? Taste, the types of products that people liked and the meaning that they associated with such commodities also had an important part to play in the global success of industrial commodities in the nineteenth and twentieth centuries. The integration of markets brought about what I call a visual and aesthetic 'convergence of taste' that came to favour European manufactured goods.

The dynamism of western industrial manufacturing relied on global markets. In pre-industrial manufacturing, new and previously unknown markets had been a true challenge for coordination and merchandising and in achieving what today we would call good levels of 'customer satisfaction'. The revolution in transport and communication helped to make the world smaller and the assessment of consumer preferences easier. Yet the result was not the production of endless customisation but the triumph of standards set by the West. As industry had emerged as the best practice in manufacturing globally, so industrial products emerged as the most popular commodities among consumers around the world.

Figure 12.4 Tie-dyed cotton cloth for a turban made in Dehi, *c.* 1880. It was acquired by Sir Caspar Purdon Clarke (1846–1911) on his tour of India in 1881–2. Clarke sent to London more than 3,000 artefacts, including architectural pieces, sculpture, paintings, manuscripts, metalwork, jewellery and textiles. He was appointed director of the South Kensington Museum (from 1899 the Victoria and Albert Museum) in 1896.

To deny that British and other European products made inroads into international markets by way of adaptations to local tastes would, however, be misleading. In the case of textiles sold to the Southeast Asian markets, British but also Dutch and other European producers started printing versions of Gujarati patola and imitations of tie-dye cloths in the style of those made in Rajasthan. Results were not always what was expected: European batiks, for instance, were neither as cheap nor as good a quality when compared with local Southeast Asian products.[67] A similar situation could be observed in Brazil, a large and popular market for cotton textiles since at least the seventeenth century. Here the problem was that British products were seen as 'too gloomy for people who laugh at themselves. Let us have no drabs – we have no Quakers here. We want no dismal colours for an English November'.[68] Success in international markets still depended on the ability to understand consumers and foresee their changing preferences.

The complexity of supplying individual markets can be considered through the correspondence of Christophe Aubin, a commercial representative of a Glasgow merchant company sent to explore Middle Eastern markets in 1812. His report is based on meticulous research into patterns, colours and the understanding of seasonal conditions. He peremptorily asked for 'only printed goods which *must* be glazed', requiring also that calicoes 'should be arrived here in August and September' while the unglazed summer calico 'should be here in March'.[69] Reading Aubin's observations, one gets a sense of the type of markets that British and European cottons aimed to furnish. It was not the market for high-quality, richly finished textiles and not even the lowest market that was efficiently supplied by domestic production. European industrial products conquered a middle market, one that was still price-sensitive and that was at the same time expanding not just in Europe but also across most of the world. Muslins, Aubin observed, were a good example of such a middle-quality product, one 'of considerable consumption' in Turkey, especially for turbans, headdresses for ladies and veils. Yet he noticed that since Britain had started producing muslin in imitation of Indian products, Turkish consumers had been 'very much prejudiced against all English Manufacture', though he also noticed that in recent times 'they have now changed their mind and buy what is cheapest. Thus the English goods have almost replaced the Indian Muslins which however many still be sold to a certain extent, but at lower rates than formerly.'[70]

It would be likewise incorrect to attribute the success of European cottons solely to their adaptability to local tastes and market circumstances. There is evidence that identical products were commercialised in different parts of the world, with similar chintz motifs being sold both to English and Japanese ladies of the first half of the nineteenth century.[71] In both areas, such chintzes were considered to be appealing and fashionable. In India, for instance, it was observed how British fabrics were conquering markets not out of innate quality but because they offered 'a greater variety of patterns which enabled people to make a more frequent change of dress'.[72] The capacity of British industry to provide cloth that could be frequently replaced seemed to be successful also in the difficult Chinese market. The Englishman John Matheson despaired at the low results of an auction of British cotton piece-goods in Canton in 1819, noticing that 'The shirting seems quite unsalable – they call it an imitation (and of course an inferior one) of their grasscloth. Stripes were not liked. They seem altogether insensible to the beauty of these.'[73] He argued that British products had to be 'domesticated' in the same way in which Indian cottons had been for Europeans a couple of

THE PROGRESS OF CIVILIZATION.

Figure 12.5 'The Progress of Civilization', from John Russell's *Around the World with General Grant* (1879). The wearing of western clothing was here criticised as a naive attempt to embrace progress and modernity.

centuries earlier. This is why Matheson was later jubilant when he observed 'some instances of wealthy merchants dressing their children in chintzes, previously only used for bedcovers, and if the taste becomes fashionable, as is by no means impossible, the field which it opens up for British industry is immense'.[74]

The capacity to propose new uses and promote the adoption of European cloth was key to the success of western products on Asian markets. And there was no better means to change consumers' preferences for cloth than to change their clothing. The penetration of industrial fabrics produced in Europe went hand in hand with the replacement of indigenous forms of dress with European styles.[75] Europe did not just sell the cloth but also showed what could be done with it. This may be seen in the case of the fashion for the wearing of European-style trousers and redingote in Iran in the 1830s.[76] In Java, factory-woven flannels, velvets and cottons of different grades became part of common attire. In Borneo, the bark cloth used for jackets and skirts was abandoned in favour of cheap European cloth, thus changing not just the materiality of textiles but also the shapes of clothing.[77] From Russia in the early eighteenth century to the Ottoman Empire and Japan in the nineteenth century (Figure 12.5), western dress was favoured by governments eager to be 'modern'. Notwithstanding attempts to resist the infiltration of European forms of attire and the import of European textiles by promoting local fabrics and modes of dress, western-style garments made of cottons and woollens made inroads into the sartorial choices of elites, a form of 'soft power' that percolated down to the popular classes in most parts of Asia, Africa and the Americas. Cotton became a western product with a global appeal.[78]

Local production, too, was not immune from European models. The nineteenth century inaugurated a phase of 'globalisation of production' which made it difficult to discern if a fabric was produced in Manchester, Bombay or Lowell, Massachusetts, a fact that, as Susan Bean observes, 'obscured the singular identities of textiles and made them less viable as repositories of distinction, wealth, and value'.[79] Design, use and the cultural value of cloth were no longer based on local idiosyncrasies, specialisation of production and customisation. Success on global markets meant that cotton manufacturing around the world 'had to adapt to the European revolution'.[80] And they seemed to have done so more readily in terms of products than in the adoption of technologies, something not much different from what had happened in Europe with Asian products and their associated technologies a couple of centuries earlier.

This picture should, however, be taken with a pinch of salt. Industrial European products conquered the middle market, but the extent of such a market differed substantially from place to place. In the case of India, for instance, the vast market producing low counts (below 24) remained the prerogative of Indian producers and did not face as hard a competition as finer fabrics.[81] The Japanese market resorted to imported products only for specific uses and in particular white bleached cottons. It is not by chance that in 1860 more than half of all British cottons imported into Japan were textiles for shirting. Japanese consumers continued instead to prefer locally woven rather than cheaper British cottons. Most English cottons were rather fine, with high counts of yarn: 30 to 60 for shirting, 40–50 for doria stripes and 36–80 for sateens. Local textiles were instead characterised by low counts, mostly around 20.[82]

Why isn't the whole world developed?

The world that cotton created was a one of increasing commercial connections, of complex economic entanglements and of political influence. The so-called 'soft globalisation' of the early modern period based on encounters, discovery and trade gave way to a phase of 'hard globalisation' measured by the integration of markets and price convergence.[83] Polycentrism was replaced by western power in economic and political affairs worldwide. Raw cotton and cotton textiles represent the major mediums through which momentous changes were achieved. Cottons did not just 'clothe the world'; they also shaped and aided the flows of raw materials and commodities – ranging from tea to opium and from silver to copper – across unparalleled geographic extensions.[84] In many ways, the world in 1913 was more globalised than it is at present.[85] The cost of transport, the rapidity of information and the ease of communication changed dramatically over the second half of the nineteenth century.[86] Today we think of our lives as being profoundly affected by the Internet, emails, social networks and satellite technologies. Yet these present-day innovations pale in comparison with those of the nineteenth century. That was a century in which railroads connected ports and industrial areas and allowed people to move fast and cheaply; steamships revolutionised trans-oceanic trade, with the cost of moving bulk commodities halving between the 1840s and 1880s.[87] The telegraph and later the telephone made communication instantaneous. One could read about cotton prices in Bombay or Canton in a New Orleans newspaper (as was done by the man in Degas' painting in Figure 12.1) the day after they were released.

The nineteenth century structured the world in which to a large extent we still live. Outcomes differed. It was a world of profound inequality, both internal to nations (as Marx would observe) and across nations and continents (as Pomeranz and many before him noticed). But why didn't the entire world industrialise and develop? This might appear a naive question if we believe the world to be a 'zero-sum' game in which only some can reap the benefits. Yet, generations of development economists, past and present, identify the central issue not in the self-interest of the West, but in the mechanisms, incentives and institutional structures conducive to economic and social development. The case of cotton textiles shows that these opposite perspectives might be a useful common ground to explain why the economy of North America flourished while China lagged behind, or why the setting up of cotton mills in India failed to trigger a process of industrialisation that led to the creation of 'a Lancashire of a new type'.[88]

To some extent, 'Lancashires of a new type' were established elsewhere in the world. Some areas were receptive not just to European technologies but also to the cultural and institutional models that had supported innovation. The newly independent United States established societies of *savants* similar to those of Europe. American manufactures were fostered through means of encouragements such as rewards, premiums, monopolies and privileges not unlike those of Europe.[89] Despite a false start in 1807–14, by the 1830s the United States had developed their own cotton textile industry, which was second in size only to that of Britain.[90] Similar developments were taking place in Europe, though results were chequered by the competition of British products. In Russia, too,

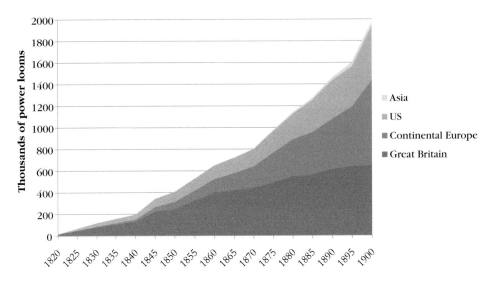

Figure 12.6 Power looms in the cotton industry in the world, 1820–1900.

cotton manufacturing developed after 1840 when the German Ludwig Knoop set up his first cotton mill.[91]

Most of the initial technologies used in North America, continental Europe and Russia came from Britain. There is little doubt that British technology was cutting edge in terms of productivity, but technological transfer encountered several barriers. The most important was the British ban on the export of machinery enacted in 1781–2 that prohibited the export of every 'machine, engine, tool, press, paper, utensil or implement' used in textile manufacturing in the United Kingdom. The laws prohibiting the export of machinery were finally repealed in 1825 and only after Britain had attained such advantages that no other nation could truly rival in cotton textile manufacturing, at least in the short term.[92]

An indication of the gap between Britain and other areas of the world in textile manufacturing can be glimpsed from the number of power looms in the cotton industry (Figure 12.6). In the mid nineteenth century, Britain accounted for two-thirds of all cotton textile mechanical looms used in the world. Fifty years later, Britain's share had declined to a still substantial one-third, with Europe and the United States accounting for the rest. Before 1900, Asia never had more than 3–4 per cent of the world's power looms. Bombay never became a Lancashire for India.[93]

Why was that the case? The original protection (the assertion of property rights) of technology was part and parcel of a system that I have defined as 'centripetal'. Yet this was something that was not sustainable in the long term. When it came to recognising that other parts of the world might start a process of economic development, the European experience was seen as a model to follow.[94] In some cases, as for US cotton manufacturing, Britain provided a model to improve on, as happened with the introduction of ring spinning, an innovation later adopted by UK producers in the second half of the nineteenth century.[95]

Some have argued against this type of interpretation, supporting the idea that East Asia – and Japan in particular – developed along a special path that was labour- rather than capital-intensive.[96] The interesting East Asian case of the adoption of labour-intensive technologies and the promotion of labour-absorbing institutions has generated debate on whether this is a different path or a deviation from a European path of industrial development that suited the specific socio-economic contexts. Yet, when one compares the world of textile manufacturing in the fifteenth and in the nineteenth centuries, some striking differences are evident. The world of the early modern Indian 'cotton sphere' was characterised by the diffusion of products and their eventual adoption in the most remote corners of Afro-Eurasia. The reception was accompanied by adaptation, changing technological solutions to suit specific working conditions and specialisation. The industrial system of the nineteenth century, by contrast, proposed one best practice (the most efficient and best quality), a unilateral standard that was sought after across the world. This was a world in which success meant if not 'be European', then to 'become European'.

Technologies explain part of the problem. They might be said to be necessary but not sufficient to create a competitive industry. A country needed its own entrepreneurial class providing fixed and circulating capital, human capital in the form of a skilled workforce, a system of credit and insurance as well as transport facilities and the ability to sell on domestic and international markets. These factors, more than mere technological aptitude, were paramount to economic development.[97] Yet by setting a western standard of economic development, non-western areas of the world could only fall short. I am here arguing that new technologies and industrial organisation of production allowed for the West to manufacture a range of products at lower real prices than those produced elsewhere in the world. This in turn allowed the West to achieve comparative advantages that became the base for setting the rules of the world economy, something that worked to the advantage of the West in the longer period.

In many cases, the technologically integrated world of production exemplified by factories was unsuited to non-European socio-economic contexts. In Latin America, for example, cotton textile manufacturing developed along the model of decentralised indigenous production that had characterised the sector before the arrival of the Europeans. The relative easiness of the supply of raw cotton made spinning the perfect domestic activity, while weaving was mostly carried out in small workshops.[98] This productive model was supported and strengthened by the imposition of tributes in kind by the Spanish crown.[99] Latin America, although an area of the world of high consumption of cottons and with a relative abundance of suitable natural resources, did not develop a large-scale cotton industry. Human capital was relatively low, with little technical expertise and an endemic lack of long-term investment. These issues, coupled with a lack of basic infrastructures for moving goods and information across vast geographies, made the coordination of markets particularly difficult vis-à-vis the responsiveness of local domestic production. Moreover, technological adoption remained difficult in a hostile anti-manufacturing climate imposed by colonial rule.[100] Until the early years of the nineteenth century, the prohibition of manufacturing of textiles in Brazil included not just high-quality silks, taffetas and satins, but also the more modest chintzes, bombazines, fustians and other types of cottons.[101] The only exception was the manufacture of coarse cotton textiles for slaves, which was already a highly developed and commercialised industry that did not affect the economic interests of the mother country.[102]

The difficulty of fitting into a European model of economic development can also be seen as something positive. The case of China is emblematic in the fact that European capitalism and products – however successful they might be – never became hegemonic. Until the end of the nineteenth century, British and European cottons achieved little popularity in China. In the age of western industrialisation and the rise of the European cotton industry, Chinese cotton textile production prospered, expanding dramatically thanks to the importation of large quantities of raw cotton from India, one of China's major imports.[103] Until the 1880s, only a small percentage of China's yarn and cloth was imported. Historians have attributed this to the survival of handicraft production. The rural household could compete both with national and international mechanised spun yarn production and cloth weaving because of the exploitation of labour internal to the household itself.[104] Labour elasticity created a labour market with no bottom. Some historians, however, do not see these dynamics as signs of economic involution. Rather, they present the survival of handicraft production in a positive light, underlining how it allocated labour efficiently and allowed the industry to innovate.[105]

Conclusion

How much did cotton influence the world economy? This chapter has emphasised the role of trade and consumption in the creation of what I have defined as a 'centripetal system'. Cotton was key in structuring a capitalist world in which the West, often through the means of political power and influence, imposed standards in production as well as consumption. The world that cotton created was one based on industrial capitalism and its prosperous core. Such a core was not just Britain but also included most of those countries that we now refer to as 'the West'. This was also a world, unlike its Indian Ocean predecessor, that had a clearly defined centre in which resources and profits converged. And much more than the Indian Ocean world, this was a 'global world' to be considered as one system of trade, exchange and socio-cultural and political entanglement.

13 CONCLUSION: FROM SYSTEM TO SYSTEM; FROM DIVERGENCE TO CONVERGENCE

Let me conclude with what might appear a rather ordinary piece of cloth (Figure 13.1). It is a bandana, a square handkerchief commonly worn in India. Indeed, this cloth was produced in South Asia in the early nineteenth century but was consumed not in Asia but in North America. We are well acquainted with bandanas as they are to be seen around the neck of cowboys in endless 1950s and 1960s movies. They might be one of the few items that we are accurate about in films of nineteenth-century adventurers living in the Wild West. What the movies do not reveal, however, is that the bandana was made of a pretty Indian cloth (sometimes made of silk but most commonly of cotton), and that such cloth was part of the hyper-masculine sartorial choices of American cowboys.

An Indian bandana appears to us to be out of place in the American Far West also because the construction of the figure of the cowboy relies on the importance of another item made of cotton: jeans. It is Californian jeans (Levi's and later other labels) that have been repeatedly presented as foundational to US national identity. Yet, when the recently independent American Republic started trading in the Indian Ocean, bandanas were the most important item of importation into the US.[1] Bandanas became a hit, with literally millions of them being sold in North America in the first couple of decades of the nineteenth century. It was such a good line of business that bandana imitations for US customers started being produced in the United States, and also in Britain and China.[2]

From system to system

This object sits so uncomfortably between Asia and the West: its identity is unclear and it defies conventional classifications. Yet, it is a good prop to reflect on the transition of cotton textiles from being an Asian sector commodity to

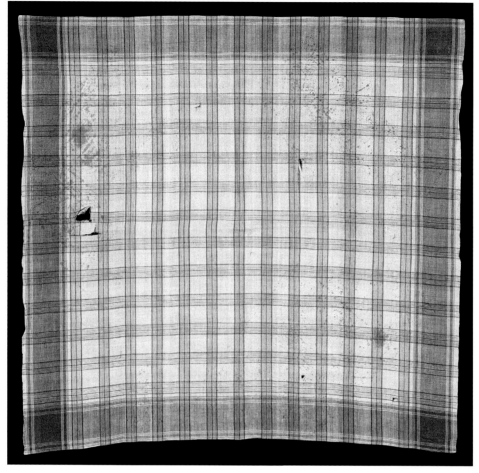

Figure 13.1 Cotton bandana with plaid of maroon and white, produced in India and probably used in the United States, nineteenth century. (See also colour plate.)

becoming central to western industry and culture. This book has mapped a shift from what I defined as the 'old cotton system' of the Indian Ocean to a 'new cotton system' created by the West (Table 13.1). In what ways are these two systems different?

The most striking dissimilarity between them is that before the eighteenth century it was India (and to a lesser extent other areas of Asia) that excelled in cotton manufacturing, trade and consumption. From the early nineteenth century, Europe and later North America emerged as the new undisputed areas of cotton textile production and trade. The main aim of this book has been to explain why this happened and how this story relates to the wider framework of divergence. But keeping ourselves to a purely descriptive level, other differences

Table 13.1 *The old and the new cotton systems.*

	Old cotton system *c.* 1000–1750	New cotton system *c.* 1750–2000
Manufacturing core	India	Northwestern Europe
Exchange	Long-distance but fragmented; sea and ocean-based	Long-distance, global; including the Atlantic and Pacific
Competition	Import substitution; does not kill off local industries	Import involution; does kill off local industries
Products	Customisation of goods	Standardisation and fashion
Resources	Mostly local	Imported from other continents

between these two systems are noticeable. Since the nineteenth century, cotton textile trade has become truly global, connecting not just Afro-Eurasia but also the Atlantic and the Pacific. Both systems were based on long-distance exchange, but while customisation of production and design were central to the success of India, Europe played with new notions of fashionability, often creating visual and aesthetic canons for other areas of the world to follow.

I have also argued that while the trade and exchange of cottons in the 'old cotton system' did not kill off local cotton manufacturing, in the new industrial system created by Europe, non-industrial production was marginalised and often destroyed by competition. I have called the 'new cotton system' centripetal because its logic is egocentric: it not only aims at selling to the entire world but is also based on the use of raw materials produced outside the boundaries of the West. It creates property rights, colonial policies and power relationships that foster the preservation of competitive advantages. Capital is an important component in the dynamics of western ascendancy, though this book has also underlined the role played by raw materials and finished commodities.

If we translate this static picture into a dynamic one, this book has attempted to understand the changing relationship between four main areas of the world that for reasons of brevity I equate with four continents (Figure 13.2). The story of cotton textiles has here been linked to that of Europe's industrialisation but also to Asia's diminishing economic importance. When in the sixteenth century trade between Asia (especially India and China) and western Europe started in full, Asia provided manufactured goods (cottons, but also porcelain, lacquer and other 'luxury goods') to Europe in exchange for bullion (silver). There was a haemorrhage of capital from the precious metal reserves that the continent acquired from the Americas (dotted lines in Figure 13.2). To a certain

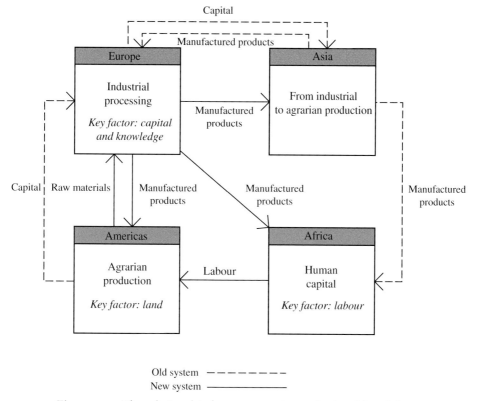

Figure 13.2 The relationship between continents in the old and the new cotton systems.

extent, Asian products also reached other continents, such as Africa and the Americas.

Europe's industrial conversion changed such relations dramatically. Central to Europe's transition to what has been defined as a 'modern economy' was the investment of capital and knowledge in innovative productive processes (continuous line in Figure 13.2). We have seen the success of European products on all the world's markets, causing a decline and a relative re-agrarianisation of Asia. But Europe's new position was also based on factors provided by other continents (Africa and the Americas) that came for the first time to be fully integrated into a global system of exchange and economic relations. In the long term, the Americas became important not for the provision of bullion but of land and raw materials: they provided new crops, abundant foodstuffs and key raw materials for the European industries. Africa instead provided untapped reserves of labour through the millions of slaves that were transported to the Americas to work on plantations. Two features of this reconfiguration should be emphasised. First, that the resulting system is more complex and articulated than the one it replaced: it is not just geographically more extensive but also larger in terms of fluxes. This is what we might call 'globalisation'. Second, this new system sees a reversal of fortunes for Europe and Asia, with the latter being marginalised. India (and to a lesser extent China) became markets for European goods, losing their manufacturing importance.

Towards divergence

How did all of this happen? This book has used cotton as a way to present a narrative but also to explain the logic of global economic and social change. It has given particular attention to three contexts.

Agrarian. As Mark Elvin noticed more than thirty years ago, 'the Chinese had no such vast new sources of cotton as the British found in the West Indies and South America'.[3] In this book, I have tried to understand in which ways such resources external to Europe came to be used for the development of the cotton textile sector. Two major points of departure were evident: first the fact that abundant quantities of raw materials allowed for prices to remain low without falling in a well-known inflationary spiral caused by burgeoning demand. Second, these abundant supplies came from 'somewhere else', allowing for the agrarian economy of Europe to be insulated from the massive changes that affected its industrial structure. The modernity of the European cotton industry lay not just in the use of machinery but also in the delinking of manufacturing from local agrarian production.

Industrial. Part and parcel of any story of divergence is the importance of technological innovation. In most stories of industrialisation, technology remains the one and only factor of transformation. In this book I have put technology in context in at least two ways. First, I have purposely played down its importance, showing for instance how without raw cotton or consumer markets, technological innovation had little potential per se. Second, I have suggested that we should not focus narrowly on spinning and weaving and on productivity, but that the assessment of the industrial transition of Europe should take into consideration issues of quality and the importance of finishing (printing). This perspective adds a comparative international dimension to European industrialisation vis-à-vis the high level of sophistication of Indian cotton textile production and finishing.

Commercial. Most histories of divergence give little or no space to consumption. They consider markets only from an aggregate point of view and presume that they are responsive to whatever is produced. My book has challenged this perspective and has considered the position of consumers, their likes and dislikes, their tastes, the vagaries of fashion and the attempt by governments to control consumption and shape markets. It has also shown the success of European products in creating their own markets around the world, often with the help of conducive policies and friendly political governments.

My explanation of divergence has two main characteristics: its connectedness and its protracted nature. Europe's divergence cannot be solely understood by looking within the borders of Europe, or by attributing it to Europe's peculiar culture, institutions, scientific and mechanical knowledge or natural endowments. This book has shown instead that divergence was a process based on a changing interaction between different areas of the world. I have also done my best to avoid falling into an opposition between 'the West' and 'the Rest' by showing how the so-called 'Rest' was integral to the rise of the West. The West (Europe and North America in particular) did not possess any 'killer apps' – as Niall Ferguson has recently defined as the presumed innate qualities of Europe.[4] The possible rise of the West was founded instead on the reframing of the workings and logic of power and exchange around the globe. These in turn made industrialisation viable. It was not just a matter of producing more or more efficiently; one had to find markets, structure trade, provide insurance, convince consumers and create fluxes of information, capital and commodities.[5] Many of these skills were learned by 'the West' from 'the Rest'. All of this could not happen in a short amount of time. It took centuries to restructure economies, understand potentials, acquire knowledge and expand markets. Although divergence remains a point of major departure, its chronological stretch is here seen as being longer than other historians have been willing to admit.

From divergence to convergence

In 1873 the Indian nationalist Bholanath Chandra predicted that by 1970 the US and India would have eclipsed industrial Britain.[6] Chandra might have been too optimistic, but he was half right. A great deal of the interest given in recent years to divergence derives from what we might call 'convergence', that is to say, the rise of China and India to be leading industrial areas in today's world economy.[7] One might see it as a return to prominence after a lull of over two centuries, with the consequent reassessment of the privileged position that the West long enjoyed in world politics, economy and society.

The discussion of the reasons for a possible convergence of the Asian economies is today a hot topic and resides well outside the remit of this book. Yet there is a somewhat misleading impression that the rise of China and India is part of (or only the result of) the development of new economic sectors. In reality, textiles and clothing (the majority made of cotton) constitute the bulk of production in both countries. Although this book has focused on the transition from an early modern world to a so-called modern world of industry in the nineteenth century, it is important to underline how cottons, other textiles, and in recent decades clothing remained key commodities in global manufacturing and trade. Cotton was fundamental to the industrialisation of Japan in the early twentieth century. In 1919, the cotton industry generated 13.4 per cent of the nation's GNP. By 1933, Japan had surpassed Great Britain and the US as the world's largest supplier of cotton textiles.[8] Perhaps even more than for Britain, cotton textiles were, for Japan, the springboard towards modern industry, ensuring not just high levels of export but also the modernisation of production and management.[9]

Cottons were also central to the economic 'take-off' of China. Until the 1950s, China's cotton industry relied only marginally on industrial production as the majority of output was generated in rural households. However, between 1950 and 1970 China overtook the US as the largest producer of cotton yarn and by 1969 also overtook Japan as the largest world exporter of cotton cloth. The records broken by China in cotton textile production were indicative of what was going to come in other sectors. In 1971 it acquired the largest spindleage in the world; in 1981 it became the largest producer of raw cotton; in 1988 it was the largest exporter of clothing; in 1991 it was the largest world exporter of textiles.[10]

Cotton textiles swung the balance of economic power back to Asia. A similar trend can be observed for India. In 2003, textiles and clothing accounted for a quarter of India's exports and *circa* 3 per cent of the world's textiles and clothing exports. It is estimated that the sector is the second largest in India, providing employment to 35 million people, *circa* 10 per cent of the country's workforce.[11]

With growth rates of between 6 and 9 per cent a year, China and India are growing at levels that are unimaginable anywhere in the western world.[12] Complaints are often voiced about the cut-throat competition of these Asian countries possibly leading to deindustrialisation and unemployment, not just in textile and clothing production in the West but also in Latin America and Korea, areas that had previously developed solid textile and clothing production that are now in decline.[13] Yet this reversal of fortunes is in some ways the fruit of what might be called a 'reversal of conditions'. Whilst at the end of the eighteenth century the textile sector emerged as one of the most capital-intensive by shifting from small-scale artisanal to factory production, today the textile sector that contributes so much to the development of Asia is relatively labour-intensive. Together with clothing, toys, furniture and consumer-good production, textile production in China and India takes advantage of relatively cheap labour while using technologies that are as efficient as those used in the West.[14] Over time, there has also been a shift in the textile industry from high to low value-added. Part of this can be explained by the fact that since the late nineteenth century only marginal technological innovations have taken place in textile manufacturing. Major exceptions have been the introduction of synthetic fibres, the use of chemical processes for printing, and, in recent years, the adoption of computer-aided design. Still, these have not substantially altered textile production as a whole.[15]

Levi's might one day, in a not so distant future, become a Chinese product, in the same ways in which palampores and bandanas became western products in the eighteenth and nineteenth centuries. The clothes of our future John Wayne (probably on a Bollywood film set) will not only be of Asian manufacture, but also recognisably Asian in appearance. But this is another story.

NOTES

1 Introduction: global cotton and global history

1 The success of cotton textiles on global markets in the early modern period is considered in two volumes that I have edited as part of the Global Economic History Network project (GEHN) funded by the Leverhulme Trust (www2.lse.ac.uk/economicHistory/Research/GEHN/Home.aspx). They provide insights into topics and areas that for the reason of brevity could not be included in this book. See Giorgio Riello and Prasannan Parthasarathi, eds., *The Spinning World: a Global History of Cotton Textiles, 1200–1850* (Oxford University Press, 2009); and Giorgio Riello and Tirthankar Roy, eds., *How India Clothed the World: the World of South Asian Textiles, 1500–1850* (Leiden: E. J. Brill, 2009). For the period post-1800, see Douglas A. Farnie and David J. Jeremy, eds., *The Fibre that Changed the World: the Cotton Industry in International Perspective, 1600–1990s* (Oxford University Press, 2004).

2 See in particular Giorgio Riello and Tirthankar Roy, 'Introduction: the World of South Asian Textiles, 1500–1850', in Riello and Roy, eds., *How India Clothed the World*, pp. 1–27.

3 On the debates over the extent and intensity of early modern globalisation, see Frederick Cooper, 'What is the Concept of Globalization Good For? An African Historian's Perspective', *African Affairs* 100 (2001): 189–213; A. G. Hopkins, ed., *Globalisation in World History* (London: Pimlico, 2002), especially the chapter by C. A. Bayly, '"Archaic" and "Modern" Globalization in the Eurasian and African Arena, c. 1750–1850', pp. 45–72; C. A. Bayly, *The Birth of the Modern World, 1780–1914* (Oxford: Blackwell, 2004), esp. pp. 23–83; Kevin H. O'Rourke and Jeffrey G. Williamson, 'When did Globalisation Begin?', *European Review of Economic History* 6/1 (2002): 23–50; Pieter Emmer, 'The Myth of Early Globalization: the Atlantic Economy, 1500–1800', *European Review* 9/1 (2003): 37–47; and Jan de Vries, 'The Limits of Globalization in the Early Modern World', *EHR* 63/3 (2010): 710–33. For a synthetic overview, see Jürgen Osterhammel and Niels P. Peterson, *Globalization: a Short History* (Princeton University Press, 2005) and Toyin Falola and Emily Brownell, eds., *Africa, Empire and Globalization: Essays in Honor of A. G. Hopkins* (Durham: University of Carolina Press, 2011), especially in part 3 the essays by Patrick K. O'Brien, Peter Cain and Sue Martin, pp. 447–92.

4 Angus Maddison, *The World Economy: a Millennial Perspective* (Paris: Development Centre Studies, 2001), p. 67.

5 Alfred P. Wadsworth and Julia de Lacy Mann, *The Cotton Trade and Industrial Lancashire 1600–1780* (Manchester University Press, 1931).

6 Kenneth Pomeranz, *The Great Divergence: China, Europe and the Making of the Modern World Economy* (Princeton University Press, 2000). On the critique of divergence see: P. H. H. Vries, 'Are Coal and Colonies Really Crucial? Kenneth Pomeranz and the Great Divergence', *JWH* 12/2 (2001): 407–46; Prasannan Parthasarathi, 'Review Article: the Great Divergence', *P&P* 167 (2002): 275–93; Joseph M. Bryant, 'The West and the Rest Revisited: Debating Capitalist Origins, European Colonialism, and the Advent of Modernity', *Canadian Journal of Sociology* 31/4 (2006): 403–44.

7 These days, such a view is deeply unfashionable. Bryant reviewing Pomeranz's divergence says that the scholarship 'that discounts or flattens variations in the institutional and the cultural is here [Pomeranz's Divergence] met by a new kind of history that dispenses with the tracking of deep lines of cumulative causation and reconfigures the past in terms of long-persisting similarities, protracted lulls, and sudden discontinuities'. This is not a perspective shared in this book. Joseph M. Bryant, 'A New Sociology for a New History? Further Critical Thoughts on the Eurasian Similarity and Great Divergence Theses', *Canadian Journal of Sociology* 33/1 (2008): 151.

8 Kristof Glamann, *Dutch-Asiatic Trade, 1620–1740* (The Hague: Martinus Nijhoff, 1958); K. N. Chaudhuri, *The English East India Company: The Study of an Early Joint-Stock Company 1600–1640* (London: Frank Cass, 1965); K. N. Chaudhuri, *The Trading World of Asia and the English East India Company 1660–1760* (Cambridge University Press, 1978); Philippe Haudrère, *La Compagnie française des Indes au XVIIIe siècle* (Paris: Librairie de l'Inde, 1986), vol. I; K. N. Chaudhuri, *Asia Before Europe: Economy and Civilisation of the Indian Ocean From the Rise of Islam to 1750* (Cambridge University Press, 1990); Om Prakash, *The New Cambridge History of India*, vol. II.V, *European Commercial Enterprise in Pre-Colonial India* (Cambridge University Press, 1998); and the University of Warwick's ERC project 'Europe's Asian Centuries', coordinated by Maxine Berg.

9 Prasannan Parthasarathi, *Why Europe Grew Rich and Asia did not: Global Economic Divergence, 1600–1850* (Cambridge University Press, 2011).

10 This is a perspective recently embraced by Robert C. Allen, *The British Industrial Revolution in Global Perspective* (Cambridge University Press, 2009) and Joel Mokyr, *The Enlightened Economy: An Economic History of Britain, 1700–1850* (New Haven, Conn.: Yale University Press, 2009).

11 Among the many, see James M. Blaut, *The Colonizer's Model of the World: Geographical Diffusionism and Eurocentric History* (New York: Guilford Press, 1993); David S. Landes, *The Wealth and Poverty of Nations: Why are Some so Rich and Others so Poor?* (New York: W. W. Norton, 1998); E. L. Jones, *The European Miracle: Environments, Economies, and Geopolitics in the History of Europe and Asia*, 3rd edn (Cambridge University Press, 2003); Ian Morris, *Why the West Rules – for now: the Patterns of History, and what they Reveal about the Future* (New York: Farrar, Straus and Giroux, 2010); Niall Ferguson, *Civilization: the West and the Rest* (London: Allen Lane, 2011).

12 For a short historical overview, see Osterhammel and Petersson, *Globalization*. On contemporary debates, see David Held and Anthony G. McGrew, *Globalization/Anti-Globalization: Beyond the Great Divide*, 2nd edn (Cambridge: Polity, 2007).

13 Immanuel M. Wallerstein, *The Modern World-System*, vol. I, *Capitalist Agriculture and the Origins of the European World-Economy in the Sixteenth Century* (New York: Academic Press, 1974); Immanuel M. Wallerstein, *The Modern World-System*, vol. II, *Mercantilism and the Consolidation of the European World-Economy, 1600–1750* (New York: Academic Press, 1980); Immanuel M. Wallerstein, *The Modern World-System*, vol. III, *The Second Great Expansion of the Capitalist World-Economy, 1730–1840's* (San Diego: Academic Press, 1989); Immanuel M. Wallerstein, *The Modern World-System*, vol. IV, *Centrist Liberalism Triumphant, 1789–1914* (University of California Press, 2011); Pomeranz, *Great Divergence*. This book has been influenced also by the work carried out with Prasannan Parthasarathi and his recent book that addresses divergence in Europe, India and China. See Parthasarathi, *Why Europe Grew Rich*.

14 William H. McNeill, 'An Emerging Consensus About World History?', *World History Connected* 1/1 (2004), online.

15 See in particular Farnie and Jeremy, eds., *Fibre that Changed the World*. A forthcoming book by Sven Beckert will also focus on the nineteenth century. See in addition Sven Beckert, 'Cotton: a Global History', in Jerry Bentley, Renate Bridenthal and Anand A. Yang, eds., *Interactions: Transregional Perspectives on World History* (Honolulu: University of Hawaii Press, 2005), pp. 48–63.

16 Again there is a vast literature on the topic. For a short, though incisive, overview, see Prasannan Parthasarathi and Ian Wendt, 'Decline in Three Keys: Indian Cotton Manufacturing from the Later Eighteenth Century', in Riello and Parthasarathi, eds., *Spinning World*, pp. 397–407.

17 See in particular Riello and Parthasarathi, eds., *Spinning World*; and Riello and Roy, eds., *How India Clothed the World*.

18 I draw here specifically on recent scholarship by Maxine Berg – 'In Pursuit of Luxury: Global History and British Consumer Goods in the Eighteenth Century', *P&P* 132 (2004): 85–142 and *Luxury and Pleasure in Eighteenth-Century Britain* (Oxford University Press, 2005); and specifically on cotton textile consumption, Beverly Lemire, *Fashion's Favourite: the Cotton Trade and the Consumer in Britain, 1660–1800* (Oxford University Press, 1991) and *Cotton* (Oxford: Berg, 2011).

19 For an academic engagement with commodities, see Steven Topik, Zephyr Frank and Carlos Marichal, eds., *From Silver to Cocaine: Latin American Commodity Chains and the Building of the World Economy, 1500–2000* (Durham, N.C.: Duke University Press, 2006).

2 Selling to the world: India and the old cotton system

1 Ruth Barnes, *Indian Block-Printed Textiles in Egypt. The Newberry Collection in the Ashmolean Museum, Oxford* (Oxford: Clarendon Press, 1997), pp. 8–9.

2 Ruth Barnes, 'Indian Trade Cloth in Egypt: the Newberry Collection', in *Textiles in Trade*, Proceedings of the Textile Society of America Biennial Symposium (Washington, DC: Textile Society of America, 1990), pp. 178–91.

3 Rudolf Pfister, *Les Toiles imprimées de Fostat et l'Hindoustan* (Paris: Editons d'Art et d'Histoire, 1938), p. 12; John Peter Wild and Felicity Wild, 'Rome and India: Early Indian Cotton Textiles from Berenike, Red Coast of Egypt', in Ruth Barnes,

ed., *Textiles in Indian Ocean Societies* (London and New York: Routledge, 2005), pp. 11–16.

4 The so-called Cairo-Geniza, an impressive series of thousands of documentary fragments, tells us the story of the merchant Abraham bin Yiju, who as early as the mid twelfth century moved as a trader from present-day Tunisia to Yemen and from there to Gujarat and Mangalore, south of Goa. See S. D. Goitein and Mordechai Friedman, *Études sur le Judaïsme mediéval* (Leiden: E. J. Brill, 2007).

5 Barnes, *Indian Block-Printed Textiles*; John Guy, *Woven Cargoes: Indian Textiles in the East* (London: Thames & Hudson, 1998); Beverly Lemire, 'Revising the Historical Narrative: India, Europe, and the Cotton Trade, *c.* 1300–1800', in Riello and Parthasarathi, eds., *Spinning World*, pp. 308–10.

6 A further example that shows striking similarities with the textiles at the Ashmolean and the Victoria and Albert is at the Tapi Collection in New Delhi, 01.335, and is reproduced in Ruth Barnes, 'Indian Textiles for Island Trade: the Trade to Eastern Indonesia', in Rosemary Crill, ed., *Textiles from India: the Global Trade* (Calcutta: Seagull, 2005), p. 109.

7 Sanjay Subrahmanyam, 'Notes on the Sixteenth-Century Bengal Trade', *IESHR* 24/3 (1987): 267–71; Ashin Das Gupta, 'Gujarati Merchants and the Red Sea Trade, 1700–1725', in Blair B. Kling and Michael N. Pearson, eds., *The Age of Partnership: Europeans in Asia Before Domination* (Honolulu: University of Hawaii Press, 1979), pp. 123–58. For an overview see K. N. Chaudhuri, 'The Structure of Indian Textile Industry in the Seventeenth and Eighteenth Centuries', in Tirthankar Roy, ed., *Cloth and Commerce. Textiles in Colonia India* (New Delhi: Sage, 1996), pp. 33–84, especially pp. 40–2.

8 Lionel Casson, *Ancient Trade and Society* (Detroit, Mich.: Wayne State University Press, 1984), p. 212.

9 Jean-Baptiste Tavernier, *Travels in India*, ed. William Crooke (Oxford University Press, 1925), vol. II, p. 5.

10 Pfister, *Toiles imprimées*, pp. 14–15; Tavernier, *Travels in India*, vol. II, p. 5.

11 Cited in Om Prakash, 'Archival Source Material in the Netherlands on the History of Gujarat in the Early Modern Period', in Ernestine Carreira, ed., *Sources européennes sur le Gujarat* (Paris: Société d'Histoire de l'Orient, 1998), pp. 147–8.

12 K. N. Chaudhuri, 'Foreign Trade: 1. European Trade with India', in Tapan Raychaudhuri and Irfan Habib, eds., *The Cambridge Economic History of India*, vol. I, *c. 1200–c. 1750* (Cambridge University Press, 1982), p. 402.

13 J. H. van Linschoten, *The Voyage of John Huyghen van Linschoten to the East Indies: from the Old English Translation of 1598*, ed. Arthur Coke Burnell and P. A. Tiele (London: Hakluyt Society, 1885), vol. I, p. 91.

14 Pfister, *Toiles imprimées*, p. 15.

15 Marie Antoinette Petronella Meilink-Roelofsz, *Asian Trade and European Influence in the Indonesian Archipelago: Between 1500 and About 1630* (The Hague: Martinus Nijhoff, 1962), p. 68.

16 Rosemary Crill, 'Indian Painted Cottons', *Hali* 10/4 (1988): 30; Mattiebelle Gittinger, *Master Dyers to the World: Technique and Trade in Early Indian Dyed Cotton Textiles* (Washington, DC: Textile Museum, 1982), p. 71.

17 Tavernier, *Travels in India*, cited in I. M. Varma, 'Calico Printing in India', *Indian Journal of History of Science* 15/1 (1980): 2.

18 Rudolf Pfister, 'The Indian Art of Calico Printing in the Middle Ages: Characteristics and Influences', *Indian Art and Letters* 13 (1939): 15.

19 Crill, 'Indian Painted Cottons', 31.

20 For a comprehensive and up-to-date analysis of trade in the Indian Ocean before the colonial period, see Prakash, *European Commercial Enterprise in Pre-Colonial India*, in particular chapter 1.

21 William Foster, ed., *The English Factories in India. A Calendar of Documents in the India Office, British Museum and Public Record Office*, 13 vols. (Oxford: Clarendon Press, 1906–27), vol. IV, pp. 124–5. See also R. W. Ferrier, 'The Trade Between India and the Persian Gulf and the East India Company in the 17th Century', *Bengal P&P* 89/1, 167 (1970): 189–98.

22 Shri Pramod Sangar, 'Export of Indian Textiles to Middle East and Africa in the Seventeenth Century', *Journal of Historical Research* 17/1 (1974): 5.

23 N. Chittick, 'East African Trade with the Orient', in D. S. Richards, ed., *Islam and the Trade of Asia. A Colloquium* (Oxford: Bruno Cassirer, 1970), p. 103.

24 John Thornton, *Africa and Africans in the Making of the Atlantic World, 1400–1680* (Cambridge University Press, 1992), pp. 49 and 51.

25 Kenneth R. Hall, 'Ports-of-Trade, Maritime Diasporas, and Networks of Trade and Cultural Integration in the Bay of Bengal Region of the Indian Ocean: c. 1300–1500', *JESHO* 53 (2010): 110.

26 Tomé Pires, *The Suma Oriental of Tomé Pires: an Account of the East, from the Red Sea to Japan, Written in Malacca and India in 1512–1515*, ed. Armando Cortesão (London: Hakluyt Society, 1944), vol. I, p. 45.

27 S. P. Sen, 'The Role of Indian Textiles in Southeast Asian Trade in the Seventeenth Century', *Journal of Southeast Asian History* 3/2 (1962): 92–110.

28 For more information on the geography of trade, see Riello and Roy, 'Introduction: the World of South Asian Textiles, 1500–1850', pp. 1–27.

29 See, for instance, Andre Gunder Frank's controversial *Reorient: Global Economy in the Asian Age* (Berkeley: University of California Press, 1998). See also Chaudhuri, *Asia Before Europe*, and Andre Gunder Frank and Barry K. Gills, *The World System: Five Hundred Years or Five Thousand?* (London and New York: Routledge, 1993).

30 This map has been revised to include the trans-Saharan trade (no. 7) and some key nodes of exchange mentioned in this chapter that are not in Abu-Lughod's original map. See also a similar map for the Eastern Indian Ocean by Hall, in which he represents smaller networks of trade: Hall, 'Ports-of-Trade', p. 111.

31 Janet L. Abu-Lughod, *Before European Hegemony: the World System AD 1250–1350* (Oxford University Press, 1989).

32 Sinnappah Arasaratnam, 'Some Notes on the Dutch in Malacca and the Indo-Malayan Trade 1641–1670', *Journal of Southeast Asian History* 10/3 (1964): 481.

33 For a critique see Riello and Roy, 'Introduction.'

34 Stephen F. Dale, 'Silk Road, Cotton Road or . . . Indo-Chinese Trade in Pre-European Times', *Modern Asian Studies* 43/1 (2009): 80 and 82.

35 Scott C. Levi, 'India, Russia and the Eighteenth-Century Transformation of the Central Asian Caravan Trade', *JESHO* 42/4 (1999): 531.

36 Paul Wheatley, 'Geographical Notes on some Commodities Involved in Sung Maritime Trade', *Journal of the Malaysian Branch of the Royal Asiatic Society* 32/2, 186 (1959): 59; Pfister, *Toiles imprimées*, p. 13.

37 Dale, 'Silk Road', 84.

38 Prithvish Nag, 'The Indian Ocean, India and Africa: Historical and Geographical Perspectives', in Satish Chandra, ed., *The Indian Ocean: Explorations in History, Commerce and Politics* (New Delhi: Sage, 1987), pp. 152–3 and 157.

39 Lotika Varadarajan, 'Syncretic Symbolism and Textiles: Indo-Thai Expressions', in Om Prakash and Denys Lombard, eds., *Commerce and Culture in the Bay of Bengal, 1500–1800* (New Delhi: Manohar, 1999), p. 361.

40 Sangar, 'Export of Indian Textiles', 2.

41 Gittinger, *Master Dyers*, p. 139.

42 Robyn Maxwell observes for the case of Southeast Asian textiles that they 'reflect...diverse influences: the ancestor figures of earlier legends, the sacred *mandala* of the Hindu-Buddhist world, the zodiac menagerie of Chinese iconography, the flowing calligraphy of Islam and the lace of the West'. Robyn Maxwell, *Textiles of Southeast Asia: Tradition, Trade and Transformation* (Melbourne: National Gallery of Victoria, 1990), p. 20.

43 John Guy, 'Sarasa and Patola: Indian textiles in Indonesia', *Orientations* 20/1 (1989), pp. 55–6.

44 See Deepika Shah, *Masters of the Cloth: Indian Textiles Traded to Distant Shores* (New Delhi: Tapi Collection, 2005), p. 18.

45 Varadarajan, 'Syncretic Symbolism', p. 361.

46 Kenneth R. Hall, 'The Textile Industry in Southeast Asia, 1400–1800', *JESHO* 39/2 (1996): 92–4.

47 Fiona Kerlogue, 'The Early English Textile Trade in South East Asia: The East India Company Factory and the Textile Trade in Jambi, Sumatra, 1615–1682', *TH* 28/2 (1997):150–1.

48 Sanjay Subrahmanyam, 'Rural Industry and Commercial Agriculture in Late Seventeenth-Century South-Eastern India', *P&P* 126 (1990): 82. The EEIC imported similar quantities to Europe only in the late 1660s and early 1670s, though the figures are for the entire Asian textiles. Chaudhuri, *Trading World of Asia and the English East India*, pp. 545–8.

49 Prasannan Parthasarathi and Giorgio Riello, 'From India to the World: Cotton and Fashionability', in Frank Trentmann, ed., *The Oxford Handbook of the History of Consumption* (Oxford University Press, 2012), pp. 151–2.

50 Chiu Hsin-hui, *The Colonial 'Civilizing Process' in Dutch Formosa, 1624–1662* (Leiden and Boston: E. J. Brill, 2008), pp. 167 and 173–5.

51 Chaudhuri, 'Structure of Indian Textile Industry', pp. 34–5.

52 Prasannan Parthasarathi, 'Cotton Textiles in the Indian Subcontinent', in Riello and Parthasarathi, eds., *Spinning World*, p. 32. See also Hameeda Khatoon Naqvi, *Urban Centres and Industries in Upper India, 1556–1803* (New York: Asia Publishing House, 1968), pp. 190–212.

53 Giorgio Riello, 'Fabricating the Domestic: the Material Culture of Textiles and Social Life of the Home in Early Modern Europe', in Beverly Lemire, ed., *The Force of Fashion in Politics and Society: Global Perspectives from Early Modern to Modern Times* (Aldershot: Ashgate, 2010), pp. 43–5. Amin Jaffer discusses the obstacles to the adoption of western-style joined furniture in India in Amin Jaffer, ed., *Furniture from British India and Ceylon: a Catalogue of the Collections in the Victoria and Albert Museum and the Peabody Essex Museum* (London: V&A Publications, 2001), introduction.

54 Saleem Kidwai, 'Mughal Art: Technologies of the Elite', in A. Rahman, ed., *India's Interaction with China, Central and West Asia* (Oxford University Press, 2002), vol. III, part 2, p. 386.

55 Nicholas Downton, *The Voyage of Nicholas Downton to the East Indies 1614–15: as Recorded in Contemporary Narratives and Letters*, ed. William Foster (London: Hakluyt Society, 1938), p. 146.

56 Irfan Habib, 'Non-Agricultural Production and Urban Economy', in Raychaudhuri and Habib, eds., *Cambridge Economic History of India*, vol. I, p. 79. See also Parthasarathi and Riello, 'From India to the World', pp. 147–50.

57 Parthasarathi, *Why Europe Grew Rich*, pp. 32–3.

58 Sebastien Manrique, *Travels of Fray Sebastien Manrique, 1629–1643*, ed. C. Eckford Luard and H. Hosten (Oxford: Hakluyt Society, 1927), vol. II, p. 42.

59 Levi, 'India, Russia', 530–1; Willem Floor, 'Economy and Society: Fibres, Fabrics, Factories', in Carol Bier, ed., *Woven from the Soul, Spun from the Heart: Textile Arts of Safavit and Qajar Iran 16th–19th Centuries* (Washington, DC: Textile Museum, 1987), p. 26.

60 Muzzaffar Alam, 'Trade, State Policy and Regional Change: Aspects of Mughal–Uzbek Commercial Relations, c. 1550–1750', *JESHO* 37/3 (1994): 206.

61 Hall, 'Textile Industry', 88.

62 Guy, *Woven Cargoes*. Data on the overall trade and prices of textiles traded by the VOC in Southeast Asia are given by Ruurgje Laarhoven, 'The Power of Cloth: the Textile Trade of the Dutch East India Company (VOC), 1600–1780', unpublished PhD thesis, Australian National University, 1994, 317–21 and appendix H.

63 Anthony Reid, *Southeast Asia in the Age of Commerce, 1450–1680*, vol. I, *The Lands Below the Winds* (New Haven, Conn.: Yale University Press, 1984), pp. 90–1; Wheatley, 'Geographical Notes', 59–60.

64 Colleen E. Kriger, 'Mapping the History of Cotton Textile Production in Pre-Colonial West Africa', *African Economic History* 33 (2005): 99 and 102.

65 Chittick, 'East African Trade', p. 103.

66 Joseph E. Inikori, 'English Versus Indian Cotton Textiles: the Impact of Imports on Cotton Textile Production in West Africa', in Riello and Roy, eds., *How India Clothed the World*, pp. 85–114.

67 Reid, *Southeast Asia*.

68 Hall, 'Textile Industry', 90.

69 Sung Ying-Hsing, *T'ien-Kung K'ai-Wu Chinese Technology in the Seventeenth Century* (Pennsylvania State University Press, 1966), p. 63.

70 Kathy Le Mons Walker, *Chinese Modernity and the Peasant Path. Semicolonialism in the Northern Yangzi Delta* (Stanford University Press, 1999), p. 31.

71 Michel Cartier, 'À propos de l'histoire du coton en Chine: approche technologique, économique et sociale', *Études Chinoises* 13/1–2 (1994): 426.

72 Francesca Bray, 'Textile Production and Gender Roles in China, 1000–1700', *Chinese Science* 12 (1995): 127.

73 Parthasarathi and Riello, 'From India to the World', pp. 152–3.

74 Kristof Glamann, 'European Trade, 1500–1750', in Carlo Maria Cipolla, ed., *The Fontana Economic History of Europe* (London and Glasgow: Fontana, 1971), vol. II, p. 15. See also Eliyahu Ashtor, 'The Venetian Cotton Trade in the Later Middle Ages', *Studi Medievali* 17/3 (1976): 675–715.

75 François Crouzet, *A History of the European Economy, 1000–2000* (Charlottesville: University Press of Virginia, 2001), p. 27.

3 'Wool growing on wild trees': the global reach of cotton

1 John Mandeville, *The Travels of Sir John Mandeville*, ed. C. Moseley (Harmondsworth: Penguin, 2005).

2 Andrew M. Watson, 'The Rise and Spread of Old World Cotton', in Veronika Gervers, ed., *Studies in Textile History in Memory of Harold B. Burnham* (Toronto: Royal Ontario Museum, 1977), p. 359. Johnson however reports the date of 781 CE. See also W. H. Johnson, *Cotton and its Production* (London: Macmillan & Co., 1926), p. 5; Reiko Mochinaga Brandon, *Country Textiles of Japan: the Art of Tsutsugaki* (New York: Weatherill, 1986), p. 39.

3 Debiprasad Chattopadhyaya, *History of Science and Technology in Ancient India: the Beginnings* (Calcutta: Firma, 1986), p. 288. Today there are at least thirty main varieties of cotton worldwide, many of which exist as a series of local sub-varieties. These varieties are divided into two broad families: 'New World cotton' (with 26 chromosomes and 8 species) and 'Old World cotton' (with 13 chromosomes and 4 species). Among the eight species of New World cotton, the North American *Gossypium hirsutum* is probably the most common in the world today. The so-called Old World species are divided into two large sub-families, which comprise *Gossypium herbaceum* (annual variety, or 'cotton plant'), originating in northern Arabia and still grown in Asia, and *Gossypium arboretum* (perennial variety, also known as 'cotton tree'), first cultivated in India and later across Asia. These varieties are the product of a millennium of genetic change as well as man-made cross-breeding. Edward H. Schafer, *The Golden Peaches of Samarkand: a Study of T'ang Exotics* (Berkeley and Los Angeles: University of California Press, 1963), p. 204; W. Bally, 'The Cotton Plant', *Ciba Review* 95 (1952): 3405. The aim was to create strands that produced good-quality lint. Quality is measured in terms of tensile resistance of the fibre (itself related to length and consistence of the staple) and the physical qualities of the fibre (colour, capacity to absorb dyes, and capacity to be spun on high counts).

4 Cited in Jack Goody, *The East in the West* (Cambridge University Press, 1996), p. 127. See also E. R. Bevan, 'India in Early Greek and Latin Literature', in E. J. Rapson, ed., *The Cambridge History of India*, vol. I, *Ancient India* (Cambridge University Press, 1922), p. 396.

5 See Linda Shaffer, 'Southernization', *JWH* 3/1 (1994): 1–21.

6 Watson, 'Rise and Spread', p. 357.

7 Maurice Lombard, *Les Textiles dans le monde musulman du VIIe au XIIe siècle* (Paris: Mouton, 1978), pp. 61–79.

8 Maureen Fennell Mazzaoui, 'L'Organizzazione delle industrie tessili nei secoli XIII–XIV: i cotonieri veronesi', *Studi Storici Veronesi Luigi Simeoni* 18–19 (1968/9): 100.

9 Watson, 'Rise and Spread', p. 357.

10 The spreading of the crop was therefore limited by its climatic tolerance. The cotton plant cannot be cultivated in climates with temperatures below 11 degrees centigrade and it needs at least 20 degrees temperature for a term of 25 to 40 days during maturation. It also needs moisture during the three months of growth, but it can

resist harsher conditions during the long period of picking, which can last over three months. Henry Hobhouse, *Seeds of Change: Five Plants that Transformed Mankind* (London: Papermac, 1985), p. 178.

11 Kriger, 'Mapping the History', 93. See also Michael Gervers, 'Cotton and Cotton Weaving in Meroitic Nubia and Medieval Ethiopia', *TH* 21/1 (1990): 13–30; and Patricia Davison and Patrick Harries, 'Cotton Weaving in South-East Africa: its History and Technology', *TH* 9 (1980): 178–9.

12 Wu Min, 'The Exchange of Weaving Technologies Between China and Central and Western Asia from the 3rd to the 8th Century. Based on New Textile Findings in Xinjiang', in Regula Schorta, ed., *Central Asian Textiles and their Contexts in the Early Middle Ages* (Riggisberg: Abegg-Stiftung, 2006), pp. 233–4.

13 Dale, 'Silk Road', 82. Kathy Walker suggests an earlier date (Han period, 202 BCE–220 CE), but there is insufficient evidence corroborating this hypothesis. Le Mons Walker, *Chinese Modernity*, p. 29.

14 Cartier, 'À propos de l'histoire du coton en Chine', 421. There are, however, textual sources that show that *Gossypium herbaceum* was already present in sixth-century China. Dieter Kuhn, *Science and Civilisation in China, vol. V, Chemistry and Chemical Technology. Part IX. Textile Technology: Spinning and Reeling* (Cambridge University Press, 1998), p. 57.

15 Cheng Weiji, *History of Textile Technology of Ancient China* (New York: Science Press, 1992), pp. 135 and 183; Ramon H. Myers, 'Cotton Textile Handicraft and the Development of the Cotton Textile Industry in Modern China', *EHR* 18/3 (1965): 614; Harriet T. Zurndorfer, 'The Resistant Fibre: Cotton Textiles in Imperial China', in Riello and Parthasarathi, eds., *Spinning World*, pp. 43–4; Harriet T. Zurndorfer, 'Cotton Textile Manufacture and Marketing in Late Imperial China and the "Great Divergence"', *JESHO* 54/4 (2011): 702–5; Watson, 'Rise and Spread', p. 359. Others have also suggested a date as early as the first-third century for the arrival of perennial cotton in southern China. See Kuhn, *Science and Civilisation in China*, pp. 57–8.

16 Reid, *Southeast Asia in the Age of Commerce*, p. 91.

17 Watson, 'Rise and Spread', p. 359.

18 Francesca Bray, 'Towards a Critical History of Non-Western Technology', in Timothy Brook and Gregory Blue, eds., *China and Historical Capitalism: Genealogies of Sinological Knowledge* (Cambridge University Press, 1999), p. 180. See also Francesca Bray, *Technology and Gender: Fabrics and Power in Late Imperial China* (Berkeley: University of California Press, 1997), p. 212.

19 Bray, 'Towards a Critical History', p. 181; Cartier, 'À propos de l'histoire du coton en Chine', 423

20 Robert Cliver, 'China', in Lex Heerma van Voss, Els Hiemstra-Kuperus and Elise van Nederveen Meerkerk, eds., *The Ashgate Companion to the History of Textile Workers* (Aldershot: Ashgate, 2010), p. 303.

21 Bray, 'Towards a Critical History', p. 181; Zurndorfer, 'Cotton Textile Manufacture', 708.

22 Gang Deng, *The Premodern Chinese Economy. Structural Equilibrium and Capitalist Sterility* (London and New York: Routledge, 1999), p. 284; Bray, 'Towards a Critical History', p. 181.

23 Philip C. C. Huang, *The Peasant Family and Rural Development in the Yangzi Delta, 1350–1988* (Stanford University Press, 1990), pp. 45 and 81.

24 Philip C. C. Huang, *The Peasant Economy and Social Change in North China* (Stanford University Press, 1985), p. 112.

25 Equal to 2 million mu of land. 1 hectare = 10,000 sqm = *c.* 15 mu; 1 mu = 666 sqm; 1 acre = 4,046 mq = 6.6 mu. Huang, *Peasant Family*, p. 45.

26 Timothy Brook, *The Confusions of Pleasure: Commerce and Culture in Ming China* (Berkeley: California University Press, 1998), p. 195.

27 Willard J. Peterson, *The Cambridge History of China*, vol. IX, Part 1, *The Ch'ing Empire to 1800* (Cambridge University Press, 2002), p. 513.

28 Prasannan Parthasarathi, *The Transition to a Colonial Economy: Weavers, Merchants and Kings in South India 1720–1800* (Cambridge University Press, 2001), pp. 50–1 and appendix 2.1.

29 Ibid., p. 51.

30 Mi Chü Wiens, 'Cotton Textile Production and Rural Social Transformation in Early Modern China', *Journal of the Institute of Chinese Studies* 7/2 (1973): 519.

31 Mark Elvin, 'The High-Level Equilibrium Trap: the Causes of the Decline of Invention in the Traditional Chinese Textile Industries', in W. E. Willmott, ed., *Economic Organization in Chinese Society* (Stanford University Press, 1972), p. 148.

32 Cartier, 'À propos de l'histoire du coton en Chine', 422.

33 Weiji, *History of Textile Technology*, p. 186.

34 Myers, 'Cotton Textile Handicraft', 614–15.

35 Cotton was rarely cultivated with wheat, as the two crops were incompatible: 'the people in this country are very busy working at cotton and don't plant wheat', commented the Zhenyang country gazetteer, 'They only plant it on the banks and borders between the fields. This is done to preserve the land's fertility and because the harvest season for wheat is too late. Those who plant wheat on all their land, are planning to plant rice'. Cited in Sadao Nishijima, 'The Formation of the Early Chinese Cotton Industry', in Linda Grove and Christian Daniels, eds., *State and Society in China. Japanese Perspectives on Ming–Qing Social and Economic History* (University of Tokyo Press, 1984), p. 38. See also Bozhong Li, *Agricultural Development in Jiangnan, 1620–1850* (New York: St Martin's Press, 1998), pp. 52–3.

36 William Milburn, *Oriental Commerce or the East India Trader's Complete Guide* (London: Kingsbury, Parbury and Allen, 1813), p. 150.

37 Sanjay Subrahmanyam, *The Political Economy of Commerce: Southern India, 1500–1650* (Cambridge University Press, 2002), pp. 26–7; Carla M. Sinopoli, *The Political Economy of Craft Production: Crafting Empire in South India, c. 1350–1650* (Cambridge University Press, 2003), p. 174.

38 Lallanji Gopal, 'Indian Agriculture – a Historical Perspective', in Rahman, ed., *India's Interaction with China, Central and West Asia*, vol. III, Part 1, p. 323; Chaudhuri, 'Structure of Indian Textile Industry', p. 70.

39 Suraiya Faroqhi, 'Notes on the Production of Cotton and Cotton Cloth in XVIth and XVIIth Century Anatolia', *JEEH* 8/2 (1979): 406–7; Kate Fleet, *European and Islamic Trade in the Early Ottoman State: the Merchants of Genoa and Turkey* (Cambridge University Press, 1999), p. 99.

40 D. Schlingloff, 'Cotton-Manufacture in Ancient India', *JESHO* 17/1 (1974): 81; William Gervase Clarence-Smith, 'The Production of Cotton Textiles in Early Modern South-East Asia', in Riello and Parthasarathi, eds., *Spinning World*, p. 130; Victor Lieberman, *Strange Parallels: Southeast Asia in Global Context, c. 800–1830* (Cambridge University Press, 2003), vol. I, p. 145.

41 Subrahmanyam, *Political Economy*, p. 333.
42 Le Mons Walker, *Chinese Modernity*, p. 34.
43 Cited in Huang, *Peasant Economy*, p. 112.
44 Brook, *Confusions of Pleasure*, pp. 196–7; Jack Goldstone, 'Gender, Work, and Culture: Why the Industrial Revolution came Early to England but Late to China', *Sociological Perspectives* 39/1 (1996): 3.
45 Bray, 'Towards a Critical History', p. 183.
46 Le Mons Walker, *Chinese Modernity*, pp. 34–5.
47 Sinnappah Arasaratnam, *Merchants, Companies and Commerce on the Coromandel Coast, 1650–1740* (Oxford University Press, 1986), p. 63.
48 Subrahmanyam, *Political Economy*, pp. 26–7.
49 Joseph Jerome Brennig, 'The Textile Trade of Seventeenth-Century Northern Coromandel: a Study of a Pre-Modern Asian Export Industry', unpublished PhD thesis, University of Wisconsin–Madison, 1975, 230–6; Subrahmanyam, *Political Economy of Commerce*, pp. 71–2; Sinopoli, *Political Economy of Craft Production*, pp. 172, 175 and 177; Parthasarathi, *Why Europe Grew Rich*, p. 77.
50 Joseph J. Brennig, 'Textile Producers and Production in Late Seventeenth Century Coromandel', *IESHR* 23/4 (1986): 335–7; Bhaswati Bhattacharya, 'The Hinterland and the Coast: the Pattern of Integration in Coromandel in the Late Eighteenth Century', in Rudrangshu Mukherjee and Lakshmi Subramanian, eds., *Politics and Trade in the Indian Ocean World: Essays in Honour of Ashin Das Gupta* (Oxford University Press, 1998), pp. 28–9.
51 Tapan Raychaudhuri, 'Non-Agricultural Production: Mughal India', in Raychaudhuri and Habib, eds., *Cambridge Economic History of India*, vol. I, p. 271; Hameeda Hossain, *The Company Weavers of Bengal: the East India Company and the Organisation of Textile Production in Bengal, 1750–1813* (Oxford University Press, 1988), p. 33.
52 Shoma Chandra, 'Textile Production in Bengal. A Case Study of Dinajpur: 1793–1815', *Bengal P&P* 110/1–2, 210–11 (1991): 51.
53 Philip P. Argenti, *The Occupation of Chios by the Genoese and their Administration of the Island, 1346–1566* (Cambridge University Press, 1958), p. 501.
54 Maureen Fennell Mazzaoui, 'The Cotton Industry of Northern Italy in the Late Middle Ages: 1150–1450', *JEH* 32/1 (1972): 264–5.
55 H. Wescher, 'Cotton Growing and Cotton Trade in the Orient During the Middle Ages', *Ciba Review* 64 (1948): 2336.
56 See for instance a cargo of three galleys sent to Venice from Beirut in 1405. Jacques Heers, 'Il commercio nel mediterraneo alla fine del sec. XIV e nei primi anni del XV', *Archivio Storico Italiano* 113 (1955): 168.
57 Ashtor, 'Venetian Cotton Trade', 675. See also Eliyahu Ashtor, 'L'Apogée du commerce vénitien au Levant. Un nouvel essai d'explication', in Hans-Georg Beck, Manoussos Manoussacas and Agostino Pertusi, eds., *Venezia centro di mediazione tra oriente e occidente (secoli XV–XVI)* (Florence: Olschki, 1977), vol. I, pp. 307–26; and Halil İnalcık, 'An Outline of Ottoman–Venetian Relations', in Manoussacas and Pertusi, eds., *Venezia*, especially pp. 83–4.
58 Eliyahu Ashtor, 'The Volume of Levantine Trade in the Later Middle Ages (1370–1498)', *JEEH* 4/3 (1975): 594–5.

59 Ashtor, 'Venetian Cotton Trade', 687–90.

60 Fleet, *European and Islamic Trade*, p. 99; Jacques, 'Il commercio', pp. 171–2. The famous Fondaco dei Tedeschi near Rialto Bridge acted as a warehouse for the German merchants especially after 1320 when the city of Ulm in Bavaria became an important centre for the production of mixed cotton linens, fustians and other mixed cotton cloths. By the end of the fourteenth century German merchants in Venice were reputed to be the largest buyers of raw cotton from Syria. Hermann Kellenbenz, 'The Fustian Industry of the Ulm Region in the Fifteenth and Early Sixteenth Centuries', in N. B. Harte and K. G. Ponting, eds., *Cloth and Clothing in Medieval Europe. Essays in Memory of Professor E. M. Carus-Wilson* (London: Heinemann Educational, 1983), p. 260.

61 This is contested by Fleet, who shows evidence that the main bottleneck could have been the availability of shipping rather than the supply of cotton. Fleet, *European and Islamic Trade*, p. 99.

62 Eliyahu, 'Venetian Cotton Trade', p. 677.

63 Diamond Jenness, *The Economics of Cyprus. A Survey to 1914* (Montreal: McGill University Press, 1962), pp. 47, 82–3.

64 Wescher, 'Cotton Growing', 2337.

65 Ying-Hsing, *T'ien-Kung K'ai-Wu*, p. 63.

66 For an overview see Angela Lakwete, *Inventing the Cotton Gin: Machine and Myth in Antebellum America* (Baltimore, Md.: Johns Hopkins University Press, 2003), pp. 1–20.

67 Ishrat Alam, 'Cotton Technology in India down to the Sixteenth Century', in Rahman, ed., *India's Interaction with China, Central and West Asia*, volume III, Part 2, pp. 445–6.

68 Eugenia Vanina, *Urban Crafts and Craftsmen in Medieval India (Thirteenth–Eighteenth Centuries)* (New Delhi: Munshiram Manoharlal, 2004), p. 30; Habib, 'Non-Agricultural Production and Urban Economy', p. 78. Schlingloff proposes the early date of mid twelfth century, while other authors suggest mid fourteenth century. Schlingloff, 'Cotton-Manufacture', 83.

69 Irfan Habib, 'Technological Changes and Society, 13th and 14th Centuries', in Debiprasad Chattodhyaya, ed., *Studies in the History of Science in India* (New Delhi: Editorial Enterprises, 1982), p. 822. This was, however, only one-tenth of the cotton that could be cleaned with a Whitney machine after its introduction in the Americas in 1794. See p. 204.

70 Weiji, *History of Textile Technology*, p. 139. In reality it is difficult to say with precision what might have been taken from India. As Kuhn points out, there were several different types of ginning devices, some of which were crank-handle operated, others fixed to a table, and others again included a flywheel. Kuhn, *Science and Civilisation in China*, pp. 191–3. See also Schlingloff, 'Cotton-Manufacture', 83 and 85.

71 Joseph Needham, *Science and Civilisation in China, vol. IV, Physics and Physical Technology, Part 2. Mechanical Engineering* (Cambridge University Press, 1962), pp. 122–4.

72 Habib, 'Non-Agricultural Production', p. 78.

73 Irfan Habib, 'The Technology and Economy of Mughal India', *IESHR* 17/1 (1980): 6–7. Vijaya Ramaswamy, however, suggests that the bow was introduced to South India between the second and the sixth century AD. Vijaya Ramaswamy, 'Notes

on the Textile Technology in Medieval India with Special Reference to the South', *IESHR* 17/2 (1980): 227.

74 Weiji, *History of Textile Technology*, pp. 136, 190.

75 Schlingloff, 'Cotton-Manufacture', 84.

76 Habib, 'Non-Agricultural Production', p. 78; O. P. Jaggi, *History of Science, Technology and Medicine in India*, vol. I, *Technology in Ancient India* (Delhi: Atma Ram & Sons, 1981), p. 95.

77 Debiprasad Chattopadhyaya, *History of Science and Technology in Ancient India: The Beginnings* (Calcutta: Firma, 1986), p. 288.

78 Kuhn, *Science and Civilisation in China*, p. 198.

79 Habib, 'Technological Changes', p. 817.

80 Ibid., p. 220.

81 Vijaya Ramaswamy, 'Interactions and Encounters: Indian Looms and Crafts Traditions Abroad – a South Indian Perspective', in Rahman, ed., *India's Interaction with China, Central and West Asia*, pp. 432–3.

82 Sinopoli, *Political Economy of Craft Production*, p. 177. By hand spinning I mean the use of a drop spindle. However, in the European literature the phrase 'hand spinning' is used for all forms of spinning that do not make use of inanimate power, and therefore include both spinning with a drop spindle and with a spinning wheel. I thank John Styles for clarifying this point.

83 Reid, *Southeast Asia*, pp. 93–4, and Clarence-Smith, 'Production of Cotton Textiles', p. 141.

84 Kriger, 'Mapping the History', 96–7; Colleen Kriger, '"Guinea Cloth": Production and Consumption of Cotton Textiles in West Africa, Before and During the Atlantic Slave Trade', in Riello and Parthasarathi, eds., *Spinning World*, p. 108.

85 Elvin, 'High-Level Equilibrium Trap', pp. 148–9. See also Dixin Xu, and Chengming Wu, *Chinese Capitalism, 1522–1840* (London: Macmillan, 2000), pp. 214–15. I thank John Styles for pointing out to me that this is possibly a wheel for doubling and not for spinning.

86 Weiji, *History of Textile Technology*, p. 134.

87 Prasannan Parthasarathi and Giorgio Riello, 'Cotton Textiles and Global History', in Riello and Parthasarathi, eds., *Spinning World*, pp. 3–4.

88 Ramaswamy, 'Notes', 230.

89 Some looms such as the 'four-cornered frame' introduced from the Muslim north in the fifteenth-sixteenth century were used only in Muslim communities of the south. Sinopoli, *Political Economy of Craft Production*, p. 178.

90 Ramaswamy, 'Notes', 231.

91 Lotika Varadarajan, 'Indian Textile Technology in the Pre-Industrial Period', in *Technology in India (Ancient and Medieval Periods). Proceedings of the Seminar Held in February 1983* (Bombay: Ananthacharya Indological Research Institute, 1984), 60.

92 The 1637 *T'ien-kung k'ai-wu (The Creation of Nature and Man)* suggested that the smaller and more practical waist-loom was not widespread in China. Ying-Hsing, *T'ien-Kung K'ai-Wu*, p. 56.

93 Habib, 'Technological Changes', p. 826.

94 There is, however, proof of draw-looms in South India from the eleventh century, though historians disagree on how widespread their use might have been. Ramaswamy, 'Notes', and compare it with Habib, 'Technological Changes.'

95 Kriger, 'Mapping the History', 102–3 and 111.

96 Reid, *Southeast Asia*, p. 94. This was also the case with the spinning wheel, the treadle loom and printing blocks that arrived in Southeast Asia mainly from China and India and were adapted locally. Venice Lamb, *Looms Past and Present: Around the Mediterranean and Elsewhere* (Hertingfordbury: Roxford Books, 2005); Clarence-Smith, 'Production of Cotton Textiles', p. 139.

97 Clarence-Smith, 'Production of Cotton Textiles', pp. 139–40.

98 Vanina, *Urban Crafts*, p. 37; Tirthankar Roy, 'Knowledge and Divergence from the Perspective of Early Modern India', *JGH* 3/3 (2008): 367–8; Parthasarathi, *Why Europe Grew Rich*, ch. 7.

4 The world's best: cotton manufacturing and the advantage of India

1 A. Rahman, 'General Ideas on Technology', in Rahman, ed., *India's Interaction with China, Central and West Asia*, vol. III, Part 1, p. 365.

2 Sushil Chaudhuri, *From Prosperity to Decline: Eighteenth Century Bengal* (Delhi: Manohar, 1995), p. 139; Subrahmanyam, 'Rural Industry', 92.

3 Raychaudhuri, 'Non-Agricultural Production: Mughal India', p. 283.

4 Rasjan Humar Gupta, 'The Growth and Decay of the Cotton Piece-Goods Industry of Berthum', *Bengal P&P* 97/1, 182 (1977): 68; Chaudhuri, *From Prosperity to Decline*, p. 138; Vijaya Ramaswamy, 'The Genesis and Historical Role of the Masterweavers in South Indian Textile Production', *JESHO* 28 (1985): 308; Ian C. Wendt, 'The Social Fabric: Textile Industry and Community in Early Modern South India', unpublished PhD, University of Wisconsin–Madison, 2005, 97.

5 Gupta, 'Growth and Decay', p. 69.

6 Subramanyam, 'Rural Industry', 112; Brennig, 'Textile Producers', 348.

7 Prakash, 'Textile Manufacturing', p. 6; Chaudhuri, *From Prosperity to Decline*, p. 148.

8 Sinnappah Arasaratnam, 'Weavers, Merchants and Company: the handloom Industry in Southeastern India 1750–1790', *IESHR* 17/3 (1980): 260–1.

9 Ibid., 263.

10 Goody, *East in the West*, p. 210.

11 Raychaudhuri, 'Non-Agricultural Production: Mughal India', pp. 279–80.

12 Chaudhuri, 'Structure', p. 44; Prakash, 'Textile Manufacturing', p. 5.

13 Arasaratnam, *Merchants, Companies and Commerce*, pp. 267–8.

14 Chaudhuri, 'Structure of Indian Textile Industry', p. 53; Chaudhuri, *From Prosperity to Decline*, p. 146; P. Sudhir and P. Swarnalatha, 'Textile Traders and Territorial Imperatives: Masulipatnam, 1750–1850', *IESHR* 29/2 (1992): 147–8.

15 Prakash, 'Textile Manufacturing', p. 7.

16 For the late eighteenth century Subramanian cites the case of a 9 per cent penalty for undelivered cloth to the EEIC. Lakshmi Subramanian, 'Power and the Weave: Weavers, Merchants and rules in Eighteenth-Century Surat', in Mukherjee and Subramanian, eds., *Essays in Honour of Ashin Das Gupta*, p. 56.

17 In what Parthasarathi calls an 'asymmetry of contracts', merchants did not possess the right to break a contract or demand the return of an advance. Parthasarathi, *Transition to a Colonial Economy*, pp. 26–7.

18 Brennig, 'Textile Producers', 351.

19 The complexity of these intermediary systems derives from the fact that different organisations were in place in different areas of the country. See Gupta, 'Growth and Decay', pp. 70–1; Arasaratnam, *Merchants, Companies and Commerce*, p. 268; Arasaratnam, 'Weavers', 265; Sinopoli, *Political Economy of Craft Production*, p. 186; Sudhir and Swarnalatha, 'Textile Traders', 148, 151; Wendt, 'Social Fabric', 145.

20 Franklin F. Mendels, 'Proto-industrialization: the First Phase of the Industrialization Process', *JEH* 32/1 (1972): 241–61; and the later Peter Kriedte, Hans Medick and Jürgen Schlumbohm, *Industrialisierung vor der Industrialisierung. Gewerbliche Waren Production auf dem Land in der Formationsperiode des Kapitalismus* (Göttingen: Vandenhoeck und Ruprecht, 1977). For a critical overview see Donald C. Coleman, 'Proto-Industrialisation: a Concept too Many', *EHR* 36/3 (1983): 435–48.

21 Vijaya Ramaswamy, 'South Indian Textiles: a Case for Proto-Industrialization?', in Deepak Kumar, ed., *Science and Empire: Essays in Indian Context (1700–1947)* (Delhi: Anamika Prakashan, 1991), pp. 41–56.

22 Sheila C. Ogilvie and Marcus Cerman, eds., *European Proto-Industrialization* (Cambridge University Press, 1996).

23 Leslie A. Clarkson, *Proto-Industrialization: the First Phase of Industrialization?* (Basingstoke: Macmillan, 1985).

24 For an overview, see Maxine Berg, 'Markets, Trade and European Manufacture', in Maxine Berg, ed., *Markets and Manufacture in Early Industrial Europe* (London: Routledge, 1990), pp. 173–201. See also Maxine Berg, Pat Hudson and Michael Sonenscher, eds., *Manufacture in Town and Country Before the Factory* (Cambridge University Press, 1983); Pat Hudson, ed., *Regions and Industries. A Perspective on the Industrial Revolution in Britain* (Cambridge University Press, 1989).

25 Giovanni Luigi Fontana, ed., *Le Vie dell'industrializzazione europea: sistemi a confronto* (Bologna: Il Mulino, 1997).

26 Frank Perlin, 'Proto-Industrial and Pre-Colonial South Asia', *P&P* 98 (1983): 30–95.

27 Chaudhuri, 'Structure of Indian Textile Industry', p. 55.

28 Arasaratnam, *Merchants, Companies and Commerce*, pp. 268–9.

29 Berg, 'Markets, Trade and European Manufacture'.

30 Chaudhuri, 'Structure of Indian Textile Industry', p. 56; Arasaratnam, *Merchants, Companies and Commerce*, p. 268.

31 Arasaratnam, 'Weavers', 265.

32 Ramaswamy, 'Genesis', 305–6; Sudhir and Swarnalatha, 'Textile Traders', 156. The Indian productive system resembled more closely what in Europe has been defined as a 'verlagg-system'.

33 Chaudhuri, 'Structure of Indian Textile Industry', p. 52.

34 In the village of Maldeh in Bengal in the closing years of the eighteenth century there were 120 weavers' households procuring fine muslin (*molmol*), but the total village had 160 looms, accounting for some weavers having up to seven looms. Chandra, 'Textile Production in Bengal', 58.

35 This was particularly the case in South India, but much less in Bengal and Gujarat. Weavers might move to avoid the dangers of warfare or to escape coercion, but were likely to return to their weaving villages. Douglas E. Haynes and Tirthankar

Roy, 'Conceiving Mobility: Weavers' Migration in Pre-Colonial and Colonial India', *IESHR* 36 (1999): 35–67. Ramaswamy, 'Genesis', 314; Brennig, 'Textile Producers', 346; David Washbrook, 'India in the Early Modern World Economy: Modes of Production, Reproduction and Exchange', *JGH* 2/1 (2007): 94; Ravi Ahuja, 'Labour Relations in an Early Colonial Context: Madras, *c.* 1750–1800', *Modern Asian Studies* 36/4 (2002): 811; John Irwin, 'Indian Textile Trade in the Seventeenth Century. II. Coromandel Coast', *Journal of Indian Textile History* 2 (1956): 28; Hossain, *Company Weavers*, p. 49.

36 Chaudhuri, 'Structure of Indian Textile Industry', p. 38; Hossain, *Company Weavers*, pp. 20–2.

37 Sinopoli, *Political Economy of Craft Production*, p. 173; Chaudhuri, *From Prosperity to Decline*, p. 152; Ramaswamy, 'South Indian Textiles', p. 45.

38 Gittinger, *Master Dyers*, p. 61.

39 Subrahmanyam, 'Rural Industry', 94; Chaudhuri, *From Prosperity to Decline*, p. 138.

40 Washbrook goes as far as to argue that this logic of exchange based on 'often-elongated patterns of trade' discouraged fixed investment in any one locale. Washbrook, 'India', 95.

41 Sidney Pollard, *The Genesis of Modern Management: a Study of the Industrial Revolution in Great Britain* (Cambridge, Mass.: Harvard University Press, 1965).

42 Subramanian, 'Power and the Weave', p. 54.

43 Arasaratnam, 'Weavers', 269; Parthasarathi, *Transition to a Colonial Economy*, p. 51.

44 Cited in Washbrook, 'India', 87–8.

45 India in 1600 might have had *c.* 140–150 million while China had between 120 and 200 million people to clothe. Population might be a misleading indicator, but it provides a rough indication of proportions, especially in an economy in which production heavily depended on labour inputs. Stephen Broadberry and Bishnupriya Gupta, 'Indian GDP, 1600–1871: some Preliminary Estimates and a Comparison with Britain', unpublished paper, University of Warwick, April 2010, 9–10 and 18 (www.warwick.ac.uk/fac/soc/economics/staff/academic/broadberry/wp/indiangdppre1870v4.pdf); Robert B. Marks, 'China's Population Size During the Ming and Qing: a Comment on the Mote Revision', unpublished paper given at the 2002 Annual Meeting of the Association of Asian Studies, Washington, DC, 3 (http://web.whittier.edu/people/webpages/personalwebpages/rmarks/pdf/env._panel_remarks.pdf).

46 Martin Heijdra, 'The Socio-Economic Development of Rural China During the Ming', in Dennis Twitchett and Frederick W. Mote, eds., *The Cambridge History of China*, vol. VIII, Part 2, *The Ming Dynasty* (Cambridge University Press, 1998), p. 507.

47 Bray, *Technology and Gender*, p. 213.

48 Bray, 'Towards a Critical History', 181; Zurndorfer, 'Resistant Fibre', p. 48.

49 Zurndorfer, 'Cotton Textile Manufacture', 708.

50 Bray, *Technology and Gender*, p. 213.

51 Deng, *Premodern Chinese Economy*, pp. 284–5; Chü Wiens, 'Cotton Textile Production', 516–17; Zurndorfer, 'Cotton Textile Manufacture', 705–6.

52 Zurndorfer, 'Resistant Fibre', pp. 55–8.

53 Only in the late sixteenth and seventeenth centuries, and following the expansion of cotton textile production, did men take charge of weaving (as well as finishing and dyeing), relegating women mostly to the cleaning, ginning and spinning of cotton. Bray, 'Towards a Critical History', p. 185. See also Lynda S. Bell, 'For Better, for Worse: Women and the World Market in Rural China', *Modern China* 20/2 (1994): 180–210 and Bray, 'Textile Production and Gender Roles in China', especially 127–8.

54 Cited in Masatoshi Tanaka, 'The Putting-Out System of Production in the Ming and Qing Periods: with a Focus on Clothing Production (I)', *Memoirs of the Research Department of the Toyo Bunko* 52 (1994): 27.

55 Xu and Wu, *Chinese Capitalism*, pp. 218–19.

56 Brook, *Confusions of Pleasure*, p. 114. On the Ming economy, see Evelyn S. Rawski, 'Ming Society and the Economy', *Ming Studies* 2 (1976): 12–19.

57 Xu and Wu, *Chinese Capitalism*, p. 222.

58 Tanaka, 'Putting-out System', 26–9.

59 Ibid.; Nishijima, 'Formation of the Early Chinese Cotton Industry', pp. 17–77. For an overview, see Zurndorfer, 'Cotton Textile Manufacture', 717–18.

60 Cited in Brook, *Confusions of Pleasure*, p. 197.

61 Li, *Agricultural Development*, pp. 107–8.

62 Elvin, 'High-Level Equilibrium Trap', p. 150; Bray, *Technology and Gender*, p. 214, Myers, 'Cotton Textile Handicraft', 616.

63 Xu and Wu, *Chinese Capitalism*, p. 215.

64 Bray, *Technology and Gender*, pp. 222–3.

65 Chü Wiens, 'Cotton Textile Production', 520; Tanaka, 'Putting-Out System', 32; Zurndorfer, 'Cotton Textile Manufacture', 713–14.

66 Elvin, 'High-Level Equilibrium Trap', p. 168.

67 Cited in Craig Dietrich, 'Cotton Culture and Manufacture in Early Ch'ing China', in Wilmott, ed., *Economic Organisation*, p. 110.

68 Donald Quataert, *Ottoman Manufacturing in the Age of the Industrial Revolution* (Cambridge University Press, 1993), p. 27. See also the map in Suraiya Faroqhi, 'Textile Production in Rumeli and the Arab Provinces: Geographical Distribution and Internal Trade (1560–1650)', in Suraiya Faroqhi, *Peasants, Dervishes and Traders in the Ottoman Empire* (London: Variorum Reprints, 1986), p. 53; and William Gervase Clarence-Smith, 'Locally Produced Textiles on the Indian Ocean Periphery 1500–1850: East Africa, the Middle East, and Southeast Asia', unpublished paper presented at Pune GEHN conference, December 2005.

69 Charles Issawi, *The Economic History of the Middle East, 1800–1914: a Book of Readings* (University of Chicago Press, 1966), pp. 180–1.

70 The traveller Ibn Battuta refers to Syrian centres like Baalbek as producers of cotton fabrics and garments for the markets of Egypt, and specialising in the production of *ihrām*, a fabric used for the cloaks traditionally worn on the pilgrimage to Mecca. Ashtor, 'Venetian Cotton Trade', 682–3.

71 Faroqhi, 'Textile Production', pp. 73–4; Abdul-Karim Rafeq, 'Craft Organisation, Work Ethics, and the Strains of Change in Ottoman Syria', *Journal of the American Oriental Society* 111/3 (1991): 508.

72 Suraiya Faroqhi, *Approaching Ottoman History. An Introduction to the Sources* (Cambridge University Press, 2000), p. 227.

73 Suraiya Faroqhi, 'Research on the History of the Ottoman Consumption: a Preliminary Exploration of Sources and Models', in Donald Quataert, ed., *Consumption Studies and the History of the Ottoman Empire, 1550–1922* (New York: SUNY Press, 2000), p. 36.

74 Daniel Goffman, *Izmir and the Levantine World, 1550–1650* (Seattle: University of Washington Press, 1990), pp. 70–1.

75 Faroqhi, 'Notes on the Production of Cotton and Cotton Cloth', 262–3.

76 Faroqhi, 'Textile Production', pp. 64–5; Issawi, *Economic History*, pp. 48–9.

77 Quataert, *Ottoman Manufacturing*, p. 34.

78 Lombard, *Textiles dans le monde*, pp. 22 and 49; Clarence-Smith, 'Locally Produced Textiles'.

79 Faroqhi, 'Notes on the Production of Cotton and Cotton Cloth', 270; Quataert, *Ottoman Manufacturing*, p. 33; Suraiya Faroqhi, *Towns and Townsmen of Ottoman Anatolia. Trade, Crafts and Food Production in an Urban Setting, 1520–1650* (Cambridge University Press, 1984), p. 155.

80 Socrates D. Petmezas, 'Patterns of Protoindustrialization in the Ottoman Empire. The Case of Eastern Thessaly, *ca.* 1750–1860', *JEEH* 19/3 (1990): 589.

81 Veronika Gervers, *The Influence of Ottoman Turkish Textiles and Costume in Eastern Europe, with Particular Reference to Hungary* (Toronto: Royal Ontario Museum, 1982), p. 9; Faroqhi, 'Textile Production', p. 62.

82 Suraiya Faroqhi, 'Ottoman Cotton Textiles: the Story of a Success that did not Last, 1500–1800', in Riello and Parthasarathi, eds., *Spinning World*, pp. 94–5 and 97.

83 Suraiya Faroqhi, 'Ottoman Textiles in European Markets', unpublished paper presented at the conference Renaissance and the Ottoman World, Warburg Institute, 26–27 April 2006). I thank Suraiya Faroqhi for providing me with a copy of this paper.

84 Gervers, *Influence of Ottoman Turkish Textiles*, pp. 5–6.

85 Ibid., pp. 7–8.

86 Faroqhi, 'Ottoman Cotton Textiles', p. 91.

87 Faroqhi, *Towns and Townsmen*, p. 127. The length of an *ell* varied from place to place, but was on average 1.1 metre.

88 For a comprehensive overview see Maureen Fennell Mazzaoui, *The Italian Cotton Industry in the Later Middle Ages, 1100–1600* (Cambridge University Press, 1981), and Maureen Fennell Mazzaoui, 'The First European Cotton Industry: Italy and Germany, 1100–1800', in Riello and Parthasarathi, eds., *Spinning World*, pp. 63–88.

89 Mazzaoui, 'Cotton Industry', 263. On the general European economy see: Jan van Luiten, *The Long Road to the Industrial Revolution. The European Economy in a Global Perspective, 1000–1800* (Leiden: E. J. Brill, 2009), especially part 1.

90 For an indication of the chronology of development of the industry, see H. Wescher, 'The Beginning of the Cotton Industry in Europe', *Ciba Review* 64 (1948): 2328–33; and Mazzaoui, 'Cotton Industry', 262–86.

91 Eugene H. Byrne, 'Genoese Trade with Syria in the Twelfth Century', *AHR* 25/2 (1920): 216.

92 Patrizia Mainoni, *Economia e politica nella Lombardia medievale: da Bergamo a Milano fra XIII e XV secolo* (Cavallermaggiore: Gribaudo Editore, 1994), p. 15. Probably the name 'fustian' derives from Fustat, a city that for Europeans was synonymous with cotton textiles. David Abulafia, *Italy, Sicily and the Mediterranean, 1100–1400* (London: Variorum Reprints, 1987), p. 237.

93 Mazzaoui, 'Organizzazione delle industrie tessili', 108.

94 Armando Sapori, 'I beni del commercio internazionale nel medioevo', *Archivio Storico Italiano* 113 (1955): 17; Hilmar C. Krueger, 'The Wares of Exchange in the Genoese–African Traffic of the Twelfth Century', *Speculum* 12/1 (1937): 59; Byrne, 'Genoese Trade', 217; Luciana Frangioni, 'Le manifatture in età comunale e signorile', in Franco Dalla Peruta, ed., *Storia illustrata di Milano* (Milan: Sellino, 1992), p. 734.

95 Fustian for instance was used on Venetian galleys, though most commonly sails were made of hemp or flax. Mazzaoui, 'Cotton Industry', 269–70.

96 Michele Daverio, 'Saggi storici sulle manifatture delle bambagine e fustagni', in C. A. Vianello, ed., *Economisti minori del Settecento lombardo* (Milan: Giuffrè, 1942), p. 450.

97 In the mid thirteenth century Venice exported a quarter of a million ducats worth of raw cotton to Lombardy's cities. Wescher, 'Cotton Growing', 2337.

98 H. Wescher, 'Fustian Weaving in South Germany from the Fourteenth to the Sixteenth Century', *Ciba Review* 64 (1948): 2341; Kellenbenz, 'Fustian Industry of the Ulm Region', p. 262.

99 Wescher, 'Schürlitz Weaving in Switzerland', *Ciba Review* 64 (1948): 2351–4.

100 Mainoni, *Mercanti lombardi*, p. 20.

101 Wescher, 'Beginning of the Cotton Industry in Europe', 2332.

102 Charles Wilson, 'Cloth Production and International Competition in the Seventeenth Century', *EHR* 13/2 (1960): 214.

103 Wood, *History of the Levant Company*, p. 74.

104 The total value of the fustian production was estimated in the region of £1,500 a year. William H. Price, 'On the Beginning of the Cotton Industry in England', *Quarterly Journal of Economics* 20/4 (1906): 608–10.

105 Bray, 'Towards a Critical History', p. 182 and Weiji, *History of Textile Technology*, p. 140; Zurndorfer, 'Resistant Fibre', p. 48. The original calculations are in Yan Zhongping, *Zhongguo mianfangzhi shikao, 1289–1937* (Beijing: Ke xue chu ban she, 1963), pp. 15–17. I thank Kent Deng for the conversion rate of bolts into western weight and linear measures. A bolt of cotton for taxation purposes weighted 1.5 kg, compared to normal bolts of 1 kg. The higher weight was due to a higher count of the thread. Notice that calculations are based on a weight of 0.1 kg per yard. See also following footnote for the Ottoman Empire.

106 Faroqhi, 'Notes on the Production of Cotton and Cotton Cloth', p. 264. The number of yards has been calculated by taking the weight of a yard of cloth to range between 0.2 and 0.33 kg.

107 Scott C. Levi, *The Indian Diaspora in Central Asia and its Trade, 1550–1900* (Leiden: E. J. Brill, 2002), p. 78; Chaudhuri, *Trading World of Asia and the English East India Company*, pp. 540–1; Femme S. Gaastra, 'The Textile Trade of the VOC: the Dutch Response to the English Challenge', *South Asia* 19/special issue (1996): 85–95.

108 The Chinese figures are based on 3.6–4 days' work for one bolt; 12 hours of work a day over 24 days a month. Xu and Wu, *Chinese Capitalism*, pp. 215–16. This comparison reveals that Chinese spinners had to work more hours than their Indian counterparts. There is no indication in fact that Indian spinners worked as long as 12 hours a day.

109 Calculations for China suggest that nearly as much work went into the cultivation of raw cotton as in spinning.

110 Other estimates for weaving in India suggest an output of 5 yards of cloth per loom a day. However, a loom needed both a weaver and an assistant, thus making 3 yards an estimate not incompatible with a productivity per loom of 5 yards a day. See in particular Brennig, 'Textile Producers', 343.

111 Kuhn, *Science and Civilisation in China*, p. 196.

112 Frederic C. Lane, 'Ritmo e rapidità di giro d'affari nel commercio veneziano del quattrocento', in *Studi in Onore di Gino Luzzatto* (Milan: Giuffrè, 1949), vol. I, pp. 262–3.

113 Mazzaoui, 'Organizzazione delle industrie tessili', 117.

114 Xu and Wu, *Chinese Capitalism*, p. 55.

115 Faroqhi, 'Notes on the Production of Cotton and Cotton Cloth', p. 135.

116 Mazzaoui, 'Cotton Industry', 272–3.

117 Bin Roy Wong, *China Transformed: Historical Change and the Limits of European Experience* (Ithaca, NY: Cornell University Press, 1996), pp. 40–1.

118 Crill, 'Indian Painted Cottons', 28. There is also evidence of the use of mordants in the Middle East and Egypt in the fourth century CE.

119 Lotika Varadarajan, 'Indian Textile Technology in the Pre-Industrial Period', *Indica* 21/2 (1984): 66–7 and note 30.

120 Alexander I. Tchitcherov, *India: Changing Economic Structure in the Sixteenth to Eighteenth Centuries* (New Delhi: Manohar, 1998), p. 72.

121 Florence M. Montgomery, *Printed Textiles: English and American Cottons and Linens, 1700–1850,* (London: Thoemmes Press Reprints, [1970] 1999), pp. 13–14; Vanina, *Urban Crafts*, p. 36. It must be said that chintzes are sometimes both printed and painted. Tchitcherov, *India*, p. 72.

122 N. A. Reath, 'Printed Fabrics', *Bulletin of the Pennsylvania Museum* 20/95 (1925), 143.

123 See Crill, 'Indian Painted Cottons', 28.

124 Zaheer Baber, *The Science of Empire: Scientific Knowledge, Civilization, and Colonial Rule in India* (New York: SUNY Press, 1996), p. 59.

125 Nishijima, 'Formation of the Early Chinese Cotton Industry', pp. 52–3.

126 Hall, 'Textile Industry in Southeast Asia', 113–14.

127 Kayoko Fujita, 'Japan Indianized: the Material Culture of Imported Textiles in Japan, 1550–1850', in Riello and Parthasarathi, eds., *Spinning World*, pp. 181–2.

128 Pfister, *Toiles imprimées*, p. 20.

129 Pitton de Tournefort, *Relation d'un voyage du Levant* (Paris, 1717), vol. II, p. 434. Cited in Amanda Phillips, 'Little known Ottoman-Period Cotton and Linen Textiles in Oxford's Ashmolean Museum', *Proceedings of the 13th International Congress of Turkish Art* (Budapest: Hungarian National Museum, 2010), p. 598.

130 Kriger, 'Mapping the History', 105. In the case of Europe, as we will see in Chapter 6, the main barrier was that printing was unsuitable for woollens. See also Giorgio Riello, 'Asian Knowledge and the Development of Calico Printing in Europe in the Seventeenth and Eighteenth Centuries', *JGH* 5/1 (2010): 1–28.

5 The Indian apprenticeship: Europeans trading in Indian cottons

1 Tavernier, *Travels in India*, vol. II, p. 23.
2 Dennis O. Flynn and Arturo Giráldez, 'Born with a "Silver Spoon": the Origin of World Trade in 1571', in Dennis O. Flynn and Arturo Giráldez, eds., *Metals and Monies in an Emerging Global Economy* (Aldershot: Ashgate, 1997), pp. 259–79.
3 Jan de Vries, 'Connecting Europe and Asia: a Quantitative Analysis of the Cape-Route Trade, 1497–1795', in Dennis O. Flynn, Arturo Giráldez and Richard von Glahn, eds., *Global Connections and Monetary History, 1470–1800* (Aldershot: Ashgate, 2003), pp. 35–106. Further figures about the overall size of the Eurasian trade are provided by Om Prakash, 'Financing the European Trade with Asia in the Early Modern Period: Dutch Initiatives and Innovations', *JEEH* 27/2 (1998): 354.
4 Vries, 'Limits of Globalization in the Early Modern World', 720.
5 The first position is represented by Williamson and O'Rourke: O'Rourke and Williamson, 'When did Globalisation Begin?', 23–50; Kevin O'Rourke and Jeffrey G. Williamson, 'After Columbus: Explaining Europe's Overseas Trade Boom, 1500–1800', *JEH* 62/2 (2002): 417–56; Ronald Findlay and Kevin H. O'Rourke, *Power and Plenty: Trade, War, and the World Economy in the Second Millennium* (Princeton University Press, 2007), especially ch. 6; while the second is championed by Maxine Berg, 'Manufacturing the Orient. Asian Commodities and European Industry 1500–1800', in Simonetta Cavaciocchi, ed., *Prodotti e tecniche d'oltremare nelle economie europee. Secc. XIII–XVIII. Atti della ventinovesima settimana di studi, 14–19 aprile 1997* (Florence: Le Monnier, 1998), 385–419; Berg, 'In Pursuit of Luxury', 85–142.
6 The nature of the Carreira da Índia was different from the later north European companies as it was a direct agency of the Portuguese crown.
7 Om Prakash observes instead a balance between competition and cooperation among the European companies and with other traders, especially in the late seventeenth and eighteenth centuries. See Om Prakash, 'Cooperation and Conflict Among European Traders in the Indian Ocean in the Late Eighteenth Century', *IESHR* 39/2–3 (2002): 131–48. A more cautious position is proposed by Tirthankar Roy, *India in the World Economy: from Antiquity to the Present* (Cambridge University Press, 2012).
8 George Bryan Souza, *The Survival of Empire: Portuguese Trade and Society in China and the South China Sea, 1630–1754* (Cambridge University Press, 1986), p. 76.
9 Quoted in Micheal N. Pearson, *Merchants and Rulers in Gujarat: the Response to the Portuguese in the Sixteenth Century* (Berkeley: University of California Press, 1976), p. 12.
10 Prakash, *European Commercial Enterprise in Pre-Colonial India*, p. 36, table 2.3; Sanjay Subrahmanyam, *The Portuguese Empire in Asia. 1500–1700: a Political and Economic History* (Harlow: Longman, 1993), pp. 63, 142 and 166.
11 James C. Boyajian, *Portuguese Trade in Asia under the Habsburgs, 1580–1640* (Baltimore, Md.: Johns Hopkins University Press, 1993), pp. 139–41; Afzal Ahmad, 'Indian Textiles and the Portuguese Trade in the Seventeenth Century (1600–1643)', *Studia* 48 (1989): 215–20; Afzal Ahmad, *Portuguese Trade and Socio-Economic Changes on the Western Coast of India (1600–1663)* (New Delhi: Originals, 2000), p. 109 and appendix 9, p. 227.
12 Ahmad, *Portuguese Trade*, p. 108.

13 Ahmad, 'Indian Textiles', 214; José Roberto do Amaral Lapa, 'Domensões do Comercio Colonial o Brasil e o Oriente', *Studia* 49 (1989): 391–2; Ahmad, *Portuguese Trade*, p. 108.

14 John Vogt, 'Notes on the Portuguese Cloth Trade in West Africa, 1480–1540', *International Journal of African Historical Studies* 8/4 (1975): 644.

15 Anthony R. Disney, *Twilight of the Pepper Empire: Portuguese Trade in Southwest India in the Early Seventeenth Century* (Cambridge, Mass.: Harvard University Press, 1978), pp. 118–19; Souza, *Survival of Empire*, p. 78.

16 Femme S. Gaastra, 'War, Competition and Collaboration: Relations Between the English and Dutch East India Company in the Seventeenth and Eighteenth Centuries', in Huw V. Bowen, Margarette Lincoln and Nigel Rigby, eds., *The Worlds of the East India Company* (Woodbridge: Boydell Press, 2002), pp. 49–68; Glamann, *Dutch-Asiatic Trade*, p. 138. On the early engagement by the EIC with cotton textiles see Chaudhuri, *English East India Company*, pp. 190–203. See also ch. 6 in this book.

17 On the American market, see Robert DuPlessis, 'Cottons Consumption in the Seventeenth- and Eighteenth-Century North Atlantic', in Riello and Parthasarathi, eds., *Spinning World*, pp. 227–46. See also Joseph E. Inikori, *Africans and the Industrial Revolution in England: A Study of International Trade and Economic Development* (Cambridge University Press, 2002); Joseph E. Inikori, 'Africa and the Globalization Process: Western Africa, 1450–1850', *JGH* 2/1 (2007): 63–86.

18 O. P. Singh, *Surat and its Trade in the Second Half of the 17th Century* (University Press of Delhi, 1977), pp. 55–78; Sangar, 'Export of Indian Textiles', 2.

19 Charles Woolsey Cole, *French Mercantilism, 1683–1700* (New York: Columbia University Press, 1943), p. 168.

20 Philippe Haudrère, 'La Compagnie française des Indes, 1719–1795', *L'Information Historique* 51 (1989): 1. For an overview of the French trade in India in the eighteenth century see Haudrère, *Compagnie française*, vol. I; and Paul Butel, 'French Traders and India at the End of the Eighteenth Century', in Sushil Chaudhuri and Michel Morineau, eds., *Merchants, Companies and Trade: Europe and Asia in the Early Modern Era* (Cambridge University Press, 1999), pp. 287–99.

21 Indrani Ray, 'The French Company and the Merchants of Bengal (1680–1730)', in Lakshmi Subramanian, ed., *The French East India Company and the Trade of the Indian Ocean: a Collection of Essays by Indrani Ray* (New Delhi: Munshiram Manoharlal, 1999), p. 84.

22 Ibid., p. 78.

23 Haudrère, 'Compagnie française des Indes', 5; Philippe Haudrère and Gérard Bouëdec, *Les Compagnies des Indes* (Rennes: Ouest France, 1999), p. 80.

24 Ole Feldbæk, 'The Danish Trading Companies of the Seventeenth and Eighteenth Centuries', *Scandinavian EHR* 34/3 (1986): 204–6.

25 Kristof Glamann, 'The Danish Asiatic Company, 1732–1771', *Scandinavian EHR* 8/2 (1960): 125–49.

26 There are several collections of published materials, for instance, for the English East India Company in the seventeenth century. See Foster, ed., *English Factories in India*, on the period 1618–69; Sir Charles Fawcett, ed., *English Factories in India*, new series, 4 vols. (Oxford: Clarendon Press, 1936–55), on the period 1670–84; Ethel Bruce Sainsbury, ed., *A Calendar of the Court Minutes of the East India Company*

1635–1679, 11 vols. (Oxford: Clarendon Press, 1907–38), covering the period 1635–79. Some selected VOC sources are published in English: Om Prakash, ed., *The Dutch Factories in India, 1617–1623: a Collection of Dutch East India Company Documents Pertaining to India* (New Delhi: Munshiram Manoharlal, 1984); and Om Prakash, ed., *The Dutch Factories in India: a Collection of Dutch East India Company Documents Pertaining to India*, vol. II, *1624–1627* (New Delhi: Manohar, 2007).

27 On the early cotton trade of the VOC, see the sales at Kamer Amsterdam in Glamann, *Dutch-Asiatic Trade*, table 26, p. 143. Between 1631 and 1658 the VOC exported from Surat on average 277,000 pieces of cotton cloth a year, but they were mostly directed towards Asian destinations. In the period between 1620 and 1650 textiles and silks accounted for no more than 15 per cent of the value of commodities imported by the VOC into Europe. Niels Steensgaard, 'The Growth and Composition of the Long-Distance Trade of England and the Dutch Republic before 1750', in James D. Tracy, ed., *The Rise of Merchant Empires: Long-Distance Trade in the Early Modern World, 1350–1750* (Cambridge University Press, 1990), pp. 114 and 124.

28 The original figures for the Carreira da India are expressed in 'bales' and Boyajian calculates that a bale weighed on average 223 pounds. This is in line with other estimates. What is problematic is that it includes both silks and cottons. However, calculations of value at 1 cruzado = 0.33 Dutch florins and £1 = 11 florins with a sale value of *c.* £0.9 per piece (as from the English post-1660 sales) give figures with a margin error of 10 per cent on Boyajian figures. I thank Dennis Flynn and George Souza for their help with these calculations.

29 Femme S. Gaastra and Jaap R. Bruijn, 'The Dutch East India Company's Shipping 1602–1795, in a Comparative Perspective', in Jaap R. Bruijn and Femme S. Gaastra, eds., *Ships, Sailors and Spices: East India Companies and their Shipping in the 16th, 17th and 18th Centuries* (Amsterdam: Neha, 1993), p. 182.

30 Anthony Reid, 'Southeast Asian Consumption of Indian and British Cotton Cloth, 1600–1850', in Riello and Roy, eds., *How India Clothed the World*, pp. 29–52 and especially table 1.1, p. 35.

31 See also Prakash, *European Commercial Enterprise in Pre-Colonial India*, p. 120, table 4.2. The figures that I calculated for the VOC are broadly in line with the figures provided by Steur with the exception of the late 1760s. J. J. Steur, *Herstel of ondergang: de woorstellen tot redres van de Verenigde Oost-Indische Compagnie 1740–1795* (Utrecht: Hes Uitgevers, 1984), especially p. 100.

32 Jan Willem Veluwenkamp, 'De buitenlandse textielhandel van de Republiek in de achttiende eeuw', *Textielhistorische Bijdragen* 34 (1994): 83.

33 Gaastra, 'Textile Trade of the VOC', 85–95; Femme S. Gaastra, 'De textielhandel en de VOC', *Textielhistorische Bijdragen* 34 (1994), 50–69; Ryuto Shimada, *The Intra-Asian Trade in Japanese Copper by the Dutch East India Company During the Eighteenth Century* (Leiden: E. J. Brill, 2006), pp. 136–7. The figures for cotton textiles exported to Europe are an average per year from the quinquennial figures for 1711–15. The general exchange rate is 1 British pound sterling to 11 guilders.

34 *Letters Received by the East India Company from its Servants in the East, 1602–1617*, vol. II, *1613–15*, ed. F. C. Danvers and Sir William Foster (London: Marston, 1896–1902), p. 269.

35 IOIR, Letter Book, vol. 3, fo. 89. Cited in Kerlogue, 'Early English Textile Trade', 154.

36 Gaastra, 'Textile Trade of the VOC', 86.

37 Cited in François Martin, *La Compagnie des Indes Orientales* (Paris: Augustin Challamel, 1908), p. 199.

38 *Correspondance du Conseil Supérieur de Pondichéry avec le Conseil de Chandernagor*, vol. I, *1728–1757*, ed. A. Martineau (Pondichéry: Société de l'Histoire de l'Inde Française, 1915), p. 271.

39 Els M. Jacobs, *Merchant in Asia: the Trade of the Dutch East India Company During the Eighteenth Century* (Leiden: CNWS Publications, 2006), p. 141.

40 Ahmad, 'Indian Textiles', 214–19.

41 Giorgio Riello, 'The Indian Apprenticeship: the Trade of Indian Textiles and the Making of European Cottons', in Riello and Roy, eds., *How India Clothed the World*, pp. 332–5.

42 Satya Prakash Sangar identifies more than 150 different types of cotton cloths produced in seventeenth-century India, excluding quilted fabric, turbans and mixed silk cotton fabrics. Satya Prakash Sangar, *Indian Textiles in the Seventeenth Century* (New Delhi: Reliance Publication House, 1998), especially pp. 1–28. The FEIC did not fare better, as it sold several dozen varieties of cotton. Arvind Sinha, *The Politics of Trade: Anglo-French Commerce on the Coromandel Coast, 1763–1793* (New Delhi: Manohar, 2002), pp. 177–82.

43 Alexandre Legoux de Flaix, *Essai historique, géographique et politique sur l'Indoustan* (Paris, 1807), vol. II, p. 3. Cited in Richard Roberts, 'West Africa and the Pondicherry Textile Industry', *IESHR* 31/2 (1994): 120.

44 K. N. Chaudhuri, 'Treasure and Trade Balance: the East India Company's Export Trade, 1660–1720', *EHR* 21/3 (1968): 483.

45 Singh, *Surat*, p. 130. See also the quantitative analysis in Dietmar Rothermund, 'The Changing Pattern of British Trade in Indian Textiles, 1701–1757', in Chaudhuri and Morineau, eds., *Merchants, Companies and Trade*, pp. 276–86.

46 Jopie van Eijkern-Balkenstein, Peter Diebels and Ebeltje Hartkamp-Jonxis, 'Orderoverzicht van door de VOC uit India "geëiste" sitsen', in Ebeltje Hartkamp-Jonxis, ed., *Sits: oost-west relaties in textiel* (Zwolle: Waanders 1987), pp. 113–21.

47 Berg, 'Manufacturing the Orient', p. 396.

48 Prakash, ed., *Dutch Factories*, vol. I, pp. 51–2.

49 Clarence-Smith, 'Production of Cotton Textiles', p. 135.

50 *Peter Floris: his Voyage to the East Indies in the 'Globe', 1611–1615*, ed. W. H. Moreland (London: Hakluyt Society, 1934), p. 71.

51 Chaudhuri, *Trading World of Asia and the English East India Company*, pp. 281–7. Also reported in John E. Wills, 'European Consumption and Asian Production in the Seventeenth and Eighteenth Centuries', in John Brewer and Roy Porter, eds., *Consumption and the World of Goods* (London and New York: Routledge, 1993), p. 137. Shirts had already been traded by the Dutch in 1622 to Batavia. However we do not know if they were a success. Prakash, ed., *Dutch Factories*, vol. I, p. 194.

52 John Styles, 'Product Innovation in Early Modern London', *P&P* 168 (2000): 137. See also Audrey W. Douglas, 'Cotton Textiles in England: the East India Company's Attempts to Exploit Developments in Fashion 1660–1721', *Journal of British Studies* 8/2 (1969): 32; and Lemire, *Fashion's Favourite*, p. 180.

53 Quoted in Styles, 'Product Innovation', 137. On the issue of the dependence of England on imported linen, see Chapter 11 below.

54 Quoted in Douglas, 'Cotton Textiles in England', 32. See also John Irwin and P. R. Schwartz, *Studies in Indo-European Textile History* (Ahmedabad: Calico Museum of Textiles, 1966), p. 36.

55 Styles, 'Product Innovation', 138–9.

56 *Voyages et aventures du capitaine Ripon aux Grandes Indes: journal inédit d'un mercenaire (1617–1627)*, ed. Yves Giraud (Thonon-les-Bains: L'Albatron, 1990), pp. 140–1.

57 See in particular the numerous examples in Barnes, ed., *Textiles in Indian Ocean Societies*; and Crill, ed., *Textiles from India*.

58 This topic is analysed in detail in my 'The Globalisation of Cotton Textiles: Indian Cottons, Europe and the Atlantic World, 1600–1850', in Riello and Parthasarathi, eds., *Spinning World*.

59 India Office Archives, Factory Records Miscellaneous, vol. 12, fo. 99. See also John Irwin, 'Origins of the "Oriental Style" in English Decorative Art', *Burlington Magazine* 97/625 (1955): 109.

60 Irwin, 'Indian Textile Trade', and Styles, 'Product Innovation', 132–40. See also Woodruff D. Smith, *Consumption and the Making of Respectability, 1600–1800* (New York and London: Routledge, 2002).

61 Riello, 'Asian Knowledge', 1–28. See also Chapter 8 below.

62 These techniques were, however, not invented or introduced in Asia. This might partly be explained by the fact that the market for white-background textiles was small and therefore there was little incentive on the part of Indian craftsmen to either invent or adopt them.

63 Jacobs, *Merchant in Asia*, p. 140.

64 Cited in Tamezo Osumi, *Printed Cottons of Asia: the Romance of Trade Textiles* (Tokyo: Bijutsu Shuppan-sha, 1963), p. 17.

65 Andrew Morall and Melinda Watt, *English Embroidery from the Metropolitan Museum of Art, 1580–1700* (New Haven, Conn.: Yale University Press, 2008), p. 272.

66 Margherita Bellezza Rosina, 'Tra oriente e occidente', in Marzia Cataldi Gallo, ed., *I mezzari: tra oriente e occidente* (Genoa: Sagep Editrice, 1988), pp. 20–1; Gittinger, *Master Dyers*, p. 186; Maxwell, *Textiles of Southeast Asia*, p. 27.

67 Osumi, *Printed Cottons of Asia*, p. 17.

68 Philippe Minard, 'Réputation, normes et qualité dans l'industrie textile française au XVIIIe siècle', in Alessandro Stanziani, ed., *La Qualité des produits en France, XVIIIe-XXe siècle* (Paris: Belin, 2004), pp. 69–92.

69 ANF, C² 67f, 189–189v, Ougly 18 Dec. 1704. Cited in Indrani Ray, 'The French Company and the Merchants of Bengal (1680–1730)', in Subramanian, ed., *French East India Company*, p. 68.

70 Cited in Ray, 'French Company', p. 78. One of the servants of the EEIC explained that 'a weaver cannot, with all the skill he hath, make a peece of bafta or stuffe soe thick and well wove, notwithstanding he have the same yarne and the same quantity, in the dry time as they can in the raines or wett time'. Foster, ed., *English Factories in India*, vol. XI (1661–4), p. 112.

71 Factory Records Miscellaneous, vol. 1, 26, 18 February 1620. Cited in Chaudhuri, *English East India Company*, p. 194.

72 Foster, ed., *English Factories in India*, vol. XI (1661–4), p. 200.

73 Ibid., p. 201.

74 Sinnappah Arasaratnam, 'The Dutch East India Company and its Coromandel Trade, 1700–1740', *Bijdragen tot de Taal-, Land- en Volkenkunde*, 123 (1967): 338.

75 *Correspondance du Conseil Supérieur, de Pondichéry et de la Compagnie, 1726–67*, vol. IV, 1744–49, ed. A. Martineau (Pondichéry: Société de l'Histoire de l'Inde Française, 1920–34), p. 73.

76 *Correspondance du Conseil Supérieur de Pondichéry avec le Conseil de Chandernagor*, p. 324.

77 Rothermund, 'Changing Pattern', p. 279.

78 Foster, ed., *English Factories in India*, vol. XI (1661–4), p. 159.

79 Ibid., p. 369.

80 Indrani Ray, 'The Trade and Traders in Ahmedabad in Late Seventeenth Century: Extracts from George Roques' MSS', in Subramanian, ed., *French East India Company*, p. 66.

81 Subramanian, 'Power and the Weave', pp. 52–82.

82 See for instance Prakash, 'Cooperation and Conflict', 133; Om Prakash, 'From Market-Determined to Coercion-Based: Textile Manufacturing in Eighteenth-Century Bengal', in Riello and Roy, eds., *How India Clothed the World*, pp. 217–50; Lakshmi Subramanian, 'The Political Economy of Textiles in Western India: Weavers, Merchants and the Transition to a Colonial Economy', in Riello and Roy, eds., *How India Clothed the World*, pp. 253–80.

83 Subramanyam, 'Rural Industry', 76–114; Parthasarathi and Wendt, 'Decline in Three Keys', pp. 397–407.

84 E. Levasseur, *Histoire du commerce de la France* (Paris: Arthur Rousseau, 1911–12), vol. I, p. 475.

85 Chaudhuri, *From Prosperity to Decline*, pp. 280–90. This explains the sudden increase in the profits of the EEIC measured as the mark up between sale price in London and purchasing prices in India. However the figures for the 1690s are difficult to interpret because the quantities traded were much below the average of previous and following decades.

86 Prasannan Parthasarathi, 'Rethinking Wages and Competitiveness in the Eighteenth Century', *P&P* 158 (1998): 79–109.

87 The FEIC's profit margins were even lower than the EEIC's. See the figures for the period 1725–68 in Henry Weber, *La Compagnie française des Indes (1604–1875)* (Paris: Arthur Rousseau, 1904), p. 402.

88 The next chapter presents similar considerations by examining the price relationship between cottons and other fabrics in the eighteenth century.

89 Cited in Jean Deloche, 'Le Mémoire de Moracin sur Macilipattanamu: un tableau des conditions économiques et sociales des provinces côtières de l'Andhra au milieu du XVIIIe siècle', *Bulletin de l'Ecole Française d'Extrême-Orient* 62 (1975): 139.

90 See Morineau and Prakash respectively on the French and Dutch policies for increasing the quality of textiles bought in India. Michel Morineau, 'Le Défi indien, XVIIe et XVIIIe siècle', *Bulletin de l'Ecole Française d'Extrême-Orient* 82 (1995): 37; Prakash, *European Commercial Enterprise in Pre-Colonial India*, p. 218.

91 Arasaratnam, 'Dutch East India Company', pp. 338–9.

92 This was the case of the Dutch in Coromandel in the 1750s. See Bhattacharya, 'Hinterland and the Coast', pp. 38–9.

93 Maxine Berg, 'Asian Luxuries and the Making of the European Consumer Revolution', in Maxine Berg and Elizabeth Eger, eds., *Luxury in the Eighteenth Century: Debates, Desires and Delectable Goods* (London: Palgrave, 2003), p. 229.

6 New consuming habits: how cottons entered European houses and wardrobes

1 The literature on the 'consumer revolution' is now vast. For an overview see Brewer and Porter, eds., *Consumption and the World of Goods*; on clothing see John Styles, *The Dress of the People: Everyday Fashion in Eighteenth-Century England* (New Haven, Conn.: Yale University Press, 2007). For a global perspective see Frank Trentmann and John Brewer, eds., *Consuming Cultures, Global Perspectives: Historical Trajectories, Transnational Exchanges* (Oxford: Berg, 2006), especially pp. 1–18.

2 An exhibition of these tokens was held at the Foundling Museum in London in 2010. See John Styles, *Threads of Feeling: the London Foundling Hospital's Textiles Tokens, 1740–1770* (London: Foundling Hospital, 2010). See also Gillian Clark, 'Infant Clothing in the Eighteenth Century: a New Insight', *Costume* 28 (1994): 47–59.

3 On Manchester production see Chapter 7 and on printing see Chapter 8. I thank John Styles, who did a microscopic analysis for me on the Foundling 220 and identified the striped cloth as having a linen warp and a cotton weft.

4 Mildred Davison, 'Printed Cotton Textiles', *Art Institute of Chicago Quarterly* 52/4 (1958): 83.

5 Domenico Sella, *Commerci e industrie a Venezia nel secolo XVII* (Venice: Istituto per la Collaborazione Culturale, 1961), p. 26.

6 Gervers, *Influence of Ottoman Turkish Textiles*, p. 7; Colette Establet and Jean-Paul Pascual, *Des Tissus et des hommes. Damas, vers 1700* (Damascus: Institut Français du Proche-Orient, 2005), p. 209; Richard Hellie, *The Economy and Material Culture of Russia, 1600–1725* (University of Chicago Press, 1999), p. 291.

7 Chaudhuri, *Trading World of Asia and the English East India Company*.

8 Huw Bowen has painstakingly gathered the entire set of trade figures for the period 1760 to the demise of the company in 1834. I thank him for providing me with a copy of his dataset. See also Vries, 'Connecting Europe and Asia', pp. 35–146, and Vries 'Limits of Globalization in the Early Modern World', 710–33.

9 Emmer, 'Myth of Early Globalization', 39.

10 Maxine Berg, 'New Commodities, Luxuries and their Consumers in Eighteenth-Century England', in Maxine Berg and Helen Clifford, eds., *Consumers and Luxury: Consumer Culture in Europe, 1650–1850* (Manchester University Press, 1999), pp. 63–85; Maxine Berg, 'From Imitation to Invention: Creating Commodities in Eighteenth-Century Britain', *EHR* 55/1 (2002): 1–30.

11 These are calculated from K. N. Chaudhuri's EIC's imports divided by the population estimated by E. A. Wrigley. Chaudhuri, *Trading World of Asia and the English East India*, pp. 540–1: Wrigley and Schofield. E. A. Wrigley, and R. S. Schofield, *The Population History of England, 1541–1871: A Reconstruction* (London: Edward Arnold, 1981), pp. 532–4. The figures are, however, much lower if we consider also the American colonies, ranging from 0.4 yards per person per year in the decade 1690–9 to 1.3 yards in the decade 1670–9. Carole Shammas, 'The Decline of Textile

Prices in England and British America Prior to Industrialization', *EHR* 47/3 (1994): 502. On cloth consumption on the Coromandel coast of India, see Brennig, 'Textile Producers', 333–55.

12 Niels Steensgaard, *Carracks, Caravans and Companies: The Structural Crisis in the European-Asian Trade in the Early 17th Century* (Copenhagen: Studentlitteratur, 1973), p. 174; and Lemire, *Fashion's Favourite*, pp. 191–7.

13 See in particular Shammas, 'Decline of Textile Prices'.

14 For a still rich overview see the classic article, Douglas, 'Cotton Textiles in England', 28–43.

15 Sarah Levitt, 'Clothing', in Mary B. Rose, ed., *The Lancashire Cotton Industry. A History Since 1700* (Preston: Lancashire County Books, 1996), pp. 154–5.

16 Cited in Lemire, *Fashion's Favourite*, p. 18.

17 On the changing concept of cleanliness, see Georges Vigarello, *Concepts of Cleanliness: Changing Attitudes in France Since the Middle Ages* (Cambridge University Press, 1988).

18 John Styles, 'Indian Cottons and European Fashion, 1400–1800', in Glenn Adamson, Giorgio Riello and Sarah Teasley, eds., *Global Design History* (London and New York: Routledge, 2011), p. 39.

19 Negley B. Harte, 'Introduction', in N. B. Harte, ed., *The New Draperies in the Low Countries and England, 1300–1700* (Oxford University Press, 1997), p. 3.

20 Wilson, 'Cloth Production and International Competition', 210–11.

21 Lemire, *Fashion's Favourite*; Styles, 'Product Innovation', 132–40.

22 K. N. Chaudhuri, 'Some Reflections on the World Trade of the XVIIth and XVIIIth Century: a Reply', *JEEH* 7/1 (1978): 224.

23 Cited in Lemire, 'Revising the Historical Narrative', p. 213.

24 Archivio di Stato di Firenze, Miscellanea Medicea, no. 107/3, c. 104, 6 October 1547. Cited in Angela Orlandi, 'Mercanti toscani nell'Andalusia del Cinquecento', *Historia, Instituciones, Documentos* 26 (1999): 366. I Thank Luca Molà bringing this article to my attention.

25 Anne Buck, 'Clothing and Textiles in Bedfordshire Inventories, 1617–1620', *Costume* 34 (2000): 27 and 29.

26 Margaret Spufford, 'Fabric for Seventeenth-Century Children and Adolescents' Clothes', *TH* 34/1 (2003): 62.

27 John Styles, 'What were Cottons for in the Industrial Revolution?', in Riello and Parthasarathi, eds., *Spinning World*, pp. 307–26; Styles, *Dress of the People*, pp. 109–32. See also Styles, 'Indian Cottons and European Fashion', pp. 37–46 and Prasannan Parthasarathi's 'Response', in Riello and Teasley, eds., *Global Design History*, pp. 47–9.

28 Anne E. McCants, 'Modest Households and Globally Traded Textiles: Evidence from Amsterdam Household Inventories', in Laura Cruz and Joel Mokyr, eds., *The Birth of Modern Europe: Culture and Economy, 1400–1800. Essays in Honour of Jan de Vries* (Leiden and Boston: E. J. Brill, 2010), pp. 124–6.

29 Daniel Roche, *La Culture des apparences: une histoire du vêtement (XVIIe–XVIIIe siècle)* (Paris: Gallimard, 1991), p. 138.

30 Fernando Ramos, 'Patterns of Textile Consumption in pre-Industrial Spain: Castille, 1750–1850. Consumption Revolution Without Industrial Revolution?', paper presented at the Economic History Society Conference, April 2004, 20.

31 Beverly Lemire, 'Fashioning Cottons: Asian Trade, Domestic Industry and Consumer Demand, 1660–1780', in David Jenkins, ed., *The Cambridge History of Western Textiles* (Cambridge University Press, 2003), vol. I, p. 494.

32 *The Trade of England Revived: and the Abuses Thereof Rectified* (London: Dorman Newman, 1681), p. 16.

33 Chaudhuri, 'Some Reflections', 226.

34 Figures for fustians, cotton cloth and linen are taken from Beveridge's analysis of prices paid by charitable institutions and therefore tend to be constant in time as they were not subject to frequent contract renegotiations. The price of Indian cotton comes instead from Chaudhuri's quantitative and price analysis. As quantities are expressed in pieces, I have used the conversion of 1 piece = 15 yards. This seems to be a plausible measure considering the variety of textiles traded with different measure units per piece: longcloths were up to 40 yards long, baftas 13–18 yards, and romalls just 0.75 yard square handkerchiefs. The resulting value per yard is in line with Shammas's figures in Shammas, 'Decline of Textile Prices', 484 and 493.

35 Margaret Spufford, *The Great Reclothing of Rural England. Petty Chapmen and their Wares in the Seventeenth Century* (London: Hambledon Press, 1985), p. 109.

36 Edgard Depitre, *La Toile peinte en France au XVIIe et au XVIIIe siècles: industries, commerce, prohibitions* (Paris: Marcel Rivière, 1912), p. 9.

37 Berg, 'Manufacturing the Orient', p. 397.

38 Gitanjli Shahani, '"A Foreigner by Birth": The Life of Indian Cloth in the Early Modern English Marketplace', in Barbara Sebek and Stephen Deng, eds., *Global Traffic: Discourses and Practices of Trade in English Literature and Culture from 1550 to 1700* (London and New York: Palgrave Macmillan, 2008), pp. 186–7.

39 Thomas Braker, *Tunbridge-Walks* (1703), cited in Beverly Lemire, *Cotton* (Oxford: Berg, 2011), p. 52.

40 TNA, CO 388/21 part 1, fo. 208.

41 William J. Ashworth, *Customs and Excise: Trade, Production and Consumption in England, 1640–1845* (Oxford University Press, 2003), pp. 5–6. See also John Brewer, *The Sinews of Power: War, Money and the English State, 1688–1783* (London: Unwin Hyman, 1989).

42 Mokyr, *Enlightened Economy*, pp. 34 and 59.

43 Possibly by Charles Davenant. Cited in Chaudhuri, *Trading World of Asia and the English East India Company*, p. 278.

44 *The Stuff Weaver's Case Against Printing Callicoes Examined* (London (?), 1704), p. 1.

45 Cited in Depitre, *Toile peinte*, p. 12.

46 For an overview of the role of European states and their commercial policies, see Mokyr, *Enlightened Economy*, especially ch. 4; Findlay and O'Rourke, *Power and Plenty*, especially ch. 5; Lars Magnusson, *Nation, State and the Industrial Revolution* (London and New York: Routledge, 2009), especially ch. 2.

47 Beverly Lemire, ed., *The British Cotton Trade, 1660–1815* (London: Pickering & Chatto, 2009), especially vol. I.

48 Tim Keirn, 'Parliament, Legislation and the Regulation of English Textile Industries, 1689–1714', in L. Davidson, Timothy Hitchcock, Tim Keirn and Robert D. Shoemakers, eds., *Stirring the Grumbling Hive: the Response to Social and Economic Problems in England, 1689–1750* (Stroud: Sutton, 1992), p. 4.

49 Raymond L. Sickinger, 'Regulation or Ruination: Parliament's Consistent Pattern of Mercantilist Regulation of the English Textile Trade, 1660–1800', *Parliamentary History* 19/2 (2000): 220–1.

50 Lemire, 'Fashioning Cottons', p. 403; James K. Thomson, 'Marketing Channels and Structures in Spain in the First Half of the Eighteenth Century: Two Contrasting Cases', in Jacques Bottin and Nicole Pellegrin, eds., *Échanges et cultures textiles dans l'Europe pré-industrielle. Actes du colloque de Rouen, 17–19 mai 1993* (Lille: Revue du Nord Supplement 12, 1996), p. 338.

51 Glamann, 'European Trade, 1500–1750', p. 87. See also Natalie Rothstein, 'The Calico Campaign of 1719–1721', *East London Papers*, 7 (1964): 3–21.

52 Cited in Lemire, *Cotton*, p. 56.

53 By 1704 duties came to include also white calicoes and muslins. Ralph Davis, 'The Rise of Protection in England, 1789–1786', *EHR* 19/2 (1966): 309; Keirn, 'Parliament', p. 4.

54 Parthasarathi, *Why Europe Grew Rich*, p. 128.

55 Between 1719 and 1748 no less than fifteen *arrêts* banned the use of Indian cottons. Levasseur, *Histoire du Commerce*, vol. I, p. 497. See also Haudrère and Bouëdec, *Compagnies des Indes*, p. 85.

56 *Ârret of the Concil of State in France for Renewing the Prohibition to Import into that Kingdom, to Deal in or Use Indian, Chinese, or Eastern Stained Callicoes or Silks …* (London, 1720), p. 2; *Edit du Roi, Qui Prononce des peines contre ceux qui introduiront dans le Royaume des Toiles peintes ou teintes, Ecorces d'arbres, ou Etoffes de la Chine, des Indes & du Levant* (1736), p. 1.

57 BNF, MSS 21778. Collection Delamare. Pièces relatives aux étoffes des Indes XVII–XVIIIe, fo. 22: 'Arrest du Conseil d'Estat du Roy, 5 Fevrier 1705'.

58 Cole, *French Mercantilism*, pp. 175–6.

59 Daniel Defoe, *A Brief State of the Question, Between the Printed and Painted Callicoes, and the Woollen and Silk Manufacture …* (London: W. Boreham, 1719), p. 5.

60 ANF, F^{12} 1405A. See also Haudrère, *Compagnie française*, vol. I, pp. 302–3.

61 Cited in Philippe Haudrère, *Les Compagnies des Indes Orientales: trois siècles de rencontre entre orientaux et occidentaux* (Paris: Editions Desjonquères, 2006), pp. 169–70.

62 Haudrère, *Compagnie française*, vol. I, p. 304.

63 BNF, MSS 21778. Collection Delamare. Pièces relatives aux étoffes des Indes XVII–XVIIIe, fos. 11–181: prosecutions in Paris between December 1727 and December 1738. See also Philippe Haudrère, 'La Contrebande des toiles indiennes à Paris au XVIIIe siècle', in René Favier, Gérard Gayot, Jean-François Klein, Didier Terrier and Denis Woronoff, eds., *Tisser l'histoire: l'industrie et ses patrons, XVIe–XXe siècles* (Valenciennes: Presses Universitaires de Valenciennes, 2009), especially pp. 172–3.

64 V. L. Bourilly, 'La Contrebande des toiles peintes en Provence au XVIIIe siècle', *Annales du Midi* (1914): 52–74.

65 ANF, F^{12} 1891, item 2: 'L'inspecteur des manufactures de Bayonne envoyai l'extrait des procès verbaux de seize d'étoffe des Indes faites pendant les 6 dernier mois de 1715'.

66 ANF, F^{12} 1891, item 3: 'Réponse de Mr de Matheux à Mr de Berlage, relativement à difficulté d'abolir l'usage des Indiennes en France'. See also Madeleine Dobie, *Trading*

Places: Colonization and Slavery in Eighteenth-Century French Culture (Ithaca, NY: Cornell University Press, 2010), pp. 103–5.

67 Paul Masson, *Histoire du commerce français dans le Levant au XVIIe siècle* (Paris: Hachette & Co., 1896), p. 278.

68 Berg, 'In Pursuit of Luxury', 116 and 123. Berg expands on the classic economic concept of 'import substitution' to show the complexity, variety and flexibility of processes that led to the imitation of Asian products and their eventual reinterpretation.

69 Linda Levy Peck, *Consuming Splendor: Society and Culture in Seventeenth-Century England* (Cambridge University Press, 2005), pp. 85–92.

70 Lien Bich Luu, *Immigrants and the Industries of London, 1500–1700* (Aldershot: Ashgate, 2005), p. 154.

71 D. C. Coleman, 'Mercantilism Revisited', *Historical Journal* 23/4 (1980): 773–91.

72 Cole, *French Mercantilism*, p. 276 and more recently Parthasarathi, *Why Europe Grew Rich*, pp. 128–9.

73 Jules Sottas, *Histoire de la Compagnie des Indes Orientales, 1666–1719* (Paris: Librairie Plon, 1905), p. 92. The import of white cotton cloth was not prohibited in France, but it could not be legally printed. Weber, *Compagnie française des Indes*, p. 236.

74 Olivier Raveux, 'Espaces et technologies dans la France méridionale d'ancien régime: l'example de l'indiennage marseillais (1648–1793)', *Annales du Midi* 116/246 (2004): 155–70 and Olivier Raveux, 'The Birth of a New European Industry: l'indiennage in Seventeenth-Century Marseilles', in Riello and Parthasarathi, eds., *Spinning World*, pp. 291–306

75 Masson, *Histoire du commerce français*, p. 278.

76 Sickinger, 'Regulation or Ruination', p. 229.

77 Beverly Lemire, 'Transforming Consumer Custom: Linen, Cotton, and the English Market, 1660–1800', in Brenda Collins and Philip Ollerenshaw, eds., *The European Linen Industry in Historical Pespective* (Oxford University Press, 2003), p. 197; Trevor Griffiths, Philip Hunt and Patrick O'Brien, 'Scottish, Irish, and Imperial Connections: Parliament, the Three Kingdoms, and the Mechanization of Cotton Spinning in Eighteenth-Century Britain', *EHR* 61/3 (2008): 633–4.

78 Willem Johannes Smit, *De katoendrukkerij in Nederland tot 1813* (Amsterdam: Ontwikkeling, 1928), p. 184, n. 38.

79 The Dutch woollen producers of Leiden settled an agreement in 1742 and 1776 with the VOC by which the Dutch company agreed to buy a certain amount of woollen cloth. Valentijn Schenk, '"Een naare en bedroefde eeuw": De verschepingen van Leidse textiel naar Azië door tussenkomst van de VOC in de periode 1770–1790 en de rol van het contract van 1776', *Textielhistorische Bijdragen* 41 (2001): 49–64; Femme S. Gaastra, 'Leiden en de VOC', in Dick E. H. de Boer, ed., *Leidse Facetten* (Zwolle: Waanders, 1982), pp. 53–64; Jan Arie Frederik de Jongste, *Onrust aan het Spaarne: Haarlem in de jaren 1747–1751* (Dieren: Bataafsche Leeuw, 1984), pp. 22–31.

80 Gaastra, 'Textile Trade of the VOC'. 93–4.

81 Serge Chassagne, *Oberkampf: un entrepreneur capitaliste au siècle des lumières* (Paris: Aubier Montaigne, 1980), p. 123.

82 Vibeke Kingma, 'De katoendrukkerijen in Amsterdam en Nieuwer-Amstel', *Textielhistorische Bijdragen* 38 (1998) : 24–5.

83 See Ann Coenen, 'Katoen en economische groei. De katoenhandel in de Oosten-rijkse Nederlanden tussen politieke ambities en economische realiteit 1759–1791', *Tijdschrift Voor Sociale en Economische Geschiedenis* 8/2 (2011): 32–60.

84 Jan de Vries and A. M. van der Woude, *The First Modern Economy: Success, Failure, and Perseverance of the Dutch Economy, 1500–1815* (Cambridge University Press, 1997).

85 Styles, 'What Were Cottons For'.

86 Adriana Turpin, 'Furnishing the London Merchant's Town House', in Mireille Galinou, ed., *City Merchants and the Arts 1670–1720* (London: Oblong, 2004), pp. 59–60.

87 Lemire, 'Domesticating the Exotic'; Ebeltje Hartkamp-Jonxis, *Sitsen uit India* (Amsterdam: Rijksmuseum, 1994), pp. 11–13; Jan van Campen and Ebeltje Hartkamp-Jonxis, *Asian Spendour: Company Art in the Rijksmuseum* (Amsterdam: Rijksmuseum, 2011), pp. 35–6.

88 Riello, 'Fabricating the Domestic', pp. 54–6.

89 Pepys' Diary, 5 September 1663; 21 November 1663 and 8 January 1664.

90 Pepys' Diary, 1 July 1661. In 1666 Pepys decided to hire an Indian gown for a portrait, but it was in all probability one made of brown silk, as it appears in his famous portrait.

91 Beverly Lemire, 'Fashioning Global Trade: Indian Textiles, Gender Meanings and European Consumers, 1500–1800', in Riello and Roy, eds., *How India Clothed the World*, especially pp. 371–81.

92 *Weekly Review*, 31 January 1708.

93 *A Brief Deduction of the Original Progress and Immense Increase of the Woollen Manufacturers* (1727), p. 50.

94 TNA, CO, 388/21, part 1, fo. 207.

95 Cited in Douglas, 'Cotton Textiles in England', 32. See also Irwin and Schwartz, *Studies in Indo-European Textile History*, p. 36; Spufford, *Great Reclothing*, pp. 121–2.

96 Cited in Spufford, *Great Reclothing*, p. 109.

97 John Cary, *A Discourse Concerning the East-India-Trade, Shewing How it Is Unprofitable to the Kindome of England …* (London: E. Baldwin, 1699), pp. 4–5.

98 Beverly Lemire and Giorgio Riello, 'East and West: Textiles and Fashion in Early Modern Europe', *Journal of Social History* 41/4 (2008): 887–916. For contrasting opinions, see Lemire, *Fashion's Favourite*; Styles, *Dress of the People*, especially pp. 110–32.

99 Riello, 'Asian Knowledge', 1–28.

100 G. Smith, *The Laboratory; or, School of Arts …* (London: C. Hitch and L. Hawes, 1756), vol. II, p. 47.

101 On this point see Styles, 'Indian Cottons', p. 41.

102 William H. Sewell Jr, 'The Empire of Fashion and the Rise of Capitalism in Eighteenth-Century France', *P&P* 206 (2010): 81–120.

103 Goulleau (avocat), *Pour les marchands merciers de la ville de Paris, contre l'usage des toiles peintes, teintes à la réserve, imprimées en façon des Indes, et autres étoffes prohibées* (Paris: P.-G. Simon, sd.). He added that 'La prévarication est universelle. A la Cour, à la Ville, à la Campagne, les vêtements & les ameublements ne sont plus que d'Etoffes étrangères & prohibées.' While their fashionability was impinged by

the fact that they had to be sold through illicit channels, people 'sans aveu & sans qualité' made profits without even paying taxes. This was a net loss for everyone.

104 Jacob Nicolas Moreau, *Examen des effets qui doivent produire dans le commerce de France, l'usage & la fabrication des toiles peintes...* (Geneva, 1759), p. 60.

105 André Morellet, *Réflexions sur les avantages de la libre fabrication et de l'usage des toiles peintes en France; pour servir de réponse aux divers mémoires des ...* (Geneva, 1758), pp. 42–3.

106 Styles, 'Product Innovation', 133 and 136.

107 Beverly Lemire, 'Plasmare la domanda, creare la moda: l'Asia, l'Europa e il commercio dei cotoni indiani (XIV–XIX secc.)', *Quaderni Storici* 46/122 (2006): 481–508.

108 Cited in Florence M. Montgomery, 'English Textile Swatches of the Mid-Eighteenth Century', *Burlington Magazine* 102/687 (1960): 243.

109 Giorgio Riello, 'The Globalization of Cotton Textiles: Indian Cottons, Europe, and the Atlantic World, 1600–1850', in Riello and Parthasarathi, eds., *Spinning World*, pp. 271–2.

7 From Asia to America: cottons in the Atlantic world

1 Ernst van den Boogaart, 'A população do Brasil Holandês retratada por Albert Eckhout 1641–1643', in Barbara Berlowicz, ed., *Albert Eckhout volta ao Brasil, 1644–2002* (Copenhagen: Nationalmuseet, 2002), pp. 117–31. This figure was copied from Zacharias Wagener, *Theatrum Rerum Naturalium*, 3 vols. See Cristina Ferrão and José Paulo Monteiro Soares, *Dutch Brazil* (Rio de Janeiro: Editoria Index, 1997).

2 See the debate on when globalisation began. O'Rourke, Findlay and Williamson support the idea that globalisation is measured by relative price convergence around the world, something that they identify only in the nineteenth century. O'Rourke, and Williamson, 'After Columbus', 417–56; O'Rourke and Williamson, 'When did Globalisation Begin?', 23–50; Findlay and O'Rourke, *Power and Plenty*, especially ch 7. By contrast Bayly and de Vries, though in different ways, see globalisation emerging in the early modern period. Bayly, '"Archaic" and "Modern" Globalization', pp. 45–72; Vries, 'Limits of Globalization in the Early Modern World', 710–33. For a critical perspective see Cooper, 'What is the Concept of Globalization Good For?', 189–213.

3 Boyajian, *Portuguese Trade in Asia under the Habsburgs*, p. 141.

4 Ibid.

5 Vogt, 'Notes on the Portuguese Cloth Trade in West Africa', 625–6.

6 Carolyn Keyes Adenaike, 'West African Textiles, 1500–1800', in Maureen Fennell Mazzaoui, ed., *Textiles: Production, Trade and Demand* (Aldershot: Ashgate, 1998), p. 257.

7 Margaret Makepeace, 'English Traders on the Guinea Coast, 1657–1668: an Analysis of the East India Company Archive', *History in Africa* 16 (1989): 240. Unlike the Portuguese who sold Indian cloth to West Africa on their way back to Europe, the EEIC, even when directly involved in the African trade, had all cloth shipped (and taxed) in London first.

8 Ibid., 265–6.

9 Inikori shows the increasing popularity of textiles in the Biafra trade in the period between 1660 and 1850 (from 16 to 32% of all commodities with a peak of 46.6% in 1791) while copper rods and cowries decreased in importance (from 67.6% of the entire cargo in 1661 to 1.2% in 1845–50). Inikori, 'English Versus Indian Cotton Textiles', pp. 102–4.

10 Herbert S. Klein, 'Economic Aspects of the Eighteenth-Century Atlantic Slave Trade', in Tracy, ed., *Rise of Merchant Empires*, p. 292.

11 Ernst van den Boogaart, 'The Trade Between Western Africa and the Atlantic World, 1600–90: Estimates of Trends in Composition and Value', *Journal of African History* 33/3 (1992): 383.

12 Harvey M. Feinberg, 'Africans and Europeans in West Africa: Elminans and Dutchmen on the Gold Coast during the Eighteenth Century', *Transactions of the American Philosophical Society* 79/7 (1989): 51.

13 Shah, *Masters of the Cloth*, p. 33.

14 Eltis and Jennings provide an overall quantification of the trade between West Africa and the Atlantic World. They estimate that African exports of slaves and commodities were worth £6.5 million in the 1680s, increasing to £31.7 million in the 1780s and £51.8 million in the 1860s. Imports for the same periods are estimated at £1.7 million for the 1680s, £18.5 million for the 1780s and £41.3 million for the 1860s. David Eltis and Lawrence C. Jennings, 'Trade Between Western Africa and the Atlantic World in the Pre-Colonial Era', *AHR* 93/4 (1988): 939–40.

15 Pierre H. Boulle, 'Marchandises de traite et développement industriel', *Revue Française d'Histoire d'Outre-Mer* 62 (1975): 312, note 13.

16 Herbert S. Klein, *The Atlantic Slave Trade* (Cambridge University Press, 1999), p. 87.

17 Sinha, *Politics of Trade*, p. 176. In the same decade the British trade of Indian cottons to Africa was worth £100,000.

18 See for instance the evidence in Wadsworth and Mann, *Cotton Trade and Industrial Lancashire*, pp. 150–1.

19 Keyes Adenaike, 'West African Textiles', pp. 258 (note 27) and 260.

20 Vogt, 'Notes on the Portuguese Cloth Trade in West Africa', 630.

21 Makepeace, 'English Traders', p. 240.

22 Ibid., p. 241.

23 Adam Jones, *From Slaves to Palm Kernels: a History of the Galinhas Country (West Africa) 1730–1890* (Wiesbaden: Franz Steiner Verlag, 1983), p. 174.

24 See the original formulation of 'triangular trade' in Eric E. Williams, *Capitalism & Slavery* (Chapel Hill: University of North Carolina Press, 1944).

25 Cooper, 'What is the Concept of Globalization Good For?', 205. See also Inikori, 'Africa and the Globalization Process', 73.

26 David Eltis, 'Precolonial Western Africa and the Atlantic Economy', in Barbara L. Solow, *Slavery and the Rise of the Atlantic System* (Cambridge University Press, 1991), p. 108.

27 Ibid., p. 107.

28 Marion Johnson, *Anglo-African Trade in the Eighteenth Century: English Statistics on African Trade 1699–1808* (Leiden: Centre for the History of European Expansion, 1990), p. 10. Eltis instead argues that imported cloth reached a wider African

market in the eighteenth century, but began to impinge on the domestic textile industry only as the slave trade was replaced by the traffic in commodities in the mid-nineteenth century'. Eltis, 'Precolonial Western Africa', p. 108.

29 Kriger, '"Guinea Cloth"', pp. 105–26; Inikori, 'English Versus Indian Cotton Textiles', pp. 85–114. See also Henry A. Gemery and Jan S. Hogendorn, 'The Economic Costs of West African Participation in the Atlantic Slave Trade: a Preliminary Sampling for the Eighteenth Century', in Henry A. Gemery and Jan S. Hogendorn, eds., *The Uncommon Market: Essays in the Economic History of the Atlantic Slave Trade* (New York: Academic Press, 1979), pp. 143–62.

30 Lapa, 'Domensões do comercio colonial', 391–2. Figures for the British trade of cotton checks to the West Indies can be found in Wadsworth and Mann, *Cotton Trade and Industrial Lancashire*, p. 153.

31 John Everaert, 'Le Commerce colonial de la "nation flamande" a Cadiz sous Charles III (*ca.* 1670–1700)', *Anuario de Estudios Americanos* 28 (1971): 144–5.

32 Boyajian, *Portuguese Trade*, pp. 141–2; Marta V. Vicente, 'Fashion, Race, and Cotton Textiles in Colonial Latin America', in Riello and Parthasarathi, eds., *Spinning World*, p. 248.

33 Arnold J. Bauer, *Goods, Power, History. Latin America's Material Culture* (Cambridge University Press, 2001), p. 110; Fernando A. Novais, 'A Proibição das manufaturas no Brasil e a política econômica portuguêsa do fim do siculo XVIII', *Revista de História* 33/67 (1966): 148 and 164.

34 Hans Pohl, 'Algunas consideraciones sobre el desarrollo de la industria hispanoamericana – specialmente la textil – durante el siglo XVII', *Annuario de Estudios Americanos* 28 (1971): 470; Vicente, 'Fashion', p. 251.

35 Ross W. Jamieson, 'Bolts of Cloth and Sherds of Pottery: Impressions of Caste in the Material Culture of the Seventeenth Century Audiencia of Quito', *The Americas* 60/3 (2004): 439 and 442.

36 Ibid., 444.

37 Abby Sue Fisher, 'Trade Textiles: Asia and New Spain', in Donna Pierce and Ronald Otsuka, eds., *Asia and Spanish America: Trans-Pacific Artistic and Cultural Exchange, 1500–1850* (Denver Art Museum, 2009), p. 180; and Donna Pierce's contribution in Joseph. J. Riesel and Susan Stratton-Pruitt, eds., *The Arts in Latin America, 1492–1820* (Philadelphia Museum of Art, 2006), p. 400.

38 Cited in Silvia Hunold Lara, 'The Signs of Color: Women's Dress and Racial Relations in Salvador and Rio de Janeiro, *ca.* 1750–1815', *Colonial Latin America Review* 6/2 (1997): 205.

39 Artemio de Valle-Arizpe, *Historia de la ciudad de México segun los relatos de sus cronistas* (Mexico: Colleccion Distrito Federal, 1998), pp. 173–4.

40 Cited in Marta V. Vicente, *Clothing the Spanish Empire: Families and the Calico Trade in the Early Modern Atlantic World* (New York: Palgrave Macmillan, 2006), p. 80.

41 Vicente, 'Fashion', pp. 247–60.

42 Abby Sue Fisher, 'Mestizaje and the Cuadros de Castas: Visual Representations of Race, and Dress in Eighteenth Century Mexico', unpublished PhD thesis, University of Minnesota, 1992, 66–7.

43 Elvira Martín de Codoni, 'Personajes de Mendoza en el siglo XVII', *Revista de Historia Americana y Argentina* 19/37 (1997): 387.

44 Beatriz Ricardina de Magalhães, 'A Demanda do Trivial; Vestuário, Alimentação e Habitação', *Revista Brasileira de Estudos Políticos*, 65 (1987): 172–3.

45 S. D. Smith, 'The Market for Manufactures in the Thirteen Continental Colonies, 1698–1776', *EHR* 51/4 (1998): 677–8.

46 Pamela V. Ulrich, 'From Fustian to Merino: the Rise of Textiles using Cotton Before and after the Gin', *Agricultural History* 68/2 (1994): 223.

47 Maureen Fennell Mazzaoui, 'Introduction', in Mazzaoui, ed., *Textiles: Production, Trade and Demand*, p. xxi.

48 Linda Eaton, 'Winterthur's Hand-Painted Indian Export Cottons – Winterthur', *Magazine Antiques* January (2002): 3.

49 F. Mason Norton, *John Norton & Sons, Merchants of London and Virginia, being the Papers from their Counting House for the Years 1750 to 1795* (Newton Abbott, 1968), pp. 22, 72, 103, 125, 150, 190, 218.

50 See for instance the merchant correspondence reported in Montgomery, *Printed Textiles*, p. 41.

51 *Journal of the House of Commons*, 14 February 1704, vol. 14, p. 336. Cited in Chaudhuri, 'Some Reflections: a Reply', 224–5.

52 Robert S. DuPlesssis, 'Cottons Consumption in the Seventeenth- and Eighteenth-Century North Atlantic', in Riello and Parthasarathi, eds., *Spinning World*, pp. 227–46.

53 P. Tomczyszyn, 'Towards a Dictionary of Canadian Textiles: the Town of Québec, 1635–1760', *Ars Textrina* 33 (2000): 113.

54 Robert DuPlessis shows that in North America, as in Latin America and Europe, richly decorated textiles found their way into men's wardrobes more readily than then wives. DuPlesssis, 'Cottons Consumption'.

55 Florence M. Montgomery, 'How America Really Looked: Textiles', *American Art Journal* 7/1 (1975): 82–92.

56 Williams, *Capitalism & Slavery*, pp. 68–72. See also Ralph Davis, 'English Foreign Trade, 1700–1774', *EHR* 15/2 (1962): 291.

57 This position supported by Inikori has been criticised by other historians. Inikori, *Africans*, especially p. 433.

58 For England, see Johnson, *Anglo-African Trade*, pp. 52–61; Elizabeth Schumpeter, *English Overseas Trade Statistics, 1697–1808* (Oxford: Clarendon Press, 1960), and Inikori, *Africans*. For France, see Ruggiero Romano, 'Documenti e prime consider-azioni intorno alle "balance du commerce" della Francia dal 1716 al 1780', in *Studi in onore di Armando Sapori* (Milan: Istituto Editoriale Cisalpino, 1957), vol. II, pp. 1267–305; and Guillaume Daudin, *Commerce et prosperité. La France au XVIIe siècle* (Paris: Presses de l'Université Paris-Sorbonne, 2005), especially pp. 224–6.

59 Chaudhuri, *Trading World of Asia and the English East India Company*, pp. 540–1 for 1710–19 and 1750–9; Database 'The East India Company: Trade and Domestic Financial Statistics, 1755–1838' compiled by Huw Bowen for 1790–9; Schumpeter, *English Overseas Trade*, p. 30, table 10, and p. 33, table 11.

60 There is the temptation of seeing export as a reaction to the ban of domestic consumption in England (and across Europe) between 1700 and 1720. In reality, increasing export is a function of the expansion of African and later North American markets for all commodities, including cottons from the second quarter of the eighteenth century.

61 See table 3.4 in Inikori, 'Indian Versus English Cotton Textiles', p. 106.

62 De Flaix, *Essai historique*, vol. II, pp. 134–5. Quoted in Richard Roberts, 'Guinée Cloth: Linked Transformations with France's Empire in the Nineteenth Century', *Cahiers d'Études Africaines* 128/32/4 (1992): 597.

63 Ibid., 602.

64 See also Inikori, 'Slavery and the Revolution'.

65 Riello, 'Indian Apprenticeship', pp. 332–4. See also Sergio Aiolfi, *Calicos und gedrucktes Zeug: die Entwicklung der englischen Textilveredelung und der Tuchhandel der East India Company, 1650–1750* (Stuttgart: Steiner, 1987), pp. 424–31, and Bala Krishn, *Commercial Relations Between India and England (1601–1757)* (London: Routledge, 1926), pp. 307–17.

66 Haudrère, *Compagnie française*, vol. I, p. 467, n. 222; Haudrère, 'Compagnie française des Indes', 5. In the period of twelve years between 1708 and 1720 France imported 728,784 cotton pieces, of which 595,560 were white. André Lespagnol, 'Cargaisons et profits du commerce indien au début du XVIIIe siècle. Les opérations commerciales des compagnies malouines', *Annales de Bretagne et des Pays de l'Ouest* (1982/3): 331 and 333.

67 Rothermund, 'Changing Pattern', p. 277.

68 Johnson, *Anglo-African Trade*, pp. 27–8. On the gum trade from Senegal to France, see Pierre Dardel, *Navires et marchandises dans les ports de Rouen et du Havre au XVIIIe siècle* (Paris: S. E. V. P. E. N., 1963), pp. 131–5.

69 On this perspective to the industrial revolution, see in particular Pat Hudson, *The Industrial Revolution* (London: Edward Arnold, 1993).

70 On the relationship between the global and the local, see Hopkins, ed., *Global History*, especially the author's introduction.

71 Wadsworth and Mann, *Cotton Trade and Industrial Lancashire*, p. 150.

72 Trevor Burnard and Kenneth Morgan, 'The Dynamics of the Slave Market and Slave Purchasing Patterns in Jamaica, 1655–1788', *William and Mary Quarterly* 58/1 (2001): 212.

73 In 1738 Lewis Paul and John Wyatt patented a roller spinning machine for spinning cotton to a more even thickness. Their invention did not have the success that they hoped for. Wadsworth and Mann, *Cotton Trade and Industrial Lancashire*, p. 149.

74 Williams, *Capitalism & Slavery*, p. 70; Inikori, *Africans*, p. 442; Hugh Thomas, *The Slave Trade: the History of the Atlantic Slave Trade: 1440–1870* (Basingstoke: Picador, 1997), p. 249.

75 Examples of the cottons produced in Manchester are to be found in the so-called 'Bower Textile Sample Book' at the Metropolitan Museum in New York. See Mary Elizabeth Burbidge, 'Documents and Sources. XIII. The Bower Textile Sample Book', *TH* 14/2 (1983): 213–21.

76 Cited in Montgomery, 'English Textile Swatches', 243.

77 Bibliothèque de la Union Centrale des Arts Décoratifs, Paris, G.C. 2: 'Le Livre d'Echantillons de John Holker, *c.* 1750'. On Holker's book see Montgomery, *Printed Textiles*, pp. 25–6; Montgomery, 'English Textile Swatches'; Florence M. Montgomery, 'John Holker's Mid-Eighteenth-Century *Livre d'Echantillons*', in Gervers, ed., *Studies in Textile*, pp. 214–31; Serge Chassagne, *Le Coton et ses patrons. France, 1760–1840* (Paris: Éditions de l'École des Hautes Études en Sciences Sociales, 1991), pp. 45–9.

78 *Le Livre d'Echantillons*: samples 54–60. My thanks to John Styles for showing me the importance of fibre analysis during our joint examination of the Holker book at the depot of the Musée des Arts Décoratifs, Paris.

79 Smith, *Laboratory; or, School of Arts*, vol. II, p. 49.

80 Cited in Montgomery, 'English Textile Swatches', 243.

81 Quoted in Inikori, *Africans*, p. 441.

82 Sickinger, 'Regulation or Ruination', 230.

83 TNA, T 1/469/54–59: 'Miscellaneous: Memorial of John Coghlan and Co., and Messrs. Bostock and Bainbridge, merchants, for a licence to import goods for the Africa trade not currently available from the East India Co.', 20 February 1769.

84 Inikori, *Africans*, p. 435. It is however unknown if such checks were made of linen both ways (warp and weft) or if they included a substantial part of cotton.

85 Judith Blow Williams, 'The Development of British Trade with West Africa, 1750 to 1850', *Political Science Quarterly* 50/2 (1935): 195.

86 Quoted in Montgomery, *Printed Textiles*, p. 24.

87 Williams, *Capitalism & Slavery*, p. 70.

88 For an overview of early cotton production and cotton printing in France, see Serge Chassagne, *La Manufacture de Toiles Imprimées de Tournemine-Les-Angers (1752–1820)* (Paris: Librarie C. Klincksieck, 1971), pp. 42–9.

89 Daudin, *Commerce et prosperité*, pp. 448–50.

90 Paul Jeulin, *L'évolution du port de Nantes: organisation et trafic depuis les origines* (Paris: Presses Universitaires de France, 1929), p. 259; Thomas, *Slave Trade*, pp. 252–3.

91 Gaston Martin, 'Capital et Travail à Nantes au cours du XVIIIe siècle', *Revue d'Histoire Economique et Sociale* 17 (1930): 61.

92 Mazzaoui, 'Introduction', p. xxxviii.

93 Daudin, *Commerce et prosperité*, pp. 448–50.

94 Chassagne, *Coton*, pp. 25–6.

95 W. Wescher, 'The "Rouannerie" Trade and its Entrepreneurs', *Ciba Review* 12 (1959): 14; Dardel, *Navires*, p. 139; J. R. Harris, *Industrial Espionage and Technology Transfer: Britain and France in the Eighteenth Century* (Aldershot: Ashgate, 1998), pp. 48–9.

96 Pierre Dardel, *Commerce, industrie et navigation à Rouen et au Havre au XVIIIème siècle* (Rouen: Société Libre d'Emulation de la Seine-Maritime, 1966), pp. 29 and 34.

97 Ann DuPont, 'Captives of Colored Cloth: the Role of Cotton Trade Goods in the North Atlantic Slave Trade (1600–1808)', *Ars Textrina* 24 (1995): 180. The value of the French trade to Africa in the early 1770s was 3.8 million livres (£157,000). This was less than half than the value of English trade (£370,000 on average per year). Johnson, *Anglo-African Trade*, pp. 53–61.

98 Parthasarathi, *Why Europe Grew Rich*, p. 149.

99 Boulle, 'Merchandises', 320, note 44.

100 Dardel, *Navires*, pp. 140–1; Gaston Martin, *L'ère des négriers (1714–1774): Nantes au XVIIIe siècle* (Paris: Karthala, 1993), p. 298; Pierre Léon, 'Structure du commerce extérieur et évolution industrielle de la France à la fin du XVIIIe siècle', in *Conjoncture Economique – Structures Sociales: Hommage à Ernest Labrousse* (Paris: La Haye, 1974), p. 420. In 1786 the major producers of printed cottons in France

were Rouen (150,000 pieces), Paris (114,000), Nantes (102,000) and Marseilles (c. 100,000). ANF, F¹² 1404A: 'Toiles peintes en Provence – Etat approximatif'.

101 Parthasarathi, *Why Europe Grew Rich*, pp. 149–50.

102 An exhibition of eighteenth-century textile samples was organised in Honfleur in 1899. Although I was able to find a copy of the brochure published at the time, it has been impossible so far to locate the samples. See Charles Bréard, *Collection d'échantillons de marchandises d'échange et de toilerie de Rouen* (Honfleur: Sescau, 1899).

103 BPP, *Report from the Committee, Appointed to Examine and State to the House, the matters of fact in the several Petitions of the Manufacturers of, and Traders and Dealers in, the Linen Manufactury*, Tenth Parliament of Great Britain: fourth session (17 January 1751–25 June 1751), p. 291.

104 Ibid., pp. 290–1. Yet, Manchester might have enjoyed even cheaper labour from Ireland and Scotland importing raw materials (linen yarn) and semi-finished products as part of what we might call a 'domestic imperial' strategy. Griffiths, Hunt and O'Brien, 'Scottish, Irish', 625–50.

105 Boulle, 'Marchandises', 328.

8 Learning and substituting: printing cotton textiles in Europe

1 John Ovington, *A Voyage to Surat in the Year 1689*, ed. H. G. Rawlinson (Oxford University Press, 1929), p. 167.

2 See George Percival Baker, *Calico Printing and Painting in the East Indies in the XVIIth and XVIIIth Centuries* (London: Edward Arnold, 1921), p. 6; Rosina, 'Tra oriente e occidente', pp. 15–17.

3 *Pour les six corps des marchands de la ville de Paris, contre l'usage des toiles Peintes, teintes à la réserve, imprimes en façon des Indes & autres Etoffes prohibées* (Paris [?]: De l'Imprimerie de J. Chardon, 1758), pp. 6–7.

4 For a critical review of the literature on the topic, see Maxine Berg, 'The Genesis of "Useful Knowledge"', *History of Science* 45 (2007): 131.

5 Joel Mokyr, *The Gifts of Athena: Historical Origins of the Knowledge Economy* (Princeton University Press, 2002); Mokyr, *Enlightened Economy*.

6 For a critique of Mokyr's work see Parthasarathi, *Why Europe Grew Rich*, pp. 185–7.

7 Patterning on the loom (by using a drawloom) was not absent in the Indian sub-continent, but it developed as a technique of decoration and ornamentation only after the arrival of Islam and never achieved the success of printing, painting and pencilling. Varadarajan, 'Indian Textile Technology', 61–2.

8 Engraved wooden blocks were used to print simple designs on linens and woollens, but this industry never expanded beyond the Rhenish provinces of Germany. An example of these early printed linens can be found at the Victoria and Albert Museum (object 1745-1888: http://collections.vam.ac.uk/item/O148454/printed-linen/). Ada K. Longfield, 'History of the Irish Linen and Cotton Printing Industry in the 18th Century', *Journal of Royal Society of Antiquaries of Ireland* 58 (1937): 26. See Also Donald King, 'Textiles and the Origin of Printing in Europe', *Pantheon* 20 (1962): 23–30; and David Mitchell and Milton E. Sonday, 'Printed Fustians: 1490–1600', *CIETA Bulletin* 77 (2000): 99–118.

9 Indian textiles were also well known for their embroideries. However, their main item of trade (especially to Europe) were printed and painted textiles.

10 A. F. Vialets', and Liudmyla Bilous, *Muzeĭ Ukraïns'koho Narodnoho Dekoratyvnoho Mystetstva. Museum of Ukrainian Folk Decorative Art* (Kyïv: Mystetstvo, 2009), pp. 156–61; Ol'ga Gordeeva, Luiza Efimova, *Marina Kuznetsova. Russkie uzornye tkani: XVII-nachalo XX veka* (Moskva: Gos. istoricheskiĭ muzeĭ, 2004), pp. 13–53.

11 Peter C. Floud, 'The Origins of English Calico Printing', *Journal of the Society of Dyers and Colourists* 76 (1960): 275; Geoffrey Turnbull, *A History of the Calico Printing Industry of Great Britain* (Altrincham: John Sherratt & Son, 1947), p. 18.

12 De Flaix, *Essai historique*, vol. I, p. 313.

13 Styles, 'Product Innovation', 124–69.

14 Cited in Shri Dharampal, ed., *Indian Science and Technology in the Eighteenth Century: Some Contemporary European Accounts* (Goa: Other India Press, 1971), p. 253. This point is however questioned by Eugenia Vanina, *Urban Crafts and Craftsmen in Medieval India (Thirteenth–Eighteenth Centuries)* (New Delhi: Munshiram Manoharlal, 2004), p. xxii.

15 Both documents are in the India Office Library at the British Library and were probably acquired in the nineteenth century. Hameeda Khatoon Naqvi, 'Dyeing of Cotton Goods in the Mughal Hindustan', *Journal of Indian Textile History* 7/1 (1967): 46–7; Vanina, *Urban Crafts*, p. 36.

16 Brennig, 'Textile Producers', 352.

17 There is also a fourth document that provides substantial information on dyeing and printing, the account of the Dutchman Daniel de Havart written *c.* 1680 and published in Dutch in 1693 that is not considered here. See Irwin, 'Indian Textile Trade', 31. Another, although much later document containing valuable information of calico painting is William Roxburgh's *Plants of the Coromandel Coast* (London, 1795). See in particular Paul R. Schwartz, 'The Roxburgh Account of Indian Cotton Painting: 1795', *Journal of Indian Textile History* 4 (1959): 47–56.

18 Paul R. Schwartz, 'French Documents on Indian Cotton Painting. I. The Beaulieu MS, *c.* 1734', *Journal of Indian Textile History* 2 (1956): 7.

19 Stuart Robinson, *A History of Printed Textiles* (London: Studio Vista, 1969), p. 112. Coeurdoux's letters from Pondicherry were partially published in 1742 in volume XIV of the *Lettres édificantes et curieurses*. Baker, *Calico Printing*, p. 11.

20 For an overview of the history of the manuscript see Paul R. Schwartz, *Printing on Cotton at Ahmedabad, India in 1678* (Ahmedabad: Calico Museum of Textiles, 1969), pp. 1–3. For a detailed analysis of Roques and printing techniques, see George Bryan Souza, 'The French Connection: Indian Cottons and their Early Modern Technology', in Riello and Roy, eds., *How India Clothed the World*, pp. 347–64.

21 Indrani Ray, 'Of Trade and Traders in the Seventeenth-Century India: an Unpublished French Memoir by Georges Roques', in Subramanian, ed., *French East India Company*, pp. 1–62, and Ray, 'Trade and Traders', pp. 63–76.

22 Cited in Claude Alphonso Alvarez, *Homo Faber: Technology and Culture in India, China and the West from 1500 to the Present Day* (The Hague: Martinus Nijhoff, 1980), p. 61.

23 Schwartz, *Printing on Cotton*, pp. 4–8.

24 P. R. Schwartz, 'L'impression su coton à Ahmedabad (Inde) en 1678', *Bulletin del la Société Industrielle de Mulhouse* 726/1 (1967): 2.

25 For a description, see *Sublime Indigo* (Paris: Editions Vilo, 1987), p. 223.

26 Schwartz, 'French Documents', pp. 6–7.
27 Figure 8.7 is stage 9 of eleven stages of production. The full list of stages reads as follows: (1) Cloth ready for preparation; drawing of lines with iron mordant (black lines) and aluminium mordant (red lines); (2) After a madder bath the red and black lines get darker; (3) Cloth after bleaching; (4) The wax lines applied on the leaf will produce a resistant effect; (5) Part of the cloth is waxed to resist dyeing; (6) Shows the unresisted parts in blue (a spot near the main flower has been caused by cracking of the wax); (7) Aluminium mordants are applied to produce red or white effects; (8) The cloth is pencilled with aluminium and diluted iron mordants; (9) Cloth after second madder bath; (10) Cloth after a second bleaching with dung; (11) Finished cloth. Yellow has been pencilled to produce green and blue.
28 The manuscript was however published only in 1865. Alvarez, *Homo Faber*, p. 61. The original Ryhiner manuscript was well known in its day and was important for the development of calico printing in the Alsace corridor (between the Netherlands and northwest Switzerland). The manuscript is now preserved at the Musée de l'Impression sur l'Étoffe in Mulhouse. I thank Jacqueline Jacquet for showing me the manuscript.
29 Cited in Alvarez, *Homo Faber*, p. 60.
30 See in particular Liliane Hilaire Pérez, 'Technology as a Public Culture in the Eighteenth Century: the Artisans' Legacy', *History of Science* 45 (2007): 137.
31 There is instead no evidence that calico printers were recruited in India to replicate their productive process in Europe. This is somewhat puzzling, as attempts were made to recruit spinners and weavers in India.
32 Schwarz, 'French Documents', pp. 3–23. The long-distance movement of skilled artisans was standard practice in early modern Europe. Pérez, 'Technology as a Public Culture', 135–53; Liliane Hilaire Pérez, 'Cultures, techniques et pratiques de l'échange, entre Lyon et le Levant: inventions et réseaux au XVIIIe siècle', *Revue d'Histoire Moderne et Contemporaine* 49/1 (2002): 89–114.
33 Pfister, *Toiles imprimées*, pp. 19–20.
34 Gervers, *Influence of Ottoman Turkish Textiles*, p. 7.
35 Olivier Raveux, 'Du commerce à la production: l'indiennage européen et l'acquisition des techniques asiatiques au XVIIe siècle', in *Féerie indienne: des rivages de l'Inde au Royaume de France* (Mulhouse: Musée de l'Impression sur Étoffes, 2008), pp. 23–5; Rabih Banat and Améziane Ferguene, 'La Production et le commerce du textile à Alep sous l'Empire ottoman: une forte contribution à l'essor économique de la ville', *Histoire, Economie & Société* 29/2 (2010): 13. See also Katsumi Fukasawa, *Toilerie et commerce du Levant d'Alep à Marseilles* (Paris: CNRS, 1987), pp. 24–6 and 46.
36 Phillips, 'Little-Known Ottoman-Period Cotton and Linen', p. 596.
37 Fukasawa, *Toilerie*, p. 48.
38 Avedis K. Sanjian, *The Armenian Communities in Syria under Ottoman Domination* (Cambridge, Mass.: Harvard University Press, 1965), p. 50; Gittinger, *Master Dyers*, p. 23.
39 Raveux, 'Birth of a New European Industry', p. 298.
40 L. A. Driessen, 'Calico Printing and the Cotton Industry in Holland', *Ciba Review* 48 (1944): 1749.
41 Marzia Cataldi Gallo, 'Indiane e mezzari a Genova', in Gallo, ed., *I mezzari*, p. 25.

42 Cited Ernst Homburg, 'From Colour Maker to Chemist: Episodes from the Rise of the Colourist, 1670–1800', in Robert Fox and Agustí Nieto-Galan, eds., *Natural Dyestuffs and Industrial Culture in Europe, 1750–1880* (Canton, Mass.: Watson Publishing, 1999), p. 221.

43 Vahan Baibourtian, 'Participation of Iranian Armenians in World Trade in the 17th Century', in Sushil Chaudhuri and Kéram Kévonian, eds., *Les Arméniens dans le commerce asiatique au début de l'ère moderne* (Paris: Editions de la Maison des Sciences de l'Homme, 2008), pp. 44–5.

44 Christian Simon, 'Labour Relations at Manufactures in the Eighteenth Century: the Calico Printers in Europe', *International Review of Social History* 39 (1994): especially 140–2. See also Liliane Pérez, 'Savoirs techniques, identités et migrations: l'histoire face aux mythes', *Documents Pour l'Histoire des Techniques* 15 (2008): 3–9.

45 Wadsworth and Mann, *Cotton Trade and Industrial Lancashire*, pp. 131; *Les Indiennes et l'impression sur étoffes du 16e au 18e siècle* (Mulhouse: Museé de l'Impression sur Étoffes, n.d.), p. 1.

46 Wadsworth and Mann, *Cotton Trade and Industrial Lancashire*, pp. 130 and 137. On the early London calico printers, see Stanley David Chapman, 'David Evans & Co. The Last of the Old London Textile Printers', *TH* 14/1 (1983): 29–56; and David Chapman, 'Les imprimeurs sur étoffes londoniens et leur "âge d'or" vers 1750–1780: le regard d'Oberkampf', in Favier, Gayot, Klein, Terrier and Woronoff, eds., *Tisser l'histoire*, pp. 285–99.

47 R. Traupel, 'The Cloth Printing Trade of Glarus', *Ciba Review* 105 (1954): 3783.

48 W. Wescher, 'The Normandy Textile Printing Industry of the Eighteenth and Nineteenth Centuries', *Ciba Review* 12/135 (1959): 30.

49 For an excellent overview, see Stanley David Chapman and Serge Chassagne, *European Textile Printers in the Eighteenth Century: a Study of Peel and Oberkampf* (London: Heinemann Educational, 1981), pp. 6–9.

50 Montgomery, *Printed Textiles*, p. 16.

51 Printshops were opened in Aberdeen (1720?), Edinburgh (1729), Schwechat near Vienna (1726), Glasgow (1730s), Hamburg (1737), Wiesenback (1738), Zschopau (1740), Schlesia, Rehin-Prussia and Berlin (1741), Mulhausen (1746), Basel (1749), Paluen in Vogtlande (1750), Loerrach (1752), St Petersburg (1753), Wesserling in Els (1760), Preston and Manchester (1764), Bohemia (1778) and Iwanowo in Russia (1780).

52 Olivier Raveux, 'Les Débuts de l'indiennage dans les pays d'Aix (1758–1770)', *Industries en Provence* 4 (2004): 1.

53 Geert Verbong, 'The Dutch Calico Printing Industry Between 1800 and 1875', in Fox and Nieto-Galan, eds., *Natural Dyestuffs*, p. 195. Vibeke Kingma calculates that twenty printshops were already operative in Amsterdam before 1700. Another thirty-three were founded in the first decade of the eighteenth century, followed by a further fourteen in 1710–20 and twenty-two in the 1720–30, but after 1740 only five new printshops were opened. Kingma, 'Katoendrukkerijen', 11–12.

54 Smit, *Katoendrukkerij in Nederland*, pp. 155–6; Veluwenkamp, 'Buitenlandse textielhandel', 80–3. Several factors have been highlighted to explain the relative decline of calico printing in the Netherland from the 1730s, including high wages compared to the rest of Europe, a drop in quality of raw materials, technological

conservatism, and the dependence of manufacturing entrepreneurs on merchants. Smit, *Katoendrukkerij in Nederland*, pp. 195–8; Kingma, 'Katoendrukkerijen', 7–30.

55 Robert Chenciner, *Madder: a History of Luxury and Trade* (Richmond, Va.: Curzon, 2000), p. 70. For a comprehensive analysis of calico printing in Barcelona, see J. K. J. Thomson, *A Distinctive Industrialisation: Cotton in Barcelona, 1728–1832* (Cambridge University Press, 1992), especially pp. 50–95.

56 Homburg, 'From Colour Maker to Chemist', pp. 219–58; Pierre Caspard, 'L'accumulation du capital dans l'indiennage au XVIIIéme siècle', *Revue du Nord* 61/240 (1979): 119.

57 Lemire and Riello, 'East and West', 898.

58 Kingma, 'Katoendrukkerijen', 15.

59 Chapman and Chassagne, *European Textile Printers*, p. 15.

60 Pierre Caspard, 'Manufacture and Trade in Calico Printing at Neuchâtel: the Example of Cortaillod (1752–1854)', *TH* 8 (1977): 151

61 Chapman and Chassagne, *European Textile Printers*, p. 224, n. 24.

62 Jean-Marie Schmitt, 'The Origins of the Textile Industry in Alsace: the Beginnings of the Manufacture of Printed Cloth at Wesserling (1762–1802)', *TH* 13/1 (1982): 100.

63 Kingma, 'Katoendrukkerijen', 14.

64 Chapman, 'Imprimeurs sur étoffes', pp. 287–9. Two of the major London printers occupied 25 and 30 acres of land respectively. This explains why calico printing could only be carried out outside city centres.

65 George Bryan Souza, 'Dyeing Red: S.E. Asian Sappanwood in the Seventeenth and Eighteenth centuries', *O Oriente* 8 (2004): 40–58; Souza, 'French Connection'.

66 Shireen Moosvi, 'Armenians in Asian Trade: 16th and 17th Centuries', in Chaudhuri and Kévonian, eds., *Arméniens*, pp. 104–5.

67 Jenny Balfour-Paul, *Indigo* (London: British Museum, 1998), pp. 56–7.

68 Susan Fairlie, 'Dyestuffs in the Eighteenth Century', *EHR* 17/3 (1965): 498.

69 See Riello, 'Indian Apprenticeship'. See also Homburg, 'From Colour Maker to Chemist', p. 233.

70 Louisa Dolza, 'How did they Know? The Art of Dyeing in Late-Eighteenth-Century Piedmont', in Fox and Nieto-Galan, eds., *Natural Dyestuffs*, pp. 139–45.

71 For a more detailed discussion, see Raveux, 'Espaces et technologies', 163–4.

72 Peter C. Floud, 'The English Contribution to the Chemistry of Calico Printing before Perkin', *Ciba Review* 1 (1961): 8–14. See also Balfour-Paul, *Indigo*, p. 160; Riello, 'Asian Knowledge', 21. G. Smith commented that 'The *Indians* in their chints still are obliged to follow the same way; they, as yet, not being possessed of the secret of printing or pencilling their blues. This has proved of singular advantage; for as before the calicoes and linens, for common wear, could only admit of black and read, when now, by pencilling the blue, and the yellow upon the blue, five colours, namely, black, red, blue, green and yellow are produced'. Smith, *Laboratory; or, School of Arts*, vol. II, p. 53.

73 Serge Chassagne, 'Calico Printing in Europe before 1780', in Jenkins, ed., *Cambridge History of Western Textiles*, vol. I, pp. 516–17.

74 Chapman and Chassagne, *European Textile*, pp. 105–6.

75 Anne-Françoise Garçon and Liliane Hilaire-Pérez, '"Open Technique" Between Community and Individuality in Eighteenth-Century France', in Ferry de Goey and Jan Willem Veluwenkamp, eds., *Entrepreneurs and Institutions in Europe and Asia, 1500–2000* (Amsterdam: Aksant, 2002), pp. 237–56.

76 R. Traupel, 'Rise and Decline of the Swiss Calico Printing Industry', *Ciba Review* 105 (1954): 3766–76.

77 Sarah Lowengard, *The Creation of Color in Eighteenth-Century Europe* (www.gutenberg-e.org/lowengard/), 'Turkey Red'.

78 Hilaire Pérez, 'Culture techniques', p. 105.

79 Ibid., pp. 105–8; W. Wescher, 'Turkey Red Dyeing', *Ciba Review* 12/135 (1959): 21–6.

80 Raveux, 'Espaces et technologies', 157.

81 Chenciner, *Madder*, p. 69.

82 W. Wescher, 'John Holker, a Promoter of the French Textile Industry', *Ciba Review* 12/135 (1959): 10.

83 Cited in Berg, 'In Pursuit of Luxury', 115.

84 The *Historische Geografische Konst- en Reis Almanak* (1753) shows a printshop with two workers in which, as the caption says, 'One prints paper, the other cotton. Both do it for the money' (D'Een drukt Papier, en d'aâr Catoen, En beiden is 't om poen te doen). It was not uncommon in the Netherlands to print both on paper and textiles. The *Amsterdamsche Courant* (8 March 1785) offered painted and printed paper with East-Indian textile designs. Smit, *Katoendrukkerij in Nederland*, pp. 199–201.

85 Floud, 'English Contribution', 425–6.

86 Chassagne, 'Calico Printing', p. 520.

87 In Ireland in 1754; England in 1756; France in 1763; Augsburg in 1766; Barcelona in 1779; Orange in 1779; Colmar in 1770; and Mulhouse in 1782.

88 Peter C. Floud, 'The Earliest Copper-Plate in India', *Journal of Indian Textile History* 5 (1960): 72.

89 Floud, 'British Calico Printing', 4.

90 Robinson, *History of Printed Textiles*, p. 26.

91 Depitre, *Toile peinte*, p. 5; Robinson, *History of Printed Textiles*, p. 24.

92 Potter, Edmund, *Calico Printing as an Art Manufacture* (London: John Chapman, 1852), p. 8.

93 Pitoiset, *Toiles imprimées*, p. 9.

94 Stanley David Chapman, 'Quality Versus Quantity in the Industrial Revolution: The Case of Textile Printing', *Northern History* 11 (1985): 179.

95 Sarah Lowengard, 'Colours and Colour Making in the Eighteenth Century', in Berg and Clifford, eds., *Consumers and Luxury*, pp. 103–17.

96 Fairlie, 'Dyestuffs', 506.

97 C. A. Bayly, 'British Orientalism and the Indian "Rational Tradition" *c.* 1780–1820', *South Asia Research* 14/1 (1994): 2.

98 Chenciner, *Madder*, p. 25.

99 Dominique Cardon, 'Textile Research: an Unsuspected Mine of Information on Some Eighteenth-Century European Textile Products and Colour Fashions around the World', *TH* 29/1 (1998): 99–101.

100 Leonard Trevengone, 'Chemistry at the Royal Society in London in the Eighteenth Century – IV', *Annals of Science* 26/4 (1970): 332.

101 Robert Fox and Agustí Nieto-Galan, 'Introduction', in Fox and Nieto-Galan, eds., *Natural Dyestuffs*, p. x.

102 T. Birch, *History of the Royal Society of London* (London, 1756–7), p. 401.

103 Mokyr, *Enlightened Economy*; Styles, 'Indian Cottons', pp. 43–4.

104 Floud, 'English Contribution'. 8–14.
105 Cardon, 'Textile Research', p. 96.
106 *Sublime Indigo*, p. 154.
107 *Instructions for Officers who Survey Printers of Calicoes &c* (London, 1777), p. 12. For France: F¹² 1404A: 'Indiennes, toiles paintes, 1785–8' with examples of plombs.
108 N. Biriukova, *West European Printed Textiles 16th–18th Century* (Moscow: Iskusstvo Publishers, 1973), p. 79.
109 In some cases, it benefitted from low duty levels on dyes as in the case of the abolition of the duty on cochineal and other dyestuffs in England in 1714. Davis, 'Rise of Protection in England', 311.
110 I discuss elsewhere how there is also a narrative aspect to this story in which over time the connection between the development of the industry and Indian knowledge was not just forgotten but consciously played down and even denigrated. See Riello, 'Asian Knowledge', pp. 1–28.
111 Tirthankar Roy, 'Regimes for the Development of Useful and Reliable Industrial Knowledge in the West and the East Before the Age of Institutionalised R&D', unpublished paper presented at the Fondation Maison des Sciences de l'Homme, Paris, 24–25 May 2007, 8.

9 Cotton, slavery and plantations in the New World

1 Francis Moore, *Travels into the Inland parts of Africa: Containing a Description of the Several Nations... up the River Gambia* (London: Edward Cave, 1738), vol. II, p. 32.
2 *Beauties of Nature and Art Displayed, in a Tour through the World ...* (London, 1774–5), vol. X, p. 61.
3 Moore, *Travels*, vol. II, p. 32.
4 Barbara L. Solow, 'Capitalism and Slavery in the Exceedingly Long Run', *Journal of Interdisciplinary History* 17/4 (1987): 732. See also Felipe Fernández-Armesto, *Before Columbus: Exploration and Colonisation from the Mediterranean to the Atlantic, 1229–1492* (Basingstoke: Macmillan, 1987).
5 George E. Brooks, *Landlords and Strangers: Ecology, Society, and Trade in Western Africa, 1000–1643* (Boulder, Col.: Westview Press, 1993), pp. 157 and 165–6.
6 Ibid., p. 165.
7 Cited in Frederick C. Knight, *Working the Diaspora: the Impact of African Labor on the Anglo-American World, 1650–1850* (New York University Press, 2010), pp. 75–6.
8 Europeans believed local African textile production to be of low quality and that therefore there was potential to sell finished cloth in exchange for ivory, gold, pepper and raw cotton. Michael Adas, *Machines as the Measure of Men: Science, Technology, and Ideologies of Western Dominance* (Ithaca, NY: Cornell University Press, 1989), pp. 178–9.
9 Philip D. Curtin, 'The Environment Beyond Europe and the European Theory of Empire', *JWH* 1/2 (1990): 131 and 138.
10 John F. Richards, *The Unending Frontier: an Environmental History of the Early Modern World* (Berkeley: University of California Press, 2003), p. 22.

11 Joseph E. Inikori, 'Slavery and Capitalism in Africa', *Indian Historical Review* 15/1-2 (1988/9): 145.

12 Henry A. Gemery and Jan S. Hogendorn, 'Comparative Disadvantage: the Case of Sugar Cultivation in West Africa', *Journal of Interdisciplinary History* 9/3 (1979): 446. See also Gemery and Hogendorn, 'Introduction', pp. 1–21.

13 Inikori, 'Slavery and Capitalism', 147.

14 Daron Acemoglu, Simon Johnson and James Robinson, 'Disease and Development in Historical Perspective', *Journal of the European Economic Association* 1/2-3 (2003): 402; John R. McNeill, *Mosquito Empires: Ecology and War in the Greater Caribbean, 1620–1914* (Cambridge University Press, 2010), p. 96. Eltis adds to this epidemiological explanation also the African military pressure on a relatively small number of European slave traders on the West African coast. Eltis, 'Precolonial Western Africa', pp. 112–13.

15 Joseph C. Miller, 'The Political Economy of the Angolan Slave Trade in the Eighteenth Century', *Indian Historical Review* 15/1-2 (1988/9): 163.

16 O. Flynn and Giráldez, 'Born with a "Silver Spoon"', pp. 259–79.

17 Alfred W. Crosby, *The Columbian Exchange: Biological and Cultural Consequences of 1492* (Westport, Conn.: Greenwood Press, 1972); Alfred W. Crosby, *Ecological Imperialism: the Biological Expansion of Europe, 900–1900* (Cambridge University Press, 1986).

18 John F. Richards, 'Early Modern India and World History', *JWH* 8/2 (1997): 202.

19 Frances F. Berdan, 'Cotton in Aztec Mexico: Production, Distribution and Uses', *Mexican Studies / Estudios Mexicanos* 3/2 (1987): 247–8.

20 Eufemio Lorenzo Sanz, *Comercio de España con América en la época de Felipe II* (Valladolid: Servicio de Publicaciones de la Diputación Provincial, 1979), p. 628; Glamann, 'European Trade 1500–1750', p. 27.

21 Barbara Gaye Jaquay, 'The Caribbean Cotton Production: an Historical Geography of the Region's Mysterious Crop', unpublished PhD thesis, Texas A&M University, 1997, 60–1.

22 For an overview see M. B. Hammond, *The Cotton Industry: an Essay in American Economic History. Part I. The Cotton Culture and the Cotton Trade* (New York: American Economic Association, 1897), pp. 4–5; Knight, *Working the Diaspora*, pp. 76–83.

23 See in particular on sugar, coffee and cocoa, Sidney W. Mintz, *Sweetness and Power: the Place of Sugar in Modern History* (Harmondsworth: Penguin, 1985); Brian W. Cowan, *The Social Life of Coffee: the Emergence of the British Coffeehouse* (New Haven, Conn.: Yale University Press, 2005); William Gervase Clarence-Smith, *Cocoa and Chocolate, 1765–1914* (London and New York: Routledge, 2000).

24 Larry D. Gragg, 'The Barbados Connection: John Parris and the Early New England Trade with the West Indies', *New England Historical and Geographical Register* 140 (1986): 99; Russell R. Menard, 'Plantation Empire: how Sugar and Tobacco Planters Built their Industries and Raised an Empire', *Agricultural History* 81/3 (2007): 311.

25 Nuala Zahedieh, *The Capital and the Colonies: London and the Atlantic Economy, 1660–1700* (Cambridge University Press, 2010), pp. 189 and 227. This was however 50 per cent of all cotton imported into Britain. Philip R. P. Coelho, 'The Profitability of Imperialism: the British Experience in the West Indies', *Explorations in Economic History* 10 (1973): 259 and 266.

26 A. Meredith John, *The Plantation Slaves of Trinidad, 1783–1816: a Mathematical and Demographic Enquiry* (Cambridge University Press, 1988), p. 18; Knight, *Working the Diaspora*, pp. 79–81.

27 Because cotton and sugar were harvested at the same time of the year, it made it more difficult for cotton to become part of plantation cultivation. An Old Planter [Gordon Turnbull], *Letters to a Young Planter; or, Observations on the Management of a Sugar-Plantation* ... (London: Stuart and Stevenson, 1785), p. 18.

28 The print was reproduced in books in several languages. It was to be found in Thomas Salmon's *A General History of the Several Nations of the World* translation into Italian (*Lo Stato presente di tutti i paesi e popoli del mondo*...(Venice: Giambattista Albrizzi, 1738) (www.istitutodatini.it/biblio/images/it/datini/?id=8256), p. 311, and was itself copied from earlier representations of the cotton plant. See for instance the plate in Cornelis de Bruin's *Reizen over Moskovie, door Persie en Indie* (1711) (New York Public Library online catalogue).

29 Joyce E. Chaplin, 'Creating a Cotton South in Georgia and South Carolina, 1760–1815', *Journal of Southern History* 57/2 (1991): 176–7 and 179.

30 Alan L. Olmstead and Paul W. Rhode, 'Biological Innovation and Productivity Growth in the Antebellum Cotton Economy', *NBER Working Papers Series* 14142 (2008): 8–9 (www.nber.org/papers/w14142). On cotton experimentation, see also Alan L. Olmstead and Paul W. Rhode, *Creating Abundance: Biological Innovation and American Agricultural Development* (Cambridge University Press, 2008), pp. 98–116.

31 ANF, F^{12} 655A: An XI – Coton de S.te Lucie. 'Copie d'une lettre du M. de la Borie a M. le Marechal de Castries, du 6 décembre 1785'.

32 Cited in Knight, *Working the Diaspora*, p. 76.

33 See in particular Peter Wood, *Black Majority: Negroes in Colonial South Carolina from 1670 through the Stono Rebellion* (New York: Alfred A. Knopf, 1974), and Judith Ann Carney, *Black Rice: the African Origins of Rice Cultivation in the Americas* (Cambridge, Mass.: Harvard University Press, 2001).

34 Knight, *Working the Diaspora*, p. 82.

35 Londa Schiebinger, *Plants and Empire: Colonial Bioprospecting in the Atlantic World* (Cambridge, Mass.: Harvard University Press, 2004). Puritan settlers on Providence Island, off the Mosquito Coast of Nicaragua, for instance, experimented with different varieties of cotton from Barbados in the 1630s. Karl Offen, 'Puritan Bioprospecting in Central America and the West Indies', *Itinerario* 35/1 (2011): 25.

36 See for instance for cotton cultivation in Trinidad, John, *Plantation Slaves of Trinidad*, pp. 12–13.

37 TNA, CO 37/40: 'Dispatch by Thomas Browne to the High Hon.ble Thomas Lord Sydney, Whitehall, from Bermuda', 5 February 1787.

38 Edwards, Bryan, *The History, Civil and Commercial, of the British Colonies in the West Indies* (London: John Stockdale, 1793), vol. I, pp. 268–71.

39 Louis Deschamps, *Le Coton, études élémentaires sur la plantation, la culture et la production de cet arbuste, par L. Deschamps* ... (Paris: Michelet, s.d. 1884), p. 46.

40 Richard H. Grove, *Green Imperialism: Colonial Expansion, Tropical Island Edens and the Origins of Environmentalism, 1600–1860* (Cambridge University Press, 1995), p. 8.

41 Jaquay, 'Caribbean Cotton', pp. 28–46.

42 Thomas Dalby, *An Historical Account of the Rise and Growth of the West India Collonies, and of the Great Advantages they are to England, in Respect to Trade* (London: J. Hindmarsh, 1690).

43 The French were rather slow at developing cotton cultivation in the West Indies, as this was still in its infancy when they lost control of vast part of their territories in the 1750s and 1760s. Marie Polderman, *La Guyane française, 1676–1763: mise en place et évolution de la société coloniale, tensions et métissages* (Petit-Bourg: Ibis Rouge, 2004), pp. 81–3. On the changing geopolitical context during the Seven Years' War, see Daniel A. Baugh, *The Global Seven Years War, 1754–1763: Britain and France in a Great Power Contest* (Harlow: Longman, 2011).

44 Javier Cuenca Esteban, 'Comparative Patterns of Colonial Trade: Britain and its Rivals', in Leandro Prados de la Escosura, ed., *Exceptionalism and Industrialisation: Britain and its European Rivals, 1688–1815* (Cambridge University Press, 2004), pp. 36 and 53; Robert Stein, 'The State of French Colonial Commerce on the Eve of the Revolution', *JEEH* 12/1 (1983): 109.

45 Thomas, *Slave Trade*, p. 515.

46 Coelho, 'Profitability', 266.

47 R. C. Nash, 'South Carolina Indigo, European Textiles, and the British Atlantic Economy in the Eighteenth Century', *EHR* 63/2 (2010): 378–9.

48 Karl Marx, *Capital: a Critique of Political Economy* (New York: International Publishers, 1967), vol. I, p. 361.

49 Solow, 'Capitalism and Slavery', p. 732.

50 Robin Blackburn, *The Making of New World Slavery: from the Baroque to the Modern, 1492–1800* (London: Verso, 1997), pp. 491–2; Thomas, *Slave Trade*, p. 540.

51 See in particular Douglas C. North, *The Economic Growth of the United States, 1790–1860* (Englewood Cliffs, N.J.: Prentice-Hall, 1961); Robert W. Fogel and Stanley L. Engerman, *Time on the Cross: the Economics of American Negro Slavery* (Boston, Mass.: Little, Brown, 1974); Robert W. Fogel, *Without Consent or Contract: the Rise and Fall of American Slavery* (New York: W. W. Norton, 1989); Gavin Wright, *Slavery and American Economic Development* (Baton Rouge: Louisiana State University Press, 2006).

52 Marco Coltellini, *Il gazzettiere americano* (Livorno, 1763), p. 235, fig. 21; Francesco Griselini, *Dizionario delle arti e de' mestieri* (Venice, 1768–78), vol. III, tav. 14. The most complete of these images is in Griselini's *Dizionario delle arti*, forty pages of which are dedicated to cotton growing and cotton textile production. Griselini's image was a compounded one. The author seemed uncertain how the operation of bowing fitted within the process and therefore decided to represent it separately performed by a man who looks distinctively Asian.

53 This was the case in India of the 1720s and 1730s, when harvest failure increased substantially both the cost of rice and cotton. Bhattacharya, 'Hinterland and the Coast', p. 33.

54 Solow, 'Capitalism and Slavery', p. 717.

55 North and Fogel highlight the importance of the gang system of production allowed by large-scale slave plantations. Gavin Wright emphasises instead scientific management and property rights. North, *Economic Growth*, especially pp. 128–9; Fogel and

Engerman, *Time on the Cross*, especially pp. 26–7; Gavin Wright, 'The Efficiency of Slavery: Another Interpretation', *AHR* 69/1 (1979): 219–26; Wright, *Slavery*, pp. 105–7.

56 Henry A. Gemery and Jan S. Hogendorn, 'The Atlantic Slave Trade: a Tentative Economic Model', *Journal of African History* 15/2 (1974): 229–30.

57 Ibid., 228.

58 John Houghton, *Husbandry and Trade Improv'd: Being a Collection of many Valuable Materials Relating to Corn, Cattle, Coals, Hops, Wool, &c.* (London: Woodman and Lyon, 1727), p. 136.

59 Griselini, *Dizionario delle arti*, vol. III, p. 137. See also Charles S. Aiken, 'The Evolution of Cotton Ginning in the Southeastern United States', *Geographical Review* 63/2 (1973): 200.

60 Houghton, *Husbandry*, p. 136.

61 Antonio Gutiérrez Escudero, *Poblacion y economia en Santo Domingo (1700–1746)* (Seville: Excma, 1985), p. 117.

62 Zahedieh, *Capital and the Colonies*, p. 227.

63 Gutiérrez Escudero, *Poblacion*, p. 116.

64 Johannes Menne Postma, *The Dutch in the Atlantic Slave Trade, 1600–1815* (Cambridge University Press, 1990), pp. 183, 213 and appendix 26, p. 411.

65 Johnson, *Bahamas*, p. 13. See also Lowell Joseph Ragatz, *The Fall of the Planter Class in the British Caribbean, 1763–1833: a Study in Social and Economic History* (New York: Century, 1928).

66 Michael J. Jarvis, *In the Eye of all Trade: Bermuda, Bermudians, and the Maritime Atlantic World, 1680–1783* (Chapel Hill: University of North Carolina Press, 2010), pp. 579–80, nn. 55 and 56.

67 De Flaix, *Essai historique*, vol. II, p. 71. Cited in G. Jouveau-Dubreuil, 'Le Commerce des tissus de coton à Pondichéry au XVIIe et XVIIIe siècles', *Revue Historique de l'Inde Française* 8 (1952): 230.

68 Johnson, *Bahamas*, pp. 10–11.

69 John, *Plantation Slaves*, pp. 14–15.

70 Gutiérrez Escudero, *Poblacion*, p. 116. In 1790 there were 705 cotton plantations in St Domingue out of 4,875 plantations of sugar, cotton, indigo and coffee. The total production was of c. 5–6 million pounds of cotton. Ragatz, *Fall of the Planter Class*, p. 204.

71 Williams, *Capitalism & Slavery*, p. 72.

72 Peter C. Mancall, Joshua L. Rosenbloom and Thomas Weiss, 'Exports and the Economy of the Lower Southern Region, 1720–1770', *Research in Economic History* 25 (2008): 62.

73 Howard, *Bahamas*, pp. 10–11, 22.

74 Patrick Colquhoun, *A Treatise on the Wealth, Power and Resources of the British Empire, in Every Quarter of the World, Including the East Indies* (London, Printed for J. Mawman, 1814), p. 364.

75 Ibid., p. 378.

76 Daniel MacKinnen, *A Tour Through the British West Indies, in the Years 1802 and 1803, Giving a Particular Account of the Bahama Islands* (London: J. White, 1804), p. 117.

77 Colquhoun, *Treatise*, p. 373.

78 Jaquay, 'Caribbean Cotton', tables 10 and 12; Henry Smithers, *Liverpool, its Commerce, Statistics and Institutions, with a History of the Cotton Trade* (Liverpool: Thomas Kaye, 1825).

79 Eugene R. Dattel, *Cotton and Race in the Making of America: the Human Costs of Economic Power* (Chicago, Il.: Ivan R. Dee, 2009), pp. 30–1; Fogel and Engerman, *Time on the Cross*, p. 90.

80 J. L. Sheffield, *Observations on the Commerce of the American States* (London, 1784), p. 116.

81 Michael Zakim, 'Sartorial Ideologies: from Homespun to Ready-Made', *AHR* 106/5 (2001): 1553–86.

82 Hammond, *Cotton Industry*, p. 6.

83 Ibid., p. 7.

84 Daniel H. Usner Jr, 'American Indians on the Cotton Frontier: Changing Economic Relations with Citizens and Slaves in the Mississippi Territory', in Sanjay Subrahmanyam, ed., *Merchant Networks in the Early Modern World* (Aldershot: Variorum, 1996), p. 363; Chaplin, 'Creating a Cotton South', 181.

85 Hammond, *Cotton Industry*, pp. 6–9.

86 Hobhouse, *Seeds of Change*, pp. 187–8.

87 Dattel, *Cotton and Race*, pp. 33–6.

88 Aiken, 'Evolution', 197–9.

89 Cited in Thomas, *Slave Trade*, p. 569.

90 Eliza Lucas Pinckney, *The Letterbook of Eliza Lucas Pinckney 1739–1762*, ed. Elise Pinckney (Columbia: University of South Carolina Press, 1997), p. 15.

91 Peter J. Hugill, *World Trade Since 1431. Geography, Technology and Capitalism* (Baltimore and London: Johns Hopkins University Press, 1993), p. 82; Gavin Wright, 'Slavery and American Agricultural History', *Agricultural History* 77/4 (2003): 527–52.

92 Usner, 'American Indians', pp. 364 and 371.

93 James Oliver Horton and Lois E. Horton, *Slavery and the Making of America* (Oxford University Press, 2005), p. 109; Ira Berlin, *Many Thousands Gone: the First Two Centuries of Slavery in North America* (Cambridge, Mass.: Belknap Press, 1998), p. 110.

94 Paul E. Johnson, *The Early American Republic, 1789–1829* (Oxford University Press, 2006), p. 90; *Statistical Abstract of the US* (www.census.gov/prod/www/abs/statab.html); Hugill, *World Trade*, p. 83. If in 1800 the West Indies produced less than 10,000 tons of cotton, in 1850 the US South produced *c.* half a million tons.

95 Horton and Horton, *Slavery*, p. 110. This was necessary after the abolition of the importation of slaves in 1808. Whilst earlier plantations had made use of the external supply of new slaves, most of the expansion of cotton plantations had to rely on transportation from elsewhere in the US and on natural reproduction. Mark Michael Smith, *Debating Slavery: Economy and Society in the Antebellum American South* (Cambridge University Press, 1998), p. 7.

96 Johnson, *Early American Republic*, p. 91. Sixty per cent of all slaves in mid-century US were employed in cotton cultivation. Fogel and Engerman, *Time on the Cross*, pp. 95 and 203.

97 Dale W. Tomich, *Slave in the Circuit of Sugar. Martinique and the World Economy, 1830–1848* (Baltimore, Md.: Johns Hopkins University Press, 1990), pp. 88–91.

98 Frederick Law Olmsted, *The Cotton Kingdom: a Traveller's Observation on Cotton and Slavery in the American Slave States*, ed. Arthur M. Schlesinger (New York: Alfred A. Knopf, 1953), p. 16.

99 Johnson, *Early American Republic*, p. 92.

100 Susan Eva O'Donovan, *Becoming Free in the Cotton South* (Cambridge, Mass.: Harvard University Press, 2007), pp. 24–5.

101 Ibid., pp. 24–32.

102 Theodore Rosengarten, *Tombee: Portrait of a Cotton Planter* (New York: William Morrow, 1986), pp. 82–3.

103 Hugh Brogan, *The Penguin History of the United States of America* (Harmondsworth: Penguin, 1990), p. 205.

104 Thomas, *Slave Trade*, p. 596.

105 Compare James Belich, *Replenishing the Earth: the Settler Revolution and the Rise of the Anglo-World, 1783–1939* (Oxford University Press, 2009), pp. 230–1.

10 Competing with India: cotton and European industrialisation

1 英国 (いきりす) の阿克来 (あくらい) ハ紡棉機 (もめんいとをよるしかけ)

を造るに數年心を苦しめて
家貧くなりけるを其妻其功な
くして徒に財を費すを憤り雛
形を打砕きければ阿克来 (あくらい) 怒
りて婦を逐出しぬ其後機器
成就して大ニ冨りとそ

Ikirisu no akurai wa momen-ito o yoru shikake
o tsukuruni sūnen kokoro o kurushimete
ie mazushiku narikeruo sono tsuma sono kō na-
kushite itazurani zai o tsuiyasu o ikidoori hina-
gata o uchikudakikereba akurai ika-
rite fu o oidashinu sononochi kiki
jōjushite ooini tomeri toso.

2 *Report of the Select Committee . . . Upon the Subject of the Cotton Manufacture of this Country* (London, 1793), p. 5.

3 On the key technological innovations affecting cotton textile production, see David S. Landes, *The Unbound Prometheus: Technological Change and Industrial Development in Western Europe from 1750 to the Present* (Cambridge University Press, 1969), especially pp. 84–5; Richard Leslie Hills, *Power in the Industrial Revolution* (Manchester University Press, 1970), pp. 54–88; Allen, *British Industrial Revolution in Global Perspective*, pp. 182–216.

4 Christine MacLeod, *Heroes of Invention: Technology, Liberalism and British Identity, 1750-1914* (Cambridge University Press, 2007).

5 J. Talboys Wheeler, *Handbook to the Cotton Cultivation in the Madras Presidency* (London: Virtue Brothers, 1863), p. 27.

6 Thomas Ellison, for instance, in his influential work of 1886 provided a genealogy of invention for the key period 1741 to 1800, mapping the progress of trade and production next to that of technological invention. Thomas Ellison, *The Cotton Trade of Great Britain: Including a History of the Liverpool Cotton Market and of the Liverpool Cotton Brokers' Association* (London: E. Wilson, 1886), p. 29.

7 Chris Freeman and Francisco Louçã, *As Time Goes By: from the Industrial Revolutions to the Information Revolution* (Oxford University Press, 2001), p. 169.

8 The importance of cotton textiles for the First Industrial Revolution has been the subject of debate between Crafts and Harley and Cuenca Esteban over the sector's rates of growth from the 1760s to the 1820s and in more qualitative discussion with Berg and Hudson over the nature and 'extension' of industrialisation. For estimates of growth rates see N. F. R. Crafts, *British Economic Growth During the Industrial Revolution* (Oxford University Press, 1985). For cotton textiles see Javier Cuenca Esteban, 'British Textile Prices, 1770–1831: are British Growth Rates Worth Revising Once Again?', *EHR* 47/1 (1994): 66–105; C. K. Harley and N. F. R. Crafts, 'Cotton Textiles and Industrial Output Growth During the Industrial Revolution', *EHR* 48/1 (1995): 134–44; Javier Cuenca Esteban, 'Further Evidence on Falling Prices of Cotton Cloth, 1768–1816', *EHR* 48/1 (1995): 145–50; C. Knick Harley, 'Cotton Textile Prices and the Industrial Revolution', *EHR* 51/1 (1999): 49–83; J. Cuenca Esteban, 'Factory Costs, Market Prices and Indian Calicos: Cotton Textile Prices Revisited, 1779–1831', *EHR* 52/4 (1999): 749–75. On the debate with Berg and Hudson, see N. R. F. Crafts and C. Knick Harley, 'Output Growth and the British Industrial Revolution: a Restatement of the Crafts–Harley View', *EHR* 45/4 (1992): 703–30; Maxine Berg and Pat Hudson, 'Rehabilitating the Industrial Revolution', *EHR* 45/1 (1992): 24–50; Maxine Berg and Pat Hudson, 'Growth and Change: a Comment on the Crafts–Harley View of the Industrial Revolution', *EHR* 47/1 (1994): 147–9.

9 Harley, 'Cotton Textile Prices'; Hobhouse, *Seeds of Change*, p. 176; Crouzet, *History of the European Economy*, p. 88.

10 Wong and Rosenthal however warn us against exaggerating the innovative nature of technologies in leading sectors: 'Although the magnitude of demand for coke and cotton textiles explains the visible success of the new technologies, it masks the fact that they developed in ways that were very similar to the development of older, less economically rewarding technologies.' Jean-Laurent Rosenthal and R. Bin Wong, *Before and Beyond Divergence: the Politics of Economic Change in China and Europe* (Cambridge, Mass.: Harvard University Press, 2011), p. 124.

11 In Britain, in particular, a prominent school of thought saw technological development as key to the nation's future. See Anne Gambles, *Protection and Politics: Conservative Economic Discourse, 1815–52* (Oxford: Boydell Press, 1999).

12 For an overview, see Hudson, *Industrial Revolution*; Martin J. Daunton, *Progress and Poverty: an Economic and Social History of Britain, 1700–1850* (Oxford University Press, 1995); Joel Mokyr, ed., *The British Industrial Revolution: an Economic Assessment*, 2nd edn (Boulder, Col.: Westview Press, 1998); Allen, *British Industrial Revolution in Global Perspective*.

13 Jack A. Goldstone, 'The Rise of the West – or Not? A Revision to Socio-economic History', *Sociological Theory* 18/2 (2000): 175–94; Jan Luitten van Zanden, 'The Great Convergence from a West-European Perspective. Some Thoughts and Hypotheses', *Itinerario* 24/3–4 (2001): 9–29; Kenneth Pomeranz, 'Is there an East Asian Development Path? Long-term Comparisons, Constraints, and Continuities', *JESHO* 44/3 (2001): 322–62; Vries, 'Are Coal and Colonies Really Crucial?', 407–46; Kenneth Pomeranz, 'Political Economy and Ecology on the Eve of Industrialization: Europe, China, and the Global Conjuncture', *AHR* 107/2 (2002): 425–46; Bin R. Wong, 'The Search for European Differences and Domination of the Early Modern World: a View from Asia', *AHR* 107/2 (2002): 447–69; Kenneth Pomeranz, 'Beyond the East–West Binary: Resituating Development Paths in the Eighteenth-Century World', *JAS* 61/2 (2002): 539–90; Jack A. Goldstone, 'Efflorescence and Economic Growth in World History: Rethinking the "Rise of the West" and the Industrial Revolution', *JWH* 13/2 (2002): 323–89; Jan Luiten van Zanden, 'The Road to the Industrial Revolution: Hypotheses and Conjunctures about the Medieval Origins of the "European Miracle"', *JGH* 3/3 (2008): 337–59; Jan Luiten van Zanden, *The Long Road to the Industrial Revolution: the European Economy in a Global Perspective, 1000–1800* (Leiden and Boston: E. J. Brill, 2009); Parthasarathi, *Why Europe Grew Rich*.

14 For some recent contributions see Jeff Horn, *The Path Not Taken: French Industrialization in the Age of Revolution, 1750–1830* (Cambridge, Mass.: MIT Press, 2006); Mokyr, *Enlightened Economy*; Allen, *British Industrial Revolution in Global Perspective*. For a critique of Allen's and Mokyr's books, see Patrick O'Brien, 'A Conjuncture in Global History or an Anglo-American Construct: the British Industrial Revolution, 1700–1850', *JGH* 5/3 (2010): 503–9; and Nicholas Crafts, 'Explaining the First Industrial Revolution: Two Views', *European Review of Economic History* 15/1 (2011): 153–68.

15 Maxine Berg, 'Product Innovation in Core Consumer Industries in Eighteenth-Century Britain', in Maxine Berg and Kristine Bruland, eds., *Technological Revolutions in Europe: Historical Perspectives* (Cheltenham: Edward Elgar, 1998), pp. 38–60; Styles 'Product Innovation', 124–68; Berg, 'From Imitation to Invention', 1–30.

16 I leave land aside here. An intensification of land use means to produce more raw cotton per acre and/or acquire it at lower prices. Some of these topics have been considered in Chapters 8 and 9.

17 I must state here that in the case of de Vries's 'industrious revolution', the intensification of labour is only one aspect of a more complex model that attempts to integrate consumption and reflects on important 'qualitative' issues, though de Vries does not address the difference between industrial commodities and goods produced within the boundaries of the household. Jan de Vries, *The Industrious Revolution: Consumer Behavior and the Household Economy, 1650 to the Present* (Cambridge University Press, 2008). There is a copious literature on proto-industrialisation. For a summary, see Ogilvie and Cerman, eds., *European Proto-Industrialization*. On Asian labour-intensive industrialization, see Kaoru Sugihara, 'The Second Noel Butlin Lecture: Labour-Intensive Industrialisation in Global History', *Australian EHR* 47/2 (2007): 121–54, and Gareth Austin and Kaoru Sugihara, eds., *Labour-Intensive Industrialization in Global History* (London and New York: Routledge, 2013).

18 Berg, 'Product Innovation', pp. 138–60.

19 Berg, 'Asian Luxuries', pp. 228–44, and Berg, 'In Pursuit of Luxury', pp. 85–142.

20 Christine MacLeod, 'European Origins of British Technological Predominance', in Escosura, ed., *Exceptionalism and Industrialisation*, p. 114.

21 ANF, F^{12} 650: 'Mémoire contenant les sues d'un Magistrat d'Alsace sur le commerce de cette province' (n.d. [before 1756]).

22 The Society of Arts and Manufactures in London was also concerned with expanding mechanised spinning. Parthasarathi, *Why Europe Grew Rich*, p. 103; Derek Hudson and Kenneth W. Luckhurst, *The Royal Society of Arts, 1754–1954* (London: John Murray, 1954), p. 129.

23 Jon Stobart, *The First Industrial Region. North-West England, c. 1700–60* (Manchester University Press, 2004), p. 66.

24 ANF, F^{12} 2195: mémoire, 22 August 1739.

25 'Project tendant a perfectionner les fabriques de France, 1752', in P. Boissonnade, 'Trois mémoires relatifs a l'amélioration des manufactures de France sous l'administration des Trudaine (1754)', *Revue d'Histoire Économique et Sociale* 17 (1914): 64.

26 Cited in R. J. Barendse, *Arabian Seas 1700–1763*, vol. III, *Men and Merchandise* (Leiden: E. J. Brill, 2009), p. 1037.

27 I am very grateful to Liliane Pérez for information provided on the Montarans (father and son) and their role in promoting several branches of manufacturing, including the dyeing and spinning of cotton.

28 ANF, F^{12} *254: 'Etablissement de tisserands indiens en France 1785–1788' (for the expenses); F^{12} 1411B: 'Cotton 1701–9'; Paul Marichal, 'Une Colonie indienne a Thieux', *Bulletin de la Société de l'Histoire de Paris et de l'Ile-de-France* 22 (1895): 44–56.

29 See Peter Hans Kriedte, Hans Medick and Jürgen Schlumbohm, *Industrialization Before Industrialization: Rural Industry in the Genesis of Capitalism* (Cambridge University Press, 1981); Peter Hans Kriedte, *Peasants, Landlords, and Merchant Capitalists: Europe and the World Economy, 1500–1800* (Cambridge University Press, 1983); Ogilvie and Cerman, eds., *European Proto-Industrialization*.

30 Jan de Vries, 'The Industrial Revolution and the Industrious Revolution', *JEH* 54/2 (1994): 249–70; Vries, *Industrious Revolution*.

31 Bin Wong, *China Transformed*, pp. 62–6; Goldstone, 'Gender, Work, and Culture', 1–21.

32 Jan de Vries, 'Great Expectations: Early Modern History and the Social Sciences', *Review: Journal of the Fernand Braudel Center* 22/2 (1999): 141; Bin Wong, *China Transformed*, p. 31.

33 Pomeranz, 'Political Economy', 431–2; Lynda S. Bell, 'Farming, Sericulture, and Peasant Rationality in Wuxi County in the Early Twentieth Century', in Thomas G. Rawski and Lillian M. Li, eds., *Chinese History in Economic Perspective* (Berkeley: University of California Press, 1992), pp. 213–14. Some sinologists are now sceptical about using the label 'proto-industry' to identify cotton textile production in Ming and Qing China. Some areas of the empire were clearly producing for distant markets, but the bulk or production and consumption remained within the household. See Zurndorfer, 'Cotton Textile Manufacture', especially 715–18. Compare Bray, *Technology and Gender*, especially p. 222 and Li Bozhong, *Agricultural Development in Jiangnan, 1620–1850* (Basingstoke: Macmillan, 1998).

34 Huang, *Peasant Family*.

35 Focusing on the cotton region of Jiangnan, Pomeranz is less pessimistic, showing continuous economic expansion throughout the eighteenth century, not just in Jiangnan but also in other Chinese cotton-producing regions. See Pomeranz, 'Is there an East Asian Development Path?', 322–62; Kenneth Pomeranz, 'Chinese Development in Long-Run Perspective', *Proceedings of the American Philosophical Society* 152 (2008): 83–100; Kenneth Pomeranz, 'Their Own Path to Crisis? Social Change, State-Building and the Limits of Qing Expansion, *c.* 1770–1840', in David Armitage and Sanjay Subrahmanyam, eds., *The Age of Revolutions in Global Context, c.1760–1840* (Basingstoke: Palgrave Macmillan, 2010), pp. 189–208.

36 See figures 2.6 and 2.7 in this book, and Elvin, 'High-Level Equilibrium Trap', pp. 142–72; Mark Elvin, *The Pattern of the Chinese Past* (Stanford University Press, 1973), pp. 298–315. It remains unclear however, if these were truly machines for spinning or for doubling.

37 Susan Mann, 'Household Handicrafts and State Policy in Qing Times', in Jane Kate Leonard and John R. Watt, eds., *To Achieve Security and Wealth: the Qing Imperial State and the Economy, 1644–1911* (Ithaca, NY: Cornell University Press, 1992), p. 89.

38 Kuhn, *Science and Civilisation in China*, p. 223. On the role of the state in shaping the political economy of China, see Kent, *Political Economy in Modern Times: Changes and Economic Consequences, 1800–2000* (London: Routledge, 2011), ch. 2.

39 Huang, *Peasant Family*, p. 46.

40 E. A. Wrigley, *Continuity, Chance and Change: the Character of the Industrial Revolution in England* (Cambridge University Press, 1988).

41 See for instance Allen, *British Industrial Revolution in Global Perspective*.

42 David A. Washbrook, 'Progress and Problems: South Asian Economic and Social History, *c.* 1720–1860', *Modern Asian Studies* 22/1 (1988): 57–96. In a very different vein, this point is also made by Adas, *Machines as the Measure of Men*.

43 Washbrook, 'Progress and Problems', 60 and 78; and Ramaswami, 'Genesis', 300. However, this point is criticised by economic historians, suggesting that cotton spinners and weavers might have not been as prosperous as previously thought. See in particular the debate between Parthasarathi and Broadberry, Gupta and Allen in note 48.

44 *Réflexions des marchands merciers, drapiers, et corps unis de la ville de Rouen, sur l'impossibilité de fabriquer en France des toiles propres pour l'impression, en concurrence avec celles des Indes* (Rouen [*c.* 1756]), p. 3.

45 Ibid., p. 2. Bleaching accounted for the remainder 4 per cent. For India, see Wendt, 'Social Fabric', 336–7.

46 *Réflexions*, p. 4.

47 TNA, CO 388/21, part 1 fo. 206 (1721).

48 Robert Allen and Stephen Broadberry and Bishnu Gupta support the view of high wages in Europe: Robert C. Allen, 'The Great Divergence in European Wages and Prices from the Middle Ages to the First World War', *Explorations in Economic History* 38 (2001): 411–47; Robert C. Allen, 'Britain's Economic Ascendancy in a European Context', in Escosura, ed., *Exceptionalism and Industrialisation*, pp. 15–34; Robert C. Allen, 'India in the Great Divergence', in Timothy J. Hatton, Kevin H. O'Rourke and Alan M. Taylor, eds., *The New Comparative Economic History: Essay in Honour of Jeffrey G. Williamson* (Cambridge, Mass.: MIT Press,

2007), pp. 9–32; Allen, *British Industrial Revolution*, especially ch. 6. Broadberry and Gupta consider factor prices more widely: Stephen Broadberry and Bishnupriya Gupta, 'The Early Modern Great Divergence: Wages, Prices and Economic Development in Europe and Asia, 1500–1800', *EHR* 59/1 (2006): 2–31; Stephen Broadberry and Bishnupriya Gupta, 'Lancashire, India and Shifting Competitive Advantage in Cotton Textiles, 1700–1850: the Neglected Role of Factor Prices', *EHR* 62/2 (2009): 279–305. By contrast, Parthasarathi supports the idea of high wages in India: Parthasarathi, 'Rethinking Wages', 79–109; Prasannan Parthasarathi, 'Historical Issues of Deindustrialisation in Nineteenth-Century South India', in Riello and Roy, eds., *How India Clothed the World*, pp. 415–36. See also Roman Studer, 'India and the Great Divergence: Assessing the Efficiency of Grain Markets in Eighteenth- and Nineteenth-Century India', *JEH* 68/2 (2008): 393–437.

49 See in particular Roy, 'Knowledge and Divergence', 361–87.

50 Patrick Karl O'Brien, 'The Micro Foundations of Macro Invention: the Case of the Reverend Edmund Cartwright', *TH* 28/2 (1997): 201–33.

51 Mary B. Rose, 'Introduction: the Rise of the Cotton Industry in Lancashire to 1830', in Rose, ed., *Lancashire Cotton Industry*, p. 13. This was accompanied by resistance from handloom weavers. See Duncan Bythell, *The Handloom Weavers: a Study in the English Cotton Industry during the Industrial Revolution* (Cambridge University Press, 1969).

52 Mokyr, *Enlightened Economy*; Ralf Meisenzahl and Joel Mokyr, 'The Rate and Direction of Invention in the British Industrial Revolution: Incentives and Institutions', *NBER Working Papers Series* 16993 (April 2011) (www.nber.org/papers/w16993). It is, however, true that England showed a particular propensity for technological solutions to cotton manufacturing: consider the 1761 reward of £50 offered by the Society of Arts for a machine that could spin six threads at once. Hills, *Power in the Industrial Revolution*, p. 55.

53 O'Brien, 'Conjuncture'.

54 Parthasarathi, *Why Europe Grew Rich*, ch. 7. See also Arun Bala, *The Dialogue of Civilizations in the Birth of Modern Science* (New York: Palgrave Macmillan, 2006).

55 Berg, 'Asian Luxuries', pp. 228–44; Berg, 'In Pursuit of Luxury', Harold Cook, *Matters of Exchange: Commerce, Medicine, and Science in the Dutch Golden Age* (New Haven, Conn.: Yale University Press, 2007); Anne Gerritsen, 'Global Design in Jingdezhen: Local Production and Global Connections', in Adamson, Riello and Teasley, eds., *Global Design History*, pp. 25–33.

56 Russell has recently revived the idea that American cotton was more suitable than other types of raw cotton for mechanised processing, as it was longer staple. He argues that American supplies allowed for the mechanisation of spinning, thus adding an ecological dimension to explanations of mechanisation and industrialisation. This suggestive hypothesis, supported by the price differential paid for the more costly American cotton, is contentious, however, as Britain was not the only importer of American cotton, nor solely relied on cotton from the West Indies and the US South. Edmund Russell, *Evolutionary History: Uniting History and Biology to Understand Life on Earth* (Cambridge University Press, 2011), pp. 116–17.

57 ANF, F^{12} 2195: untitled mémoire, August 1779.

58 In spinning, the breakthrough to high-quality yarn came with Crompton's mule. See Hills, *Power in the Industrial Revolution*, p. 60.

59 For an overview, see James K. Thomson, 'Invention in the Industrial Revolution: the Case of Cotton', in Escosura, ed., *Exceptionalism and Industrialisation*, pp. 132–42.

60 ANF, F^{12} 2195: 'Brisout de Barneville, demande de secours ou d'aide pour établir à Nancy une manufacture de mousselines et de baptistes utilisant une machine nouvelle inventé par son père, 1779–80'.

61 Maxine Berg, 'Quality, Cotton and the Global Luxury Trade', in Riello and Roy, eds., *How India Clothed the World*, pp. 391–414; Prasannan Parthasarathi, 'The European Response to Indian Cottons', paper presented at the GEHN Conference 'Cotton Textiles in the Indian Ocean', Pune, December 2005; Parthasarathi, *Why Europe Grew Rich*, especially pp. 94–103.

62 D. Rasbotham, *Thoughts on the Use of Machines, in the Cotton Manufacture. Addressed to the Working People in that Manufacture, and to the Poor in General* (Manchester, 1780), p. 13.

63 Cited in R. S. Fitton and A. P. Wadsworth, *The Strutts and the Arkwrights, 1758–1830. A Study of the Early Factory System* (Manchester University Press, 1958), p. 70. The parliamentary act of 1774 allowed the production and use of British all-cotton cloth. This cloth had to have three blue threads woven into the selvages to distinguish it from Indian cotton textiles. Natalie Rothstein, 'Cotton', in Jane Turner, *The Dictionary of Art* (London: Macmillan, 1996), vol. VIII, p. 37.

64 Allen, *British Industrial Revolution in Global Perspective*, pp. 207–8. Harley, 'Cotton Textile Prices', 49–83. See also the debate that followed between Harley and Cuenca Esteban. Esteban, 'Factory Costs, Market Prices', 749–55; and C. Knick Harley, 'Cotton Textile Prices Revisited: a Response to Cuenca Esteban', *EHR* 52/4 (1999): 756–65.

65 This point was already argued by Chapman and Chassagne in the 1980s. Chapman and Chassagne, *European Textile Printers*; and Chapman, 'Quality Versus', 175–92.

66 Stanley D. Chapman, 'Fixed Capital Formation in the British Cotton Industry, 1770–1815', *EHR* 23/2 (1970): 235–66; Stanley D. Chapman, 'Industrial Capital Before the Industrial Revolution: an Analysis of the Assets of a Thousand Textile Entrepreneurs, *c.* 1730–50', in N. B. Harte and K. G. Ponting, eds., *Textile History and Economic History: Essays in Honour of Miss Julia de Lacy Mann* (Manchester University Press, 1973), pp. 113–37; and Chapman and Chassagne, *European Textile Printers*.

67 Rose, 'Introduction', p. 19. See also Stanley D. Chapman, *The Cotton Industry in the Industrial Revolution* (London: Macmillan, 1972).

68 For the reaction of foreign visitors, see Giorgio Riello and Patrick K. O'Brien, 'The Future is Another Country: Offshore Views of the British Industrial Revolution', *Journal of Historical Sociology* 22/1 (2009): 1–29

69 Roger Lloyd-Jones and A. A. LeRoux, 'The Size of Firms in the Cotton Industry: Manchester in 1815', *EHR* 33/1 (1980): 75.

70 Benjamin Silliman, *A Journal of Travels in England, Holland and Scotland and of Two Passages over the Atlantic in the Years 1805 and 1806* (Boston: T. B. Wait & Co., 1812), vol. I, pp. 78–9.

71 See Clark Nardinelli, *Child Labor and the Industrial Revolution* (Bloomington: Indiana University Press, 1990); Katrina Honeyman, *Women, Gender and Industrialisation in England, 1700–1870* (Houndmills: Macmillan, 2000); Joyce Burnette, *Gender,*

Work and Wages in Industrial Revolution Britain (Cambridge University Press, 2008); Jane Humphries, *Childhood and Child Labour in the British Industrial Revolution* (Cambridge University Press, 2010).

72 Lloyd-Jones and LeRoux, 'Size of Firms', 76.

73 Rose, 'Introduction', pp. 13–14.

74 Ibid., pp. 16–17.

75 Chaudhuri, 'Structure of Indian Textile Industry', p. 72.

76 ANF, F¹² 650: 'Mémoire', pp. 6–7.

77 See, for instance, the classic work by Sidney Pollard, 'Factory Discipline in the Industrial Revolution', *EHR* 16/2 (1963): 254–71; E. P. Thompson, 'Time, Work-Discipline, and Industrial Capitalism', *P&P* 38 (1967): 56–97; and Eric Hopkins, 'Working Hours and Conditions During the Industrial Revolution: a Re-Appraisal', *EHR* 35/1 (1982): 52–66; David S. Landes, 'What do Bosses Really do?', *JEH* 46/3 (1986): 585–623. On gender see Burnette, *Gender, Work and Wages*.

78 Styles argues that high levels of standardisation were already achieved by putting-out systems. John Styles, 'Manufacturing, Consumption and Design in Eighteenth-Century England', in Brewer and Porter, eds., *Consumption and the World of Goods*, pp. 527–54. However, the strong regional specialisation of production substantially decreased with industrialisation.

79 For an analysis of the aesthetic and architectural impact of such large buildings, see Celina Fox, *The Arts of Industry in the Age of Enlightenment* (New Haven, Conn.: Yale University Press, 2009), pp. 399 and 434–5, including the two famous paintings by Joseph Wright of Derby of Arkwright's cotton mills, *c.* 1782–3.

80 Nathaniel Hazeltine Carter, *Letter from Europe, Comprising the Journal of a Tour through Ireland, England, Scotland, France, Italy, and Switzerland, in 1825, '26 and '27* (New York: G. & C. Carvill, 1827), vol. I, p. 76.

81 The swatches preserved at the Musée de l'Impression sur Étoffes in Mulhouse show a truly kaleidoscopic view of design patterns used for early nineteenth-century French cottons. They also show the importance of storing design information. When several hundred designs were in production in every single year, books containing information on specific motifs, colours and quantities of production were a necessity. See also Philip Sykas, 'Calico Catalogues: Nineteenth-Century Printed Dress Fabrics from Pattern Books', *Costume* 33 (1999): 58.

82 Josette Brédif, *Toiles de Jouy. Classic Printed Textiles from France 1760–1843* (London: Thames & Hudson, 1989); Mélanie Riffel and Sophie Rouart, *Toile de Jouy: Printed Textiles in the French Classic Style* (London: Thames & Hudson, 2003); Starr Siegele, *Toiles for all Seasons: French and British Printed Textiles* (Boston: Bunker Hill Publishing, 2004).

83 In Britain it led to the passing of the 1787 Copyright Act that protected design. Chapman and Chassagne, *European Textile Printers*, pp. 205–6 See Toshio Kusamitsu, 'British Industrialization and Design Before the Great Exhibition', *TH* 12 (1981): 77–95; David Greysmith, 'Patterns, Piracy and Protection in the Textile Printing Industry 1787–1850', *TH* 14/2 (1983): 165–94; Lara Kriegel, 'Culture and the Copy: Calico, Capitalism, and Design Copyright in Early Victorian Britain', *Journal of British Studies* 43/2 (2004): 233–65. For France see Katie Scott, 'Art and Industry: a Contradictory Union. Authors, Rights and Copyrights During the Consulat', *Journal of Design History* 13/1 (2000): 1–21.

84 Kriegel, 'Culture', 244.

85 Liliane Hilaire Pérez, *L'invention technique au siècle des lumières* (Paris: Albin Michel, 2000).

86 Thomson, 'Marketing Channels and Structures in Spain', pp. 335–57.

87 Marta Vicente, 'Artisans and Work in a Barcelona Cotton Factory', *International Review of Social History* 45/1 (2000): 2.

88 M. Antonia Cillezuelo Uzquiza, 'Los fabricantes: su ennoblecimiento. Los Canals: la fábrica de Indianas. De "Payes a Barón". Otros fabricantes ennobleados', *Pedralbes: Revista d'Història Moderna* 8/1 (1988): 49–56.

89 Carlos Martìnez Shaw, 'Los Orìgenes de la industria algodonera catalana y el comercio colonial', in Jordi Nadal and Gabriel Tortella, eds., *Agricultura, comercio colonial y crecimiento económico en la España contemporánea* (Barcelona: Editorial Ariel, 1974), pp. 247, 260–4.

90 Chassagne, *Manufacture de Toiles Imprimées*.

91 Jorge Miguel Pedreira, 'Indústria e negócio: a estamparia da região de Lisboa, 1780–1880', *Anàlise Social* 27/112–113 (1991): 553.

92 Eugenio Lo Sardo, 'Cotton Industry and Public Intervention in Rome in the Second Half of the Eighteenth Century', *TH* 20/1 (1990): 79–90; Daverio, 'Saggi storici', pp. 449–54.

93 F. W. Carter, 'The Cotton Printing Industry in Prague, 1766–1873', *TH* 6 (1975): 134–5.

94 Landes, *Unbound Prometheus*, pp. 139–40.

95 TNA, BT6/111, unpaginated.

96 Wadsworth and Mann, *Cotton Trade and Industrial Lancashire*, pp. 195–9. Allen argues that it was rational for the French (and indeed even more for Indian manufacturers) not to adopt spinning jennies and other spinning equipment as it was economically inefficient because of the low cost of labour. Allen, *British Industrial Revolution in Global Perspective*, pp. 188–95.

97 ANF, F^{12} 2195: 'Lafau, à Lyon, demande de récompense pour un moulin à filer le coton, 1756'; Charles Schmidt, 'Les Débuts de l'industrie cotonnière en France, 1760–1806', *Revue d'Histoire Economique et Sociale* 6 (1913): 268–9. On Holker, see W. Wescher, 'John Holker, a Promoter of the French Textile Industry', *Ciba Review* 12/135 (1959): 10–13; John R. Harris, *Industrial Espionage and Technology Transfer: Britain and France in the Eighteenth Century* (Aldershot: Ashgate, 1998), especially pp. 43–55, 153–4, 361–89. See also the classic analysis by Landes, *Unbound Prometheus*, pp. 159–70.

98 France and Britain had different systems for the protection of inventions. Whilst the French *privilège* was a royal guarantee, the English patent did guarantee protection against possible economic exploitation. The English 'regime of invention' was not necessarily better at fostering higher rates of invention (in fact many in Britain believed the French system to be much more thorough), but had the effect of fostering inventive application on a scale that was not visible in France. France seems to have been mired with organisational problems, something frequently mentioned in petitions for privileges. Hilaire Pérez, *Invention technique*, pp. 114–24; Christine MacLeod, *Inventing the Industrial Revolution: the English Patent System, 1660–1800* (Cambridge University Press, 1988), pp. 41, 80–1.

99 Harris, *Industrial Espionage*.

100 ANF, F^{12} 533: 'Department de l'Escaut'.

101 Geneviève Dufresne, 'Les Filatures et tissages de coton sous la révolution et l'empire: l'example de l'Eure-et-Loir', in Favier, Gayot, Klein, Terrier and Woronoff, eds., *Tisser l'histoire*, pp. 57–69.

102 ANF, F^{12} 2195: 'William Douglas, entrepreneur de mousselines à Manchester: proposition d'installer en France des machines à filer à eau dites "grandes machines", 1789'.

103 François Crouzet, 'Wars, Blockade, and Economic Change in Europe, 1792–1815', *JEH* 24/4 (1964): 571–2.

104 In 1803 there were just six spinning mills in the French capital, but eight years after, in 1811, there were sixty-four, some of which were of substantial size, as in the case of the factory of Richard-Lenoir in the Parisian area of Charonne that employed 750 workers. Jean-Pierre Poussou, 'Les Activités commerciales des villes françaises de 1789 à 1815', *Histoire, Economie et Société* 12/1 (1993): 109.

105 Pedreira, 'Indústria', pp. 553–5.

106 John J. Monaghan, 'The Rise and Fall of the Belfast Cotton Industry', *Irish Historical Studies* 3 (1942/3): 1–17.

11 'The wolf in sheep's clothing': the potential of cotton

1 The text reads 'A subtile Wolfe, more saf[e]ly to betray / In a sheepes Clothing does himself aray / And unexpected now whole flocks destroys / Till a kind halter ends his stoln joys / Morall: The zealous Cheat has wrought the land more woe / than bare fac'd villaine could ever doe'.

2 William Marshall, *The Rural Economy of the Midland Counties* . . . (London: Nicol, 1796), p. 364.

3 Crafts, *British Economic Growth*, p. 17. Still in 1975 the consumption of cotton alone surpassed that of all other fibres taken together. Douglas A. Farnie, 'The Role of Merchants as Prime Movers in the Expansion of the Cotton Industry, 1760–1990', in Farnie and Jeremy, eds., *Fibre that Changed the World*, p. 24.

4 Phyllis Deane and W. A. Cole, *British Economic Growth, 1688–1959* (Cambridge University Press, 1962), p. 51; Crafts, *British Economic Growth*, p. 23.

5 An exception is Russell, *Evolutionary History*, pp. 103–31.

6 *Report Relating to Chequered and Striped Linens* (1751), p. 293. Cited in Lemire, 'Transforming Consumer Custom', p. 198.

7 Between 1750 and 1810 European cotton consumption increased between sixfold and eightfold. Paul Bairoch, *Economics and World History: Myths and Paradoxes* (Hemel Hempstead: Harvester Wheatsheaf, 1993), p. 158.

8 The method is based on the 'ghost acreages' model first applied by E. L. Jones and later by Kenneth Pomeranz. See Jones, *European Miracle*, ch. 1; Pomeranz, *Great Divergence*, pp. 275–7. It is also based on the assumption of constant prices and stocking rates.

9 Michael G. Mullhall, *The Dictionary of Statistics*, 4th edn (London: Routledge, 1909), p. 109.

10 See in particular Vaclav Smil, *Energy in World History* (Boulder, Col.: Westview Press, 1994), ch. 1.

11 Wrigley, *Continuity, Chance and Change*.

12 Paolo Malanima, 'Energy Systems in Agrarian Societies: the European Deviation', in Simonetta Cavaciocchi, ed., *Economia e energia, secc. XIII–XVIII. Atti della 'Trentaquattresima Settimana di Studi', 15–19 aprile 2002* (Florence: Le Monnier, 2003), p. 63.

13 Chester Whitney Wright, *Wool-Growing and the Tariff: a Study in the Economic History of the United States* (New York: Houghton Mifflin Company, 1910).

14 Virginia DeJohn Anderson, *Creatures of Empire: How Domestic Animals Transformed Early America* (Oxford University Press, 2004), pp. 105–6.

15 Giovanni Federico, *Feeding the World: an Economic History of Agriculture, 1800–2000* (Princeton University Press, 2005), pp. 49–51, 90.

16 E. Rievsanem, 'The US Great Plains', in B. L. Turner, ed., *The Earth as Transformed by Human Action: Global and Regional Changes in the Biosphere over the Past* (Cambridge University Press, 1990), p. 562.

17 Federico, *Feeding the World*, p. 50.

18 Philip McMichael, *Settlers and the Agrarian Question: Foundations of Capitalism in Colonial Australia* (Cambridge University Press, 1984), pp. 146–8.

19 Stephen H. Roberts, *History of Australian Land Settlement, 1788–1920* (London: Frank Cass, 1969), pp. 163–5.

20 Pomeranz, *Great Divergence*, pp. 275–6. Pomeranz's original calculations are based on the substitution of a 'pound for a pound' of raw material and do not take into consideration that one pound of cotton did not produce the same amount of textiles (in linear yards) as one pound of flax. This means that the estimated land in table 9.4 is double that of the figures provided by Pomeranz.

21 Mullhall, *Dictionary of Statistics*, p. 280; James M. Dempsey, *Fiber Crops* (Gainesville: University of Florida Press, 1975), pp. 6–7. Even considering that flax could only be fruitfully grown without depleting the soil only one year out of five, with rotation we might estimate that less than 5 per cent of cultivable land was needed. Alexander Johnston A. Warden, *The Linen Trade, Ancient and Modern* (London: Longman, Roberts & Green, 1867), p. 14.

22 For an overview of the processes, see Jane Schneider, 'Rumpelstiltskin's Bargain: Folklore and the Merchant Capitalism Intensification of Linen Manufacture in Early Modern Europe', in Annette B. Weiner and Jane Schneider, eds., *Cloth and Human Experience* (Washington, DC: Smithsonian Institution Press, 1989), pp. 201–2.

23 Leslie Clarkson, 'The Linen Industry in Early Modern Europe', in Jenkins, ed., *Cambridge History of Western Textiles*, vol. I, pp. 473–92.

24 Negley B. Harte, 'The Rise of Protection and the English Linen Trade, 1690–1790', in Harte and Ponting, eds., *Textile History and Economic History*, p. 104. See also Lemire, 'Transforming Consumer Custom'.

25 Alastair J. Durie, *The Scottish Linen Industry in the Eighteenth Century* (Edinburgh: John Donald, 1979); Thomas M. Truxes, *Irish-American Trade, 1660–1783* (Cambridge University Press, 1988), pp. 276–7.

26 David Ormrod, *The Rise of Commercial Empires: England and the Netherlands in the Age of Mercantilism, 1650–1770* (Cambridge University Press, 2002), pp. 169–72.

27 Vries, *Industrious Revolution*.

28 Craig Muldrew, '"Th'Ancient Distaff" and the Whirling Spindle: Measuring the Contribution of Spinning to Household Earnings and the National Economy in England, 1550–1770', *EHR* 65/2 (2012): 498–526.

29 This is, of course, hypothetical, as one might imagine that without cotton and subject to the demographic expansion of the period post 1750, there might have been a strong incentive towards technological innovation in the processing of flax and hemp.

30 I adopt here the same methodology used by Pomeranz, according to which the productivity per hectare remained the same over the eighteenth and nineteenth centuries. Peter Solar argues instead that the higher productivity of the land of the American cotton plantations (possibly twice as high as in the West Indies) should be taken into consideration. This means that the impact on European land (again if cotton could be grown and the land was as fertile as in the Americas) would have been even smaller. Peter M. Solar, 'The Triumph of Cotton in Europe', unpublished paper, January 2011. I am grateful to Professor Solar for providing me with a copy of his paper.

31 I used the index of physical output of US cotton production by David Eltis and attributed a 250 lb of ginned cotton per slave in 1810. This means that the average cotton production per slave per year was, 116 lb in 1800, 250 lb in 1820, 280 lb in 1820 and 1830, 338 lb in 1840 and 350 lb in 1850. I have also estimated a productivity of 120 lb in 1780 and 1790, before the introduction of Whitney's gin. David Eltis, *Economic Growth and the Ending of the Transatlantic Slave Trade* (Oxford University Press, 1989), pp. 189 and 287 (figures for unginned cotton).

32 However, these figures are commensurable with the number of slaves in the US in the period before 1850. *Distribution of Slaves in the United States, US Census Bureau.*

33 This estimate is approximately correct, as four million slaves were employed in the American South and *c.* 40–60 per cent of the cotton production was sold to Britain. Horton and Horton, *Slavery*, p. 109.

34 Mullhall, *Dictionary of Statistics*, pp. 7–8 and 157. See also Wright, *Slavery*.

35 We have to remember, however, that while Britain had 7–8 million inhabitants by the end of the eighteenth century, France had nearly three times as many inhabitants.

36 Esteban, 'Comparative Patterns of Colonial Trade', pp. 42–3.

37 Giorgio Riello, 'The Ecology of Cotton in the Eighteenth Century: Possibilities and Potentials', unpublished paper, October 2005 (www2.lse.ac.uk/economicHistory/Research/GEHN/GEHNPDF/RielloPadua.pdf), 6.

38 David T. Jenkins and Kenneth G. Ponting, *The British Wool Textile Industry, 1770–1914* (London: Heinemann Educational, 1982); Julia de L. Mann, *The Cloth Industry in the West of England from 1640 to 1880* (Oxford: Clarendon Press, 1971), especially pp. 37–62; Pat Hudson, *The Genesis of Industrial Capital: a Study of the West Riding Wool Textile Industry, c. 1750–1850* (Cambridge University Press, 1986). One might agree with Allen's high wage hypothesis, as England exported goods that were less labour-intensive and imported goods that were more labour-intensive. Allen, *British Industrial Revolution in Global Perspective*, pp. 25–56.

39 Daniel Defoe, *A Plan of the English Commerce, Being a Compleat Prospect of the Trade of this Nation* (London, 1730), p. 190.

40 George Andrew Patrick Briton (pseud.), *Some Impartial Thoughts on the Woollen Manufactures …* (London: T. Cooper, 1742), p. 2.

41 M. Jubb, 'Economic Policy and Economic Development', in Jeremy Black, ed., *Britain in the Age of Walpole* (London: Macmillan, 1984), pp. 124–6; Pat Hudson, 'The

Limits of Wool and the Potential of Cotton in the Eighteenth and Early Nineteenth Centuries', in Riello and Parthasarathi, eds., *Spinning World*, pp. 337–40.

42 England imported finished linen from continental Europe as well as increasing quantities of linen spun yarn from Scotland and Ireland. See Griffiths, Hunt and O'Brien, 'Scottish, Irish', 625–50.

43 Cited in Ormrod, *Rise of Commercial Empires*, p. 152.

44 Robert Stephenson, *Observations on the Present State of the Linen Trade of Ireland: in a Series of Letters* ... (Dublin: n.p., 1784), p. 17.

45 Griffiths, Hunt and O'Brien, 'Scottish, Irish', 632.

46 Trevor Griffiths, Philip Hunt and Patrick O'Brien, 'Political Components of the Industrial Revolution: English Cotton Textile Industry, 1660–1774', *EHR* 44/3 (1991): 413–14.

47 Griffiths, Hunt and O'Brien, 'Scottish, Irish', 11.

48 If in 1751–6 Silesia exported 4 million thalers worth of linen per year, a decade later, in 1761, its export did not exceed 1 million thalers.

49 Conrad Gill, *The Rise of the Irish Linen Industry* (Oxford: Clarendon Press, 1925), p. 92.

50 Ormrod, *Rise of Commercial Empires*, p. 154, figure 5.1; Adam Anderson, *An Historical and Chronological Deduction of the Origin of Commerce, from the Earliest Accounts* (London: J. Walter, 1787–9), p. 174.

51 Patrick O'Brien, 'The Geopolitics of a Global Industry: Eurasian Divergence and the Mechanisation of Cotton Textile Production in England', in Riello and Parthasarathi, eds., *Spinning World*, pp. 355–8.

52 Joan Thirsk, *Economic Policy and Projects: the Development of a Consumer Society in Early Modern England* (Oxford: Clarendon Press, 1978), pp. 30–1.

53 Jacques-Pierre Brissot de Warville, *The Commerce of America with Europe, Particularly with France and Great-Britain, Comparatively Stated and Explained* (New York: Swords, 1795), pp. 86–7.

54 Hudson, 'Limits of Wool', pp. 327–50.

55 Marshall, *Rural Economy*, p. 364.

56 Hudson, 'Limits of Wool', pp. 333–4.

57 De Lacy Mann, *Cloth Industry*, pp. 37–62. See for instance Samuel Webber, *An Account of a Scheme for Preventing the Exportation of our Wool* ... (London: T. Cooper, 1740); George Bridges, *A Letter... Upon the Decay of the Woollen Manufactories in Great Britain and Ireland* ... (London: R. Viney, 1739).

58 Jubb, 'Economic Policy', pp. 126–7.

59 Arthur Young, *Political Essays Concerning the Present State of the British Empire*... (London: W. Straham and T. Cadell, 1772), p. 192; see also Phyllis Deane, 'The Output of the British Woollen Industry in the Eighteenth Century', *JEH* 17/2 (1957): 207–23.

60 David Seward, 'The Wool Textile Industry, 1750–1960', in J. Geraint Jenkins, ed., *The Wool Textile Industry in Great Britain* (London: Routledge & Kegan Paul, 1972), pp. 35–6.

61 R. M. Hartwell, 'A Revolution in the Character and Destiny of British Wool', in Harte and Ponting, eds., *Textile History and Economic History*, p. 322.

62 Ibid., pp. 328–9. For a detailed analysis of the causes and effects of such 'genetic' changes see British Parliamentary Papers, Session Papers, vol. 8, no. 515 (1828):

'Report from the Select Committee of the House of Lords on the State of the British Wool Trade'.

63 Hudson, 'Limits of Wool', p. 332.

64 Mazzaoui, 'Introduction', pp. xx–xxi.

65 Hudson, 'Limits of Wool', pp. 329–30.

66 As such it should be taken with a pinch of salt, as Middle Eastern cotton was expensive but not of very good quality; West Indian cotton was more similar to American Upland. However the figure provides sufficient overlaps in the price series to delineate clear trends.

67 Fogel and Engerman, *Time on the Cross*, pp. 90–1.

68 France controlled 56.5 per cent of the total production of cotton in the West Indies in 1770, followed by Britain with 35 per cent, Denmark with 6.5 per cent and the Dutch Republic with 2 per cent. David Eltis, 'The Salve Economies of the Caribbean: Structure, Performance, Evolution and Significance', in Franklin W. Knight, ed., *General History of the Caribbean*, vol. III, *The Slave Society* (London: Unesco, 1997), pp. 113–14.

69 Ragatz, *Fall of the Planter Class*, p. 204. After the slave revolts of 1791, a great deal of the raw cotton produced in the French West Indies was exported to Britain.

70 For the British West Indies, see Jaquay, 'Caribbean Cotton Production', tables 8 and 9. For the French West Indies, see Jean Tarrade, *Le Commerce colonial de la France à la fin de l'ancien régime. L'évolution du régime de 'l'exclusif' de 1763 à 1789* (Paris: Presses Universitaires de France, 1972), pp. 748–9.

71 Elena Frangakis, 'The Ottoman Port of Izmir in the Eighteenth and Early Nineteenth Centuries, 1695–1820', *Revue de l'Occident Musulman et de la Méditerranée* 39/1 (1985): 149–62; Ü. Necmi, 'The Emergence of Izmir as a Mediterranean Commercial Center for the French and English Interests, 1698–1740', *International Journal of Turkish Studies* 4/1 (1987): 1–37; Elena Frangakis-Syrett, 'The Trade of Cotton and Cloth in Izmir: from the Second Half of the Eighteenth Century to the Early Nineteenth Century', in Çağlar Keyder and Faruk Tabak, eds., *Landholding and Commercial Agriculture in the Middle East* (SUNY Press, 1991), pp. 98–111; Serap Yilmaz, 'Le Traffic portuaire d'Istanbul dans la seconde moitié du XVIIIe siècle: la journée du 23 avril 1772', in Daniel Panzac, ed., *Histoire économique et sociale de l'Empire ottoman et de la Turquie (1326–1960)* (Paris: Peeters, 1995), pp. 288–94.

72 A. M. Arnould, *De la balance du commerce et des relations commerciales extérieures de la France* ... (Paris, 1791), pp. 254–5.

73 J. K. J. Thomson, 'La Política del algodón en la España del siglo XVIII', *Revista de Historia Industrial* 17/2 (2008): 15–44; J. K. J. Thomson, 'The Spanish Trade of American Cotton: Atlantic Synergies in the Age of Enlightenment', *Revista de Historia Economica* 26/2 (2008): 277–313; J. K. J. Thomson, *A Distinctive Industrialization: Cotton in Barcelona, 1728–1832* (Cambridge University Press, 1992), pp. 164, 204 and 236.

74 See Carlos Matinez-Shaw, 'Entre orient et occident: l'approvisionnement en coton et l'industrialisation de la Catalogne', in Bottin and Pellegrin, eds., *Échanges et cultures textiles*, pp. 227–45.

75 This is notwithstanding the fact that the French government had attempted to encourage the use of American cotton by imposing heavy duties on cotton yarn from the

Levant. C. Issawi, 'The Decline of Middle Eastern Trade, 1100–1850', in Richards, ed., *Islam and the Trade of Asia*, p. 258.

76 Parthasarathi, *Why Europe Grew Rich*, table 5.1.

77 N. W. Posthumus, *Nederlandsche Prijsgeschiedenis* (Leiden: E. J. Brill, 1943), pp. 183–4 and 281–3; Gaston Rambert, ed., *Histoire du commerce de Marseille; Tome V. De 1660 à 1789: le Levant* (Paris: Librairie Plon, 1949–66), pp. 510–11.

78 This is a position recently supported by Russell but already present in Wadsworth and Mann. Russell, *Evolutionary History*, pp. 103–31. It must be said that it is contentious especially when it is argued that pure cotton cloth was produced in Europe before Arkwright's water frame. It is more likely that pure cotton cloth could be produced only by doubling the warp, as in Holker's samples of cottons from Manchester, *c.* 1750. See pp. 152–3.

79 *Observations adressé au Premier Consul, par les manufacturiers et Entrepreneurs de la filature du coton, touchant les inconvénients de l'arrête du 6 brumaire an 12 ...* (n.p., 1805?), p. 21. See also François Crouzet, *Britain Ascendant: Comparative Studies in Franco-British Economic History* (Cambridge University Press, 1990), pp. 289–93, and John V. C. Nye, *War, Wine, and Taxes: the Political Economy of Anglo-French Trade, 1689–1900* (Princeton University Press, 2007), pp. 44–59; Blackburn, *Making of New World Slavery*, p. 570.

80 Poussou, 'Activités commerciales des villes françaises', 105–7.

81 Alain Blondy, 'La Culture du coton en Provence sous le 1er Empire', *Provence Historique* 56/224 (2006): 251–79. Joseph Horan at Florida State University is currently completing a PhD dissertation entitled 'Fibre d'Empire. La culture du coton à l'époque napoléonienne'.

82 The price of raw cotton fluctuated greatly between 1780 and 1810. However, by the early 1820s cotton could be purchased at half the price of a generation earlier. The price of cotton in the late 1830s was less than a third of what it had been in the early 1780s. C. Knick Harley, 'Cotton Textiles and the Industrial Revolution: Competing Models and Evidence of Prices and Profits', unpublished paper presented at St Antony's College, Oxford, 2006, table 1.1.

83 *Minutes of the Evidence Taken before a Committee of the House of Commons, Being a Committee of the Whole House to Whom it was Referred to Consider of the Circumstances of the Slave Trade* (London, 1789), p. 63.

84 Daniel Barros Dominguez da Silva and David Eltis, 'The Slave Trade to Pernambuco, 1561–1851', in David Eltis and David Richardson, eds., *Extending the Frontiers: Essays on the New Transatlantic Slave Trade Database* (New Haven, Conn.: Yale University Press, 2008), p. 111. Brazil's cotton ouput was already 1.6 million pounds in 1777 and increased to 3.5 million in 1788. But the real expansion of Brazil's cotton production happened with the crisis of the West Indian plantations in the 1790s. By 1798 Brazil's production had more than doubled to reach 7.4 million pounds, more than doubling again over the following decade to reach 17.3 million in 1807. By then it was worth more than a quarter of all Portugal's colonial re-export. Blackburn, *Making of New World Slavery*, pp. 491–2.

85 James Lang, *Portuguese Brazil: the King's Plantation* (New York: Academic Press, 1979), p. 185.

86 José Jobson de Andrade Arruda, 'Brazilian Raw Cotton as a Strategic Factor in Global Textile Manufacturing During the Industrial Revolution', unpublished

paper presented at the Helsinki World History Congress, August 2006, 1–2. In 1821–3 cotton accounted for a quarter of the country's export, exceeding even the export of sugar. Over the following two decades cotton cultivation expanded thanks to the influx of 370,000 slaves (1840–51). Maddison, *World Economy*, pp. 76–7.

87 See also Eltis, *Economic Growth*, pp. 194–5.

88 Fogel, *Without Consent*, p. 64.

89 Fogel and Engerman, *Time on the Cross*, pp. 166–7.

90 North, *Economic Growth of the United States*, pp. 128–9.

91 Olmstead and Rhode, 'Biological Innovation and Productivity Growth', 3.

92 Cited in Fogel, *Without Consent*, pp. 26–7.

93 Slaves worked on average 281 days a year, well below the potential maximum. Fogel, *Without Consent*, pp. 28 and 77. See also Jacob Metzer, 'Rational Management, Modern Business Practices, and Economies of Scale in the Ante-bellum Southern Plantations', *Explorations in Economic History* 12/2 (1975): 123–50.

94 Olmstead and Rhode, 'Biological Innovation and Productivity Growth', 6–14.

95 North, *Economic Growth*, pp. 126–7.

96 Fogel, *Without Consent*, pp. 65–6.

97 C. Knick Harley, 'Ocean Freight Rates and Productivity, 1740–1913: the Primacy of Mechanical Invention Reaffirmed', *JEH* 48/4 (1988): 857.

98 Stanley D. Chapman, 'Cottons and Printed Textiles', in *Textiles in Trade* (Washington, DC: Proceedings of the Textile Society of America Biennial Symposium, 1990), p. 34; Peter Maw, 'Yorkshire and Lancashire Ascendant: England's Textile Exports to New York and Philadelphia, 1750–1805', *EHR* 63/3 (2010): 734–68.

99 Sven Beckert, 'Emancipation and Empire: Reconstructing the Worldwide Web of Cotton Production in the Age of the American Civil War', *AHR* 109/5 (2005), online, paragraph 7. See also Brian Schoen, *The Fragile Fabric of Union: Cotton, Federal Politics, and the Global Origins of the Civil War* (Baltimore, Md.: Johns Hopkins University Press, 2009), pp. 45–7.

100 Hugill, *World Trade*, p. 82; David G. Surdam, 'Cotton', in Joel Mokyr, ed., *The Oxford Encyclopedia of Economic History* (Oxford University Press, 2003), vol. II, p. 19.

101 William O. Henderson, *The Lancashire Cotton Famine, 1861–1865* (New York: A. M. Kelley, 1969), p. 26.

102 George Frederick Young, *Free-Trade and the Navigations Laws Practically Considered* (London: P. Richardson, 1849), p. 5. A similar point was supported by Manchester manufacturers. See John Taylor, *Money and Morals: a Book for the Times* (London: J. Chapman 1852), p. 185.

103 Henderson, *Lancashire Cotton Famine*, pp. 41–3. Egypt emerged as an important supplier of raw cotton only in the second half of the nineteenth century and in response to the productive crisis caused by the American Civil War. Long-staple cotton was introduced in Egypt only after 1820, and became a major item of export over the decade. Roger Owen, *The Middle East in the World Economy, 1800–1914: a Study of Trade and Development* (Oxford: Clarendon Press, 1993), p. 69. See also Roger Owen, *Cotton and the Egyptian Economy, 1820–1914: a Study in Trade and Development* (Oxford: Clarendon Press, 1969).

104 Tench Coxe, *A Memoir, of February, 1817, Upon the Subject of the Cotton Wool Cultivation, the Cotton Trade, and the Cotton Manufactories of the United States of America* (Philadelphia, 1817).

105 Coxe, *Memoir*, pp. 3–7.

106 William Sandford, *On Cotton Growing in Turkey and Syria* (London, 1862), p. 15; Russell, *Evolutionary History*, p. 119.

107 BL, IOR/H/374: 'Extract from Dr Hove's Journal 1787' and Pantaleon Hove, *Tours for Scientific and Economical Research made in Guzerat, Kattiawar, and the Conkuns, in 1787–88* (Bombay: Bombay Education Society's Press, 1855), p. 37.

108 *Observations on the Advantages which this Country Derives from a Free and Unfettered Importation of the Raw Material of Cotton Wool* (London, 1789), p. 2.

109 Tirthankar Roy, *India in the World Economy: from Antiquity to the Present* (Cambridge University Press, 2012), p. 136.

110 The import of Indian cotton into China tripled over the period 1780–85 and tripled again between 1795 and 1815. Robert Marks, *Tigers, Rice, Silk, and Silt: Environment and Economy in Late Imperial South China* (Cambridge University Press, 2006), pp. 178–9. See also Alain Le Pichon, *China Trade and Empire: Jardine, Matheson & Co. and the Origins of British Rule in Hong Kong, 1827–1843* (British Library and Oxford University Press, 2006), p. 11; H. V. Bowen, 'British Exports of Raw Cotton from India to China during the Late Eighteenth and Early Nineteenth Centuries', in Riello and Roy, eds., *How India Clothed the World*, pp. 115–37.

111 Satpal Sangwan, *Science, Technology and Colonisation: an Indian Experience, 1757–1857* (New Delhi: Anamika Prakashan, 1991), pp. 101–2.

112 A. B. Cunningham, 'The Journal of Christophe Aubin: a Report on the Levant Trade in 1812', *Archivum Ottomanicum* 8 (1983): 67.

113 Roy, *India in the World Economy*, pp. 136–7.

114 Select Committee on the Petition of the East India Company for Relief, Parliamentary Papers, 1840, vol. 7, Q 191. Cited K. N. Chaudhuri, ed., *The Economic Development of India under the East India Company 1814–58: a Selection of Contemporary Writings* (Cambridge University Press, 1971), p. 27.

115 Ibid., p. 26.

116 Pieter C. Emmer, *The Dutch in the Atlantic Economy, 1580–1880: Trade, Slavery and Emancipation* (Aldershot: Ashgate, 1998), p. 262.

117 TNA, PRO 30/12/31/12: 'Papers and Letters regarding Cotton Cultivation, 1842'; and PRO 30/12/30/18: 'Press Cuttings etc. Relating to the Experiment with Growing American Cotton in India, 1842'.

118 Sandford, *On Cotton Growing*, p. 9; Deschamps, *Coton, études élémentaires sur la plantation*, pp. 70 and 75.

119 Arthur W. Silver, *Manchester Men and Indian Cotton, 1847–1872* (Manchester University Press, 1966), especially pp. 201–24; Henderson, *Lancashire Cotton Famine*, pp. 35–8.

120 Peter Harnetty, *Imperialism and Free Trade: Lancashire and India in the Mid-Nineteenth Century* (Vancouver: University of British Columbia Press, 1972), especially pp. 36–58. See also the case of Western India: Sandip Hazareesingh, 'Cotton, Climate and Colonialism in Dharwar, Western India, 1840–1880', *Journal of Historical Geography* 38/1 (2012): 1–17.

121 Cited in Ratcliffe, 'Cotton Imperialism', p. 91.
122 Henderson, *Lancashire Cotton Famine*, p. 40.

12 Global outcomes: the West and the new cotton system

1 Some figures might explain the scale of this phenomenon. In *c.* 1760 colonial empires accounted for 18 per cent of the earth's surface and 3 per cent of the world population. In 1913 they had grown to 39 per cent of the surface and 31 per cent of the population. Meanwhile, the gap between industrial and third world countries had increased from a benchmark of 1 in the 1750s to 2.5 in 1880, 3.4 in 1913 and 5.1 in 1950. Bouda Etemad, *Possessing the World: Taking the Measurements of Colonisation from the Eighteenth to the Twentieth Century* (New York: Berghahn Books, 2007), pp. 3 and 6.

2 Alice Amsden, *The Rise of 'The Rest': Challenges to the West from Late-Industrializing Economies* (Oxford University Press, 2001), especially part 1.

3 Bhaswati Bhattacharya, 'Making Money at the Blessed Place of Manila: Armenians in the Madras–Manila Trade in the Eighteenth Century', *JGH* 3/3 (2008): 13 and 19.

4 Peter M. Solar, 'The Triumph of Cotton', unpublished paper, January 2012, 2–3. I thank Peter Solar for providing me with a copy of this paper.

5 Peter J. Huggill, 'Structural Changes in the Core Regions of the World-Economy, 1830–1945', *Journal of Historical Geography* 14/2 (1988): 111–27.

6 Christopher A. Bayly, 'South Asia and the "Great Divergence"', *Itinerario* 24/3–4 (2000): 99.

7 Bairoch, *Economics and World History*, pp. 68–9.

8 In 2010 China produced 29.5 million bales of raw cotton, follow by India (25), the United States (18.1), Brazil (9.0), Pakistan (8.7), Uzbekistan (4.6), Australia (4.5), Turkey (2.1), Turkmenistan (1.5) and Argentina (1.2). *National Cotton Council of America Report* (www.cotton.org/econ/cropinfo/cropdata/rankings.cfm).

9 Bairoch, *Economics and World History*, p. 70.

10 Paul Bairoch, *Commerce extérieur et développement économique de L'Europe au XIXe siècle* (Paris: Mouton, 1976), p. 83. See also Etemad, *Possessing the World*, chs. 8–11.

11 Douglas A. Farnie, 'Cotton Industry', in Mokyr, ed., *Oxford Encyclopedia of Economic History*, vol. II, p. 21.

12 Esteban, 'Comparative Patterns of Colonial Trade', pp. 36–7.

13 Ibid., pp. 50–1. Peter Hill underlines how this was a missed opportunity caused by the failure of the French to provide goods that suited American taste in terms of size, shape and colour. Peter P. Hill, *French Perceptions of the Early American Republic, 1783–1793* (Philadelphia: American Philosophical Society, 1988), p. 60.

14 On the economic consequences, see Patrick K. O'Brien, 'Inseparable Connections: Economy, Fiscal State, and the Expansion of Empire, 1688–1815', in Peter J. Marshall, ed., *The Oxford History of the British Empire*, vol. II, *The Eighteenth Century* (Oxford University Press, 1998), pp. 53–77.

15 ANF, F^{12} 534: 'A sa majesté Napoléon, Empereur des Français et Roi d'Italie', Bordeaux 6 July 1807.

16 Norton, *Norton & Sons, merchants*, pp. 22, 72, 103, 125, 150, 190, 218.

17 Chapman, 'Cottons and Printed Textiles', pp. 35–6.
18 Bauer, *Goods, Power, History*, p. 130. In the case of Peru, cotton textiles accounted for 95 per cent of all its imports in the first decade of independence of the country.
19 Vicente, *Clothing the Spanish Empire*, especially ch. 4.
20 Patrick K. O'Brien and Stanley L. Engerman, 'Exports and the Growth of the British Economy from the Glorious Revolution to the Peace of Amiens', in Solow, ed., *Slavery and the Rise of the Atlantic System*, p. 184; Freeman and Louçã, *As Time Goes By*, p. 155; Ralph Davis, 'The English Export Trade: Textiles from 1784 to 1856', in Stanley D. Chapman, ed., *The Textile Industries*, vol. II, *Cotton, Linen, Wool and Worsted* (London and New York: I. B. Tauris, 1997), p. 235.
21 Crafts, *British Economic Growth*, p. 143.
22 Bairoch, *Commerce extérieur*, p. 94.
23 Broadberry and Gupta, 'Lancashire, India', 279–305.
24 Beckert, 'Cotton: a Global History', p. 55.
25 Maria Graham, *Journal of a Residence in India* (Edinburgh, 1813), p. 33. Cited in Medha M. Kudaisya, ed., *The Oxford India Anthology of Business History* (Oxford University Press, 2011), p. 50. Graham incorrectly thought that British chintzes were produced by using Indian raw cotton
26 Sudhir and Swarnalatha, 'Textile Traders', 167.
27 Prasannan Parthasarathi, 'Historical Issues of Deindustrialization in Nineteenth-Century South India', in Riello and Roy, eds., *How India Clothed the World*, p. 423.
28 Bairoch, *Economics and World History*, p. 54.
29 Giorgio Borsa, *La Nascita del mondo moderno in Asia Orientale. La penetrazione europea e la crisi delle società tradizionali in India, Cina e Giappone* (Milan: Rizzoli, 1996), pp. 133–4.
30 Banat and Ferguene, 'Production et le commerce du textile', 11.
31 Alfred C. Wood, *A History of the Levant Company* (London: Frank Cass, 1965), p. 193.
32 Cited in İnalcık, 'When and How British Cotton Goods Invaded', p. 380.
33 Quataert, *Ottoman Manufacturing*, p. 23.
34 Kaoru Sugihara, 'The Resurgence of Intra-Asian Trade, 1800–1850', in Riello and Roy, eds., *How India Clothed the World*, in particular Singapore's trade, p. 162.
35 Douglas A. Farnie, 'The Role of the Cotton Industry in Economic Development', in Farnie and Jeremy, eds., *Fibre that Changed the World*, pp. 557–66.
36 O'Brien and Engerman, 'Exports', p. 191.
37 Cited in Parthasarathi, 'Historical Issues', p. 429.
38 For an overview of the different positions, see Parthasarathi and Wendt, 'Decline in Three Keys', pp. 397–407.
39 Subrahmanyam, 'Rural Industry', especially 107–8.
40 Jon E. Wilson, 'Early Colonial India Beyond Empire', *Historical Journal* 50/4 (2007): especially pp. 954–5.
41 Rila Mukherjee, 'The Last Commercial Frontier: French and English Presence in South Eastern Bengal and Beyond', *Indian Historical Review* 34/1 (2007): 169. See also Subramanian, 'Power and the Weave', pp. 52–82; Subramanian, 'Political Economy of Textiles in Western India', pp. 253–80; Prakash, 'From Market-Determined to Coercion-Based', pp. 217–52.

42 Parthasarathi and Wendt, 'Decline in Three Keys'.

43 Roger Owen, 'Introduction', in Thomas Naff and Roger Owen, eds., *Studies in 18th-Century Islamic History* (London and Amsterdam: Ferrer & Simons, 1977), p. 150; Onur Yildirim, 'Ottoman Guilds in the Early Modern Era', *International Review of Social History* 53/supplement (2008): 86.

44 Şevket Pamuk and Jeffrey G. Williamson, 'Ottoman De-industrialization, 1800–1913: Assessing the Magnitude, Impact, and Response', *EHR* 64/supplement 1 (2011): 164–7 and Şevket Pamuk, 'Evolution of Monetary and Fiscal Institutions Across the Ottoman Empire, 1500–1800', GEHN Conference 7: Imperialism and Colonialism, Istanbul, 11–12 September 2005 (www2.lse.ac.uk/economicHistory/Research/GEHN/Conferences/conference7.aspx).

45 Karl Marx, *Capital* (London: J. M. Dent, 1974), ch. 15, sec. 5.

46 Cited in K. A. Arora, 'Colonialism and the Decline of the Cotton Industry in 19th Century India', *Papers of the University of Greenwich Business School* 17 (1992): 19.

47 Clingingsmith and Williamson, for instance, argue for a two-period decline for South Asia, first caused by the decline of the Mughal state and then after 1810 by the competition of western cotton textiles. David Clingingsmith and Jeffrey G. Williamson, 'India's De-industrialization under British Rule: New Ideas, New Evidence', *CEPR Discussion Paper* 5066 (2005) (www.cepr.org.ezproxy.eui.eu/pubs/dps/DP5066.asp). See also Riello and Roy, 'Introduction: the World of South Asian Textiles, 1500–1800', pp. 16–17.

48 Britain enjoyed only a short 'free trade spell' between 1882 and 1894, when preferential duties for the mother country were repealed. K. N. Chaudhuri, 'Foreign Trade and Balance of Payments (1757–1947)', in Dharma Kumar and Meghnad Desai, eds., *The Cambridge Economic History of India*, vol. II, *1757–1970* (Cambridge University Press, 1983), pp. 865–8.

49 *A Gazetteer of Southern India with the Tenasserim Provinces and Singapore* (Madras: Pharoah & Co., 1855), pp. 22 and 285. Cited in Parthasarathi, 'Historical Issues', p. 427.

50 L. C. A. Knowles, *The Economic Development of the British Overseas Empire*, 2nd edn (London: George Routledge, 1928), p. 308.

51 Tirthankar Roy, 'Out of Tradition: Master Artisans and Economic Change in Colonial India', *JAS* 66/4 (2007): 963. See also Tirthankar Roy, *Rethinking Economic Change in India: Labour and Livelihood* (London: Routledge, 2005), and Tirthankar Roy, 'The Long Globalisation and Textile Producers in India', in van Voss, Hiemstra-Kuperus and van Nederveen Meerkerk, eds., *History of Textile Workers*, pp. 253–74.

52 Roy, 'Out of Tradition', 964.

53 See in particular Gregory Clark, 'Why isn't the Whole World Developed? Lessons from the Cotton Mills', *JEH* 47/1 (1987): 141–73.

54 Bairoch, *Economics and World History*, p. 54; Amsden, *Rise of 'The Rest'*, p. 34.

55 We do not however have good estimates for China's cotton output. The Chinese cotton sector might have been as large as the Indian one.

56 The table also reveals the very different number of weavers employed in non-mechanised Asian economies and in mechanised European factories. In the 1840s, for every weaver employed in a British mill, fifteen Indian weavers were necessary

to produce the same length of cloth. Overall this is in line with recent calculations by Broadberry and Gupta, although their recent estimates of domestic Indian cotton production are higher than those provided here in table 11.1. See Stephen Broadberry and Bishnupriya Gupta, 'Indian GDP Before 1870: Some Preliminary Estimates and a Comparison with Britain', *CEPR Discussion Paper Series 8007* (2010), table 5 p. 21.

57 Parthasarathi, *Why Europe Grew Rich*, pp. 118–19; Suraiya Faroqhi, *Towns and Townsmen of Ottoman Anatolia. Trade, Crafts and Food Production in an Urban Setting, 1520–1650* (Cambridge University Press, 1984), p. 129.

58 André Raymond, 'The Sources of Urban Wealth in 18th-Century Cairo', in Naff and Owen, eds., *Studies in 18th-Century Islamic History*, p. 193.

59 Şevket Pamuk, *The Ottoman Empire and European Capitalism, 1820–1913* (Cambridge University Press, 1987), p. 119; Şevket Pamuk, 'The Decline and Resistance of Ottoman Cotton Textiles, 1820–1913', *Explorations in Economic History* 23/2 (1986): 206. See also Issawi, 'Decline of Middle Eastern Trade', p. 256.

60 Halil İnalcık, 'When and How British Cotton Goods Invaded the Levant Markets', in Islamoğlu-Inan, ed., *Ottoman Empire*, p. 375.

61 Pamuk and Williamson, 'Ottoman De-industrialization', p. 169.

62 Quataert, *Ottoman Manufacturing*, p. 28.

63 Jeremy Prestholdt, *Domesticating the World: African Consumerism and the Genealogies of Globalization* (Berkeley: University of California Press, 2008), pp. 67 and 80.

64 Sonia Ashmore, 'Colour and Corruption: Issues in the Nineteenth-Century Anglo-Indian Textile Trade', unpublished paper, AHRC Diasporas Migrations and Identities Programme, 7–8.

65 John Forbes Watson created *The Collection of the Textile Manufactures of India* (1866), a collection of Indian textile samples in eighteen volumes that were produced in thirteen sets to be distributed in Britain with the purpose of improving industrial design. Felix Driver and Sonia Ashmore, 'The Mobile Museum: Collecting and Circulating Indian Textiles in Victorian Britain', *Victorian Studies* 52/3 (2010): 353–85.

66 Christopher A. Bayly, 'The Origins of Swadeshi (Home Industry): Cloth and Indian Society, 1700–1930', in Arajun Appadurai, ed., *The Social Life of Things: Commodities in Cultural Perspective* (Cambridge University Press, 1986), pp. 285–321. See also Victor Margolin, 'Where in the World of Design? The Case of India, 1900–1945', in Adamson, Riello and Teasley, eds., *Global Design History*, pp. 110–18.

67 Maxwell, *Textiles of Southeast Asia*, pp. 367 and 369.

68 Cited in Herbert Heaton, 'A Merchant Adventurer in Brazil', *JEH* 6/1 (1946): 13.

69 A. B. Cunningham, 'The Journal of Christophe Aubin: a Report on the Levant Trade in 1812', *Archivum Ottomanicum* 8 (1983): 70–1.

70 Ibid., 67.

71 I refer here to a forthcoming article by Kayoko Fujita that explores the shift of Japanese textile aesthetics from Indian to British motifs in the early part of the nineteenth century. The similarity of patterns in different markets is however

difficult to connect to precise strategies. Chapter 2 started with two identical pieces of cloth produced by Gujarati printers and traded to markets in Egypt and Southeast Asia.

72 Cited in Willem Floor, *Textile Import into Qajar Iran: Russia Versus Great Britain. The Battle for Market Domination* (Costa Mesa, Calif.: Mazda Publishers, 2009), p. 20.

73 Cited in Michael Greenberg, *British Trade and the Opening of China, 1800–42* (New York and London: Monthly Review Press, 1951), pp. 99–100.

74 Ibid., p. 101.

75 There was also a worldwide shift from buying whole apparels from the weaver or cloth producer to buying pieces of fabric produced in factories and having garments tailored at home (through the use of sewing machines after 1850) or in neighbourhood shops. This had devastating for traditional cloth producers, as in the case of India. I thank Tirthankar Roy for discussing this point with me.

76 Floor, *Textile Import into Qajar*, p. 19.

77 Maxwell, *Textiles of Southeast Asia*, p. 366.

78 Wilburn Zelinsky, 'Globalization Reconsidered: the Historical Geography of Modern Western Male Attire', *Journal of Cultural Geography* 22/1 (2004): 83–134; Robert Ross, *Clothing: a Global History, or, the Imperialists' New Clothes* (Cambridge: Polity, 2009).

79 Susan S. Bean, 'Bandana: on the Indian Origins of an All-American Textile', in Peter Benes, ed., *Textiles in Early New England: Design, Production, and Consumption* (Boston University Press, 1997), pp. 180–1.

80 Parthasarathi and Wendt, 'Decline in Three Keys', p. 406.

81 Heita Kawakatsu, 'International Competition in Cotton Goods in the Late Nineteenth Century: Britain Versus India and East Asia', in Wolfram Fischer, R. Marvin McInnis and Jürgen Schneider, eds., *The Emergence of a World Economy 1500–1914: Papers of the IX International Congress of Economic History* (Nuremberg: Anschrift der Schriftleitung, 1986), p. 630.

82 The count refers to the number of hanks (1 hank being equal to 840 yards) contained in a pound of cotton yarn. The higher the count, the finer the yarn. Kawakatsu, 'International Competition', pp. 623–5.

83 For an overview of the debate, see Vries, 'Limits of Globalization in the Early Modern World', 710–33. See also Kevin H. O'Rourke and Jeffrey G. Williamson, *Globalization and History: the Evolution of a Nineteenth-Century Atlantic Economy* (Cambridge, Mass.: MIT Press, 1999).

84 See the Commodity of Empire Project (www.open.ac.uk/Arts/ferguson-centre/commodities-of-empire/index.shtml) and the special issues on 'Commodities of Empire' *JGH* 4/1 (2009).

85 Martin Daunton, 'Presidential Address. Britain and Globalisation since 1850: 1. Creating a Global Order, 1850–1914', *Transactions of the Royal Historical Society* 16 (2006): especially pp. 1–3. Between 1820 and 1914 the level of trade on world GDP passed from 2 to 18 per cent. This 1914 peak was reached again only in the 1970s with the start of the present-day phase of contemporary globalisation. David Dollar, 'Globalization, Poverty, and Inequality', in Michael M. Weinstein, ed., *Globalization: What's New?* (New York: Columbia University Press, 2005), pp. 98–9.

86 Liverpool cotton prices were 57 per cent higher than in Bombay in 1870 and were only 20 per cent higher in 1913. Similarly Liverpool cotton prices were 41 per cent higher than in Alessandria in the 1860s, but just 5 per cent higher at the end of the century. Guillaume Daudin, Matthias Morys and Kevin H. O'Rourke, 'Europe and Globalization, 1870–1914', *OFCE Document de Travail* 17 (2008): 2 (www.ofce.sciences-po.fr/pdf/dtravail/WP2008-17.pdf).

87 O'Rourke and Williamson, 'When did Globalisation Begin?', 36–7.

88 Farnie, 'Role of the Cotton Industry', p. 573.

89 Piero Bairati, 'The Transfer of Technology from Europe to the United States, 1775–1820', in *La Révolution Américaine et l'Europe* (Paris: Éditions du CNRS, 1979), pp. 424–7. Among the most active societies were the Pennsylvania Society for the Encouragement of Useful Manufactures (1787) and the United Company of Philadelphia for Promoting American Manufactures (1775). The former acquired in the late 1780s an Arkwright carding machine together with two jennies and a fly-shuttle loom. On technological diffusion, see David J. Jeremy, *Transatlantic Industrial Revolution: the Diffusion of Textile Technologies Between Britain and America, 1790–1830s* (Cambridge, Mass.: MIT Press, 1981).

90 Joshua L. Rosenbloom, 'Path Dependence and the Origins of Cotton Textile Manufacturing in New England', in Farnie and Jeremy, eds., *Fibre that Changed the World*, pp. 365–91.

91 Stuart Thompstone, 'Ludwig Knoop, "The Arkwright of Russia"', *TH* 15/1 (1984): 46–7.

92 Bairati, 'Transfer of Technology', p. 427.

93 The number of power looms might however be a misleading indicator of industrial development as India relied on a different 'industrial system' in which yarn was produced in mills but was then largely woven and finished by handlooms. A graph chartering the British share of world factory spindles for the period 1770 to 1920 is presented in Beckert, 'Emancipation and Empire', table 3.

94 I should make it clear here that I do not support the old-fashioned view that economic development around the world followed a British model. My point is that some key aspects of it (as for instance mechanisation, use of capital, sale on international markets) became established criteria in the process of economic development around the world. The model to follow was that of industrial capitalism, rather than the specific experience of any individual country.

95 Jeremy, *Transatlantic Industrial Revolution*, ch. 13.

96 Sugihara, 'Second Noel Butlin Lecture', 121–54; Kaoru Sugihara, 'The East Asian Path of Economic Development: a Long-Term Perspective', in Giovanni Arrighi, Takeshi Hamashita and Mark Selden, eds., *The Resurgence of East Asia: 500, 150 and 50 Year Perspectives* (London: Routledge: 2003), pp. 78–123.

97 David J. Jeremy, 'The International Diffusion of Cotton Manufacturing Technology, 1750–1990s', in Farnie and Jeremy, eds., *Fibre that Changed the World*, especially pp. 125–7. The argument proposed by Clark in his famous 1987 article is that the efficiency of labour employed in the mills of most non-western countries was so low that it more than compensated for the advantage that they had in terms of low wages. Yet his controversial conclusion is that the causes were to be found not in 'skill', 'aptitude' or 'dexterity' of individual workers, but in the wider context of labour relations, cultural expectations and established norms. Clark, 'Why isn't the Whole World Developed?'

98 Jan Bazant, 'Evolution of the Textile Industry of Puebla, 1544–1845', in Michael Adas, ed., *Technology and European Overseas Enterprise* (Aldershot: Variorum, 1996), pp. 262–76; Frank T. Proctor III, 'Afro-Mexican Slave Labor in the Obrajes de Paños of New Spain, Seventeenth and Eighteenth Centuries', *The Americas* 60/1 (2003): 36–7.

99 Margaret A. Villanueva, 'From Calpixqui to Corregidor: Appropriation of Women's Cotton Textile Production in Early Colonial Spain', *Latin America Perspectives* 12/1 (1985): 17–40.

100 Pohl, 'Algunas consideraciones', 464–7. See also Richard J. Salvucci, *Textiles and Capitalism in Mexico: an Economic History of the 'Obrajes', 1539–1840* (Princeton University Press, 1987), pp. 47–52; and Bauer, *Goods, Power, History*, p. 108.

101 Novais, 'Proibição das manufaturas no Brasil', 147–8 and 164.

102 Ibid., 164.

103 Greenberg, *British Trade and the Opening of China*, p. 81.

104 Xu Xinwu and Byung-Kun Min, 'The Struggle of the Handicraft Cotton Industry Against Machine Textiles in China', *Modern China* 14/1 (1988): 31–49.

105 For instance with the adoption of an improved hand-pulled loom introduced from Japan and the later foot-pedalled, iron-gear loom to produce what was called 'improved native cloth'. Ibid., 44.

13 Conclusion: from system to system; from divergence to convergence

1 On US trade in Asia see James R. Fichter, *So Great a Proffit: How the East Indies Trade Transformed Anglo-American Capitalism* (Cambridge, Mass.: Harvard University Press, 2010).

2 Bean, 'Bandana', pp. 169 and 180.

3 Elvin, 'High-Level Equilibrium Trap', p. 152.

4 Ferguson, *Civilization: the West and the Rest*.

5 See for instance Beckert, 'Cotton: a Global History', pp. 48–63.

6 Bayly, 'South Asia and the "Great Divergence"', 89.

7 So far, however, historians have contributed little to the discussion over convergence. A rare exception is Kenneth L. Sokoloff and Stanley L. Engerman, 'Institutions, Factor Endowments, and Paths of Development in the New World', *Journal of Economic Perspectives* 14/3 (2000): 217–32.

8 Farnie, 'Cotton Industry', pp. 22–3.

9 Farnie, 'Role of Merchants as Prime Movers', pp. 578–9.

10 Farnie, 'Cotton Industry', p. 23.

11 Sonali Jain-Chandra and Ananthakrishnan Prasad, 'Realizing the Potential: the Case of India's Textile Sector', in Catriona Purfield and Jerald Schiff, eds., *India Goes Global: its Expanding Role in the World Economy* (Washington, DC: International Monetary Fund, 2006), pp. 180–1.

12 Minqi Li, *The Rise of China and the Demise of the Capitalist World-Economy* (London: Pluto Press, 2008), pp. 120–7.

13 Rhys Jenkins, 'China's Global Growth and Latin American Exports', in Amela U. Santos-Paulino and Ghuaghua Wan, eds., *The Rise of China and India: Impacts, Prospects and Implications* (Basingstoke: Palgrave Macmillan, 2010), p. 220.

14 Peter Sheehan, 'Beyond Industrialization: New Approaches to Development Strategy Based on the Service Sector', in Amela U. Santos-Paulino and Ghuaghua Wan, eds., *The Rise of China and India: Impacts, Prospects and Implications* (Basingstoke: Palgrave Macmillan, 2010), p. 72.

15 *A New World Map in Textiles and Clothing: Adjusting to Change* (OECD Publishing, 2004), pp. 1–10.

SELECT BIBLIOGRAPHY

Abu-Lughod, Janet L., *Before European Hegemony: the World System, AD 1250–1350* (Oxford University Press, 1989).

Aiolfi, Sergio, *Calicos und gedrucktes Zeug: die Entwicklung der englischen Textilveredelung und der Tuchhandel der East India Company, 1650–1750* (Stuttgart: Steiner, 1987).

Alam, Ishrat, 'Cotton Technology in India Down to the Sixteenth Century', in A. Rahman, ed., *India's Interaction with China, Central and West Asia,* volume III, part 2 (Oxford University Press, 2002), pp. 445–63.

Allen, Robert C., 'Britain's Economic Ascendancy in a European Context', in Leandro Prados de la Escosura, ed., *Exceptionalism and Industrialisation: Britain and its European Rivals, 1688–1815* (Cambridge University Press, 2004), pp. 15–34.

    The British Industrial Revolution in Global Perspective (Cambridge University Press, 2009).

    'The Great Divergence in European Wages and Prices from the Middle Ages to the First World War', *Explorations in Economic History* 38/4 (2001): 411–47.

    'India in the Great Divergence', in Timothy J. Hatton, Kevin H. O'Rourke and Alan M. Taylor, eds., *The New Comparative Economic History: Essay in Honour of Jeffrey G. Williamson* (Cambridge, Mass.: MIT Press, 2007), pp. 9–32.

Amsden, Alice, *The Rise of 'The Rest': Challenges to the West from Late-Industrializing Economies* (Oxford University Press, 2001).

Arasaratnam, Sinnappah, *Merchants, Companies and Commerce on the Coromandel Coast, 1650–1740* (Oxford University Press, 1986).

    'Weavers, Merchants and Company: the Handloom Industry in Southeastern India 1750–1790', *Indian Economic and Social History Review* 17/3 (1980): 257–81.

Ashtor, Eliyahu, 'The Venetian Cotton Trade in the Later Middle Ages', *Studi Medievali* 17/3 (1976): 675–715.

Bag, A. K., 'Technology in India in the Eighteenth–Nineteenth Century', *Journal of Indian Textile History* 17/1 (1982): 82–90.

Bairoch, Paul, *Commerce extérieur et développement économique de l'Europe au XIXe siècle* (Paris: Mouton, 1976).

    Economics and World History: Myths and Paradoxes (Hemel Hempstead: Harvester Wheatsheaf, 1993).

Baker, George Percival, *Calico Printing and Painting in the East Indies in the XVIIth and XVIIIth Centuries* (London: Edward Arnold, 1921).

'Indian Cotton Prints and Paintings of the 17th and 18th Centuries', *Transactions of the Newcomen Society* 3 (1922/3): 52–6.

Baker, Patricia L., *Islamic Textiles* (London: British Museum, 1995).

Bala, Arun, *The Dialogue of Civilizations in the Birth of Modern Science* (New York: Palgrave Macmillan, 2006).

Balfour-Paul, Jenny, *Indigo* (London: British Museum, 1998).

'Indigo in South and South-East Asia', *Textile History* 30/1 (1999): 98–112.

Bally, W., 'The Cotton Plant', *Ciba Review* 95 (1952): 3402–7.

Barendse, R. J., *Arabian Seas 1700–1763*, volume III, *Men and Merchandise* (Leiden: E. J. Brill, 2009).

Barnes, Ruth, *Indian Block-Printed Textiles in Egypt. The Newberry Collection in the Ashmolean Museum, Oxford* (Oxford: Clarendon Press, 1997).

Barnes, Ruth, ed., *Textiles in Indian Ocean Societies* (London and New York: Routledge Curzon, 2005).

Bayly, C. A., '"Archaic" and "Modern" Globalisation in the Eurasian and African Arena, *c.* 1750–1850', in A. G. Hopkins, ed., *Globalization in World History* (London: Palgrave, 2002), pp. 45–72.

The Birth of the Modern World, 1780–1914 (Oxford: Blackwell, 2004).

'South Asia and the "Great Divergence"', *Itinerario* 24/3–4 (2000): 89–101.

Bean, Susan S., 'The American Market for Indian Textiles, 1785–1820: in the Twilight of Traditional Cloth Manufacture', in *Textiles in Trade* (Washington, DC: Proceedings of the Textile Society of America, Biennial Symposium, 1990), pp. 43–52.

'Bandana: On the Indian Origins of All-American Textile', in Peter Benes, ed., *Textiles in Early New England: Design, Production, and Consumption* (Boston University Press, 1997), pp. 168–83.

Beckert, Sven, 'Cotton: a Global History', in Jerry Bentley, Renate Bridenthal and Anand A. Yang, eds., *Interactions: Transregional Perspectives on World History* (Honolulu: University of Hawaii Press, 2005), pp. 48–63.

'Emancipation and Empire: Reconstructing the Worldwide Web of Cotton Production in the Age of the American Civil War', *American Historical Review* 109/5 (2005): 1405–38.

Belich, James, *Replenishing the Earth: the Settler Revolution and the Rise of the Anglo-World, 1783–1939* (Oxford University Press, 2009).

Bellezza, Rosina Margherita, 'Tra oriente e occidente', in Marzia Cataldi Gallo, ed., *I Mezzari: tra Oriente e Occidente* (Genoa: Sagep Editrice, 1988), pp. 15–24.

Berg, Maxine, 'The Genesis of "Useful Knowledge"', *History of Science* 45 (2007): 123–33.

'In Pursuit of Luxury: Global History and British Consumer Goods in the Eighteenth Century', *Past & Present* 132 (2004): 85–142.

Luxury and Pleasure in Eighteenth-Century Britain (Oxford University Press, 2005).

'Manufacturing the Orient: Asian Commodities and European Industry 1500–1800', in Simonetta Cavaciocchi, ed., *Prodotti e tecniche d'oltremare nelle economie europee. Secc. XIII–XVIII. Atti della Ventinovesima Settimana di Studi, 14–19 aprile 1997* (Florence: Le Monnier, 1998), pp. 385–419.

'Quality, Cotton and the Global Luxury Trade', in Riello and Roy, eds., *How India Clothed the World*, pp. 391–414.

Berg, Maxine, and Pat Hudson, 'Growth and Change: a Comment on the Crafts-Harley View of the Industrial Revolution', *Economic History Review* 47/1 (1994): 147–9.

'Rehabilitating the Industrial Revolution', *Economic History Review* 45/1 (1992): 24–50.

Bhardwaj, H. C., and Kamal K. Jain, 'Indian Dyes and the Dyeing Industry During the 18th–19th Centuries', *Indian Journal of History of Science* 17/1 (1982): 70–81.

Bier, Carol, 'Textile and Society', in C. Bier, ed., *Woven from the Soul*, 1987), pp. 1–6.

Bier, Carol, ed., *Woven from the Soul, Spun from the Heart: Textile Arts of Safavit and Qajar Iran 16th–19th Centuries* (Washington, DC: Textile Museum, 1987).

Bigwood, George, *Cotton* (London: Constable & Co., 1918).

Blackburn, Robin, *The Making of New World Slavery: from the Baroque to the Modern, 1492–1800* (London: Verso, 1997).

Borlandi, F., 'Fustaniers et fustaines dans l'Italie du moyen age', in *Éventail de l'histoire vivante: hommage a Lucien Lebvre*, volume II (Paris: Colin, 1953), pp. 133–40.

Borsa, Giorgio, *La Nascita del mondo moderno in Asia orientale. La penetrazione europea e la crisi delle società tradizionali in India, Cina e Giappone* (Milan: Rizzoli, 1996).

Bowen, H. V., 'British Exports of Raw Cotton from India to China During the Late Eighteenth and Early Nineteenth Centuries', in Riello and Roy, eds., *How India Clothed the World*, pp. 115–37.

The Business of Empire: the East India Company and Imperial Britain, 1756–1833 (Cambridge University Press, 2006).

Boyajian, James C., *Portuguese Trade in Asia under the Habsburgs, 1580–1640* (Baltimore, Md.: Johns Hopkins University Press, 1993).

Bray, Francesca, *Technology and Gender: Fabrics and Power in Late Imperial China* (Berkeley: University of California Press, 1997).

'Textile Production and Gender Roles in China, 1000–1700', *Chinese Science* 12 (1995): 115–37.

Brennig, Joseph Jerome, 'Chief Merchants and European Enclaves of 17th-Century Coromandel', *Modern Asian Studies* 11/3 (1977): 321–46.

Broadberry, Stephen, and Bishnupriya Gupta, 'The Early Modern Great Divergence: Wages, Prices and Economic Development in Europe and Asia, 1500–1800', *Economic History Review* 59/1 (2006): 2–31.

'Lancashire, India, and Shifting Competitive Advantage in Cotton Textiles, 1700–1850: the Neglected Role of Factor Prices', *Economic History Review* 62/2 (2009): 279–305.

Brook, Timothy, *The Confusions of Pleasure: Commerce and Culture in Ming China* (Berkeley: University of California Press, 1998).

Brooks, George E., *Landlords and Strangers: Ecology, Society, and Trade in Western Africa, 1000–1643* (Boulder, Col.: Westview Press, 1993).

Brunello, Franco, *L'Arte della tintura nella storia dell'umanità* (Vicenza: Neri Pozza, 1968).

Cartier, Michel, 'À Propos de l'histoire du coton en Chine: approche technologique, économique et sociale', *Études Chinoises* 13/1–2 (1994): 417–35.

Cataldi Gallo, Marzia, 'Indiane e mezzari a Genova', in Marzia Cataldi Gallo, ed.,
    I Mezzari: tra oriente e occidente (Genoa: Sagep Editrice, 1988), pp. 25–50.
Chandra, Shoma, 'Textile Production in Bengal: a Case Study of Dinajpur: 1793–1815',
    Bengal Past & Present 110/1–2, 210–11 (1991): 50–74.
Chao, Kang, *The Development of Cotton Textile Production in China* (Cambridge,
    Mass.: Harvard University Press, 1977).
Chapman, Stanley David, 'The Cost of Power in the Industrial Revolution: the Case of
    the Textile Industry', *Midland History* 1/1 (1970): 1–23.
    'David Evans & Co. The Last of the Old London Textile Printers', *Textile History*
    14/1 (1983): 29–56.
    'Quality Versus Quantity in the Industrial Revolution: the Case of Textile Printing',
    Northern History 21(1985): 175–92.
    'The Textile Factory Before Arkwright: a Typology of Factory Development',
    Business History Review 48/4 (1974): 451–78.
Chapman, Stanley David, and Serge Chassagne, *European Textile Printers in the
    Eighteenth Century: a Study of Peel and Oberkampf* (London: Heinemann
    Educational and Pasold Research Fund, 1981).
Chassagne, Serge, 'Calico Printing in Europe Before 1780', in Jenkins, ed., *Cambridge
    History of Western Textiles*, volume I, pp. 513–27.
    La Manufacture de toiles imprimées de Tournemine-Les-Angers (1752–1820) (Paris:
    Librarie C. Klincksieck, 1971).
Chaudhuri, K. N., *The English East India Company: the Study of an Early Joint-Stock
    Company, 1600–1640* (London: Frank Cass, 1965).
    'Foreign Trade: 1. European Trade with India', in Tapan Raychaudhuri and Irfan
    Habib, eds., *The Cambridge Economic History of India*, volume I, *c. 1200 – c.
    1750* (Cambridge University Press, 1982), pp. 382–406.
    'Some Reflections on the World Trade of the XVIIth and XVIIIth Century: a Reply',
    Journal of European Economic History 7/1 (1978): 223–31.
    'The Structure of Indian Textile Industry in the Seventeenth and Eighteenth
    Centuries', in Tirthankar Roy, ed., *Cloth and Commerce. Textiles in Colonial
    India* (New Delhi: Sage, 1996), pp. 33–84.
    The Trading World of Asia and the English East India Company 1660–1760
    (Cambridge University Press, 1978).
Chaudhuri, Sushil, 'European Companies and the Bengal Textile Industry in the
    Eighteenth Century: the Pitfall of Applying Quantitative Techniques', *Modern
    Asian Studies* 27/2 (1993): 321–40.
    'Textile Trade and Industry in Bengal Suba, 1650–1720', *Indian Historical Review*
    1/2 (1974): 262–78.
Chenciner, Robert, *Madder Red: a History of Luxury and Trade. Plant Dyes and
    Pigments in World Commerce and Art* (Richmond, Va.: Curzon, 2000).
Chittick, N., 'East African Trade with the Orient', in D. S. Richards, ed., *Islam and the
    Trade of Asia. A Colloquium* (Oxford: Bruno Cassirer, 1970), pp. 97–104.
Çizakça, Murat, 'Incorporation of the Middle East into the European World-Economy',
    Review: a Journal of the Fernand Braudel Center 8/3 (1985): 353–77.
Clarence-Smith, William Gervase, 'The Production of Cotton Textiles in Early Modern
    South-East Asia', in Riello and Parthasarathi, eds., *Spinning World*, pp. 127–42.
Clark, Gregory, 'Why isn't the Whole World Developed? Lessons from the Cotton
    Mills', *Journal of Economic History* 47/1 (1987): 141–73.

Clarkson, Leslie, 'The Linen Industry in Early Modern Europe', in Jenkins, ed., *Cambridge History of Western Textiles*, volume I, pp. 473–92.

Clouzot, Henri, *La Manufacture de Jouy et la toile imprimée au XVIIIe siècle* (Paris and Brussels: G. Van Oest, 1926).

Collins, Brenda and Philip Ollerenshaw, eds., *The European Linen Industry in Historical Pespective* (Oxford University Press and Pasold Research Fund, 2003).

'The European Linen Industry Since the Middle Ages', in Collins and Ollerenshaw, eds., *European Linen Industry*, pp. 1–42.

Cooper, Frederick, 'What is the Concept of Globalization Good For? An African Historian's Perspective', *African Affairs* 100 (2001): 189–213.

Le Coton et la mode: 1000 ans d'aventures: Musée Galliera, musée de la mode de la ville de Paris (Paris: Somogy Editions d'Art, 2000).

Crafts, N. F. R., *British Economic Growth During the Industrial Revolution* (Oxford University Press, 1985).

Crafts, N. F. R., and C. Knick Harley, 'Output Growth and the British Industrial Revolution: a Restatement of the Crafts-Harley View', *Economic History Review* 45/4 (1992): 703–30.

Crawford, M. D. C., *The Heritage of Cotton: the Fibre of Two Worlds and Many Ages* (New York: Putnams Sons, 1924).

Crill, Rosemary, 'Indian Painted Cottons', *Hali* 10/4 (1988): 28–35.

Crill, Rosemary, ed., *Textiles from India: the Global Trade* (Calcutta: Seagull, 2005).

Crill, Rosemary, and Ian Thomas, *Chintz: Indian Textiles for the West* (London: Victoria and Albert Museum, 2008).

Crouzet, François, *Britain Ascendant: Comparative Studies in Franco-British Economic History* (Cambridge University Press, 1990).

Cuenca Esteban, Javier, 'Comparative Patterns of Colonial Trade: Britain and its Rivals', in Leandro Prados de la Escosura, eds., *Exceptionalism and Industrialisation: Britain and its European Rivals, 1688–1815* (Cambridge University Press, 2004), pp. 35–66.

'Factory Costs, Market Prices and Indian Calicos: Cotton Textile Prices revisited, 1779–1831', *Economic History Review* 52/4 (1999): 749–55.

'Further Evidence on Falling Prices of Cotton Cloth, 1768–1816', *Economic History Review* 48/1 (1995): 145–50.

Dale, Stephen F., 'Silk Road, Cotton Road or . . . Indo-Chinese Trade in Pre-European Times', *Modern Asian Studies* 43/1 (2009): 79–88.

Dattel, Eugene R., *Cotton and Race in the Making of America: the Human Costs of Economic Power* (Chicago, Il.: Ivan R. Dee, 2009).

David, Jeremy, 'The International Diffusion of Cotton Manufacturing Technology, 1750–1990s', in Farnie and Jeremy, eds., *Fibre that Changed the World*, pp. 85–127.

Davis, Ralph, *Aleppo and Devonshire Square: English Traders in the Levant in the Eighteenth Century* (London: Macmillan, 1967).

The Rise of the Atlantic Economies (London: Weidenfeld & Nicolson, 1973).

The Rise of the English Shipping Industry in the Seventeenth and Eighteenth Centuries (Newton Abbot: David & Charles, 1962).

Davison, Patricia, and Patrick Harries, 'Cotton Weaving in South-East Africa: its History and Technology', *Textile History* 9 (1980): 175–93.

Deane, Phyllis, and W. A. Cole, *British Economic Growth, 1688–1959* (Cambridge University Press, 1962).

Delgado Ribas, Josep M., 'Mercado interno versus mercado colonial en la primera industrializacion española', *Revista de Historia Económica* 13/1 (1995): 11–31.

Deng, Kent, *China's Political Economy in Modern Times: Changes and Economic Consequences, 1800–2000* (London and New York: Routledge, 2011).

Deng, Gang [Kent], *The Premodern Chinese Economy. Structural Equilibrium and Capitalist Sterility* (London and New York: Routledge, 1999).

Depitre, Edgard, *La Toile peinte en France au XVIIe et au XVIIIe siècles: industries, commerce, prohibitions* (Paris: Marcel Rivière, 1912).

Dietrich, Craig, 'Cotton Culture and Manufacture in Early Qing China', in W. E. Willmott, ed., *Economic Organization in Chinese Society* (Stanford University Press, 1972), pp. 109–41.

Dixin, Xu, and Wu Chengming, *Chinese Capitalism, 1522–1840* (London: Macmillan, 2000).

Dobie, Madeleine, *Trading Places: Colonization and Slavery in Eighteenth-Century French Culture* (Ithaca, NY: Cornell University Press, 2010).

Douglas, Audrey W., 'Cotton Textiles in England: the East India Company's Attempts to Exploit Developments in Fashion 1660–1721', *Journal of British Studies* 18/2 (1969): 28–43.

Driver, Felix, and Sonia Ashmore, 'The Mobile Museum: Collecting and Circulating Indian Textiles in Victorian Britain', *Victorian Studies* 52/3 (2010): 353–85.

DuPlessis, Robert, 'Cottons Consumption in the Seventeenth- and Eighteenth-Century North Atlantic', in Riello and Parthasarathi, eds., *Spinning World*, pp. 227–46.

'Transatlantic Textiles: European Linens in the Cloth Culture of Colonial North America', in Collins and Ollerenshaw, eds., *European Linen Industry*, pp. 123–37.

DuPont, Ann, 'Captives of Colored Cloth: the Role of Cotton Trade Goods in the North Atlantic Slave Trade (1600–1808)', *Ars Textrina* 24 (1995): 177–83.

Eijkern-Balkenstein, Jopie van, Peter Diebels and Ebeltje Hartkamp-Jonxis, 'Orderoverzicht van door de VOC uit India "geëiste" sitsen', in Ebeltje Hartkamp-Jonxis, ed., *Sits: oost-west relaties in textiel* (Zwolle: Waanders 1987), pp. 113–21.

Eltis, David, *Economic Growth and the Ending of the Transatlantic Slave Trade* (Oxford University Press, 1989).

Elvin, Mark, 'The High-Level Equilibrium Trap: the Causes of the Decline of Invention in the Traditional Chinese Textile Industries', in W. E. Willmott, ed., *Economic Organization in Chinese Society* (Stanford University Press, 1972), pp. 142–72.

The Pattern of the Chinese Past (Stanford University Press, 1973).

Emmer, Pieter, 'The Myth of Early Globalization: the Atlantic Economy, 1500–1800', *European Review* 9/1 (2003): 37–47.

Etemad, Bouda, *Possessing the World: Taking the Measurements of Colonisation from the Eighteenth to the Twentieth Century* (New York: Berghahn, 2007).

Farnie, Douglas. A., 'The Cotton Harverst of India and the World Market, 1770–2005', in A. J. H. Latham and Heita Kawakatsu, eds., *Intra-Asian Trade and Industrialization: Essays in Memory of Yasukichi Yasuba* (London and New York: Routledge, 2009), pp. 79–110.

'Cotton Industry', in Joel Mokyr, ed., *The Oxford Encyclopedia of Economic History*, volume II (Oxford University Press, 2003), pp. 20–4.

'The Role of Merchants as Prime Movers in the Expansion of the Cotton Industry, 1760–1990', in Farnie and Jeremy, eds., *Fibre that Changed the World*, pp. 15–55.

Farnie, Douglas A., and David J. Jeremy, eds., *The Fibre that Changed the World: the Cotton Industry in International Perspective, 1600–1990s* (Oxford University Press and Pasold Research Fund, 2004).

Faroqhi, Suraiya, 'Notes on the Production of Cotton and Cotton Cloth in Sixteenth- and Seventeenth-Century Anatolia', in Huri Islamoğlu-Inan, ed., *The Ottoman Empire and the World-Economy* (Cambridge University Press and Paris: Éditions de la Maison des Sciences de l'Homme, 1986), pp. 262–70.

'Notes on the Production of Cotton and Cotton Cloth in XVIth- and XVIIth-Century Anatolia', *Journal of European Economic History* 8/2 (1979): 405–17.

'Ottoman Cotton Textiles: the Story of a Success that did not Last, 1500–1800', in Riello and Parthasarathi, eds., *Spinning World*, pp. 89–104.

Towns and Townsmen of Ottoman Anatolia. Trade, Crafts and Food Production in an Urban Setting, 1520–1650 (Cambridge University Press, 1984).

Feldbæk, Ole, 'The Danish Trading Companies of the Seventeenth and Eighteenth Centuries', *Scandinavian Economic History Review* 34/3 (1986): 204–18.

Ferrier, R. W., 'The Trade Between India and the Persian Gulf and the East India Company in the 17th Century', *Bengal Past & Present* 89/1, 167 (1970): 189–98.

Fitton, R. S., and A. P. Wadsworth, *The Strutts and the Arkwrights, 1758–1830: a Study of the Early Factory System* (Manchester University Press, 1958).

Fleet, Kate, *European and Islamic Trade in the Early Ottoman State: the Merchants of Genoa and Turkey* (Cambridge University Press, 1999).

Floor, Willem, *Textile Import into Qajar Iran: Russia Versus Great Britain. The Battle for Market Domination* (Costa Mesa, Calif.: Mazda Publishers, 2009).

Floud, Peter C., 'The Development of Design in English Printed Textiles', *Ciba Review* 1 (1961): 15–20.

'The English Contribution to the Chemistry of Calico Printing Before Perkin', *Ciba Review* 1 (1961): 8–14.

'The Origins of English Calico Printing', *Journal of the Society of Dyers and Colourists* 76 (1960): 275–81.

Fogel, Robert W., *Without Consent or Contract: the Rise and Fall of American Slavery* (New York: W. W. Norton, 1989).

Fogel, Robert W., and Stanley L. Engerman, *Time on the Cross: the Economics of American Negro Slavery* (Boston, Mass.: Little, Brown, 1974).

Fontana, Giovanni Luigi, ed., *Le Vie dell'industrializzazione europea: sistemi a confronto* (Bologna: Il Mulino, 1997).

Fox, Robert, and Agustí Nieto-Galan, eds., *Natural Dyestuffs and Industrial Culture in Europe, 1750–1880* (Canton, Mass.: Watson Publishing, 1999).

Frangakis-Syrett, Elena, 'The Trade of Cotton and Cloth in Izmir: from the Second Half of the Eighteenth Century to the Early Nineteenth Century', in Çağlar Keyder and Faruk Tabak, eds., *Landholding and Commercial Agriculture in the Middle East* (State University of New York, 1991), pp. 98–111.

Frangioni, Luciana, 'Sui Modi di produzione e sul commercio dei fustagni milanesi alla fine del Trecento. Problemi economici e giuridici', *Nuova Rivista Storica* 61/5–6 (1977): 493–554.

Fujita, Kayoko, 'Japan Indianized: the Material Culture of Imported Textiles in Japan, 1550–1850', in Riello and Parthasarathi, eds., *Spinning World*, pp. 181–204.

Fukasawa, Katsumi, *Toilerie et commerce du Levant, d'Alep à Marseille* (Paris: Editions du Centre National de la Recherche Scientifique, 1987).

Gaastra, Femme S., 'De textielhandel en de VOC', *Textielhistorische Bijdragen* 34 (1994): 50–69.

'The Textile Trade of the VOC: the Dutch Response to the English Challenge', *South Asia*, 19/special issue (1996): 85–95.

Garçon, Anne-Françoise, and Liliane Hilaire Pérez, '"Open Technique" Between Community and Individuality in Eighteenth-Century France', in Ferry de Goey and Jan Willem Veluwenkamp, eds., *Entrepreneurs and Institutions in Europe and Asia, 1500–2000* (Amsterdam: Aksant, 2002), pp. 237–56.

Geijer, Agnes, *Oriental Textiles in Sweden* (Copenhagen: Rosenkilde and Bagger, 1951).

Gemery, Henry A., and Jan S. Hogendorn, 'The Atlantic Slave Trade: a Tentative Economic Model', *Journal of African History* 15/2 (1974): 223–46.

'Comparative Disadvantage: the Case of Sugar Cultivation in West Africa', *Journal of Interdisciplinary History* 9/3 (1979): 429–49.

eds., *The Uncommon Market: Essays in the Economic History of the Atlantic Slave Trade* (New York: Academic Press, 1979).

Genç, Mehmet, 'Ottoman Industry in the Eighteenth Century: General Framework, Characteristics, and Main Trends', in Donald Quataert, ed., *Manufacturing in the Ottoman Empire and Turkey 1500–1950* (State University of New York Press, 1994), pp. 59–86.

Gervers, Michael, 'Cotton and Cotton Weaving in Meroitic Nubia and Medieval Ethiopia', *Textile History* 21/1 (1990): 13–30.

Gervers, Veronika, *The Influence of Ottoman Turkish Textiles and Costume in Eastern Europe, with Particular Reference to Hungary* (Toronto: Royal Ontario Museum, 1982).

Gittinger, Mattiebelle, *Master Dyers to the World: Technique and Trade in Early Indian Dyed Cotton Textiles* (Washington, DC: Textile Museum, 1982).

Glamann, Kristof, *Dutch–Asiatic Trade, 1620–1740* (The Hague: Martinus Nijhoff, 1958).

Goffman, Daniel, *Izmir and the Levantine World, 1550–1650* (Seattle: University of Washington Press, 1990).

Goiten, S. D., *Letters of Medieval Jewish Traders* (Princeton University Press, 1973).

Goldstone, Jack, 'Efflorescence and Economic Growth in World History: Rethinking the "Rise of the West" and the Industrial Revolution', *Journal of World History* 13/2 (2002): 323–89.

'Gender, Work, and Culture: Why the Industrial Revolution Came Early to England but Late to China', *Sociological Perspectives* 39/1 (1996): 1–21.

Greysmith, David, 'Patterns, Piracy and Protection in the Textile Printing Industry 1787–1850', *Textile History* 14/2 (1983): 165–94.

Griffiths, Trevor, Philip A. Hunt and Patrick K. O'Brien, 'Inventive Activity in the British Textile Industry, 1700–1800', *Journal of Economic History* 52/4 (1992): 881–906.

'Scottish, Irish, and Imperial Connections: Parliament, the Three Kingdoms, and the Mechanisation of Cotton Spinning in Eighteenth-Century Britain', *Economic History Review* 61/3 (2008): 625–50.

Grove, Richard H., *Green Imperialism: Colonial Expansion, Tropical Island Edens and the Origins of Environmentalism, 1600–1860* (Cambridge University Press, 1995).

Guha, Amalendu, 'The Decline of India's Cotton Handicrafts, 1800–1905; a Quantitative Macro-Study', *Calcutta Historical Journal* 17/1 (1995): 41–81.

Gupta, Ashin Das, 'Gujarati Merchants and the Red Sea Trade, 1700–1725', in Blair B. Kling, and Michael N. Pearson, eds., *The Age of Partnership: Europeans in Asia Before Domination* (Honolulu: University of Hawaii Press, 1979), pp. 123–58.

Gupta, Bishnupriya, 'Competition and Control in the Market for Textiles: Indian Weavers and the English East India Company in the Eighteenth Century', in Riello and Roy, eds., *How India Clothed the World*, pp. 281–306.

Guy, John, 'Sarasa and Patola: Indian Textiles in Indonesia', *Orientations* 20/1 (1989): 48–60.

Woven Cargoes: Indian Textiles in the East (London: Thames & Hudson, 1998).

Habib, Irfan, 'Capacity of Technological Change in Mughal India', in Aniruddha Roy and S. K. Bagchi, eds., *Technology in Ancient and Medieval India* (New Delhi: Sundeep Prakashan, 1986), pp. 1–13.

'Non-Agricultural Production and Urban Economy', in Tapan Raychaudhuri and Irfan Habib, eds., *The Cambridge Economic History of India*, volume I, *c. 1200 – c. 1750* (Cambridge University Press, 1982), pp. 76–92.

'Technological Changes and Society, 13th and 14th Centuries', in Debiprasad Chattodhyaya, ed., *Studies in the History of Science in India* (New Delhi: Editorial Enterprises, 1982), pp. 816–44.

'The Technology and Economy of Mughal India', *Indian Economic and Social History Review* 17/1 (1980): 5–34.

Hall, Kenneth R., 'The Textile Industry in Southeast Asia, 1400–1800', *Journal of the Economic and Social History of the Orient* 39/2 (1996): 87–135.

Hanchao, Lu, 'Arrested Development: Cotton and Cotton Markets in Shanghai, 1350–1843', *Modern China* 18/4 (1992): 468–99.

Handler, Jerome S., and Frederick W. Lange, *Plantation Slavery in Barbados: an Archaeological and Historical Investigation* (Cambridge, Mass.: Harvard University Press, 1978).

Hanson, John R. II, 'World Demand for Cotton During the Nineteenth Century: Wright's Estimates Re-examined', *Journal of Economic History* 39/4 (1979): 1015–21.

Hariharan, Shantha, *Cotton Textile and Corporate Buyers in Cottonpolis: a Study of Purchase and Prices in Gujarat 1600–1800* (New Delhi: Manak, 2002).

Harley, C. Knick, 'Cotton Textile Prices and the Industrial Revolution', *Economic History Review* 51/1 (1998): 49–83.

'International Competitiveness of the Antebellum American Cotton Textile Industry', *Journal of Economic History* 53/3 (1992): 559–84.

Harley, C. Knick, and N. F. R. Crafts, 'Cotton Textiles and Industrial Output Growth During the Industrial Revolution', *Economic History Review* 48/1 (1995): 134–44.

Harnetty, Peter, '"DeIndustrialization" Revisited: the Handloom Weaver of the Central Provinces of India, *c.* 1800–1947', *Modern Asian Studies* 25/3 (1991): 455–510.

Imperialism and Free Trade: Lancashire and India in the Mid-Nineteenth Century (Vancouver: University of British Columbia Press, 1972).

Harte, Negley B., 'The Rise of Protection and the English Linen Trade, 1690–1790', in N. B. Harte and K. G. Ponting, eds., *Textile History and Economic History* (Manchester University Press, 1973), pp. 75–112.

Harte, Negley B., ed., *The New Draperies in the Low Countries and England, 1300–1700* (Oxford University Press and Pasold Research Fund, 1997).

Hartkamp-Jonxis, Ebeltje, *Sitsen uit India* (Amsterdam: Rijksmuseum, 1994).

Hartwell, R. M., 'A Revolution in the Character and Destiny of British Wool', in N. B. Harte and K. G. Ponting, eds., *Textile History and Economic History* (Manchester University Press, 1973), pp. 320–38.

Haudrère, Philippe, *La Compagnie française des Indes au XVIIIe siècle, 3 volumes* (Paris: Librairie de l'Inde, 1986).

Haudrère, Philippe, and Gérard Bouëdec, *Les Compagnies des Indes* (Rennes: Ouest France, 1999).

Hazareesingh, Sandip, 'Cotton, Climate and Colonialism in Dharwar, Western India, 1840–1880', *Journal of Historical Geography* 38/1 (2012): 1–17.

Heers, Jacques, 'Il Commercio nel mediterraneo alla fine del sec. XIV e nei primi anni del XV', *Archivio Storico Italiano* 113 (1955): 159–209.

Henderson, William O., *The Lancashire Cotton Famine, 1861–1865* (New York: A. M. Kelley, 1969).

Hills, Richard Leslie, *Power in the Industrial Revolution* (Manchester University Press, 1970).

Hobhouse, Henry, *Seeds of Change: Five Plants that Tranformed Mankind* (London: Papermac, 1985).

Hood, Adrienne D., 'Flax Seed, Fibre and Cloth: Pennsylvania's Domestic Linen Manufacture and its Irish Connection, 1700–1830', in Collins and Ollerenshaw, eds., *European Linen Industry in Historical Pespective*, pp. 139–58.

Horn, Jeff, *The Path Not Taken: French Industrialization in the Age of Revolution, 1750–1830* (Cambridge, Mass.: MIT Press, 2006).

Huang, Philip C. C., *The Peasant Economy and Social Change in North China* (Stanford University Press, 1985).

The Peasant Family and Rural Development in the Yangzi Delta, 1350–1988 (Stanford University Press, 1990).

Hudson, Pat, 'The Limits of Wool and the Potential of Cotton in the Eighteenth and Early Nineteenth Centuries', in Riello and Parthasarathi, eds., *Spinning World*, pp. 327–50.

Huggill, Peter J., 'Structural Changes in the Core Regions of the World-Economy, 1830–1945', *Journal of Historical Geography* 14/2 (1988): 111–27.

İnalcık, Halil, 'When and how British Cotton Goods Invaded the Levant Markets', in Huri Islamoğlu-Inan, ed., *The Ottoman Empire and the World-Economy* (Cambridge University Press and Paris: Éditions de la Maison des Sciences de l'Homme, 1986), pp. 374–83.

Inikori, Joseph E., 'Africa and the Globalization Process: Western Africa, 1450–1850', *Journal of Global History* 2/1 (2007): 63–86.

Africans and the Industrial Revolution in England: a Study of International Trade and Economic Development (Cambridge University Press, 2002).

'English Versus Indian Cotton Textiles: the Impact of Imports on Cotton Textile Production in West Africa', in Riello and Roy, eds., *How India Clothed the World*, pp. 85–114.

'Slavery and the Revolution in Cotton Textile Production in England', *Social Science History* 23/4 (1989): 343–79.

Irwin, Douglas A., 'Mercantilism as Strategic Trade Policy: the Anglo-Dutch Rivalry for the East India Company', *Journal of Political Economy* 99/6 (1991): 1296–314.

Irwin, John, 'Indian Textile Trade in the Seventeenth Century. II. Coromandel Coast', *Journal of Indian Textile History* 2 (1956): 24–42.

Irwin, John, and Margaret Hall, *Indian Painted and Printed Fabrics* (Ahmedabad: Calico Museum of Textile, 1971).

Irwin, John, and P. R. Schwartz, *Studies in Indo-European Textile History* (Ahmedabad: Calico Museum of Textile, 1966).

Jenkins, David, ed., *The Cambridge History of Western Textiles*, 2 vols. (Cambridge University Press, 2003).

Jenkins, David T., and K. G. Ponting, *The British Wool Textile Industry, 1770–1914* (London: Heinemann Educational and Pasold Research Fund, 1982).

Jeremy, David J., 'British Textile Technology Transmission to the United States: the Philadelphia Region Experience, 1770–1820', *Business History Review* 47/1 (1973): 24–52.

Transatlantic Industrial Revolution: the Diffusion of Textile Technologies Between Britain and America, 1790–1830s (Cambridge, Mass.: MIT Press, 1981).

Johnson, Marion, *Anglo-African Trade in the Eighteenth Century* (Leiden: Centre for the History of European Expansion, 1990).

Johnson, W. H., *Cotton and its Production* (London: Macmillan & Co., 1926).

Jones, E. L., *The European Miracle: Environments, Economies, and Geopolitics in the History of Europe and Asia, 3rd edn* (Cambridge University Press, 2003).

Kawakatsu, Heita, 'The Emergence of a Market for Cotton Goods in East Asia in the Early Modern Period', in A. J. H. Latham and Heita Kawakatsu, eds., *Japanese Industrialization and the Asian Economy* (London and New York: Routledge, 1994), pp. 9–34.

'International Competition in Cotton Goods in the Late Nineteenth Century: Britain versus India and East Asia', in Wolfram Fischer, R. Marvin McInnis and Jürgen Schneider, eds., *The Emergence of a World Economy 1500–1914: Papers of the IX International Congress of Economic History* (Nuremberg: Anschrift der Schriftleitung, 1986), pp. 619–43.

Keirn, Tim, 'Parliament, Legislation and the Regulation of English Textile Industries, 1689–1714', in Lee Davidson, Tim Hitchcock, T. Keirn and Robert D. Shoemakers, eds., *Stilling the Grumbling Hive: the Response to Social and Economic Problems in England, 1689–1750* (Stroud: Sutton, 1992), pp. 1–24.

Kellenbenz, Hermann, 'The Fustian Industry of the Ulm Region in the Fifteenth and Early Sixteenth Centuries', in N. B. Harte and K.G. Ponting, eds., *Cloth and Clothing in Medieval Europe. Essays in Memory of Professor E. M. Carus-Wilson* (London: Heinemann Educational and Pasold Research Fund, 1983), pp. 259–76.

Kerlogue, Fiona, 'The Early English Textile Trade in South East Asia: the East India Company Factory and the Textile Trade in Jambi, Sumatra, 1615–1682', *Textile History* 28/2 (1997): 149–60.

Keyes Adenaike, Carolyn, 'West African Textiles, 1500–1800', in Maureen Fennell Mazzaoui, ed., *Textiles: Production, Trade and Demand* (Aldershot: Ashgate, 1998), pp. 251–61.

Kingma, Vibeke, 'De katoendrukkerijen in Amsterdam en Nieuwer-Amstel', *Textielhistorische Bijdragen* 38 (1998): 7–30.

Knight, Frederick C., *Working the Diaspora: the Impact of African Labor on the Anglo-American World, 1650–1850* (New York University Press, 2010).

Kriegel, Lara, 'Culture and the Copy: Calico, Capitalism, and Design Copyright in Early Victorian Britain', *Journal of British Studies* 43/2 (2004): 233–65.

Kriger, Colleen, '"Guinea Cloth": Production and Consumption of Cotton Textiles in West Africa Before and During the Atlantic Slave Trade', in Riello and Parthasarathi, eds., *Spinning World*, pp. 105–26.

'Mapping the History of Cotton Textile Production in Pre-Colonial West Africa', *African Economic History* 33 (2005): 87–116.

Kuhn, Dieter, *Science and Civilisation in China*, volume V, *Chemistry and Chemical Technology. Part IX. Textile Technology: Spinning and Reeling* (Cambridge University Press, 1998).

Kurmuş, Orhan, 'The Cotton Famine and its Effects on the Ottoman Empire', in Huri Islamoğlu-Inan, ed., *The Ottoman Empire and the World-Economy* (Cambridge University Press and Paris: Éditions de la Maison des Sciences de l'Homme, 1986), pp. 160–9.

Kusamitsu, Toshio, 'British Industrialization and Design Before the Great Exhibition', *Textile History* 12 (1981): 77–95.

Lakwete, Angela, *Inventing the Cotton Gin: Machine and Myth in Antebellum America* (Baltmore, Md.: Johns Hopkins University Press, 2003).

Lamb, Venice, *West African Weaving* (London: Duckworth, 1975).

Landes, David S., *The Unbound Prometheus: Technological Change and Industrial Development in Western Europe from 1750 to the Present* (Cambridge University Press, 1969).

The Wealth and Poverty of Nations: why are some so Rich and others so Poor? (New York: W. W. Norton, 1998).

'What do Bosses Really Do?', *Journal of Economic History* 46/3 (1986): 585–623.

Lemire, Beverly, *Cotton* (Oxford: Berg, 2011).

'Domesticating the Exotic: Floral Culture and the East India Calico Trade with England, *c.* 1600–1800', *Textile: the Journal of Cloth and Culture* 1/1 (2003): 65–85.

Fashion's Favourite: the Cotton Trade and the Consumer in Britain, 1660–1800 (Oxford University Press and Pasold Research Fund, 1991).

'Fashioning Cottons: Asian Trade, Domestic Industry and Consumer Demand, 1660–1780', in Jenkins, ed., *Cambridge History of Western Textiles*, volume I, pp. 493–512.

'Fashioning Global Trade: Indian Textiles, Gender Meanings and European Consumers, 1500–1800', in Riello and Roy, eds., *How India Clothed the World*, pp. 365–90.

'Revising the Historical Narrative: India, Europe, and the Cotton Trade, *c.* 1300–1800', in Riello and Parthasarathi, eds., *Spinning World*, pp. 205–26.

'Transforming Consumer Custom: Linen, Cotton, and the English Market, 1660–1800', in Collins and Ollerenshaw, eds., *European Linen Industry in Historical Pespective*, pp. 187–207.

Lemire, Beverly, ed., *The British Cotton Trade, 1660–1815* (London: Pickering & Chatto, 2009).

Lemire, Beverly, and Giorgio Riello, 'East and West: Textiles and Fashion in Early Modern Europe', *Journal of Social History* 41/4 (2008): 887–916.

Leunig, Timothy, 'Cotton: Technological Change', in Joel Mokyr, ed., *The Oxford Encyclopedia of Economic History*, volume II (Oxford University Press, 2003), pp. 24–9.

Levi, Scott C., 'India, Russia and the Eighteenth-Century Transformation of the Central Asian Caravan Trade', *Journal of the Economic and Social History of the Orient* 42/4 (1999): 519–48.

Li, Bozhong, *Agricultural Development in Jiangnan, 1620–1850* (New York: St Martin's Press, 1998).

Lloyd-Jones, Roger, and A. A. LeRoux, 'The Size of Firms in the Cotton Industry: Manchester in 1815', *Economic History Review* 33/1 (1980): 72–82.

Lyons, John Stephen, 'The Lancashire Cotton Industry and the Introduction of the Powerloom, 1815–1850', *Journal of Economic History* 37/1 (1978): 283–4.

Lombard, Maurice, *Les Textiles dans le monde musulman du VIIe au XIIe siècle* (Paris: Mouton, 1978).

Longfield, Ada K., 'History of the Irish Linen and Cotton Printing Industry in the 18th Century', *Journal of Royal Society of Antiquaries of Ireland* 58 (1937): 26–56.

Lowengard, Sarah, 'Colour Quality and Production: Testing Colour in Eighteenth-Century France', *Journal of Design History* 14/2 (2001): 91–103.

McCants, Anne E., 'Modest Households and Globally Traded Textiles: Evidence from Amsterdam Household Inventories', in Laura Cruz and Joel Mokyr, eds., *The Birth of Modern Europe: Culture and Economy, 1400–1800. Essays in Honour of Jan de Vries* (Leiden and Boston: E. J. Brill, 2010), pp. 109–31.

Machado, Pedro, 'Awash in a Sea of Cloth: Gujarat, Africa, and the Western Indian Ocean, 1300–1800', in Riello and Parthasarathi, eds., *Spinning World*, pp. 161–80.

Maddison, Angus, *The World Economy: a Millennial Perspective* (Paris: Organisation for Economic Co-operation and Development, 2001).

Mancall, Peter C., Joshua L. Rosenbloom and Thomas Weiss, 'Exports and the Economy of the Lower Southern Region, 1720–1770', *Research in Economic History* 25 (2008): 1–68.

Mann, Susan, 'Household Handicrafts and State Policy in Qing Times', in J. K. Leonard and J. R. Watt, eds., *To Achieve Security and Wealth: the Qing Imperial State and the Economy, 1644–1911* (Cornell, NY: Cornell East Asia Series, 1992), pp. 75–95.

Matinez-Shaw, Carlos, 'Entre orient et occident: l'approvisionnement en coton et l'industrialisation de la Catalogne', in Jacques Bottin and Nicole Pellegrin, eds., *Échanges et cultures textiles dans l'Europe pré-industrielle. Actes du colloque de Rouen, 17–19 mai 1993* (Lille: Revue du Nord Supplement 12, 1996), pp. 227–45.

'Los Orígenes de la industria algodonera catalana y el comercio colonial', in Jordi Nadal and Gabriel Tortella, eds., *Agricultura, comercio colonial y crecimiento económico en la España contemporánea* (Barcelona: Editorial Ariel, 1974), pp. 243–67.

Maw, Peter, 'Yorkshire and Lancashire Ascendant: England's Textile Exports to New York and Philadelphia, 1750–1805', *Economic History Review* 63/3 (2010): 734–68.

Maxwell, Robyn, *Textiles of Southeast Asia: Tradition, Trade and Transformation* (Melbourne: Australian National Gallery and Oxford University Press, 1990).

Mazzaoui, Maureen Fennell, 'The Cotton Industry of Northern Italy in the Late Middle Ages: 1150–1450', *Journal of Economic History* 32/1 (1972): 262–86.

'The First European Cotton Industry: Italy and Germany, 1100–1800', in Riello and Parthasarathi, eds., *Spinning World*, pp. 63–88.

The Italian Cotton Industry in the Later Middle Ages, 1100–1600 (Cambridge University Press, 1981).

Meredith John, A., *The Plantation Slaves of Trinidad, 1783–1816: a Mathematical and Demographic Enquiry* (Cambridge University Press, 1988).

Mokyr, Joel, *The Enlightened Economy: an Economic History of Britain, 1700–1850* (New Haven, Conn.: Yale University Press, 2009).

The Gifts of Athena: Historical Origins of the Knowledge Economy (Princeton University Press, 2002).

Montgomery, Florence M., *Printed Textiles: English and American Cottons and Linens, 1700–1850* (New York: Thoemmes Press [1970] 1999).

Morineau, Michel, 'The Indian Challenge: Seventeenth to Eighteenth Centuries', in Sushil Chaudhuri and Michel Morineau, eds., *Merchants, Companies and Trade: Europe and Asia in the Early Modern Era* (Cambridge University Press and Paris: Éditions de la Maison des Sciences de l'Homme, 1999), pp. 243–75.

Mukerji, Chandra, *From Graven Images: Patterns of Modern Materialism* (New York: Columbia University Press, 1983).

Myers, Ramon H., 'Cotton Textile Handicraft and the Development of the Cotton Textile Industry in Modern China', *Economic History Review* 18/3 (1965): 614–32.

Nadal, Jordi, and Alex Sanchez, 'En los orígenes del éxito algodonero catalán', in Geneviève Gavignaud-Fontaine, Henri Michel and Elie Pélaquier, eds., *De la fibre à la fripe: le textile dans la France méridionale et l'Europe méditerranéenne (XVIIe–XXe siècles). Actes du colloque du 21 et du 22 mars 1997* (Montpellier: Université Paul-Valéry, 1998), pp. 35–60.

Nam, Jong-Kuk, *Le Commerce du coton en Méditerranée à la fin du moyen age* (Leiden and Boston: E. J. Brill, 2007).

Naqvi, Hameeda Khatoon, 'Colour Making and Dyeing of Cotton Textiles in Medieval Hindustan', *Journal of Indian Textile History* 15/1 (1980): 58–70.

'Dyeing of Cotton Goods in the Mughal Hindustan', *Journal of Indian Textile History* 7/1 (1967): 45–55.

Nash, R. C., 'South Carolina Indigo, European Textiles, and the British Atlantic Economy in the Eighteenth Century', *Economic History Review* 63/2 (2010): 362–92.

Nieto-Galan, Agustí, 'Dyeing, Calico Printing, and Technical Exchanges in Spain: the Royal Manufactures and the Catalan Textile Industry, 1750–1820', in Robert Fox and Agustí Nieto-Galan, eds., *Natural Dyestuffs and Industrial Culture in Europe, 1750–1880* (Canton, Mass.: Watson Publishing, 1999), pp. 101–28.

North, Douglas C., *The Economic Growth of the United States, 1790–1860* (Englewood Cliffs, N.J.: Prentice-Hall, 1961).

O'Brien, Patrick, 'A Conjuncture in Global History or an Anglo-American Construct: the British Industrial Revolution, 1700–1850', *Journal of Global History* 5/3 (2010): 503–9.

'European Economic Development: The Contribution of the Periphery', *Economic History Review* 35/1 (1982): 1–18.

'The Foundations of European Industrialization: from the Perspective of the World', in José Casas Pardo, ed., *Economic Effects of the European Expansion, 1492–1824* (Stuttgart: Franz Steiner, 1992), pp. 463–502.

'The Geopolitics of a Global Industry: Eurasian Divergence and the Mechanisation of Cotton Textile Production in England', in Riello and Parthasarathi, eds., *Spinning World*, pp. 351–66.

'The Micro Foundations of Macro Invention: the Case of the Reverend Edmund Cartwright', *Textile History* 28/2 (1997): 201–33.

'Path Dependency, or why Britain became an Industrialized and Urbanized Economy Long Before France', *Economic History Review* 49/2 (1996): 213–49.

O'Brien, Patrick K., and S. L. Engerman, 'Exports and the Growth of the British Economy from the Glorious Revolution to the Peace of Amiens', in Barbara L. Solow, ed., *Slavery and the Rise of the Atlantic System* (Cambridge University Press, 1991), pp. 177–209.

O'Brien, Patrick K., Trevor Griffith and Philip Hunt, 'Political Components of the Industrial Revolution: English Cotton Textile Industry, 1660–1774', *Economic History Review* 44/3 (1991): 395–423.

O'Donovan, Susan Eva, *Becoming Free in the Cotton South* (Cambridge, Mass.: Harvard University Press, 2007).

Olmstead, Alan L., and Paul W. Rhode, *Creating Abundance: Biological Innovation and American Agricultural Development* (Cambridge University Press, 2008).

Ormrod, David, *The Rise of Commercial Empires: England and the Netherlands in the Age of Mercantilism, 1650–1770* (Cambridge University Press, 2002).

O'Rourke, Kevin H., and Jeffrey G. Williamson, 'After Columbus: Explaining Europe's Overseas Trade Boom, 1500–1800', *Journal of Economic History* 62/2 (2002): 417–56.

Globalization and History: the Evolution of a Nineteenth-Century Atlantic Economy (Cambridge, Mass.: MIT Press, 1999).

'When Did Globalisation Begin?', *European Review of Economic History* 6/1 (2002): 23–50.

Osumi, Tamezo, *Printed Cottons of Asia: the Romance of Trade Textiles* (Tokyo: Bijutsu Shuppan-sha, 1963).

Owen, E. R. J., *Cotton and the Egyptian Economy, 1820–1914: A Study in Trade and Development* (Oxford: Clarendon Press, 1969).

Owen, Roger, *The Middle East in the World Economy, 1800–1914: a Study of Trade and Development* (Oxford: Clarendon Press, 1993).

Pamuk, Şevket, 'The Decline and Resistance of Ottoman Cotton Textiles, 1820–1913', *Explorations in Economic History* 23/2 (1986): 205–25.

The Ottoman Empire and European Capitalism, 1820–1913 (Cambridge University Press, 1987).

Pamuk, Şevket, and Jeffrey G. Williamson, 'Ottoman De-industrialization, 1800–1913: Assessing the Magnitude, Impact, and Response', *Economic History Review* 64/supplement 1 (2010): 159–84.

Parthasarathi, Prasannan, 'Cotton Textiles in the Indian Subcontinent, 1200–1800', in Riello and Parthasarathi, eds., *Spinning World*, pp. 17–42.

'Historical Issues of Deindustrialisation in Nineteenth-Century South India', in Riello and Roy, eds., *How India Clothed the World*, pp. 415–36.

'Rethinking Wages and Competitiveness in the Eighteenth Century', *Past & Present* 158 (1998): 79–109.

'Review Article: The Great Divergence', *Past & Present* 167 (2002): 275–93.

The Transition to a Colonial Economy: Weavers, Merchants and Kings in South India, 1720–1800 (Cambridge University Press, 2001).

Why Europe Grew Rich and Asia did not: Global Economic Divergence, 1600–1850 (Cambridge University Press, 2011).

Parthasarathi, Prasannan, and Ian Wendt, 'Decline in Three Keys: Indian Cotton Manufacturing from the Later Eighteenth Century', in Riello and Parthasarathi, eds., *Spinning World*, pp. 397–407.

Pearson, Michael N., *The Indian Ocean* (London and New York: Routledge, 2003).

Pérez, Liliane Hilaire, 'Cultures, techniques et pratiques de l'échange, entre Lyon et le Levant: inventions et réseaux au XVIIIe siècle', *Revue d'Histoire Moderne et Contemporaine* 49/1 (2002). 89–114.

L'Invention technique au siècle des lumières (Paris: Albin Michel, 2000).

Perlin, Frank, 'Proto-Industrial and Pre-Colonial South Asia', *Past & Present* 98 (1983): 30–95.

Petmezas, Socrates D., 'Patterns of Protoindustrialization in the Ottoman Empire. The Case of Eastern Thessaly, ca. 1750–1860', *Journal of European Economic History* 19/3 (1990): 575–603.

Pfister, Rudolf, 'The Indian Art of Calico Printing in the Middle Ages: Characteristics and Influences', *Indian Art and Letters*, 13 (1939): 23–9.

Les Toiles imprimées de Fostat et l'Hindoustan (Paris: Editons d'Art et d'Histoire, 1938).

Phillips, Amanda, 'Little-Known Ottoman-Period Cotton and Linen Textiles in Oxford's Ashmolean Museum', in *Proceedings of the 13th International Congress of Turkish Art* (Budapest: Hungarian National Museum, 2010), pp. 593–608.

Pitoiset, Gilles, *Toiles imprimées XVIIIe–XIXe siècles* (Paris: Bibliothèque Forney, 1982).

Pomeranz, Kenneth, *The Great Divergence: China, Europe and the Making of the Modern World Economy* (Princeton University Press, 2000).

'Is there an East Asian Development Path? Long-term Comparisons, Constraints, and Continuities', *Journal of the Economic and Social History of the Orient* 44/3 (2001): 322–62.

'Political Economy and Ecology on the Eve of Industrialization: Europe, China, and the Global Conjuncture', *American Historical Review* 107/2 (2002): 425–46.

'Women's Work, Family, and Economic Development in Europe and East Asia: Long-term Trajectories and Contemporary Comparisons', in Giovanni Arrighi, Takeshi Hamashita and Mark Selden, eds., *The Resurgence of East Asia: 500, 150, and 50 Year Perspectives* (London and New York: Routledge, 2003), pp. 124–72.

Ponting, K. G., 'Important Natural Dyes of History', *Industrial Archaeology Review* 2/2 (1973): 154–9.

The Wool Trade: Past and Present (Manchester and London: Columbine Press, 1961).

Prakash, Om, 'Bengal Textiles in Seventeenth Century International Trade', in *Studies on Bengal. Papers Presented at the Seventh Annual Bengal Studies Conference, University of Minnesota 28–30 May 1971* (Michigan State University Press, Asian Studies Center, 1975), pp. 73–84.

'Cooperation and Conflict among European Traders in the Indian Ocean in the Late Eighteenth Century', *Indian Economic and Social History Review* 39/2–3 (2002): 131–48.

'From Market-Determined to Coercion-Based: Textile Manufacturing in Eighteenth-Century Bengal', in Riello and Roy, eds., *How India Clothed the World*, pp. 217–52.

'The Indian Maritime Merchant, 1500–1800', *Journal of Economic and Social History of the Orient* 47/3 (2004): 435–57.

The New Cambridge History of India, volume V, *European Commercial Enterprise in Pre-Colonial India* (Cambridge University Press, 1998).

Prakash Sangar, Satya, *Indian Textiles in the Seventeenth Century* (New Delhi: Reliance Publishing House, 1998).

Prestholdt, Jeremy, *Domesticating the World: African Consumerism and the Genealogies of Globalization* (Berkeley: University of California Press, 2008).

'On the Global Repercussions of East African Consumerism', *American Historical Review* 109/3 (2004): 755–82.

Quataert, Donald, *Ottoman Manufacturing in the Age of the Industrial Revolution* (Cambridge University Press, 1993).

Ragatz, Lowell Joseph, *The Fall of the Planter Class in the British Caribbean, 1763–1833: a Study in Social and Economic History* (New York: Century, 1928).

Rahman, A., 'General Ideas on Technology', in A. Rahman, ed., *India's Interaction with China, Central and West Asia*, volume III, *Part 2* (Oxford University Press, 2002), pp. 358–72.

Ramaswamy, Vijaya, 'Interactions and Encounters: Indian Looms & Crafts Traditions Abroad – a South Indian Perspective', in A. Rahman, ed., *India's Interaction with China, Central and West Asia*, volume III, *Part 2* (Oxford University Press, 2002), pp. 428–44.

'Notes on the Textile Technology in Medieval India with Special Reference to the South', *Indian Economic and Social History Review* 17/2 (1980): 227–41.

'South Indian Textiles: a Case for Proto-Industrialization?', in Deepak Kumar, ed., *Science and Empire: Essays in Indian Context (1700–1947)* (New Delhi: Anamika Prakashan, 1991), pp. 41–56.

Raveux, Olivier, 'The Birth of a New European Industry: l'indiennage in Seventeenth-Century Marseilles', in Riello and Parthasarathi, eds., *Spinning World*, pp. 291–306.

'Les Débuts de l'indiennage dans les pays d'Aix (1758–1770)', *Industries en Provence* 4 (2004): 1–8.

'Espaces et Technologies dans la France méridionale d'ancien régime: l'example de l'indiennage marseillais (1648–1793)', *Annales du Midi* 116/246 (2004): 155–70.

Ray, Indrani, 'Of Trade and Traders in the Seventeenth-Century India: an Unpublished French Memoir by Georges Roques', in Lakshmi Subramanian, ed., *The French*

East India Company and the Trade of the Indian Ocean: a Collection of Essays by Indrani Ray (New Delhi: Munshiram Manoharlal, 1999), pp. 1–62.

'The Trade and Traders in Ahmedabad in Late Seventeenth Century: Extracts from George Roques' MSS', in Lakshmi Subramanian, ed., *The French East India Company and the Trade of the Indian Ocean: a Collection of Essays by Indrani Ray* (New Delhi: Munshiram Manoharlal, 1999), pp. 63–76.

Raychaudhuri, Tapan, 'Inland Trade', in Tapan Raychaudhuri and Irfan Habib, eds., *The Cambridge Economic History of India*, volume I, *c. 1200 – c. 1750* (Cambridge University Press, 1982), pp. 325–59.

'Non-Agricultural Production: Mughal India', in Tapan Raychaudhuri and Irfan Habib, eds., *The Cambridge Economic History of India*, volume I, *c. 1200 – c. 1750* (Cambridge University Press, 1982), pp. 261–307.

Raymond, André, *Artisans et commerçants au Caire au XVIIIe siècle* (Paris: Damas, 1973).

Reid, Anthony, *Southeast Asia in the Age of Commerce, 1450–1680*, volume I, *The Lands Below the Winds* (New Haven, Conn.: Yale University Press, 1984).

'Southeast Asian Consumption of Indian and British Cotton Cloth, 1600–1850', in Riello and Roy, eds., *How India Clothed the World*, pp. 29–52.

Richards, John F., *The Unending Frontier: an Environmental History of the Early Modern World* (Berkeley: University of California Press, 2003).

Riello, Giorgio, 'Asian Knowledge and the Development of Calico Printing in Europe in the Seventeenth and Eighteenth Centuries', *Journal of Global History* 5/1 (2010), pp. 1–28.

'The Globalization of Cotton Textiles: Indian Cottons, Europe, and the Atlantic World, 1600–1850', in Riello and Parthasarathi, eds., *Spinning World*, pp. 261–87.

'The Indian Apprenticeship: the Trade of Indian Textiles and the Making of European Cottons', in Riello and Roy, eds., *How India Clothed the World*, pp. 307–46.

Riello, Giorgio, and Prasannan Parthasarathi, eds., *The Spinning World: A Global History of Cotton Textiles, 1200–1850* (Oxford University Press, 2009).

Riello, Giorgio, and Tirthankar Roy, eds., *How India Clothed the World: the World of South Asian Textiles, 1500–1850* (Leiden: E. J. Brill, 2009).

'Introduction: The World of South Asian Textiles, 1500–1850', in Riello and Roy, eds., *How India Clothed the World*, pp. 1–27.

Roberts, Richard, 'Guinée Cloth: Linked Transformations in Production within France's Empire in the Nineteenth Century', *Cahiers d'Études Africaines* 32–128 (1992): 597–627.

Robinson, Stuart, *A History of Printed Textiles* (London: Studio Vista, 1969).

A History of Dyed Textiles (London: Studio Vista, 1969).

Rose, Mary B., ed., *The Lancashire Cotton Industry. a History Since 1700* (Preston: Lancashire County Books, 1996).

Rosenthal, Jean-Laurent, and Roy Bin Wong, *Before and Beyond Divergence: the Politics of Economic Change in China and Europe* (Cambridge, Mass.: Harvard University Press, 2011).

Rothermund, Dietmar, 'The Changing Pattern of British Trade in Indian Textiles, 1701–1757', in Sushil Chaudhuri and Michel Morineau, eds., *Merchants, Companies and Trade: Europe and Asia in the Early Modern Era* (Cambridge University Press and Paris: Éditions de la Maison des Sciences de l'Homme, 1999), pp. 276–86.

Rothstein, Natalie, 'The Calico Campaign of 1719–1721', *East London Papers* 7 (1964): 3–21.

Roy, Tirthankar, *Company of Kinsmen: Enterprise and Community in South Asian History, 1700–1940* (Oxford University Press, 2010).

'Did Globalisation Aid Industrial Development in Colonial India? A Study of Knowledge Transfer in the Iron Industry', *Indian Economic and Social History Review* 46/4 (2009): 570–613.

India in the World Economy: From Antiquity to the Present (Cambridge University Press, 2012).

'Knowledge and Divergence from the Perspective of Early Modern India', *Journal of Global History* 3/3 (2008): 361–87.

'The Long Globalisation and Textile Producers in India', in Lex Heerma Van Voss, Els Hiemstra-Kuperus, and Elise Van Nederveen Meerkerk, eds., *Ashgate Companion to the History of Textile Workers, 1650–2000* (Farnham: Ashgate, 2010), pp. 253–74.

'Out of Tradition: Master Artisans and Economic Change in Colonial India', *Journal of Asian Studies* 66/4 (2007): 963–91.

Traditional Industry in the Economy of Colonial India (Cambridge University Press, 1999).

Russell, Edmund, *Evolutionary History: Uniting History and Biology to Understand Life on Earth* (Cambridge University Press, 2011).

Sadao, Nishijima, 'The Formation of the Early Chinese Cotton Industry', in Linda Grove and Christian Daniels, eds., *State and Society in China. Japanese Perspectives on Ming/Qing Social and Economic History* (University of Tokyo Press, 1984), pp. 17–77.

Sangar, Shri Pramod, 'Export of Indian Textiles to the Middle East and Africa in the Seventeenth Century', *Journal of Historical Research* 17/1 (1974), pp. 1–5.

Sangwan, Satpal, *Science, Technology and Colonisation: an Indian Experience, 1757–1857* (New Delhi: Anamika Prakashan, 1991).

Schlingloff, D., 'Cotton Manufacture in Ancient India', *Journal of the Economic and Social History of the Orient* 17/1 (1974): 81–90.

Schoen, Brian, *The Fragile Fabric of Union: Cotton, Federal Politics, and the Global Origins of the Civil War* (Baltimore, Md.: Johns Hopkins University Press, 2009).

Schulze-Gaevenitz, G. von, *The Cotton Trade in England and on the Continent. A Study in the Field of the Cotton Industry* (London: Simpkin, Marshall, Hamilton, Kent & Co., 1895).

Schumpeter, Elizabeth, *English Overseas Trade Statistics, 1697–1808* (Oxford: Clarendon Press, 1960).

Schwartz, Paul R., 'French Documents on Indian Cotton Painting', *Journal of Indian Textile History* 2 (1956): 5–23.

Printing on Cotton at Ahmedabad, India in 1678: from an Unedited Manuscript in the Bibliothèque Nationale, Paris (Ahmedabad: Calico Museum of Textiles, 1969).

Sen, S. P., 'The Role of Indian Textiles in Southeast Asian Trade in the Seventeenth Century', *Journal of Southeast Asian History* 3/2 (1962): 92–110.

Sewell, William H., Jr, 'The Empire of Fashion and the Rise of Capitalism in Eighteenth-Century France', *Past & Present* 206 (2010): 81–120.

Shah, Deepika, *Masters of the Cloth: Indian Textiles Traded to Distant Shores* (New Delhi: Tapi Collection, 2005).

Shammas, Carole, 'The Decline of Textile Prices in England and British America Prior to Industrialization', *Economic History Review* 48/3 (1994): 483–507.

Sickinger, Raymond L., 'Regulation or Ruination: Parliament's Consistent Pattern of Mercantilist Regulation of the English Textile Trade, 1660–1800', *Parliamentary History* 19/2 (2000): 211–32.

Silver, Arthur W., *Manchester Men and Indian Cotton, 1847–1872* (Manchester University Press, 1966).

Simon, Christian, 'Labour Relations at Manufactures in the Eighteenth Century: the Calico Printers in Europe', *International Review of Social History* 39 (1994): 115–44.

Singleton, John, 'The Lancashire Cotton Industry, the Royal Navy, and the British Empire, c. 1700–1960', in Farnie and Jeremy, eds., *Fibre that Changed the World*, pp. 57–83.

Sinopoli, Carla M., *The Political Economy of Craft Production: Crafting Empire in South India, c.1350–1650* (Cambridge University Press, 2003).

Smith, Woodruff D., *Consumption and the Making of Respectability, 1600–1800* (New York and London: Routledge, 2002).

Solar, Peter, 'The Irish Linen Trade, 1852–1914', *Textile History* 36/1 (2005): 46–68.

Solow, Barbara L., 'Capitalism and Slavery in the Exceedingly Long Run', *Journal of Interdisciplinary History* 17/4 (1987): 711–39.

Souza, George Bryan, 'The French Connection: Indian Cottons and Their Early Modern Technology', in Riello and Roy, eds., *How India Clothed the World*, pp. 347–64.

Steensgaard, Niels, *Carracks, Caravans and Companies: the Structural Crisis in the European–Asian Trade in the Early 17th Century* (Copenhagen: Studentlitteratur, 1973).

Studer, Roman, 'India and the Great Divergence: Assessing the Efficiency of Grain Markets in Eighteenth- and Nineteenth-Century India', *Journal of Economic History* 68/2 (2008): 393–437.

Styles, John, 'Clothing the North: the Supply of Non-Elite Clothing in the Eighteenth-Century North of England', *Textile History* 25/2 (1994): 139–66.

The Dress of the People: Everyday Fashion in Eighteenth-Century England (New Haven, Conn.: Yale University Press, 2007).

'Indian Cottons and European Fashion, 1400–1800', in Glenn Adamson, Giorgio Riello and Sarah Teasley, eds., *Global Design History* (London and New York: Routledge, 2011), pp. 37–46.

'Involuntary Consumers? Servants and their Clothes in Eighteenth-Century England', *Textile History* 33/1 (2002): 9–21.

'Product Innovation in Early Modern London', *Past & Present* 168 (2000): 124–69.

Threads of Feeling: The London Foundling Hospital's Textiles Tokens, 1740–1770 (London: Foundling Hospital, 2010).

'What were Cottons for in the Industrial Revolution?', in Riello and Parthasarathi, eds., *Spinning World*, pp. 307–26.

Subrahmanyam, Sanjay, *The Political Economy of Commerce: Southern India, 1500–1650* (Cambridge University Press, 2002).

Subramanian, Lakshmi, 'The Political Economy of Textiles in Western India: Weavers, Merchants and the Transition to a Colonial Economy', in Riello and Roy, eds., *How India Clothed the World*, pp. 253–80.

'Power and the Weave: Weavers, Merchants and Rules in Eighteenth-Century Surat', in Rudrangshu Mukherjee and Lakshmi Subramanian, eds., *Politics and Trade in the Indian Ocean World: Essays in Honour of Ashin Das Gupta* (Oxford University Press, 1998), pp. 52–82.

Sugana Sarma, V., *Studies in Indian Textiles (Collection in Salarjung Museum & State Museum, Hyderabad)* (New Delhi: Bharatiya Kala Prakashan, 1998).

Sugihara, Kaoru, 'The East Asian Path of Economic Development: a Long-term Perspective', in Giovanni Arrighi, Takeshi Hamashita and Mark Selden, eds., *The Resurgence of East Asia: 500, 150 and 50 Year Perspectives* (London and New York: Routledge, 2003), pp. 78–123.

'Labour-Intensive Industrialization in Global History', *Australian Economic History Review* 47/2 (2007): 121–54.

'The Resurgence of Intra-Asian Trade, 1800–1850', in Riello and Roy, eds., *How India Clothed the World*, pp. 139–70.

Tanaka, Masatoshi, 'The Putting-Out System of Production in the Ming and Qing periods: with a Focus on Clothing Production (I)', *Memoirs of the Research Department of the toyo Bunko*, 52 (1994): 21–43.

'The Putting-Out System of Production in the Ming and Qing periods: with a Focus on Clothing Production (II)', *Memoirs of the Research Department of the toyo Bunko*, 53 (1995): 29–65.

Tarrant, Naomi E. A., 'The Turkey Red Dyeing Industry in the Vale of Leven', in John Butt and Kenneth Ponting, eds., *Scottish Textile History* (Aberdeen University Press, 1987), pp. 37–47.

Tchitcherov, Alexander I., *India: Changing Economic Structure in the Sixteenth to Eighteenth Centuries: Outline History of Crafts and Trade* (New Delhi: Manohar, 1998).

Thomas, P. J., *Mercantilism and the East India Trade* (London: Frank Cass, 1926).

Thomson, James K. J., *A Distinctive Industrialisation: Cotton in Barcelona, 1728–1832* (Cambridge University Press, 1992).

'Invention in the Industrial Revolution: the Case of Cotton', in Leandro Prados de la Escosura, ed., *Exceptionalism and Industrialisation: Britain and its European Rivals, 1688–1815* (Cambridge University Press, 2004), pp. 127–44.

'The Spanish Trade of American Cotton: Atlantic Synergies in the Age of Enlightenment', *Revista de Historia Economica* 26/2 (2008): 277–313.

'Transferring the Spinning Jenny to Barcelona: an Apprenticeship in the Technology of the Industrial Revolution', *Textile History* 34/1 (2003): 21–46.

Turnbull, Geoffrey, *A History of the Calico Printing Industry of Great Britain* (Altrincham: John Sherratt & Son, 1947).

Ulrich, Pamela V., 'From Fustian to Merino: the Rise of Textiles Using Cotton Before and After the Gin', *Agricultural History* 68/2 (1994): 219–31.

Van Campen, Jan, and Ebeltje Hartkamp-Jonxis, *Asian Splendour: Company Art in the Rijksmuseum* (Amsterdam: Rijksmuseum, 2011).

Vanina, Eugenia, *Urban Crafts and Craftsmen in Medieval India (Thirteenth–Eighteenth Centuries)* (New Delhi: Munshiram Manoharlal, 2004).

Van Zanden, Jan Luiten, 'The Great Convergence from a West-European Perspective: Some Thoughts and Hypotheses', *Itinerario* 24/3–4 (2000): 9–28.

The Long Road to the Industrial Revolution: the European Economy in a Global Perspective, 1000–1800 (Leiden and Boston: E. J. Brill, 2009).

'The Road to the Industrial Revolution: Hypotheses and Conjectures about the Medieval Origins of the "European Miracle"', *Journal of Global History* 3/3 (2008): 337–59.

Varadarajan, Lotika, 'Impact of European Traders on Indian Handicrafts and Industries', *Indica* 16 (1979): 213–20.

'Indian Textile Technology in the Pre-Industrial Period', *Indica* 21/2 (1984): 61–9.

'Syncretic Symbolism and Textiles: Indo-Thai Expressions', in Om Prakash and Denys Lombard, eds., *Commerce and Culture in the Bay of Bengal, 1500–1800* (New Delhi: Manohar, 1999), pp. 361–78.

Verbong, Geert, 'The Dutch Calico Printing Industry Between 1800 and 1875', in Robert Fox and Agustí Nieto-Galan, eds., *Natural Dyestuffs and Industrial Culture in Europe, 1750–1880* (Canton, Mass.: Watson Publishing, 1999), pp. 193–218.

Verna, I. N., 'Calico Printing in India', *Journal of Indian Textile History* 15/1 (1980): 1–5.

Vicente, Marta, 'Artisans and Work in a Barcelona Cotton Factory', *International Review of Social History* 45 (2000): 1–23.

Clothing the Spanish Empire: Families and the Calico Trade in the Early Modern Atlantic World (New York: Palgrave Macmillan, 2006).

Vogt, John, 'Notes on the Portuguese Cloth Trade in West Africa, 1480–1540', *International Journal of African Historical Studies* 8/4 (1975): 623–51.

Von Dieter, Kuhn, 'Some Notes Concerning the Textile Technology Pictured in the Kêng-chih-t'u', *Zeitschrift der Deutschen Morgenländischen Gesellschaft* 130 (1980): 408–16.

Vries, Jan de, 'Connecting Europe and Asia: a Quantitative Analysis of the Cape-Route Trade, 1497–1795', in Dennis O. Flynn, Arturo Giráldez and Richard von Glahn, eds., *Global Connections and Monetary History, 1470–1800* (Ashford: Ashgate, 2003), pp. 35–106.

'The Industrial Revolution and the Industrious Revolution', *Journal of Economic History* 54/2 (1994): 249–70.

The Industrious Revolution: Consumer Behavior and the Household Economy, 1650 to the Present (Cambridge University Press, 2008).

'The Limits of Globalization in the Early Modern World', *Economic History Review* 63/3 (2010): 710–33.

Vries, P. H. H., 'Are Coal and Colonies Really Crucial? Kenneth Pomeranz and the Great Divergence', *Journal of World History* 12/2 (2001): 407–46.

Wadsworth, Alfred P., and Julia de Lacy Mann, *The Cotton Trade and Industrial Lancashire, 1600–1780* (Manchester University Press, 1931).

Wallerstein, Immanuel M., *The Modern World-System*, volume I, *Capitalist Agriculture and the Origins of the European World-Economy in the Sixteenth Century* (New York: Academic Press, 1974).

The Modern World-System, volume II, *Mercantilism and the Consolidation of the European World-Economy, 1600–1750* (New York: Academic Press, 1980).

The Modern World-System, volume III, *The Second Great Expansion of the Capitalist World-Economy, 1730–1840s* (San Diego: Academic Press, 1989).

The Modern World-System, volume IV, *Centrist Liberalism Triumphant, 1789–1914* (University of California Press, 2011).

Washbrook, David A., 'From Comparative Sociology to Global History: Britain and India in the Pre-History of Modernity', *Journal of the Economic and Social History of the Orient* 40/4 (1997): 410–43.

'Progress and Problems: South Asian Economic and Social History, *c.* 1720–1860', *Modern Asian Studies* 22/1 (1988): 57–96.

Watson, Andrew M., 'The Rise and Spread of Old World Cotton', in Veronika Gervers, ed., *Studies in Textile History in Memory of Harold B. Burnham* (Toronto: Royal Ontario Museum, 1977), pp. 355–68.

Weber, Henry, *La Compagnie française des Indes (1604–1875)* (Paris: Arthur Rousseau, 1904).

Weiji, Cheng, *History of Textile Technology of Ancient China* (New York: Science Press, 1992).

Wendt, Ian C., 'Four Centuries of Decline? Understanding the Changing Structure of the South Indian Textile Industry', in Riello and Roy, eds., *How India Clothed the World*, pp. 193–216.

Wescher, W., 'Turkey Red Dyeing', *Ciba Review* 12/135 (1959): 21–6.

Wiens, Mi Chü, 'Cotton Textile Production and Rural Social Transformation in Early Modern China', *Journal of the Institute of Chinese Studies* 7/2 (1973): 515–34.

Wills, John E., 'European Consumption and Asian Production in the Seventeenth and Eighteenth Centuries', in J. Brewer and R. Porter, eds., *Consumption and the World of Goods* (London and New York: Routledge, 1993), pp. 133–47.

Wong, Bin Roy, *China Transformed: Historical Change and the Limits of European Experience* (Ithaca, NY: Cornell University Press, 1996).

'The Search for European Differences and Domination of the Early Modern World: a View from Asia', *American Historical Review* 107/2 (2002): 447–69.

Woolsey Cole, Charles, *French Mercantilism, 1683–1700* (New York: Columbia University Press, 1943).

Wright, Gavin, *Slavery and American Economic Development* (Baton Rouge: Louisiana State University Press, 2006).

'World Demand for Cotton During the Nineteenth Century: Reply', *Journal of Economic History* 39/4 (1979): 1023–4.

Wrigley, E. A., *Continuity, Chance and Change: the Character of the Industrial Revolution in England* (Cambridge University Press, 1988).

Xinwu, Xu, and Byung-Kun Min, 'The Struggle of the Handicraft Cotton Industry Against Machine Textiles in China', *Modern China* 14/1 (1988): 31–49.

Zahedieh, Nuela, *The Capital and the Colonies: London and the Atlantic Economy, 1660–1700* (Cambridge University Press, 2010).

Zurndorfer, Harriet T., 'Cotton Textile Manufacture and Marketing in Late Imperial China and the "Great Divergence"', *Journal of the Economic and Social History of the Orient* 54/4 (2011): 701–38.

'The Resistant Fibre: Cotton Textiles in Imperial China', in Riello and Parthasarathi, eds., *Spinning World*, pp. 43–62.

INDEX

Printed in the United States
by Baker & Taylor Publisher Services